## A TAILORED SARI
*Avalon Fotheringham*

1. Alexandra Marshall, 'Jean-Paul Gaultier in India', *Travel and Leisure* (Apr 2009): https://www.travelandleisure.com/trip-ideas/jean-paul-gaultier (accessed 2 Mar 2020)
2. Divya Gursahani, 'Why Jean Paul Gaultier is Obsessed with the Sari', *Elle* (14 Nov 2017): https://elle.in/article/jean-paul-gaultier-sari-obsession/ (accessed 16 Mar 2020)
3. See Chandra 1973 for an expansive overview of the history of ancient and medieval Indian dress and its influences.
4. Kumar 1999, p. 150
5. Boyden, Harding and Guy 1997, p. 120
6. Sandhu 2015
7. Cohn 2006, pp. 121–7; Tarlo 1996, p. 42
8. Tarlo 1996, p. 34
9. Ibid., p. 23
10. Tarlo 1991, p. 134
11. Chaudhuri 1976, pp. 6–7
12. See Ashmore 2010 for an overview of Indian influence on twentieth-century European fashion design.

## A BROKEN SUIT
*Marta Franceschini*

1. The expression was published in the September 1992 issue of Italian magazine *Domus*. Quoted in Monti 2017, p. 145.
2. Hartzell 2009, p. 52
3. Lupano 2018, p. 46
4. Mort 1996, p. 142
5. Jenss 2015, p. 40
6. White 2000
7. Amies 1994
8. Colaiacomo 2007
9. Breward 2014, p. 182
10. Elena Fava, 'MareModa Capri and the Story of Made in Italy', paper presented at XI AISU Congress, Bologna, September 2019
11. 'Per i ragazzi l'abito tradizionale veniva violentato in tutti i modi, perfino con maniche di colore diverso o con inserti di vari tessuti… Era questo il periodo e il clima che ha favorito e permesso la nascita e il successo di questa testata… In Italia *L'Uomo Vogue* fu la bandiera del cambiamento.' Flavio Lucchini, 'Rivoluzione Condé Nast. Chiude L'Uomo Vogue,' *artribune.com* (8 Aug 2017): https://www.artribune.com/editoria/2017/08/conde-nast-uomo-vogue/ (accessed 5 May 2020). All the translations are the author's own.
12. Many scholars have discussed the geographical specificity of the term *stilista*, deeming it impossible to translate. See for example Stanfill 2014.
13. Amies 1994, p. 39
14. 'La mia non è una moda unisex, è la rivendicazione sulla dolcezza per l'uomo e della forza per la donna.' Giorgio Armani, 'Armani disarmato', *Emporio Armani Magazine. Style Atlas* (14 Sep 1995 – Feb 1996), pp. I–XVI
15. Versace 1995
16. This tension was individuated by Valerie Steele 1999, p. 91.
17. Breward 2016, p. 155
18. Extract from Gucci's Autumn/Winter 2020 collection press release.

## THE JACKET ERODED, BORROWED, EVOLVED
*Alistair O'Neill*

1. Jones 1995, p. 21
2. Hooker 1998, pp. 70–1
3. Margolin 1997, p. 87
4. Jones 1995, p. 22
5. Lord 1997, p. 49
6. Edwards 2020
7. Katsahnias 1990, pp. 34–7
8. Drira 2012, pp. 66–71
9. Patrick Hollington, in conversation with the author, 13 Jan 2020
10. Reinach 2017
11. 'Cardin Designs Bright Plumage for the Males', *New York Times* (15 Mar 1960)
12. Associated Press press release, 2 Mar 1960
13. Jean Nathan, 'Scenes: A Celebration in Black', *New York Times* (29 Nov 1992)
14. Lilian Ross, 'How Do You Like It Now, Gentlemen?: the Moods of Ernest Hemingway', *New Yorker* (6 May 1950)
15. Louis Botto, 'The Great Safari Suit Flap', *New York Times* (15 Sep 1974)
16. Simon Doonan, 'Bill Cunningham: An Enigma in a Blue Sanitation Worker's Jacket', *New York Times* (6 Sep 2018)
17. *Antonio Lopez 1970: Sex, Disco, Fashion* (2017), dir. James Crump
18. Ibid.
19. Robert Armstrong, 'John Fetterman and the Politics of Workwear', *Financial Times* (21/22 Nov 2020)
20. This essay is dedicated to Patrick Hollington (1937–2020).

## WHAT EVER HAPPENED TO CONTEMPORARY MENSWEAR?
*Charlie Porter*

1. *The Face*, Apr 1986
2. Ibid.
3. Scarlett Conlon, 'Dior's Kim Jones: "These Jobs Are Not an Easy Ride"', *The Guardian* (6 Apr 2019): https://www.theguardian.com/fashion/2019/apr/06/kim-jones-dior-menswear-designer-alexander-mcqueen-streetwear (accessed 23 Apr 2021)
4. Stephen Spear, 'Kim Jones', *drapersonline*, (8 Mar 2008): https://www.drapersonline.com/news/kim-jones/909409.article (accessed 23 Apr 2021)
5. Sarah Mower, 'Kim Jones Spring 2004 Ready-to-Wear', *Vogue* (22 Sep 2003): https://www.vogue.com/fashion-shows/spring-2004-ready-to-wear/kim-jones (accessed 23 Apr 2021)
6. Marc Karimzadeh, 'The Scoop on the 2020 CFDA Fashion Awards Winners!', *cdfa*, (19 Sep 2020): https://cfda.com/news/the-scoop-on-the-2020-cfda-fashion-awards-winners (accessed 23 Apr 2021)
7. Interview with the author: http://charlieporter.net/stories/7321 (accessed 23 Apr 2021)
8. Sarah Schulman, *Gentrification of the Mind* (Berkeley 2013), p. 15
9. Suzanne Moore, 'A Generation of Artists Were Wiped Out by Aids and We Barely Talk About It', *The Guardian* (20 Apr 2016): https://www.theguardian.com/society/commentisfree/2016/apr/20/a-generation-of-artists-were-wiped-out-by-aids-and-we-barely-talk-about-it-robert-mapplethorpe (accessed 23 Apr 2021)
10. 'Eight for 1984', *The Face* (Dec 1983)
11. Ibid.
12. Nick Duffy, 'Lord Tebbit: It's Perfectly Sensible to Think Gay Acts Are Sinful', *PinkNews* (3 Jul 2017): https://www.pinknews.co.uk/2017/07/03/lord-tebbit-its-perfectly-sensible-to-think-gay-acts-are-sinful (accessed 23 Apr 2021)
13. Sarah Mower, 'Bianca Saunders: Fall 2020 Menswear', *Vogue* (6 Jan 2020): https://www.vogue.com/fashion-shows/fall-2020-menswear/bianca-saunders (accessed 23 Apr 2021)

## EPILOGUE
*Gus Casely-Hayford*

1. Miller 1998
2. Hoffman 2005

# BIBLIOGRAPHY


Adamo 2011
Grace Ebunlola Adamo, 'Nigerian Dress as a Symbolic Language', *Semiotica*, Vol. 184 (2011), pp. 1–9

Adams 2009
Ellen Adams, 'Defining and Displaying the Human Body: Collectors and Classics during the British Enlightenment', *Hermathena*, No. 187 (Winter 2009), pp. 65–97

Addison 1705
Joseph Addison, *Remarks on Several Parts of Italy* (London 1705)

Alberti 1956
Leon Battista Alberti, *On Painting* (New Haven and London 1956)

Aldrich 1993
Robert Aldrich, *The Seduction of The Mediterranean: Writing, Art and Homosexual Fantasy* (London 1993)

Allestree 1682
Richard Allestree, *The Whole Duty of Man* (London 1682)

Amies 1994
Hardy Amies, *The Englishman's Suit* (London 1994)

Andry 1743
Nicholas Andry, *Orthopaedia, or the Art of Preventing and Correcting Deformities in Children* (London 1743)

Ångström Grandien 2018
Inga Lena Ångström Grandien, '"She was Naught ... of a Woman except in Sex:" The Cross-Dressing of Queen Christina of Sweden', *Journal of Dress History*, Vol. 2, No. 1, (Spring 2018), pp. 2–13

Anon. 1555
Anonymous, *The Institucion of a Gentleman* (London 1555)

Anon. 1675a
Anonymous, *The Character of a Town-Gallant* (London 1675)

Anon. 1675b
Anonymous, *News from Covent-Garden* (London 1675)

Anon. 1699
Anonymous, *The Country Gentleman's Vade Mecum* (London 1699)

Anon. 1706
Anonymous, *The Roving Husband Reclaim'd* (London 1706)

Anon. 1747
Anonymous, *A General Description of all Trades* (London 1747)

Anon. 1763
Anonymous, *A True, Genuine and Authentic Account of ... Paul Lewis, the Famous Highwayman* (London 1763)

Anon. 1818
Anonymous, *Neckclothitania or Tietania, Being an Essay on Starchers by One of the Cloth* (London 1818)

Ansell 2018
Richard Ansell, 'Reading and Writing Travels: Maximilien Misson, Samuel Waring and the Afterlives of European Voyages, *c.*1687–1714', *English Historical Review*, Vol. 133 (2018), pp. 1446–77

Ashmore 2010
Sonia Ashmore, 'Hippies, Bohemians & Chintz' in Christopher Breward, Philip Crang and Rosemary Gill, *British Asian Style: Fashion & Textiles, Past & Present* (London 2010)

Ashton 1890
John Ashton, *Social England Under the Regency* (London 1890)

Aston 1988
Elaine Aston, 'Male Impersonation in the Music Hall: The Case of Vesta Tilley', *New Theatre Quarterly*, Vol. 4, No. 15 (15 Aug 1988), pp. 247–57

Audran 1683
Gérard Audran, *Les Proportions Du Corps Humain, Mesurées sur les plus belles Figures de l'Antiquité* (Paris 1683)

Bailey 2007
Amanda Bailey, *Flaunting: Style and the Subversive Male Body in Renaissance England* (Toronto 2007)

Bailey 2012
Ann Bailey, 'The Clothing and Footwear Industries and Professional Football Clubs in England 1950–1957', *Costume: A Volume for the London Olympics* (London 2012), pp. 180–96

Bailey and Hentschell 2010
Amanda Bailey and Roze Hentschell, *Masculinity and the Metropolis of Vice, 1550–1650* (Basingstoke 2010)

Banks 2010
Stephen Banks, *A Polite Exchange of Bullets: The Duel and the English Gentleman 1750–1850* (Woodbridge 2010)

Barrell 1989
John Barrell, 'The Dangerous Goddess': Masculinity, Prestige, and the Aesthetic in Early Eighteenth-Century Britain,' *Cultural Critique*, No. 12 (1989) pp. 101–31

Bax 1932
Clifford Bax, *Pretty Witty Nell* (London 1932)

Beeber 2015
Matthew Beeber, 'Fashionable Misconceptions: The Creation of the East in Virginia Woolf's *Orlando*' in Pamela L. Caughie and Diana L. Swanson (eds), *Virginia Woolf: Writing the World* (Liverpool 2015)

Begiato 2016
Joanne Begiato, 'Between Poise and Power: Embodied Manliness in Eighteenth and Nineteenth-Century British Culture', *Transactions of the Royal Historical Society*, Vol. 26, (2016) pp. 125–47

Ben-Amos 1994
Ilana Krausman Ben-Amos, *Adolescence and Youth in Early Modern England* (London 1994)

Benjamin 1989
Walter Benjamin, *Charles Baudelaire: A Lyric Poet In The Era Of High Capitalism* (London 1989)

Bennett-England 1967
Rodney Bennett-England, *Dress Optional: The Revolution in Menswear* (London 1967)

Benyon 2002
John Benyon, *Masculinities and Culture* (Milton Keynes 2002)

Biddle-Perry 2017
Geraldine Biddle-Perry, *Dressing for Austerity: Aspiration, Leisure and Fashion in Post-War Britain* (London 2017)

Bolich 2007
Gregory G. Bolich, *Crossdressing in Context. Vol. 4: Transgender & Religion* (Raleigh 2007)

Bordo 1999
Susan Bordo, *The Male Body: A New Look at Men in Public and in Private* (New York 1999)

Bourland 2019
W. Ian Bourland, *Bloodflowers: Rotimi Fani-Kayode, Photography, and the 1980s* (Durham 2019)

Bowron and Kerber 2008
Edgar Peters Bowron and Peter Björn Kerber, *Pompeo Batoni: Prince of Painters in Eighteenth-Century Rome* (New Haven and London 2008)

Boyden, Harding and Guy 1997
Peter Boyden, Marion Harding and Alan Guy (eds), *Soldiers of the Raj: The Indian Army, 1600–1947* (London 1997)

Braun, Costigliolo, North, Thornton and Tiramani 2016
Melanie Braun, Luca Costigliolo, Susan North, Claire Thornton and Jenny Tiramani, *17th-Century Men's Dress Patterns, 1600–1630* (London 2016)

Breitenberg 1996
Mark Breitenberg, *Anxious Masculinity in Early Modern England* (Cambridge 1996)

Breukink-Peeze 1989
Margaretha Breukink-Peeze, 'Japanese Robes: A Craze' in Stefan van Raay (ed.), *Imitation and Inspiration: Japanese Influence on Dutch Art* (Amsterdam 1989)

Breward 1995
Christopher Breward, *The Culture of Fashion* (Manchester 1995)

Breward 1999
Christopher Breward, *The Hidden Consumer: Masculinities, Fashion and City Life 1860–1914* (Manchester 1999)

Breward 2004
Christopher Breward, *Fashioning London: Clothing and the Modern Metropolis* (Oxford 2004)

Breward 2014
Christopher Breward, 'The Return of the Courtier: Men and Menswear' in Sonnet Stanfill (ed.), *The Glamour of Italian Fashion since 1945* (London 2014)

Breward 2016
Christopher Breward, *The Suit: Form, Function and Style* (London 2016)

Brooke 1681
Humphrey Brooke, *The Durable Legacy* (London 1681)

Brown 2010
Jeffrey A. Brown, *The Modern Superhero in Film and Television: Popular Genre and American Culture* (London 2010)

Brown 1989
Peter Brown, 'Late Antiquity' in Philippe Ariès and Georges Duby (eds), *A History of Private Life. Vol. 1: From Pagan Rome to Byzantium* (Cambridge, Massachusetts and London 1989), pp. 245–6

Bruna 2015
Denis Bruna, *Fashioning the Body: An Intimate History of the Silhouette* (New Haven and London 2015)

Bryant 2019
Julius Bryant, *Creating the V&A. Victoria and Albert's Museum (1851–1861)* (London 2019)

Buckley 2008
Veronica Buckley, *Christina, Queen of Sweden: The Restless Life of a European Eccentric* (London 2008)

Budd 1997
Michael A. Budd, *The Sculpture Machine: Physical Culture and Body Politics in the Age of Empire* (New York 1997)

Bullough and Bullough 1993
Vern L. Bullough and Bonnie Bullough, *Cross Dressing, Sex, and Gender* (Philadelphia 1993)

Bulwer-Lytton 1842
Edward Bulwer-Lytton, *Pelham, Or the Adventures of a Gentleman* (Leipzig 1842)

Burton 1999
Anthony Burton, *Vision and Accident. The Story of the Victoria and Albert Museum* (London 1999)

Callen 2018
Anthea Callen, *Looking at Men: Art, Anatomy and the Modern Male Body* (New Haven and London 2018)

Calvi 2002
Giulia Calvi, 'Abito, genere, cittadinanza nella Toscana moderna', *Quaderni Storici*, Vol. 37, No. 110 (2002) pp. 477–503

Campbell *c.*1937
Heyworth Campbell (ed.), *Modern Masters of Photography. Series 1: Pictorialists* (New York *c.*1937)

Campbell 1747
R. Campbell, *The London Tradesman* (London 1747)

Carden-Coyne 2009
A. Carden-Coyne, *Reconstructing the Body: Classicism, Modernism and the First World War* (Oxford 2009)

Carter 2003
Michael Carter, *Fashion Classics from Carlyle to Barthes* (Oxford 2003)

Carter 2001
Philip Carter, *Men and the Emergence of Polite Society, Britain 1660–1800* (London 2001)

Casa, Peterson (trans.) 1576
John Della Casa, Robert Peterson (trans.), *Galateo* (London 1576)

Castiglione, Singleton (trans.) 1959
Baldassare Castiglione and C.S. Singleton (trans.), *The Book of the Courtier* (New York 1959)

Celant and Ippolitov 2004
Germano Celant and Arkady Ippolitov (eds), *Robert Mapplethorpe and the Classical Tradition: Photographs and Mannerist Prints* (exh. cat., Deutsche Guggenheim, Berlin and Guggenheim, New York 2004)

Chambers 2016
Eddie Chambers, *Roots & Culture* (London 2016)

Chandler and Chandler Smith 2005
Robin M. Chandler and Núrí Chandler Smith, 'Flava in Ya Gear: Transgressive Politics and the Influence of Hip-hop on Contemporary Fashion' in Linda Welters and Patricia Cunningham (eds), *Twentieth-Century American Fashion* (Oxford 2005)

Chandra 1973
Moti Chandra, *Costumes, Textiles, Cosmetics and Coiffure* (Delhi 1973)

Chapman 1994
David Chapman, *Sandow the Magnificent. Eugen Sandow and the Beginnings of Body Building* (Urbana 1994)

Chard 1999
Chloe Chard, *Pleasure and Guilt on the Grand Tour* (Manchester 1999)

Chaudhuri 1976
Nirad C. Chaudhuri, *Culture in the Vanity Bag, Being an Essay on Clothing and Adornment in Passing and Abiding India* (Mumbai 1976)

Chenoune 1993
Farid Chenoune, *A History of Men's Fashion* (Paris 1993)

Churchyard 1593
Thomas Churchyard, *Churchyard's Telling* (London 1593)

Clark 1985
Sandra Clark, '"Hic Mulier," "Haec Vir," and the Controversy over Masculine Women', *Studies in Philology*, Vol. 82, No. 2 (Spring 1985), pp. 157–83

Clarke 1972
William H. Clarke, *Travels and Exploration in Yorubaland 1854–1858* (London 1972)

Cleland (1612) 1948
James Cleland, *The Scottish Academie (1612)* (New York 1948)

Cohen 1996
Michèle Cohen, *Fashioning Masculinity: National Identity and Language in the Eighteenth Century* (London 1996)

Cohn 2006
Bernard S. Cohn, *Colonialism and Its Forms of Knowledge: The British in India* (Princeton 2006)

Colaiacomo 2007
Paola Colaiacomo, *Factious Elegance: Pasolini and Male Fashion* (Venice 2007)

Cole 1978
Hubert Cole, *Beau Brummell* (Newton Abbot 1978)

Cole 2020
Michael W. Cole, *Sofonisba's Lesson: A Renaissance Artist and Her Work* (Princeton 2020)

Collins 1981
Philip Collins (ed.), *Dickens: Interviews and Recollections. Volume 1* (London 1981)

Collyer 1761
Joseph Collyer, *The Parent's and Guardian's Directory* (London 1761)

Coltman 2009
Viccy Coltman, *Classical Sculpture and the Culture of Collecting in Britain since 1760* (Oxford 2009)

Coltman 2019
Viccy Coltman, *Art and Identity in Scotland: A Cultural History from the Jacobite Rising of 1745 to Walter Scott* (Cambridge 2019)

Constable 1738
John Constable, *The Conversation of Gentlemen Considered* (London 1738)

Coop 2019
Elizabeth Coop, 'The Designer Reimagining Traditional West African Fabrics for a New Generation', *New York Times Style Magazine* (1 May 2019)

Cortazzi 2001
Hugh Cortazzi (ed.), *Mitford's Japan: Memories and Recollections, 1866–1906* (London 2001)

de Courtin 1671
Antoine de Courtin, *The Rules of Civility* (London 1671)

Cunningham, Eshun and Lazarides (eds) 2001
Jake Cunningham, Ekow Eshun and Steve Lazarides (eds), *Seen: Black Style UK* (London 2001)

Cunnington and Cunnington 1992
Cecil Willett Cunnington and Phillis Cunnington, *The History of Underclothes* (New York 1992)

Currie 2016
Elizabeth Currie, *Fashion and Masculinity in Renaissance Florence* (London 2016)

Currie 2019
Elizabeth Currie, 'Health Hazards: Clothing's Impact on the Body in Italy and England, 1550–1650', *Bulletin of the John Rylands Library*, Vol. 95, No. 2 (Autumn 2019)

Dalby 1993
Liza Dalby, *Kimono: Fashioning Culture* (New Haven and London 1993)

Dare 1673
Josiah Dare, *Counsellor Manners, His Last Legacy to His Son* (London 1673)

Davidson 2019
Hilary Davidson, *Dress in the Age of Jane Austen: Regency Fashion* (New Haven and London 2019)

Davis 1991
Melody Davis, *The Male Nude in Contemporary Photography* (Philadelphia 1991)

Defoe 1742
Daniel Defoe, *A History of the Lives and Exploits of the Most Famous Pirates, Highwaymen, Murderers, Street-robbers, &c* (Birmingham 1742)

Dekke and van de Pol 1989
Rudolf M. Dekke and Lotte C. van de Pol, *The Tradition of Female Transvestism in Early Modern Europe* (London 1989)

Dendy 1895
F.W. Dendy (ed.), *Extracts from the Records of the Merchant Adventurers of Newcastle-upon-Tyne*, The Surtees Society, Vol. 1 (1895), p. 20

Doan 2001
Laura Doan, *Fashioning Sapphism: The Origins of a Modern English Lesbian Culture* (New York 2001)

Drira 2012
Samuel Drira, 'Michel Schreiber', *Encens* (Fall/Winter 2012), pp. 66–71

Dutton 1995
Kenneth R. Dutton, *The Perfectible Body: The Western Ideal of Physical Development* (London 1995)

Earle 1628
John Earle, *Micro-cosmographie* (London 1628)

Edwards 2020
Lydia Edwards, *How to Read a Suit: A Guide to Changing Men's Fashion from the 17th to the 20th Century* (London 2020)

Eisen and McHugh 2019
Cliff Eisen and Dominic McHugh (eds), *The Letters of Cole Porter* (New Haven and London 2019)

Eliav-Feldon 2009
Miriam Eliav-Feldon, 'Vagabonds or Vermin: Attitudes to Gypsies in Early Modern Europe' in Miriam Eliav-Feldon, Benjamin Isaac and Joseph Ziegler (eds), *The Origins of Racism in the West* (Cambridge 2009)

Elyot (1531) 1970
Thomas Elyot, *The Book Named the Governor* (1531) (Menston 1970)

Etherege 1676
George Etherege, *The Man of Mode, or, Sr. Fopling Flutter* (London 1676)

Evans 2020
Caroline Evans, 'Chanel, la nouvelle femme en dandy' in *Chanel: Manifeste de Mode* (exh. cat., Palais Galliera, Paris, 2020) pp. 106–11

Evelyn 1661
John Evelyn, *Tyrannus, or, The Mode in a Discourse of Sumptuary Lawes* (London 1661)

Falls 2014
Susan Falls, *Clarity, Cut and Culture: The Many Meanings of Diamonds* (New York and London 2014)

Fani-Kayode 1988
Rotimi Fani-Kayode, 'Traces of Ecstasy', *Ten. 8*, No. 28 (1988)

Farington, Cave (ed.) 1982
Joseph Farington, Kathryn Cave (ed.), *The Diary of Joseph Farington. Vol. IX (January 1808 – December 1810)* (New Haven 1982)

Farrell 1992
Jeremy Farrell, *Socks and Stockings* (London 1992)

Fiala 2018
Andrew Fiala, 'A Critique of Thug Culture' in Fuat Gursozlu (ed.), *Peace, Culture, and Violence* (Leiden and Boston 2018), pp. 18–20

Fielding 1763
John Fielding, *The Universal Mentor* (Dublin 1763)

Flügel 1966
John Carl Flügel, *The Psychology of Clothes* (London 1966)

Friedman 2016
Vanessa Friedman, 'Prince's Heels Elevated Him as a Style Icon', *New York Times* (22 April 2016)

Fryer 2010
Peter Fryer, *Staying Power* (London 2010)

Funnell 2011
Peter Funnell, 'Lawrence among Men: Friends, Patrons and the Male Portrait' in A. Cassandra Albinson, Peter Funnell and Lucy Peltz (eds), *Thomas Lawrence: Regency Power and Brilliance* (New Haven and London 2011)

Gaines and Churcher 1994
Steven Gaines and Susan Churcher, *Obsession: The Lives and Times of Calvin Klein* (New York 1994)

Garber 1998
Eric Garber, 'Gladys Bentley: The Bulldagger Who Sang the Blues', *OUTLook: National Lesbian and Gay Quarterly*, No. 1 (1998), pp. 52–61

Garber 1992
Marjorie Garber, *Vested Interests: Cross-Dressing and Cultural Anxiety* (London 1992)

Garrard 1994
Mary D. Garrard, 'Here's Looking at Me: Sofonisba Anguissola and the Problem of the Woman Artist', *Renaissance Quarterly*, Vol. 47, No. 3, (Autumn 1994), pp. 556–622

Gernerd 2015
Elisabeth Gernerd, 'Pulled Tight and Gleaming: The Stocking's Position within Eighteenth-century Masculinity', *Textile History*, Vol. 46, No. 1 (2015), pp. 3–27

Gilroy 1987
Paul Gilroy, 'The Myth of Black Criminality' in Phil Scraton (ed.), *Law, Order and the Authoritarian State* (Milton Keynes 1987)

Gilroy 2002
Paul Gilroy, *There Ain't No Black in the Union Jack* (London 2002)

Glover 2019
Michael Glover, *Thrust: A Spasmodic Pictorial History of the Codpiece in Art* (New York 2019)

Goldsmith 2020
Sarah Goldsmith, *Masculinity and Danger on the Eighteenth-Century Grand Tour* (London 2020)

Goldsmith 2021
Goldsmith, 'Making the Body Beautiful' in Karen Harvey (ed.), *A Cultural History of Beauty in the Age of Enlightenment (1700–1800). Vol. 4: A Cultural History of Beauty* (London 2021)

Griffiths 1996
Paul Griffiths, *Youth and Authority: Formative Experiences in England 1560–1650* (Oxford 1996)

Grimes 2013
Kyle Grimes, '"Fit Audience, Though Few": Romanticism and Physical Education in the 1820s', *Romanticism*, Vol. 19, No. 3 (2013), pp. 261–72

Gundle 2008
Stephen Gundle, *Glamour: A History* (Oxford 2008)

Hall 1987
Stuart Hall, 'Minimal Selves' in *Identity: The Real Me* (exh. cat., ICA, London, 1987)

Hall 1993
Stuart Hall, 'What Is This "Black" in Black Popular Culture?' *Social Justice*, Vol. 20, No. 1/2 (1993), pp. 104–14

Hall 2006
Stuart Hall, 'New Ethnicities' in David Morley and Kuan-Hsing Chen (eds), *Critical Dialogues in Cultural Studies* (London 2006)

Hall 2011
Stuart Hall, *Different: A Historical Context. Contemporary Black Photographers and Black Identity* (London and New York 2011)

Harris 1931
Frank Harris, *Bernard Shaw* (London 1931)

Hart 1998
Avril Hart, *Ties* (London 1998)

Hartzell 2009
Freyja Hartzell, 'The Velvet Touch: Fashion, Furniture, and the Fabric of the Interior', *Fashion Theory*, Vol. 13 (2009), pp. 52–81

Harvey 2013
John Harvey, *The Story of Black* (London 2013)

Harvey 2005
Karen Harvey, 'The History of Masculinity, circa 1650–1800', *Journal of British Studies*, Vol. 44, No. 2 (2005), pp. 296–311

Harvey 2015
Karen Harvey, 'Men of Parts: Masculine Embodiment and the Male Leg in Eighteenth-Century England', *Journal of British Studies*, Vol. 54, No. 4 (2015), pp. 797–821

Haskell and Penny 1981
Francis Haskell and Nicholas Penny, *Taste and the Antique: The Lure of Classical Sculpture, 1500–1900* (New Haven and London 1981)

Hau 2003
Michael Hau, *The Cult of Health and Beauty in Germany: A Social History, 1890–1930* (Chicago 2003)

Hayward 2020
Maria Hayward, *Stuart Style: Monarchy, Dress and the Scottish Male Elite* (New Haven and London 2020)

Hazlitt 1868
William Carew Hazlitt (ed.), *Inedited Tracts: Illustrating the Manners, Opinions and Occupations of Englishmen* (Roxburghe Library 1868)

Hebdige 1979
Dick Hebdige, *Subculture* (London 1979)

Hills 2018
Paul Hills, *Veiled Presence: Body and Drapery from Giotto to Titian* (New Haven and London 2018)

Hobson 2004
Marian Hobson, 'Measuring Statues, or, Special Neutrality', *Paragraph*, Vol. 27, No. 1 (Mar 2004), pp. 33–49

Hoffman 2005
Fred Hoffman, 'The Defining Years: Notes on Five Key Works' in Marc Mayer (ed.), *Basquiat* (Brooklyn 2005), pp. 129–39

Hogarth, Paulson (ed.) 1997
William Hogarth, Ronald Paulson (ed.), *The Analysis of Beauty* (New Haven 1997)

Hollander 1994
Anne Hollander, *Sex and Suits: The Evolution of Modern Dress* (London 1994)

Holm 2019
Julia Holm, 'How to Dress a Female King: Manifestations of Gender and Power in the Wardrobe of Christina of Sweden' in Erin Griffey (ed.), *Sartorial Politics in Early Modern Europe* (Amsterdam 2019), pp. 183–205

Honeyman 1993
Katrina Honeyman, 'Montague Burton Ltd.: The Creators of Well-Dressed Men', *Leeds City Business 1893–1993: Essays Marking the Centenary of the Incorporation* (Leeds 1993), pp. 186–217

Honeyman 2000
Katrina Honeyman, *Well Suited: A History of the Leeds Clothing Industry, 1850–1990* (Oxford 2000)

Honour 2019
Hugh Honour, 'Studies' in David Bindman and Henry Louis Gates Jr (ed.), *The Image of the Black in Western Art. Vol. 4: From the American Revolution to World War I, Part 2: Black Models and White Myths* (Cambridge 2019), pp. 8–12

Hooker 1998
Denise Hooker, *Nina Hamnett: Queen of Bohemia* (London 1998)

hooks 2004
bell hooks, *We Real Cool: Black Men and Masculinity* (London 2004)

Horsley 2017
Jeffrey Horsley, 'The Absent Shadow: Reflections on the Incidence of Menswear in Recent Fashion Exhibitions', *Critical Studies in Men's Fashion*, Vol. 4, No. 1 (2017), pp. 11–29

Hughes 1940
Langston Hughes, *The Big Sea* (New York 1940)

Hurd 1764
Richard Hurd, *Dialogues on the Uses of Foreign Travel* (Dublin 1764)

Huysmans 1959
Joris-Karl Huysmans, *Against Nature* (Harmondsworth 1959)

Jackson 2000
Anna Jackson, 'Orient and Occident' in Paul Greenhalgh (ed.), *Art Nouveau 1890–1914* (London 2000), pp. 100–13

Jackson 2020
Anna Jackson, 'Status, Style and Seduction' in Anna Jackson (ed.), *Kimono: Kyoto to Catwalk* (London 2020), pp. 37–78

Jesse 1844
William Jesse, *The Life of George Brummell, Esq., Commonly Called Beau Brummell* (London 1844)

Jenss 2015
Heike Jenss, *Fashioning Memory: Vintage Style and Youth Culture* (London 2015)

Jones 1995
Amelia Jones, '"Clothes Make the Man": The Male Artist as a Performative Function', *Oxford Art Journal*, Vol. 18, No. 2 (1995), pp. 18–32

Jones 1735
Erasmus Jones, *The Man of Manners* (London 1735)

Jonsson 2018
Lovisa Willborg Jonsson, 'How to Cross-Dress in Eighteenth-Century Sweden: Skills, Props, and Audiences', *Journal of Dress History*, Vol. 2, No. 1 (Spring 2018), pp. 44–55

Kaiser, Rabine, Hall and Ketchum 2004
Susan Kaiser, Leslie Rabine, Carol Hall and Karyl Ketchum, 'Beyond Binaries: Respecting the Improvisation in African American Style' in Carol Tulloch (ed.), *Black British Style* (London 2004)

Kates 2001
Gary Kates, *Monsieur d'Eon is a Woman: A Tale of Political Intrigue and Sexual Masquerade* (Baltimore 2001)

Katsahnias 1990
Iannis Katsahnias, 'Les nouvelles jeunesses situationnistes', *Cahiers du cinéma*, No. 435 (Sep 1990), pp. 34–7

Kelly 2005
Ian Kelly, *Beau Brummell: The Ultimate Man of Style* (London 2005)

Kestner 1995
Joseph A. Kestner, *Masculinities in Victorian Painting* (Aldershot 1995)

Kuhn 2006
William Kuhn, *The Politics of Pleasure, A Portrait of Benjamin Disraeli* (London 2006)

Kumar 1999
Ritu Kumar, *Costumes and Textiles of Royal India* (London 1999)

Kureishi and Savage (eds) 1995
Hanif Kureishi and John Savage (eds), *The Faber Book of Pop* (London 1995)

Langdon 1998
Helen Langdon, *Caravaggio: A Life* (London 1998)

Laver 1968
James Laver, *Dandies* (London 1968)

Leoussi 2016
Athena S. Leoussi, 'Making Nations in the Image of Greece: Classical Greek Conceptions of the Body in the Construction of National Identity in Nineteenth-Century England, France and Germany' in Thorsten Fö and Richard Warren (eds), *Graeco-Roman Antiquity and the Idea of Nationalism in the Nineteenth-Century: Case Studies* (Berlin 2016)

Lewis 2010
Van Dyk Lewis, 'Hip-hop Fashion' in Valerie Steele (ed.), *The Berg Companion to Fashion* (Oxford 2010)

Lichtenstein 1993
Jacqueline Lichtenstein, *The Eloquence of Color: Rhetoric and Painting in the French Classical Age* (Berkeley 1993)

Lord 1985
James Lord, *Giacometti: A Biography* (New York 1985)

Lupano 2018
Mario Lupano, 'Vestibilità sartoriale nella confezione in serie' in Mario Lupano and Marta Franceschini (eds), *Uomini all'italiana. La confezione Zegna dalla sartoria all'industria* (Venice 2018)

Mackenzie 2003
Michael Mackenzie, 'From Athens to Berlin: The 1936 Olympics and Leni Riefenstahl's Olympia', *Critical Inquiry*, Vol. 29, No. 2 (Winter 2003), pp. 302–36

Mackie 2009
Erin Mackie, *Rakes, Highwaymen, and Pirates: The Making of the Modern Gentleman in the Eighteenth Century* (Baltimore 2009)

Mancinus 1570
Dominicus Mancinus, *The Mirrour of Good Maners* (London 1570)

Mandeville 1715
Bernard Mandeville, *The Fable of the Bees* (London 1715)

Mangan 1981
James A. Mangan, *Athleticism in the Victorian and Edwardian Public School. The Emergence and Consolidation of an Educational Ideology* (London 1981)

Mangan 2013
James A. Mangan (ed.), *Shaping the Superman: Fascist Body as Political Icon* (London 2013)

Mansel 2005
Philip Mansel, *Dressed to Rule: Royal and Court Costume from Louis XIV to Elizabeth II* (London 2005)

Margolin 1997
Victor Margolin, *The Struggle for Utopia* (Chicago 1997)

Martin and Koda 1992
Richard Martin and Harold Koda, 'Jockey: The Invention of the Classic Brief', *Textile and Text*, Vol. 15, No. 2 (1992)

Matthews David 2007
Alison Matthews David, 'Made to Measure? Tailoring the "Normal" body in Nineteenth-century France', in Waltraud Ernst (ed.), *Histories of the Normal and Abnormal: Social and Cultural Histories of Norms and Normativity* (London 2007), pp. 142–64

McKnight 2000
Penny McKnight, *Stockport Hatting* (Stockport 2000)

McNeil 2000
Peter McNeil, 'Macaroni Masculinities', *Fashion Theory*, Vol. 4, No. 4 (2000), pp. 374–8

McNeil 2018
Peter McNeil, *Pretty Gentlemen: Macaroni Men and the Eighteenth-century Fashion World* (London 2018)

McNeil and Riello 2005
Peter McNeil and Giorgio Riello, 'The Art and Science of Walking: Gender, Space, and the Fashionable Body in the Long Eighteenth Century', *Fashion Theory*, Vol. 9, No. 2 (2005), pp. 175–204

Meech-Pekarik 1986
Julia Meech-Pekarik, *The World of the Meiji Print: Impressions of a New Civilization* (New York and Tokyo 1986)

Meeker 2006
Martin Meeker, *Contacts Desired: Gay and Lesbian Communications and Community, 1940s–1970s* (Chicago 2006)

Melville 2019
Caspar Melville, *It's a London Thing* (Manchester 2019)

Mercer 1991
Kobena Mercer, 'Looking for Trouble', *Transition*, No. 51 (1991), pp. 184–97

Miller 1998
Jacques-Alain Miller (ed.), 'The Seminar of Jacques Lacan', *Book XI: The Four Fundamental Concepts of Psychoanalysis* (New York 1998)

Miller 2009
Monica L. Miller, *Slaves to Fashion: Black Dandyism and the Styling of Black Diasporic Identity* (Durham and London 2009)

Misson 1714
Maximilien Misson, *A New Voyage to Italy* (London 1714)

Mitchell Snow 2019
K. Mitchell Snow, 'Does This Fig Leaf Make Me Look Gay? Strongmen, Statue Posing and Physique Photography', *Early Popular Visual Culture*, Vol. 17, No. 2 (2019), pp. 135–55

Mizer 1954
Bob Mizer, *Physique Pictorial*, Vol. 4, No. 3 (1954)

Moffitt 2004
John F. Moffitt, *Caravaggio in Context: Learned Naturalism and Renaissance Humanism* (North Carolina and London 2004)

Montagu, Heffernan and O'Quinn (eds) 2012
Lady Mary Wortley Montagu, with Teresa Heffernan and Daniel O'Quinn (eds), *Turkish Embassy Letters* (Peterborough, Ontario 2012)

Monti 2017
Gabriele Monti, 'The Discipline of Freedom in Fashion Design', *Fashion Practice*, Vol. 9, No. 1 (2017), pp. 143–55

Montrose 1983
Louis Adrian Montrose, '"Shaping Fantasies": Figurations of Gender and Power in Elizabethan Culture', *Representations*, No. 2 (Spring 1983), pp. 61–94

Morley 1852
Henry Morley, 'A House Full of Horrors', *Household Words*, Vol. VI, No. 141 (4 Dec 1852), pp. 265–70

Morrisroe 2016
Patricia Morrisroe, *Mapplethorpe* (New York 2016)

Mort 1996
Frank Mort, *Cultures of Consumption: Commerce, Masculinities and Social Space* (London 1996)

Mort 2010
Frank Mort, *Capital Affairs: London and the Making of the Permissive Society* (New Haven and London 2010)

Mort and Thompson 1994
Frank Mort and Peter Thompson, 'Retailing, Commercial Culture and Masculinity in 1950s Britain: The Case of Montague Burton, the "Tailor of Taste"', *History Workshop*, Vol. 38, No. 1 (Autumn 1994), pp. 106–28

Mostow, Ikeda and Matsuba 2016
Joshua S. Mostow, Asato Ikeda and Ryoko Matsuba, *A Third Gender: Beautiful Youths in Japanese Edo-period Prints and Paintings 1600–1868*, (exh. cat., Royal Ontario Museum, Toronto 2016)

Muir 2019
Rory Muir, *Gentlemen of Uncertain Fortune: How Younger Sons Made Their Way in Jane Austen's England* (New Haven and London 2019)

Myrone 2005
Martin Myrone, *Bodybuilding: Reforming Masculinities in British Art, 1750–1810* (New Haven and London 2005)

Napier 1902
Lady Sarah Lennox Bunbury Napier, *The Life and Letters of Lady Sarah Lennox, 1745–1826* (London 1902)

Nead 2017
Lynda Nead, *The Tiger in the Smoke: Art and Culture in Post-War Britain* (New Haven and London 2017)

Newton 1974
Stella Mary Newton, *Health, Art and Reason: Dress Reform of the Nineteenth Century* (London 1974)

Nicholson 1973; reprint 1990
Nigel Nicholson, *Portrait of a Marriage* (1973; reprint, London 1990)

North 2009
Susan North in Karen Hearn (ed.), *Van Dyck & Britain* (London 2009)

North 2020
Susan North, 'Geographically Confused but Familiarly Exotic: The Influence of Kimono in Seventeenth-century England' in Anna Jackson (ed.), *Kimono: Kyoto to Catwalk* (London 2020), pp. 37–78

Nwafor 2011
Okechukwu Nwafor, 'Photography and the Spectacle of *Aṣọ Ebì* in Lagos, 1960–2010' (unpublished PhD thesis, University of the Western Cape, 2011)

Nwafor 2012
Okechukwu Nwafor, 'Of Mutuality and Copying: Fashioning *Aṣọ Ebì* through Fashion Magazines in Lagos', *Fashion Theory*, Vol. 16, No. 4 (2012) pp. 493–520

Oware 2018
Matthew Oware, *I Got Something to Say: Gender, Race and Social Consciousness in Rap Music* (Basingstoke 2018)

Oyama 2020
Yuzuruha Oyama, 'The Nippon Kimono Voyages to Europe' in Anna Jackson (ed.), *Kimono: Kyoto to Catwalk* (London 2020), pp. 129–36

Palmer 2017
Lisa Amanda Palmer, '"Men Cry Too": Black Masculinities and the Feminisation of Lovers' Rock in the UK' in Jon Stratton and Nabeel Zuberi (eds), *Black Popular Music in Britain Since 1945* (London 2017)

Park 2005
Roberta J. Park, 'Muscles, Symmetry and Action: "Do You Measure Up?" Defining Masculinity in Britain and America from the 1860s to the Early 1900s', *The International Journal of the History of Sport*, Vol. 22, No. 3 (2007), pp. 1604–36

Patterson 2009
Angus Patterson, *Fashion and Armour in Renaissance Europe: Proud Lookes and Brave Attire* (London 2009)

Petersen 2008
Freya Petersen, 'Aussiebum: Down Under Designs in More Ways Than One', *International Herald Tribune* (21 Jan 2008)

Pino, Pardo (ed.) 1984
Paolo Pino, Mary Pardo (ed.), *Dialogo della pittura* (Pittsburgh 1984)

Pointon 1978
Marcia Pointon, 'Painters and Pugilism in Early Nineteenth-Century England', *Gazette des Beaux Arts*, Vol. 92 (1978), pp. 131–3

Pointon 1993
Marcia Pointon, *Hanging the Head: Portraiture and Social Formation in Eighteenth-Century England* (New Haven and London 1993)

Pointon 2013
Marcia Pointon, 'Accessories in Portraits: Stockings, Buttons and the Construction of Masculinity in the Eighteenth Century' in Marcia Pointon, *Portrayal and the Search for Identity* (London 2013), pp. 121–80

Postle 1997
Martin Postle, 'Naked Authority? Reproducing Antique Statuary in the English Academy from Lely to Haydon' in Anthony Hughes and Erich Ranfft (eds), *Sculpture and Its Reproductions* (London 1997)

Potts 1994
Alex Potts, *Flesh and the Ideal: Wincklemann and the Origins of Art History* (New Haven and London 1994)

Radford 2012
Peter Radford, 'The Olympic Games in the Long Eighteenth Century', *Journal for Eighteenth-Century Studies,* Vol. 35, No. 2 (2012), pp. 161–84

Raguenet 1723
François Raguenet, *Roma Illustrata* (London 1723)

Razzall 2006
Lucy Razzall, 'The Pockets of Henry Fielding's Writing', *The Cambridge Quarterly*, Vol. 35, No. 4 (2006) pp. 361–77

Redford 1996
Bruce Redford, *Venice and the Grand Tour* (New Haven and London 1996)

Reinach 2017
Simona Segre Reinach 'Ethnicity' in Alexandra Palmer, (ed.), *A Cultural History of Dress and Fashion in the Modern Age* (London 2017), pp. 151–70

Reynolds 2013
Anna Reynolds, *In Fine Style: The Art of Tudor and Stuart Fashion* (London 2013)

Reynolds 1988
Sir Joshua Reynolds, *Discourses on Art* (New Haven and London 1988)

Ribeiro 2012
Aileen Ribeiro, 'Gustave Caillebotte: Paris Street; Rainy Day' in Gloria Groom (ed.), *Impressionism, Fashion and Modernity* (exh. cat., Art Institute of Chicago, Chicago, Metropolitan Museum of Art, New York, Musée d'Orsay, Paris 2012)

Richardson 1754
Jonathan Richardson, *An Account of the Statues, Bas-reliefs, Drawings and Pictures in Italy, France, &c.* (London 1754)

Riello 2006
Giorgio Riello, *A Foot in the Past: Consumers, Producers and Footwear in the Long Eighteenth Century* (Oxford 2006)

Rout 2020
Josephine Rout, 'Behind the Screen: Kimono as Costume' in Anna Jackson (ed.), *Kimono: Kyoto to Catwalk* (London 2020), pp. 231–41

Saccardi 2018
Nadia Saccardi, 'Who Wore the Breeches?: An Insight into Early Modern Female Cross-Dressing, between the 1570s and 1625', *Critical Studies in Men's Fashion*, Vol. 5, Nos 1–2 (2018), pp. 55–70

Salzmann 1800
C.G. Salzmann [Johann Friedrich GutsMuths], *Gymnastics for Youth...* (London 1800)

Sand, Jurgrau (trans.) 1991
George Sand, Thelma Jurgrau (trans.), *Story of My Life: The Autobiography of George Sand* (New York 1991)

Sandhu 2015
Arti Sandhu, 'A Brief History of Dress, Difference and Fashion Change in India' in Arti Sandhu, *Indian Fashion: Tradition, Innovation, Style* (London 2015), pp. 25–48

Scarce 1987
Jennifer Scarce, *Women's Costume of the Near and Middle East* (London and Sydney, 1987)

Scott 2004
Jonathan Scott, *The Pleasure of Antiquity: British Collections of Greece and Rome* (New Haven and London 2004)

Semmelhack 2017
Elizabeth Semmelhack, *Shoes: The Meaning of Style* (London 2017)

Seshagiri 2010
Urmila Seshagiri, *Race and the Modernist Imagination* (Ithaca 2010)

Seward 2020
Mahoro Seward, 'Kenneth Ize Wants to See More "Vulnerability in Men, Less Power"', *i-D Magazine* (6 Oct 2020)

Shepard 2005
Alexandra Shepard, 'From Anxious Patriarchs to Refined Gentlemen? Manhood in Britain, circa 1500–1700', *Journal of British Studies*, Vol. 44, No. 2 (2005), pp. 281–95

Sherwood 2010
James Sherwood, *Savile Row: The Master Tailors of British Bespoke* (London 2010)

Shove 2003
Elizabeth Shove, *Comfort, Cleanliness and Convenience: The Social Organization of Normality* (Oxford 2003)

Siegfried and Finkelberg 2020
Susan L. Siegfried and John Finkelberg, 'Fashion in the Life of George Sand', *Fashion Theory* (2020)

Sigsworth 1990
Eric M. Sigsworth, *Montague Burton: The Tailor of Taste* (Manchester 1990)

van Slyke 1998
Gretchen van Slyke, 'The Sexual and Textual Politics of Dress: Rosa Bonheur and Her Cross-Dressing Permits', *Nineteenth-Century French Studies*, Vol. 26, Nos 3–4 (Spring–Summer 1998), pp. 321–35

Snell 1750
Hannah Snell, *The Female Soldier: Or, the Surprising Life and Adventures of Hannah Snell* (London 1750)

Spence 1755
Joseph Spence, *Polymetis* (London 1755)

Sprecher 2020
Danielle Sprecher, 'Demob Suits: One Uniform for Another? Burtons and the Leeds Multiple Tailors' Production of Men's Demobilization Tailoring after the Second World War', *Costume*, Vol. 54, No. 1 (2020), pp. 108–30

Squire 1970
Geoffrey Squire, 'Liberty, Equality and Antiquity. Dress 1785–1820' in *The So-Called Age of Elegance: Costume 1785–1820* (London 1970)

Stanfill 2014
Sonnet Stanfill (ed.), *The Glamour of Italian Fashion since 1945* (London 2014)

Stanhope 1860
Philip Dormer Stanhope, *The Works of Lord Chesterfield including His Letters to His Son, &c.* (New York 1860)

Statt 1995
Daniel Statt, 'The Case of the Mohocks: Rake Violence in Augustan London', *Social History*, Vol. 20, No. 2 (1995), pp. 179–99

# INDEX

Illustrations and captions are in *italics*.

THE COMPLETE ENCYCLOPEDIA OF

# WORLD MOTORCYCLES

**De Dion Bouton 1900 Trike**
Deutsches-Zweirad Museum
and NSU Museum
Neckarsulm, Germany

Harley-Davidson 1929 JDH
Owner – Otis Chandler
Ojai, California

THE COMPLETE ENCYCLOPEDIA OF

# WORLD MOTORCYCLES

EDITED BY
MIRCO DE CET

BMW 1957 R60 with Steib sidecar
National Motor Museum
Beaulieu, England

GREENWICH
EDITIONS

This edition published in 2004 by
Greenwich Editions
The Chrysalis Building
Bramley Road
London W10 6SP



An imprint of **Chrysalis** Books Group plc

ISBN 0-86288-681-3

1 3 5 7 9 8 6 4 2



All correspondence concerning the content of this volume should be addressed to Salamander Books Ltd.

## CREDITS

**Editorial Director:** Will Steeds **Project Manager:** Ray Bonds
**Art Director:** John Heritage **Designer:** Mark Holt
**Photographer:** Neil Sutherland **Colour reproduction:** Studio Tec
**Production:** Phillip Chamberlain
Produced by SNP Leefung
Printed In China

**NSU 1939 Kompressor**
Deutsches-Zweirad Museum
and NSU Museum
Neckarsulm, Germany

# ACKNOWLEDGMENTS

We recognize that some words, model names and designations for example, mentioned herein are the property of the trademark holder. We use them for identification purposes only. This is not an official publication.

Photographs identified as such are copyright Harley-Davidson Motor Company and are provided courtesy of Dr. Martin Jack Rosenblum, Historian, Harley-Davidson Juneau Avenue Archives.

In addition the publishers are grateful to the many individuals and organizations credited as owners of the motorycles shown in the photographs, and/or those who have made them available for photography, including the following museums and commercial outlets:

**USA:** Glenn H. Curtiss Museum, American Motorcycle Heritage Foundation, Chandler Vintage Museum, Guggenheim Museum, Wheels Through Time Museum, and Antique Motorcycle Club of America.

**UK:** Doug Hill of National Motor Museum, National Motorcycle Museum, Marcus Blackburn of P&H Motorcycles Ltd., Lee Waddell and Graham Sanderson of Three Cross Motorcycles, Conquest Restorers, Powerhouse Motorcycles.

**Germany:** Igor Sachs of BMW Mobile Tradition Museum, Peter Kuhn and Dr. Klaus-Dieter Roos of Deutsches-Zweirad Museum and NSU Museum, Karlheinz Böckle at Auto & Technic Museum.

**Triumph 1954 TR5 Trophy**
Owner – Tony East of A.R.E. Ltd
England

# THE EDITOR

Mirco De Cet was introduced to motorcycles at a very early age, as his parents and other relatives used small-capacity Morinis, Moto Guzzis and the like as a cheap means of transportation in the Dolomite mountains in northern Italy. After moving to England his dream came true when he began work for the motorcycle magazine *On Two Wheels*. Ever since, he has not only had the opportunity to photograph countless motorcycles but also to ride, test and write about them. He has contributed to many books on classic motorcycles from all periods and from many continents, and his photographs have illustrated several international specialist motorcycle magazines and books, in particular the much-acclaimed *Classic British Bikes*.

In the preparation of the text for this book, he has drawn on the text of *The Complete Illustrated Encyclopedia of American Motorcycles* by Tod Rafferty (who, apart from being proprietor of the American Garage, has written several books on aspects of motorcycles, including what have now become standard works on Harley-Davidson machines), and *The Complete British Motorcycle* by John Carroll (who has written a number of books on Indian and Harley-Davidson motorcycles, and worked for a variety of two- and four-wheeled publications including a spell editing *Back Street Heroes*, the cult English custom bike magazine).

**Derbi Senda R**
Powerhouse Motorcycles Ltd
Kent, England

# CONTENTS

**Moto Guzzi 2000 California EV**
Three Cross Motorcycles
Dorset, England

# INTRODUCTION

This book describes and illustrates some truly magnificent motorcycles that designers and engineers from most parts of the globe have created over the last hundred years or so. It is also the story of pioneers of personal transportation who to begin with more or less came up with different ways to make bicycles move forward without effort by the rider, and then with increasingly sophisticated ways to make them faster and safer and more comfortable, as well as to stop when required. It is a record of the evolution of the motorcycle as it developed from a motorized bicycle (except, of course, the "Erstes Einrad-Motoradd" shown below) to what has now become a technologically sophisticated push-button machine. Along the way, natural human competitiveness has played its part, on the racing circuit and in the marketplace; wars have intervened, as well as prejudices against "noisy, smelly machines"; and, above all, overriding competition from the all-enclosed comfort of the automobile has had an effect to varying degrees and at different times on the success of the motorcycle.

Many of the manufacturers featured within these pages have long gone, along with the brilliant engineers and fearless racers. Fortunately, many of the results of their ingenious inventions, and stories of their exploits, remain to enthral us today.

Deciding on a list of bikes to be featured could only have been a subjective business, considering the thousands that have leapt off the drawings boards and hit the roads or racetracks of the world. Most if not all of the major marques are represented here. When I initially wrote down the names, I came up with bikes that would probably be on any motorbike enthusiast's list, but I wanted this book to be different

**"Erstes Einrad-Motorrad"**
Auto & Technic Museum
Sinsheim, Germany

**Left:** The "Erstes Einrad-Motorrad" is considered by many to be the world's first "motorcycle." It is a single-cylinder, 150cc (9.92cu in), 3.5hp machine, in which the wheel revolves around the rider and the engine. It dates from 1894 – and apparently it still goes!

from all those that have gone before. So I set to, and arrived at a much more varied range of motorcycles, including some that might be regarded as obscure (such as the one-off TS 500), or even bizarre, like the Kreidler Zigarre, and the unusual, like the 1948 Imme. I wanted them to sit alongside the classic Harleys and Indians, the Nortons and the Yamahas. The result, I believe, is a really interesting selection from around the world and from different periods of motorcycle development.

There are big bikes and small bikes, old bikes and new bikes; bikes for motorcycle sports enthusiasts, on-road and off-road; fun bikes; run-around bikes for commuters, and long-distance cruisers; soldiers' bikes; kids' bikes and first bikes; cheap bikes, and those that few could afford; bikes that a mechanically-minded rider could tinker with, and those that would need a rocket scientist to service. There are bikes that have been lovingly and for the most part faithfully restored, and also the latest bikes which still have the manufacturers' or retailers' stickers on them.

The next task was to go out and find the bikes and have them photographed. And what a joyful experience that has been. We have enjoyed the most helpful assistance from private owners, museums, restorers, and busy retail outlets who have taken the time and trouble to make their bikes available for long and arduous photographic sessions, wheeling their light, or heavy, or awkward, and often tremendously valuable motorcycles in front of the camera and away again. And, especially with the older models, each has had a story to be mulled over, a specific point of interest to be described. It's sure been a lengthy and fascinating journey.

Mirco De Cet
2001

**Right:** Showing how much the motorcycle has evolved since the machine on the left was first ridden, Honda's fabulous SP-1 is a four-stroke V-twin designed to win world superbike races, which it has achieved at speeds close on 200mph (320kph).

**Honda SP-1**
P&H Mototcycles
Sussex, England

# Ace

**Founded:** 1920
**Factory location:** Philadelphia, Pennsylvania, USA
**Manufacturing lifespan:** 1920 - 1927

1923 Ace XP4
Owner – Dr. John Patt
Gilbertsville, Pennsylvania, USA

Many collectors reckon the Ace (which, along with others, owes fealty to the FN marque of Belgian origin) was the best inline four ever built. The line stands in history as the final products of William Henderson's design and engineering, which first appeared under his own name in 1912. Henderson, the foremost four-cylinder engineer in the United States, was killed in an automobile accident in December 1922. The XP4 special built by Arthur Lemon and Everett De Long established a record in 1923 when, with test rider Red Wolverton aboard, it ran just a few ticks shy of 130mph (209kph), and the XP3 hauled a sidecar and passenger up to 106mph (171kph). But the company's financial foundation had crumbled by then and it dissolved in 1924. In 1927 the assets were purchased by the Indian Motorcycle Company, which restored the fours to production. For a period the bikes were renamed the Indian Ace but by 1929 the name Ace was consigned to the history books.

**Specifications (XP4)**
**Engine:** Air-cooled inline four
**Displacement:** 1262cc (77.01cu in)
**Horsepower:** 45 @ 5400rpm
**Wheelbase:** 59in (150cm)
**Weight:** 295lb (134kg)
**Top speed:** 129mph (208kph)

**Above:** The XP4 was a one-off Ace built specifically for top speed, and regardless of expense. All moving parts were drilled or shaved for lightness.

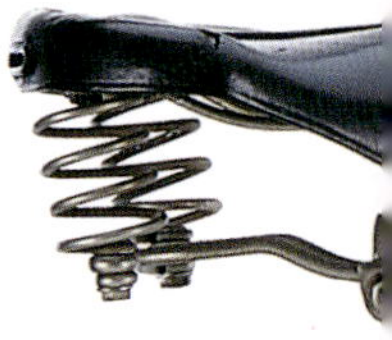

# Adler

**Founded:** 1900
**Factory location:** Frankfurt, Germany
**Manufacturing lifespan:** 1900 - 1957

Adler produced motorcycles with engines of their own manufacture for the first decade of the 20th century. From around 1910 until the outbreak of World War II in 1939, the company concentrated on the production of other items, including typewriters. In 1949 production of motorcycles was taken up once more with the manufacture of a lightweight two-stroke. From this Adler progressed to produce and market, for a short period, a range of slightly higher displacement machines. The 1953 MB 250 machine was a development of Adler's successful two-stroke 195cc (11.89cu in) twin MB 200 of 1951. The increased capacity was achieved by both bore and stroke being 54mm. The engine, fitted with a 180° crankshaft, was noted for its reliability. The clutch was on the crankshaft end and primary drive to the gearbox was by means of helical gears. The MB 250 had a leading link front fork assembly, a plunger-style frame and the final drive chain was fully enclosed. Despite this obvious quality the difficulties faced by German motorcycle manufacturers toward the end of the 1950s meant that production of the MB 250 was short-lived. Adler's return to motorcycle production ended completely when it became part of Grundig. Once again production was switched back solely to typewriters.

**Specifications (1902 Model)**
**Engine:** IOE single
**Displacement:** 370cc (23cu in)
**Horsepower:** 2.5
**Wheelbase:** N/A
**Weight:** N/A
**Top speed:** N/A

**Right:** All early Adlers used their own engines. They were of 3, 3.5 and 5 horsepower. This machine is belt driven, which can be seen running back to the large rear wheel pulley.

**Specifications (1952 200)**

**Engine:** Two-stroke twin
**Displacement:** 195cc (11.89cu in)
**Horsepower:** 9 @ 5600rpm
**Wheelbase:** N/A
**Weight:** 300lb (135kg)
**Top speed:** 60mph (95kph)

**Right:** This 1952 model has an enclosed front drum brake and chain guard. These items helped to maintain the chain and keep the brake in good working order.

**Adler 1952 Model**
Deutsches-Zweirad Museum
and NSU Museum
Neckersulm, Germany

**Left:** It looks like you might need more than two hands to ride this machine. All the engine controls are placed above the tank on the crossbar.

**Adler 1902 Model**
Deutsches-Zweirad Museum
and NSU Museum
Neckarsulm, Germany

**Above:** Looking nicely in proportion from the front, this bike has a large front light to help visibility at night.

# Aermacchi

**Founded:** 1912
**Factory location:** Varese, Italy
**Manufacturing lifespan:** 1912 - 1978

1961 Sprint
Owner – Otis Chandler
Ojai, California

Aermacchi was founded by Giulio Macchi in 1912 to build aircraft. Motorcycle manufacture came with the arrival of designer, Ing Lino Tonti, whose first model, in 1950, was an unorthodox, open-frame lightweight 123cc (7.50cu in) two-stroke engine with a single horizontal cylinder. Subsequently, a 246cc (15cu in) variant was produced through the use of two 123cc (7.50cu in) engines siamesed together.

The company had its first forays into competition with entries in the International Six Days Trial. When Tonti left, his place was taken by Ing Alfredo Bianchi, whose first, futuristic design, the Chimera, was highly acclaimed at the 1956 Milan Show, although it proved a costly flop in terms of sales. However, undressed of its bodywork, the bike became the basis for Aermacchi's sports and racing machines.

Harley-Davidson acquired a 50 percent stake in Aermacchi in 1960, and the racing motorcycle business prospered, while its range of road bikes was not inconsiderable with eight varying models. Much of the production went to the USA.

In 1972 Harley-Davidson acquired control of Aermacchi, redesigned the range, and replaced the name with AMF Harley-Davidson. But the company was put into receivership in 1978 and was acquired by Cagiva, who produced variants of the existing models under the new tank badge.

**Specifications (1961 Sprint)**
**Engine:** Ohv horizontal single
**Displacement:** 246cc (15.01cu in)
**Horsepower:** 18
**Wheelbase:** 52in (132cm)
**Weight:** 275lb (125kg)
**Top speed:** 75mph (121kph)

**Above:** Aermacchi helped fulfill a persistent urge of Harley-Davidson's to offer a lightweight motorcycle.

# AJS

**Founded:** 1909
**Factory location:** Wolverhampton/London, England
**Manufacturing lifespan:** 1909 – to date

The Stevens family owned a screw company, based in Wolverhampton, and also made engines. The four Stevens brothers built the first AJS motorcycle in 1909. Their first bike featured a 298cc (18.17cu in) side valve engine, designed by them. Following this came the 348cc (21.24cu in) and 498cc (30.37cu in) side-valve versions and there were also models with V-twin side-valve engines of 550cc (30.50cu in) through 990cc (60.41cu in).

The 348cc (21.24 cu in) ohv single was one of the first English machines with this configuration. A 498cc (30.37cu in) ohv engine was produced in 1925. AJS also designed a special 743cc (45.34cu in) engine for racing at Brooklands and a 996cc (60.78cu in) V-twin with two chain-driven camshafts to tackle world records. For the TT there was also 248cc (15.13cu in) ohc engine.

But 1931 saw things going badly for AJS and the company was sold to the Collier brothers, makers of the Matchless motorcycle. They moved AJS to Plumstead, London, where Matchless was based. ▶

**Specifications (1915 Model D)**
**Engine:** Four-stroke V-twin
**Displacement:** 748cc (45.62cu in)
**Horsepower:** N/A
**Wheelbase:** N/A
**Weight:** 276lb (125kg)
**Top speed:** N/A

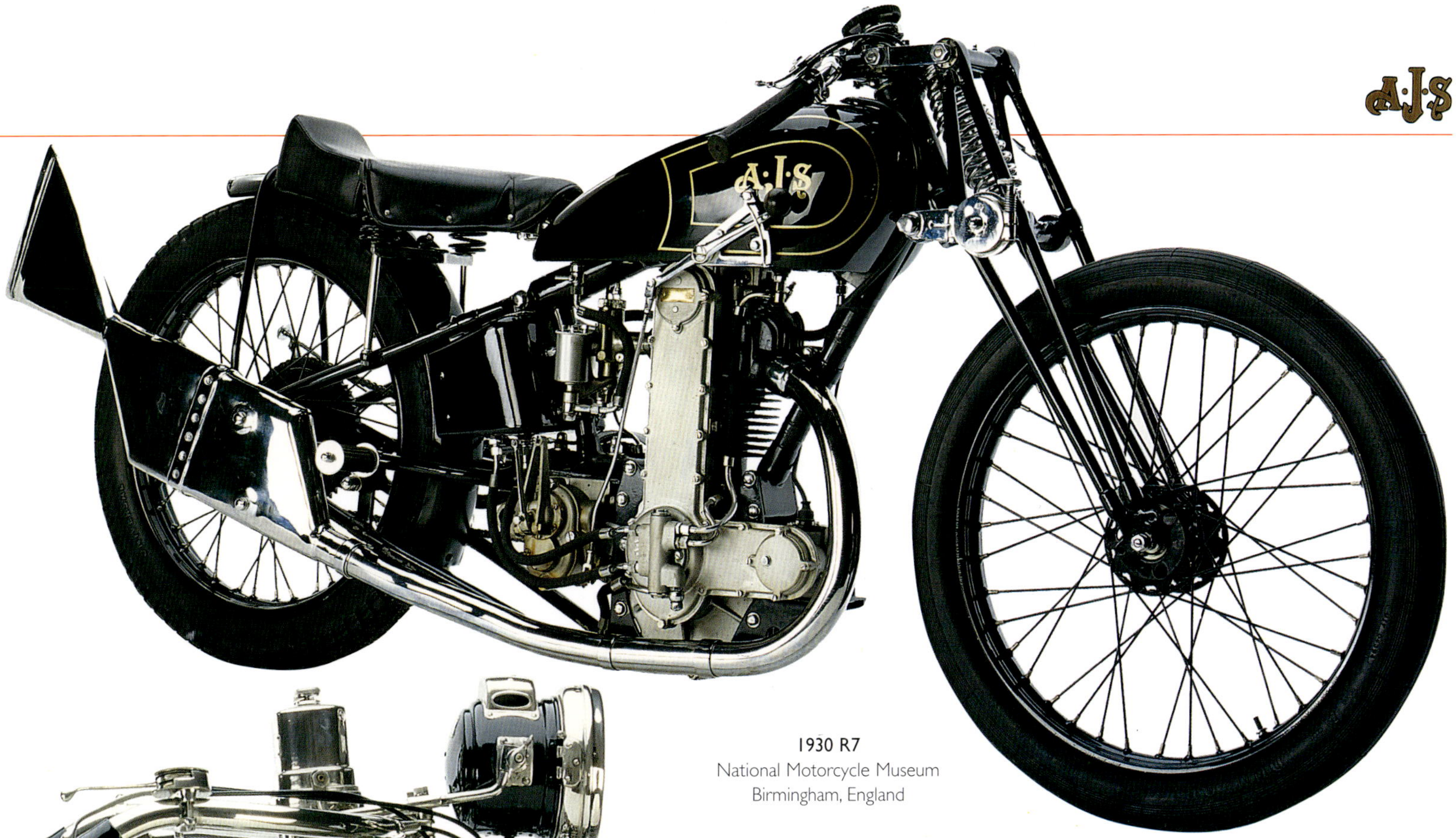

1930 R7
National Motorcycle Museum
Birmingham, England

**Specifications (1930 R7)**
**Engine:** Four-stroke ohc single
**Displacement:** 346cc (21cu in)
**Horsepower:** N/A
**Wheelbase:** N/A
**Weight:** 290lb (132kg)
**Top speed:** N/A

**Above:** The R7 had a chain-driven overhead camshaft. The chain reached from the crankcase to the cambox in the alloy case on the side of the cylinder barrel.

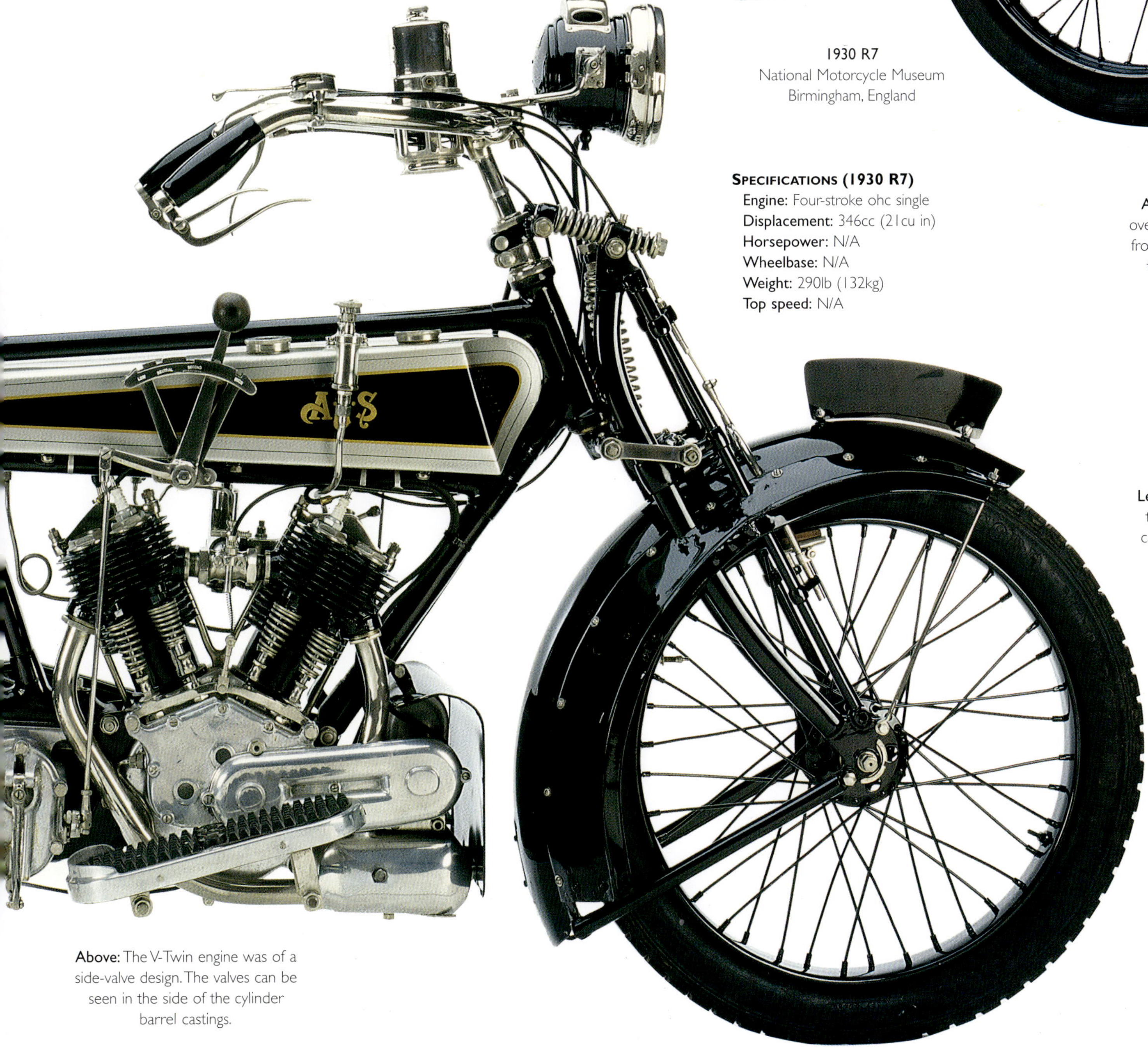

**Left:** Acetylene lights that relied on the reaction between water and calcium carbide were fitted to the front and rear of the bike.

**Above:** The V-Twin engine was of a side-valve design. The valves can be seen in the side of the cylinder barrel castings.

1915 Model D
National Motorcycle Museum
Birmingham, England

From this time AJS and Matchless shared many of the same parts. During the 1930s there were trials and racing models. At the Olympia exhibition, in London, the company even showed an air-cooled 495cc (30.21cu in) ohc V four, the racing version of which competed in the 1936 TT. Prior to the breakout of war AJS produced some of the fastest road racing machines of the period.

Soon after the war AJS presented the Porcupine, which was raced by the works team. In 1954 the factory withdrew from racing, and limited developments. By then a part of Associated Motor Cycles Ltd., along with Norton and Matchless, they moved to a new factory in Andover in 1969. Taken over by Manganese Bronze Holdings, AJS moved into the sphere of Norton-Villiers Ltd., of Wolverhampton. At this time all AJS four-strokes were dropped and only trials and motocross machines were built in the new works. Although faded out, AJS is not entirely gone. Fluff Brown heads the AJS concern whose backbone of business today is world-wide supply of AJS Stormer and Villiers Starmaker spares, from their works in Andover.

**Specifications (1954 Porcupine)**
**Engine:** Four-stroke dohc parallel twin
**Displacement:** 499cc (30.37cu in)
**Horsepower:** 55 @ 7600rpm
**Wheelbase:** N/A
**Weight:** N/A
**Top speed:** N/A

1954 Porcupine
National Motorcycle Museum
Birmingham, England

**Below:** The Porcupine nickname came about as a result of the number of fins cast into the engine to aid cooling. The name stuck even when these fins were later discontinued.

## Aprilia

**Founded:** 1968
**Factory location:** Noale, Venice, Italy
**Manufacturing lifespan:** 1968 to date

This Italian company is a relative newcomer, founded as recently as 1968. It started out producing small-capacity motorcycles for trials and motocross. During the 1980s the company began campaigning Grand Prix motorcycles in the 125cc (7.62cu in) and 250cc (15.26cu in) classes.

Initially the race bikes used Austrian Rotax engines but later the company used its own design. Co-operation with Rotax helped to realise the Pegaso, a machine that clearly derived from the Paris-Dakar style of on/off road bikes that enter that race. The first 250 World Championship came in 1994 with Max Biaggi as the rider. Following this the company introduced a road bike of the same capacity and clearly inspired by racing technology. This machine was the RS 250. Aprilia continued to produce new models into the new millennium with such bikes as the RST1000 Futura sports tourer, the CapoNord maxi trail bike, the Mille and Mille R, which are already by now considered modern classics.

**Specifications (RS 250)**
**Engine:** Two-stroke V-twin
**Displacement:** 249cc (15.19cu in)
**Horsepower:** N/A
**Wheelbase:** N/A
**Weight:** 308.6lb (140kg)
**Top speed:** N/A

**SPECIFICATIONS (RSV MILLE R)**
- **Engine:** Four-stroke longitudinal 60 V-twin
- **Displacement:** 997.62cc (60.88cu in)
- **Horsepower:** N/A
- **Wheelbase:** N/A
- **Weight:** 403.4lb (183kg)
- **Top speed:** N/A

**Right:** The Aprilia RSV Mille R uses standard components of the highest possible level; everything has been set-up and modified technically so as to achieve a balance of technology and performance and riding efficiency.

RSV Mille R
Courtesy of Aprilia
Venice, Italy

**Below:** The technology and experience that have led Aprilia to world championships are rigorously applied to the RS 250 road bike.

Aprilia RS 250
Powerhouse Motorcycles
Ashford, England

**Above:** The 90 degree V-twin two-stroke of the RS 250 is hidden behind a very neat and aerodynamic fairing. Buying one of these bikes allows the rider to take part in the 250 challenge, organised by Aprilia to spotlight new talent.

**Left:** The RS 250 has twin disc brakes on the front and a single on the rear. Single rear shock absorber and twin silencers give a neat finish to the rear end.

# Aprilia

Aprilia also concentrated on their range of scooters, reacting to an ever increasing demand brought about by emission and traffic controls. Hardly new to this style of transport, they continued to enhance their model range. One example for the year 2001 was the SR50 Ditech, which could cover over 60 miles (100 kilometers) with as little as half a gallon (2 liters) of fuel and with emission levels that were much lower than that required by legislation.

The new DITECH direct electronic injection is one generation ahead of the rest. Unlike traditional two-stroke engines, the fuel is no longer mixed with the oil and air in the crankcase, but rather injected directly into the combustion chamber by a sophisticated injector, managed by an electronic control unit. The fuel is injected only when the exhaust ports are closed: this significantly minimizes the emission of unburned fuel and oil into the exhaust, and thus the environment. The "heart" of the DITECH technology is the Air-Fuel-Rail, made up of the Fuel Injector, which doses the exact amount of fuel, and the Direct Injector, which mixes the fuel and the air from the compressor, and sends it into the combustion chamber. The fuel/air mix is atomized into particles measuring just 8 microns (against the approx. 50 microns in automobile injection systems), the density of which is controlled so as to maintain ideal combustion, drastically cutting fuel consumption and further improving performance. The entire process is managed by a sophisticated electronic control unit, which optimizes the operation of the engine at all times, and signals any faults instantly; in this way, the performance is always "top", and maintenance is much simpler and less costly.

**Specifications (SR50LC Scooter)**
- **Engine:** Two-stroke single
- **Displacement:** 50cc (3.051cu in)
- **Horsepower:** N/A
- **Wheelbase:** N/A
- **Weight:** 196.2 lb (89kg)
- **Top speed:** N/A

SR50LC Scooter
Courtesy of Aprilia
Venice, Italy

**Left:** This little scooter is already a legend and now Aprilia have given it even more power, reduced consumption and kept polluting gases to a minimum. All thanks to their DITECH (Direct Injection Technology) system.

# Ardie

| | |
|---|---|
| **Founded:** | 1919 |
| **Factory location:** | Nuremberg, Germany |
| **Manufacturing lifespan:** | 1919 - 1958 |

Ardie took its name from the founder Arno Dietrich, who was previously a designer for Premier. The first Ardie machines used the company's own 305cc (18.61cu in) and 348cc (21.24cu in) two-stroke deflector-type engines. Arno Dietrich was tragically killed in a racing accident in 1922. After this the factory was taken over by the Bendit company and from 1925 used a variety of British-made JAP four-stroke engines. The bikes were fitted with singles and V-twins that ranged from 246cc (15.01cu in) through 996cc (60.78cu in) but the most popular used an overhead-valve 490cc (29.90cu in) single.

Ardies were known for being very well made with many luxury details. Their advanced specification included one of the earliest uses of aluminum-alloy frames on a mass-produced motorcycle.

**Specifications (1927 Model)**
- **Engine:** Four-stroke twin
- **Displacement:** 750cc (45.77cu in)
- **Horsepower:** 16
- **Wheelbase:** N/A
- **Weight:** N/A
- **Top speed:** N/A

**Right:** During this period it was not strange to see bikes with two stands, one that clipped down from behind the front wheel and another which came from the back wheel.

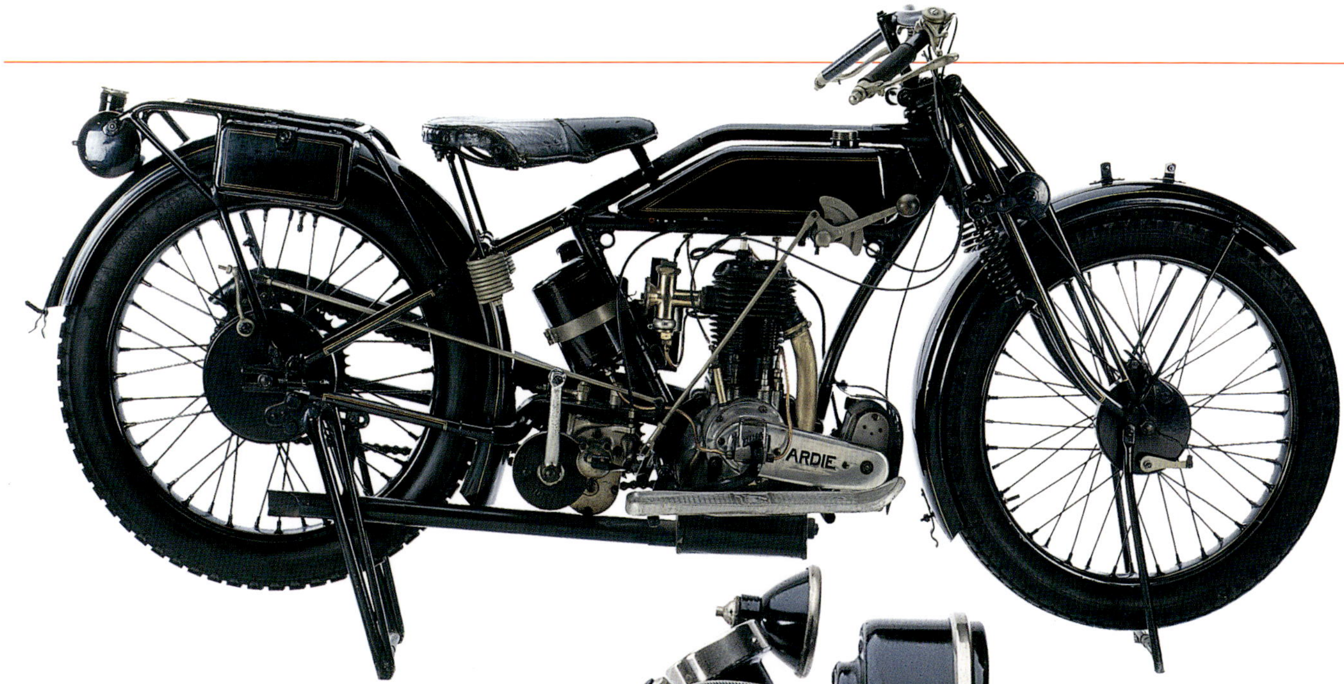


**Specifications (1928 Touremodel)**

**Engine:** Four-stroke single
**Displacement:** 484cc (29cu in)
**Horsepower:** 9.5
**Wheelbase:** N/A
**Weight:** N/A
**Top speed:** N/A

**Left:** This is the Touremodel of 1928. During this period Ardie were making machines with engines of up to 500cc (30.50cu in). This single was classed as one of the best German machines of its period.

**Above:** This machine had footboards and hand gearchange; note lever on side of the tank. It used its own 484cc (29cu in) 9.5hp engine.

**1928 Ardie Touremodel**
Deutsches-Zweirad Museum
and NSU Museum
Neckarsulm, Germany

**Below:** Up to 1925 Ardie used their own engines. This 1927 model is fitted with a JAP V-twin. This was not unique to this company; many motorcycle companies would shop around for their engines.

**1927 Ardie**
Deutsches-Zweirad Museum
and NSU Museum
Neckarsulm, Germany

# ARDIE

From the early 1930s, Ardie began to use engines supplied by German makers Bark, Kuchen, and Sachs, as well as the British Sturmey Archer factory. The bikes' alloy frames were also abandoned during the 1930s, in favor of more conventional tubular steel designs. An unconventional machine was built in 1938 using a transversely mounted 348cc (21.24cu in) V-twin ohv engine but the model never went into serious quantity production.

The company competed well in the 1920s and early 1930s, gaining many wins, among them the TT in Austria and Hungary.

After World War II, the Ardie company was taken over by the Durkopp factory based in Bielefeld, but continued under its own management. Unusually for the time, the factory also built its own two-stroke engines, designed by Ardie's engineering director Dr. Noack. The smallest machines used 122cc (7.44cu in) engines and the larger capacity bikes went up to a 344cc (20.99cu in) twin. A boom in the 1950s led the company into moped production in 1953 and sales hit a record high in 1955. However, Ardie was one of many German bike makers hit by a rapid downturn in the industry in the late 1950s and went into liquidation in 1958.

**SPECIFICATIONS (1937 MODEL)**
- **Engine:** Four-stroke single
- **Displacement:** 200cc (12.2cu in)
- **Horsepower:** 9
- **Wheelbase:** N/A
- **Weight:** 330lb (130kg)
- **Top speed:** N/A

**Right:** In 1922 Arno Dietrich was killed in an accident and the Ardie company was run by the Bendit family. Although engines were bought in, this 1928 type TM uses a factory engine of 500cc (30.5cu in).

**Below:** Times were hard in the late 1930s and a small capacity machine like this little 9hp 200cc (12.2cu in) model would have sold well.

**Ardie 1937 RZ 200**
Deutsches-Zweirad Museum
and NSU Museum
Neckarsulm, Germany

Ardie 1928 TM28
Deutsches-Zweirad Museum
and NSU Museum
Neckarsulm, Germany

**Specifications (1928 TM28)**
**Engine:** Four-stroke single
**Displacement:** 500cc (30.27cu in)
**Horsepower:** 9
**Wheelbase:** N/A
**Weight:** N/A
**Top speed:** N/A

**Left:** The 500cc Ardie engine was a very popular motor, although the company also bought in V-twins from JAP in England.

**Above:** Like the headlamp on the front of this machine, Ardie motorcycles came large but were never very effective.

## Ariel

**Founded:** 1902
**Factory location:** Selly Oak, Birmingham, England
**Manufacturing lifespan:** 1898 - 1970

This concern, which started in 1898, produced De Dion-engined three-wheelers in Birmingham, England. In 1902 production of single-cylinder White & Poppe-engined motorcycles commenced. Initially these bikes were powered by Kerry engines, and had magneto ignition and a float-type carburetor. By 1905 Charles Sangster had acquired the Ariel company and he designed a lightweight two-stroke, which was called the Arielette. It carried several advanced features such as a three-speed gearbox but unfortunately the outbreak of World War I put a stop to sales.

After the war the company introduced a 4hp single-cylinder White & Poppe-engined machine. Expansion of the range continued into the 1920s, during which time Edward Turner joined the company as a technician working under chief designer Val Page. Jack Sangster, son of Charles and now head of the Ariel works, was one of the few to entertain Turner's idea for the sophisticated Square Four.

The Square Four, which was powered by an air-cooled four-cylinder engine, had four vertical cylinders arranged in a square configuration. Production started in 1931. ▶

1949 Square Four
Owner – Tony East of A.R.E. Ltd
England

**Specifications (1949 Square Four)**
**Engine:** Four-stroke four
**Displacement:** 498cc (30.37cu in)
**Horsepower:** N/A
**Wheelbase:** N/A
**Weight:** N/A
**Top speed:** 95mph (152kph) est.

**Above:** The engine was revised several times during the production run. In 1949 it was an all-alloy unit of 995cc (60.70cu in) displacement with a bore and stroke of 65 x 75mm.

The first model had a 500cc (30.51cu in) engine, which was soon joined by a 600cc (36.61cu in) version. The engine capacity was increased to 997cc (60.84cu in) in 1937 and the Square Four stayed in production in this form until 1958. Alongside the "Squariel," as it was fondly known, were the Red Hunter singles.

The world recession of the early thirties hit Ariel hard and the factory had to close in 1932. Jack Sangster decided to take the company into his own hands and, keeping only one part of the factory, he sold off all the rest to raise money. The company became known as Ariel Motors (JS) Ltd. Designer Val Page was one of several who left at this stage. When war broke out again, the company produced the W/NG, based on the 1939 Red Hunter and built for the British Army.

After World War II the range consisted of Red Hunter singles, ohv twins, and the Square Four. Val Page rejoined Ariel and the 1950s saw the introduction of the twin-cylinder Huntmaster range. In 1954 the Square Four became a MkII "four piper," with two separate exhaust pipes placed on each side of the bike. With the company looking for a new direction, much investment went into a two-stroke that Val Page was working on. This was the Ariel Leader 250cc (15.26cu in). It had a revolutionary frame in which the engine was suspended from the bottom of a pressed-steel box member that stretched from the steering head back to the rear suspension mountings. It had a parallel-twin two-stroke engine, enclosed on both sides by panels and leg shields, a windshield and panniers and several other new ideas. The fully equipped bike was well received but never sold well.

Ariel decided therefore to strip the panels and do away with leg shields, and made several other changes. The stripped-down version was called the Ariel Arrow and the factory also included a sports version with gold and white paintwork and whitewall tyres. The redesigned model did sell well.

The company also took some interest in scrambling and trials events. Among the regulars who rode a much-modified Ariel single was a young Ulsterman who would become a legend in his own time, Sammy Miller.

**SPECIFICATIONS (1949 NH HUNTER)**

**Engine:** Four-stroke single
**Displacement:** 346cc (21.10cu in)
**Horsepower:** N/A
**Wheelbase:** N/A
**Weight:** N/A
**Top speed:** 75mph (120kph) est.

**SPECIFICATIONS (1958 FH HUNTSMASTER)**

**Engine:** Four-stroke vertical twin
**Displacement:** 647cc (39.5cu in)
**Horsepower:** 34bhp @ 5750rmp
**Wheelbase:** 56in (1422mm)
**Weight:** 365lb (166kg)
**Top speed:** 100mph (161kph)

1958 FH Huntsmaster
Owner – Tony East of A.R.E. Ltd
England

**Below:** The Ariel twin engine was bolted into a steel tubular cradle frame, but the swingarm was manufactured from welded steel pressings.

1958 FH Huntsmaster
Owner – Tony East of A.R.E. Ltd
England

**Specifications (1964 Leader)**
- **Engine:** Four-stroke single
- **Displacement:** 247cc (15.06cu in)
- **Horsepower:** 17.5 @ 6750rpm
- **Wheelbase:** N/A
- **Weight:** N/A
- **Top speed:** 70mph (112kph)

**Above:** Much of the styling of the Leader drew its inspiration from the Italian scooters popular in the early 1960s. The engine remained in the conventional motorcycle position but it was all enclosed like a scooter.

**Below:** The panniers seen fitted each side of the rear wheel of this machine were an optional extra aimed at further increasing the practical application of the Leader as a commuter motorcycle.

**Above:** This 1949 NH Hunter was built to what was in reality a prewar specification – rigid frames, half width hub brakes, tank-mounted instruments and switches.

**1964 Leader**
National Motorcycle Museum
Birmingham, England

# Ariel

Ariel 3
Owner – Tony East of A.R.E. Ltd
England

By the early 1960s, the BSA group, of which Ariel was now part, found itself in financial difficulties. One of the last bikes produced by Ariel and designed by Val Page was the 50cc (3.051cu in) Pixie. With the need to rationalize, the production version was turned out with a 50cc (3.051cu in) BSA Beagle engine. The Selly Oak factory was by now a thing of the past, and Ariel manufacturing had been moved to Small Heath. Production of the Arrow started again but did not last for long. A three-wheeler had been developed with a Dutch-made Anker 50cc (3.051cu in) engine, but this, the Ariel 3, never caught the public eye and finally the Ariel name came to an end.

**Specifications (Ariel 3)**
**Engine:** Two-stroke single
**Displacement:** 49cc (2.99cu.in)
**Horsepower:** N/A
**Wheelbase:** N/A
**Weight:** N/A
**Top speed:** N/A

**Right:** The Ariel 3 was another attempt to offer a functional machine to the British public, rather than something styled as a motorcycle. It was novel but unsuccessful.

# Armstrong

**Founded:** 1980
**Factory location:** Bolton, Lancashire, England
**Manufacturing lifespan:** 1980 - 1987

In 1980 Armstrong, a manufacturer of automotive components, moved into motorcycle production through the acquisition of Cotton, a company which had intermittently produced motorcycles since 1919, including Rotax-powered machines from 1976. Armstrong subsequently acquired CCM (Clews Competition Motorcycles) in 1981. The new company produced Rotax-powered road racers, off-road competition machines, and military motorcycles. The military machines were based on the off-road competition bikes since the thinking behind the design of military motorcycles had changed radically. Previously, military motorcycles were essentially militarized versions of roadgoing singles and twins, but by the time Armstrong came to supply military machines, the advantages of a lighter, off-road type of machine had been perceived. The design of off-road bikes had progressed rapidly during the 1970s, so the Armstrong MT500 bore little resemblance to the BSAs and Nortons ridden by previous generations of soldiers.

Armstrong withdrew from motorcycle manufacture in 1987, although Harley-Davidson acquired rights in the design of the MT500 and went on to produce a machine that was very similar to it for military use. Motorcycles such as these saw action in the Gulf War of 1991.

1985 Model
National Motorcycle Museum
Birmingham, England

**Specifications (1985 Model)**
**Engine:** Four-stroke single
**Displacement:** 482cc (29cu in)
**Horsepower:** 31.5 @ 6200rpm
**Wheelbase:** N/A
**Weight:** 315lb (150kg)
**Top speed:** 90mph (144kph)

**Left:** The Armstrong MT500 was powered by a 485cc two-stroke engine that gave it a top speed of 95mph (153kph) The whole machine was designed to be simple and rugged.

# ATK

**Founded:** 1983
**Factory location:** Centerville, Utah, USA
**Manufacturing lifespan:** 1983 – to date

The ATK company was founded in 1983 by Austrian transplant Horst Leitner in southern California. His first design was a chain-tensioning device for dirt bikes, which in English-German was called the Anti-Tension Kettenantrieb, and abbreviated was ATK.

Leitner began building motorcycles in 1987, using Honda engines and selling frame kits to home builders. The next generation ATK employed the Austrian-built Rotax engines, which remain the powerplants today. The company was among the first to offer specialized four-stroke machines for off-road recreational and competition use. In 1993 ATK was purchased by investors, and operations moved to Centerville, Utah, near Salt Lake City.

ATK also builds a 50cc (3.051cu in) mini-motocrosser; 250cc (15.26cu in) enduro (the 245lb/111kg 260E with liquid-cooled two-stroke single engine giving 28hp and a top speed of 95mph/153kph); 350cc (21.35cu in) and 490cc (29.9cu in) four-stroke cross-country and enduro models; and 500cc (30.50cu in) /600cc (36.61cu in) dirt-track machines.

**Specifications (1998 605E)**
**Engine:** Four-stroke single
**Displacement:** 598cc (36.49cu in)
**Horsepower:** 38
**Wheelbase:** 59in (150cm)
**Weight:** 305lb (138kg)
**Top speed:** 110mph (177kph)

**Below:** Rotax four-stroke engines have had wide application in custom dirt bikes worldwide. The 605 has a Paioli 1.8in (46mm fork), Ohlins shock, and Brembo brakes.

**1998 ATK 605E**
Courtesy of ATK
Centerville, Utah

# Benelli

**Founded:** 1911
**Factory location:** Pesaro, Italy
**Manufacturing lifespan:** 1911 – to date

One of the oldest surviving motorcycle builders in Italy, the company was set up as a repair business by six brothers and gradually moved on to producing components for various diverse industries. After World War I the company began production of lightweight motorcycles. Larger capacity models followed, including a 250cc four-cylinder racing bike. World War II intervened during which the factory made parts for the military. The factory was destroyed during the war but soon got back to producing small capacity machines. Of note were the two- and four-stroke versions of the Leoncino 125. The Motobi name emerged in 1950 as a separate concern when Giuseppe Benelli left the company to start up the new marque.

Benelli were active on the racing front, with regular riders including Renzo Passolini, Mike Hailwood, Tarquino Provini, and of course Kel Caruthers, who claimed the World 250cc Championship in 1969. During the 1960s Benelli (who by now had the Motobi concern under their wing) began exporting considerable numbers of machines to the USA. Motobi inspired singles, vertical singles in two- and four-stroke versions, and of course what could be judged as the last real Benelli prior to the De Tomaso takeover, the 650 Tornado.

Benelli were having financial difficulties by the early 1970s and were bought out by the Argentinian Alejandro De Tomaso. A range of four- and six-cylinder bikes were produced to complement the existing products, ranging from the four-cylinder 250cc to the mighty 750cc and later 900cc six-cylinder machines. These continued through to the 1980s when the 125 Jarno street racer was introduced. More financial problems arose at this time, but fortunately Benelli were sold to an enthusiastic businessman, Andrea Merloni, and today the factory produces a range of modern scooters, and intends to build a superbike sometime in the future.

**Specifications (1978 Sei - 750)**
**Engine:** Four-stroke six
**Displacement:** 747.7cc (45.52cu in)
**Horsepower:** 71 @ 8900rpm
**Wheelbase:** N/A
**Weight:** 485lb (219kg)
**Top speed:** 113mph (181.9kph)

**Right:** When first put on the market, the 750 Sei was the only six-cylinder bike in production. A full tank gave it a range of about 250 miles (400km), ideal for touring.

**Specifications (2000 491 Scooter)**
**Engine:** Two-stroke single
**Displacement:** 49.2cc (3cu in)
**Horsepower:** N/A
**Wheelbase:** N/A
**Weight:** 190lb (85kg)
**Top speed:** 35mph (56kph) restricted; 55mph (88kph) unrestricted

**Right:** The Benelli 491 is a sporty little water-cooled 49cc (3cu in) scooter, with 7.5in (190mm) brake discs at the front and rear, and aluminum wheels.

**2000 491 Scooter**
Powerhouse Motorcycles
Ashford, England

**Left:** If you want space to store your helmet, look no further than under the seat where there is room. Or if you prefer you can, for a little extra cost, purchase a small rear rack and box.

**1978 Sei - 750**
National Motor Museum
Beaulieu, England

**Below:** Twin disc brakes at the front help to stop the bike which has a top speed of 113mph (180kph). It has telescopic forks with coil springs and dampers as front suspension.

**Above:** Even a rear end shot of the bike allows you to see the sides of the six-cylinder engine. The exhausts also distinguish it from other machines.

## BIMOTA

bimota

**Founded:** 1972
**Factory location:** Rimini, Italy
**Manufacturing lifespan:** 1972 - 2001

Deciding they could improve on the handling of the big four-cylinder Japanese machines, three Italians formed the Bimota company, naming it after the first two letters of the founders' names, Bianchi, Morri, and Tamburini. Their first bike was based on the Honda CB750 four and called the HB1 (H for Honda, B for Bimota). Nearly all their bikes were designated this way. Clever engineering solutions, immaculate construction, attention to handling and weight factors all contributed to some of the very best machines produced.

One example of such innovative engineering was the 1982 Tesi prototype which comprised a Honda V4 engine in a carbon fiber frame. Production started in 1990, by which time Bimota had moved from using only Japanese engines to those from Ducati. For the Tesi 1D model they chose the state-of-the-art 90deg V-twin. Bimota also made their mark in racing, winning the World 350cc Grand Prix championship in 1980 and the 1987 TT-F1 championship with their YB4, ridden by Virginio Ferrari. The following year saw the launch of the first bike with a Bimota engine, the 500 V-Due. Unfortunately, financial problems pushed the company into voluntary liquidation by 2001.

**Specifications (HB2)**
**Engine:** Four-stroke four
**Displacement:** 900cc (54.92cu in)
**Horsepower:** 95 @ 9000rpm
**Wheelbase:** N/A
**Weight:** 480lb (219kg)
**Top speed:** 147mph (235kph)

**Above:** Bimota were well known for taking Japanese bikes, and later Italian ones too, and improving on the overall performance and handling. This is a Honda-engined machine.

**HB2**
Courtesy Mirco De Cet

# BMW

**Founded:** 1917
**Factory location:** Munich, Germany
**Manufacturing lifespan:** 1917 – to date

To this day, BMW's logo represents a spinning propeller, signifying its roots as an aircraft engine manufacturer. At these roots were two companies, Rapp Motorenwerke and Otto Werke, and on 20 July 1917 the former was renamed the Bayerische Motorenwerke GmbH. At the beginning of 1917 Max Friz had joined the Rapp company from Daimler, at the request of Franz-Joseph Popp, the technical director. Rapp had built itself a bad reputation for making unreliable engines for the military and it was partly to shed this reputation that the name was changed. Under Popp and Friz the new joint-stock company reversed its fortunes and gained new military orders, but ran into financial difficulties while running at full capacity, which it was overcoming just as World War I came to an end. After the war, BMW's shares were taken over by Knorr-Bremse AG who wanted the company to produce mainly air brakes and the like, not something that Popp and Friz really wanted. Popp joined forces with one of the old shareholders, Camillo Castiglioni, and convinced him to re-acquire the name BMW. This they did along with all construction rights and production facilities not required for the manufacture of air products. With a move to the Bayerisch Flugzeugwerke premises, Popp was eventually able to concentrate solely on engines under the name of BMW.

At the instigation of engineer Karl Ruhmer, the production of a simple motorized bicycle, called the Flink, was started. Ruhmer designed the machine but the engine was bought in from Carl Hanland of Berlin. In 1923 BMW's very first motorcycle designed and built by chief engineer Max Friz, the R32, made its debut at the motor shows in Paris and Berlin. It already had the classic two-cylinder characteristics, a boxer engine fitted in the crosswise position, transmission connected directly to the engine and shaft drive, all wrapped up in a double loop frame. The R47 followed in 1927. The ohv sports model benefited from modified running gear and suspension. It had gray cast iron cylinders and a two-slide carburetor that replaced the complicated three-slide version. ▶

**SPECIFICATIONS (1921 FLINK)**
**Engine:** Two-stroke single
**Displacement:** 143cc (8.72cu in)
**Horsepower:** 1.5
**Wheelbase:** N/A
**Weight:** 90lb (40kg)
**Top speed:** 32mph (50kph)

**1921 Flink**
BMW Mobile Tradition Museum
Munich, Germany

**Above:** Although the "Flink" was designed by Karl Ruhmer, it used an engine that was bought in from Carl Hanland in Berlin.

**SPECIFICATIONS (1923 R32)**
**Engine:** Four-stroke flat twin
**Displacement:** 494cc (30.10cu in)
**Horsepower:** 8.5
**Wheelbase:** N/A
**Weight:** 270lb (120kg)
**Top speed:** 60mph (90kph)

**Right:** Making its world debut in 1923, at the Paris show, the R32 was the first ever vehicle to be developed and built in the history of Bayerische Motoren Werke (BMW).

**Specifications (1927 R47)**
Engine: Four-stroke flat twin
Displacement: 494cc (30.10cu in)
Horsepower: 18 @ 400rpm
Wheelbase: N/A
Weight: N/A
Top speed: 65mph (96kph)

**Right:** The sporting ohv R47 was introduced in 1926. One change for this model came in the way of a band brake on the drive shaft instead of the old block and pulley brake on the rear wheel.

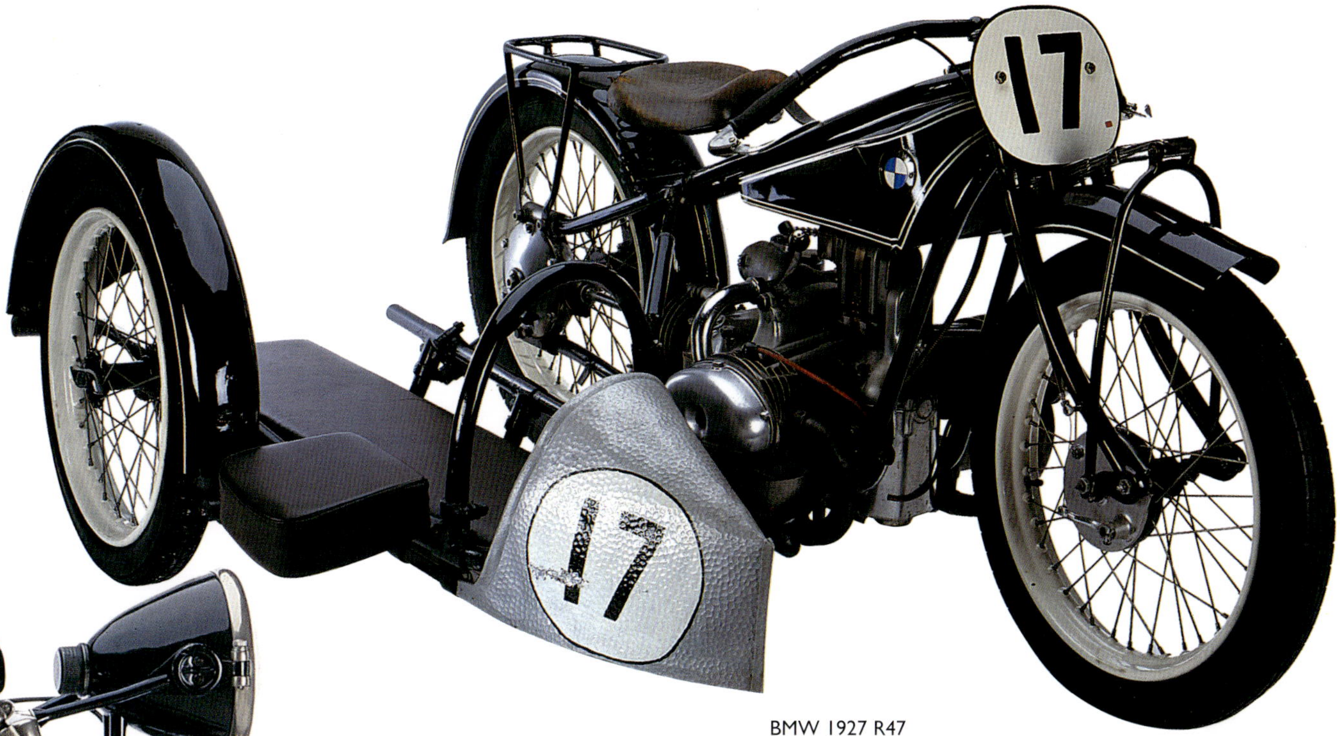


BMW 1927 R47
Auto & Technic Museum
Sinsheim, Germany

BMW 1923 R32
BMW Mobile Tradition Museum
Munich, Germany

**Left:** The connection between the gearbox and the rear hub was via shaft drive and final bevel gears. By centering the rear hub around a removable wheel spindle, taking the wheel off was made easier.

**Above:** The R32 was not particularly light for that period, but by redesigning the engine Friz managed to increase the output, enabling the bike to reach 56mph (90kph).

# BMW

During late 1923, graduate engineer Rudolf Schleicher designed a light-alloy cylinder head with enclosed overhead valves. Installed in the 1925 R37 it developed maximum output of 16bhp and provided the basis for racing machines that were destined to make the BMW brand famous both on the race track and in off-road motorcycle events. It was basically this machine that provided the starting point in 1929 for BMW's attempt at the world motorcycle speed record. Best known of the record breakers was Ernst Henne who on 19 September 1929 achieved 134mph (216kph) on a 750cc (45.77cu in) model BMW equipped with a supercharger. This was just over 6mph (10kph) more than the previous record. Almost exactly one year later Henne also broke the record for the "flying mile." Between him and various English riders, the records were broken again and again.

All BMWs built before 1929, except the R39 (dropped in 1927), had half-litre (30cu in) side-valve and overhead-valve engines. The first 750cc-class (45cu in) model, the R62, went into production in 1929 and this remained the maximum engine size until the 1970s. The engine's actual capacity was 733cc (44.73cu in) and all but the engine size was the same as the smaller machines. The R63, introduced during the same period, was also available as a 750cc machine and its power could be boosted further for racing. Following up was the R11, using a pressed-steel frame. Development of the engine culminated in the 5th series in 1934, featuring a chain-driven camshaft and two carburetors. In 1931 came a new single-cylinder 198cc (12.08cu in) model, the R2, which featured a lightweight pressed-steel frame and drum brake on the rear wheel. More power was supplied by the 1934 model.

1928 R63
National Motor Museum
Beaulieu, England

**Specifications (1928 R63 750)**
- **Engine:** Four-stroke flat twin
- **Displacement:** 745cc (45.462cu in)
- **Horsepower:** 24 @ 4000rpm
- **Wheelbase:** N/A
- **Weight:** 342lb (155kg)
- **Top speed:** 75mph (47kph)

**Specifications (1929 R11)**
- **Engine:** Four-stroke flat twin
- **Displacement:** 745cc (45.462cu in)
- **Horsepower:** 18 @ 3400rpm
- **Wheelbase:** N/A
- **Weight:** N/A
- **Top speed:** N/A

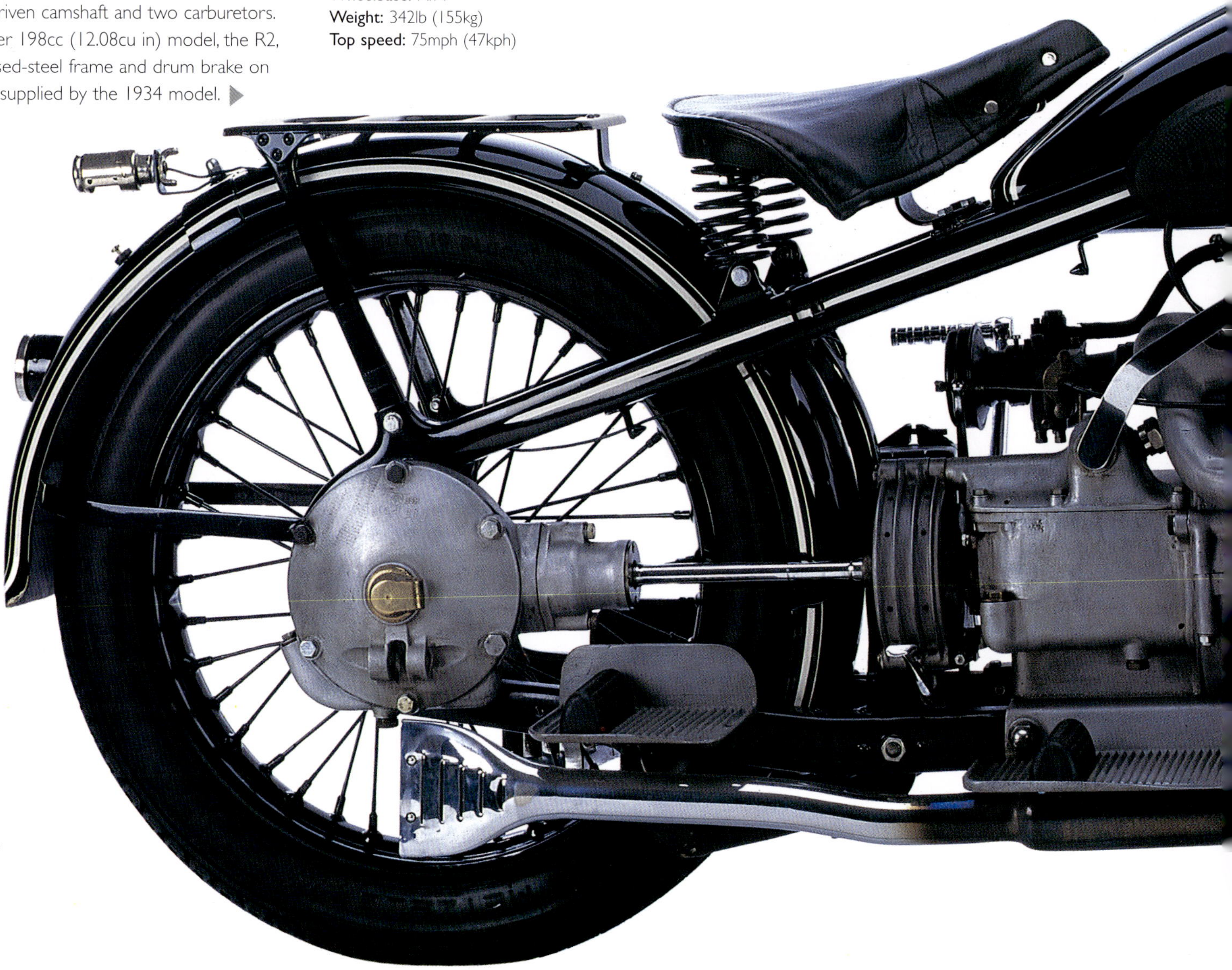

**Right:** The BMW R11 motorcycle was introduced at a time when machines started to appear with many items as standard – the lighting, a horn, speedometer and floating wheel spindles front and rear, just to name a few.

Left: The R62 and R63 (shown) were the first 750cc (45.77cu in) twins from BMW. The latter was capable of 75mph (120kph) and became the basis for the record breaking machines used by Ernst Henne between 1929 through 1935.

Below: Timing gears were replaced by a quieter chain and the carburetor even acquired an air filter. Shrouded with extras, the machines should have sold well. Unfortunately one of the biggest economic world crises was just around the corner.

**Specifications (1930 R2)**
**Engine:** Four-stroke single
**Displacement:** 198cc (12.082cu in)
**Horsepower:** 6 @ 3500rpm
**Wheelbase:** N/A
**Weight:** 242lb (110kg)
**Top speed:** 59mph (37kph)

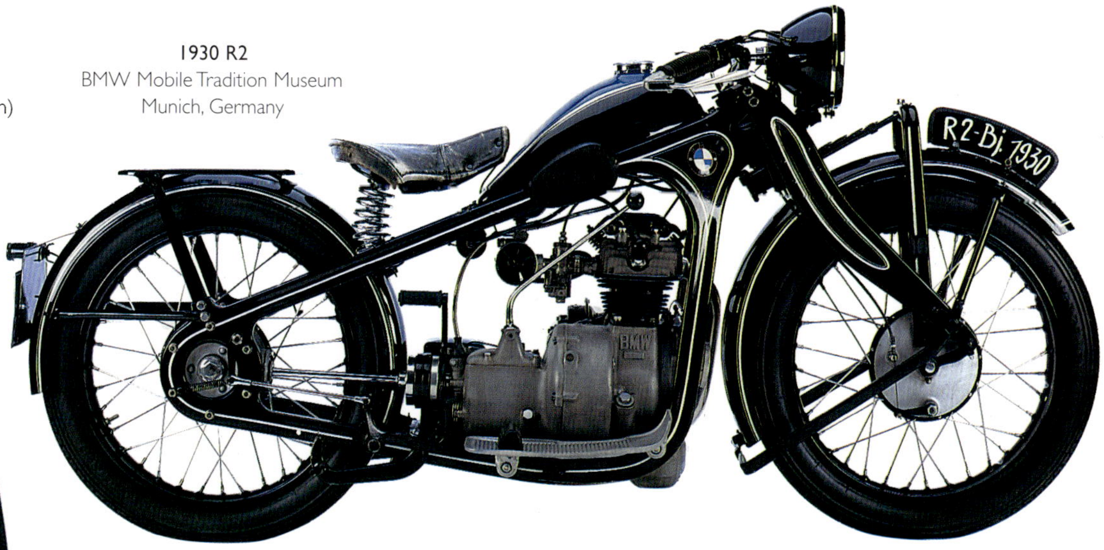


1930 R2
BMW Mobile Tradition Museum
Munich, Germany

Above: The R2 was known as the "People's" model. Brought in during one of the world's most crippling economic times, it used a small capacity, 200cc (12.2cu in) engine in a pressed-steel frame.

Left: With the R11 came the age of the pressed-steel frame. This was developed when BMW decided to go into car manufacture and bought the Dixie factory. Constructional techniques used by the car company were applied to motorcycles, hence the new frame.

Left: The drive shaft on the R11 had new flexible couplings fitted inside.

1929 R11
BMW Mobile Tradition Museum
Munich, Germany

1935 World Record Machine
Deutsches-Zweirad Museum and NSU Museum Neckarsulm, Germany

**Specifications (1935 Record Machine)**
**Engine:** Four-stroke twin boxer with compressor
**Displacement:** 750cc (45.77cu in)
**Horsepower:** 100hp
**Wheelbase:** N/A
**Weight:** N/A
**Top speed:** 150mph (240kph)

**Left:** This is the machine on which Ernst Henne smashed so many records in Germany, Austria and Hungary. It was the holder of the flying 750/1000cc (45.77/61.02cu in) record in 1935, at 160.05mph (256.08kph).

**Specifications (1952 R25/2)**
**Engine:** Four-stroke single
**Displacement:** 247cc (15.07cu in)
**Horsepower:** 12 @ 5600rpm
**Wheelbase:** 53.9in (137cm)
**Weight:** 309lb (140kg)
**Top speed:** 73mph (45.6kph)

BMW launched the R12 in 1935, introducing the first hydraulically dampened telescopic front fork in motorcycle construction. It used the same side-valve engine as in the R11, dropped into a pressed-steel frame and supplied with either a single Sum or two Amal carburetors. The R12 was built exclusively for the military from 1938. The R17 became not only Germany's most expensive motorcycle but also its fastest. Using a more powerful engine, it was marketed as an exclusive sports model. By 1936 a crankshaft-driven supercharger was fitted to BMW racing machines. The R5 was launched, a completely new Schleicher design featuring a thoroughly modified boxer engine with two camshafts, seamless tubular frame, and footrests in place of footboards. It also had a foot gearchange mechanism. Ernst Henne set up yet another world speed record for motorcycles in 1937: the "Eternal" record of 173.3mph (279.5kph) which stood for a further 14 years.

In 1938 BMW's 55bhp supercharged machine hit headlines all over European race circuits. Georg Meier finally brought home the European Championship. Then in 1939 he astounded the world with his win in the Isle of Man TT, the first non-British rider on a foreign machine to achieve this. But when war broke out in Europe in 1939, BMW became the largest manufacturer to supply motorcycles to the Wehrmacht, who in 1938 had issued a specification for a sidecar outfit intended for cross-country use. BMW satisfied it with the machine that became the R75. During the war, the Munich factory was destroyed and BMW's remaining plant later found itself inside the Russian Occupied Zone. All the company's drawings had been lost but by dismantling a prewar machine to take measurements BMW was able to start producing motorcycles again. The R24 single ready in 1947, but it was not allowed to be delivered to customers until 1948.

The R25 singles were introduced in 1950 and modified during a six-year period to become the R25/2 and R25/3, the latter becoming BMW's most produced model, with a total of 47,700 units. During 1950 the company once again launched a twin-cylinder machine the R51/2, a new and upgraded version of the prewar R51, which was followed swiftly by the 590cc (36cu in) R67.

**Right:** The R67 used a 600cc (36.61cu in) engine and was the first new twin machine to be produced after the war.

**1953 R67/2**
Auto & Technic Museum
Sinsheim, Germany

**SPECIFICATIONS (1953 R67/2)**

**Engine:** Four-stroke flat twin
**Displacement:** 594cc (36.248cu in)
**Horsepower:** 26 @ 5500rpm
**Wheelbase:** N/A
**Weight:** 423lb (192kg)
**Top speed:** 90mph (56kph)

**Left:** The R67 with its large capacity was ideal for pulling a sidecar outfit. The bike was steadily improved over the next few years.

**Below:** It was a while after World War II that the Allies allowed Germany to get back into motorcycle manufacture. The R25 was developed from the R24, one of the first BMWs to be made after the war.

**Above:** The R67 was known as 'the angel of the road.' It transported the gangs of men and women who went around the country repairing all the roads that had been damaged by bombs during the war.

**Left:** The R25 was an improvement on the R24, the frame was strengthened and it was given telescopic rear suspension. It had such a strong frame that a sidecar could be fitted without worries.

**1952 R25/2**
Auto & Technic Museum
Sinsheim, Germany

# BMW

A new model generation was launched in 1955 with the R26, R50, and R69, with full swinging arm suspension and leading-link Earles-type forks. One year earlier had seen the launch of the RS model, built for motorsport. It achieved a top speed of 124mph (200kph). That same year the company also started its 20-year domination of the world sidecar championship. As the 1960s approached, the motorcycle boom in Germany faded. Motorcycle production had to make way for cars, but as the 1970s dawned, the two-wheel market started to pick up again and BMW introduced its /5 series, using redesigned 500cc (30.50cu in), 600cc (36.61cu in), and 750cc (45.77cu in) engine units. The 50th anniversary of production came in 1973 and the company turned out its 500,000th machine since 1923. BMW also produced its first machines larger than 750cc: the R90/6 and R90S used a 900cc (54.92cu in) engine, followed in 1977 with the one-liter (61.023cu in) 100/7, 100S, and R100RS. The latter was the first machine in the world to have a full fairing as standard. The RS was backed up by a touring model, the R100RT.

BMW raced again in 1976, this time in off-road events, gaining the German off-road title in 1979 and 1980, when a version of the off-road racer also entered the market as a refined production enduro model, the R80G/S. Success also came in the Paris-Dakar race. A new direction and a brand new bike came in 1983, the K series, first of which was the K100, a water-cooled straight four, shaft-driven via a monolever swinging arm. Two years later saw a smaller brother, the K75, a 750cc three-cylinder, and the K1, a high-performance version of the K100. ABS was introduced to the K100 and K75, another first for BMW. As environmental concerns grew, BMW added catalytic converters to its K series models. The millionth motorcycle came of the production line in 1991.

In 1993 BMW introduced a new boxer-engined generation of machines, with oil- nd air-cooled four-valve cylinder heads. With all its new technology and additions, the R1100RS was voted "Motorcycle of the Year." BMW also launched a new single-cylinder recreational on/off-road bike, the Funduro, featuring a 650cc (39.665cu in) engine. The old air-cooled boxer finally retired in 1996 but more new models followed: the largest capacity model yet in the 1996 K1200S and BMW's first ever cruiser, R1200C, in 1997. In the new millennium, BMW produced what it saw as the ultimate commuter bike in the enclosed C1 scooter, using a small-capacity engine.

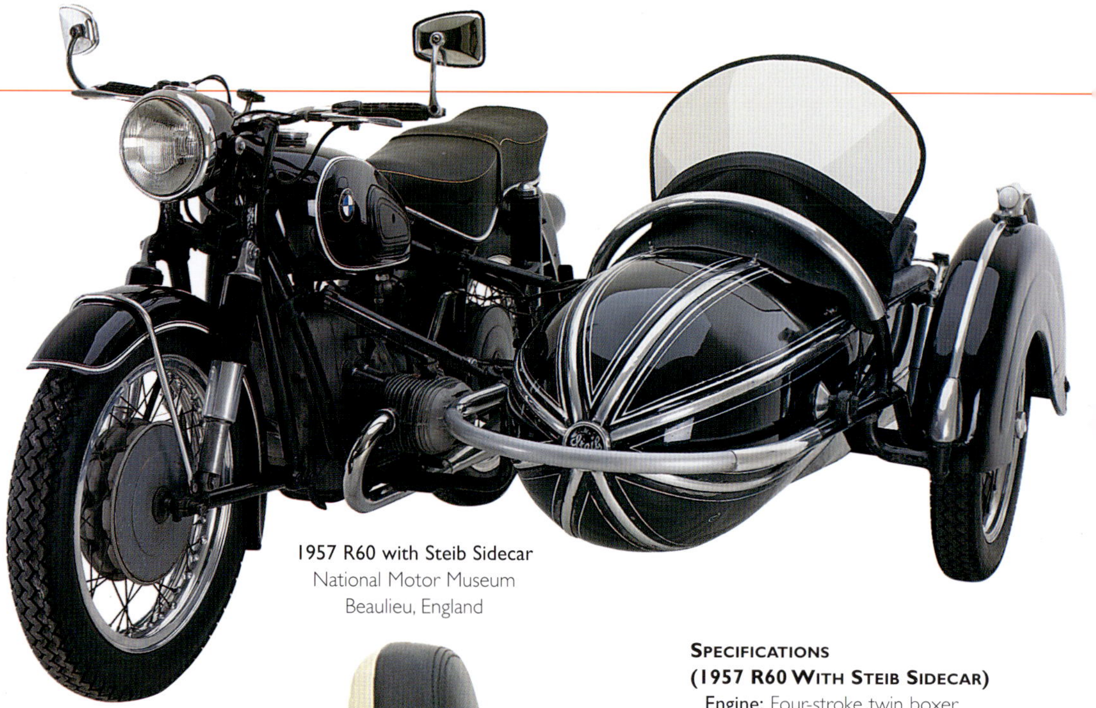

**1957 R60 with Steib Sidecar**
National Motor Museum
Beaulieu, England

**Above:** Sidecars were very popular in the late 1950s; this one is a Steib, manufactured in Nuremberg, Germany.

**Specifications (1957 R60 with Steib Sidecar)**
**Engine:** Four-stroke twin boxer
**Displacement:** 490cc (29.0cu in)
**Horsepower:** 26
**Wheelbase:** N/A
**Weight:** 430lb (195kg) – 705lb (320kg) with sidecar
**Top speed:** 70mph (112kph)

**Right:** The comfortable-looking upholstered backrest of the rider's seat can be folded back in such a way that it becomes an extra seat for a passenger.

1997 R1200C
National Motor Museum
Beaulieu, England

**Specifications (1977 R100RS)**
**Engine:** Four-stroke flat twin
**Displacement:** 980cc
**Horsepower:** N/A
**Wheelbase:** N/A
**Weight:** 500lb (227kg)
**Top speed:** 121mph (75.6kph)

**Right:** When announced in September of 1976, the R100RS looked completely different from any other BMW. The reason for this was the full fairing, which was wind-tunnel developed.

1977 R100RS
Deutsches-Zweirad Museum
and NSU Museum
Neckarsulm, Germany

**Below:** Quite obviously a BMW, this front end shot clearly shows the two distinctive cylinders protruding each side of the machine.

**Specifications (1997 R1200C)**
**Engine:** Four-stroke Boxer
**Displacement:** 1170cc (71.37cu in)
**Horsepower:** 61 @ 5000 rpm
**Wheelbase:** N/A
**Weight:** 584lb (265kg)
**Top speed:** 105mph (168kph)

**Above:** Distinctive Telelever front suspension, high US style handlebars, top speed of 105mph (168kph) and five speed gearbox – all part of the 1200's package.

**Left:** Powerful Brembo twin disc front brakes are operated via the lever on the upswept right-hand handlebar. Instrumentation is kept to a minimum but quite adequate.

## BÖHMERLAND

**Founded:** 1925
**Factory location:** Czechoslovakia
**Manufacturing lifespan:** 1925 - 1939

These machines, also supplied under the Czechie name, were designed by Albin Liebisch in an altogether unconventional way. Unlike most other motorcycles, they had a very long wheelbase, the frame was of tubular steel, and the forks were unusual in that, although they were leading-link, the suspension was by springs under tension. Solid wheels cast from light alloy have become commonplace, but they were novel when the Böhmerland featured them for the first time on a motorcycle.

A three-seater extra-long version was made, which had two fuel tanks mounted not over the engine in conventional fashion, but one each side of the rear wheel. There was also a racing version with shortened wheelbase, used for hillclimbs.

All machines used a single-cylinder 598cc (36.49cu in) ohv Liebisch engine with open pushrods and valve gear, but 1938 saw a 348cc two-stroke single with a lighter frame.

Not many Böhmerlands were built due to the start of war in Europe in 1939.

**Specifications (1928 Model)**
**Engine:** Four-stroke single
**Displacement:** 598cc (36.47cu in)
**Horsepower:** 16 @ 3000rpm
**Wheelbase:** N/A
**Weight:** N/A
**Top speed:** 59mph (95kph)

## BRITTEN

Britten

**Founded:** 1992
**Factory location:** Christchurch, New Zealand
**Manufacturing lifespan:** 1992 – to date

What started out as a dream by one man and a few friends turned out to be a successful motorcycle company. John Britten set up Britten Motorcycle Company from his workshop/garage where he started developing a new machine. After moving to other premises, development continued both there and on the race circuit. After many disappointments, wins did start to come both in international racing and national record breaking.

Britten designed a bike using two different engine sizes, the V1000 and the V1100.

Good results came, such as the 2nd and 3rd places in 1991 at The Battle Of The Twins, Daytona, USA.

Sadly John Britten died in 1995 after a short illness. The company scaled down after his death but his one desire, to build 10 bikes, has now been completed. The last was shipped to Las Vegas where the owner still has it in a crate. The others are scattered around the world – three in New Zealand, one in Italy, one in Holland, and four in the USA. A new motocross bike has been developed but a new engine is still being worked on.

Britten Racer
Courtesy of Britten Motorcycle Company
Christchurch, New Zealand

**Below:** The Britten has no frame, everything hangs from its very strong V-twin engine in which the cylinders are also part of the upper crankcase half to increase strength.

**Specifications (Racer)**
**Engine:** Four-stroke 60 V-twin
**Displacement:** 985cc (60cu in)
**Horsepower:** 153 @ 12,700rpm
**Wheelbase:** N/A
**Weight:** 300lb (136kg)
**Top speed:** 190mph (304kph)

**1928 Böhmerland**
Deutsches-Zweirad Museum
and NSU Museum
Neckarsulm, Germany

**Left:** Wholly unconventional in appearance, the Böhmerland was a Czech-manufactured design with the fuel tanks each side of the wheel at the back of the machine.

## Brough Superior

| | |
|---|---|
| **Founded:** 1921 | |
| **Factory location:** Nottingham, England | |
| **Manufacturing lifespan:** 1921 - 1940 | |

William E. Brough built single- and V-twin-engined motorcycles from 1908, but later concentrated on flat-twins. Not favoring these, his son George left the company and set up Brough Superior in 1921. He built the "Rolls-Royce of motorcycles" almost regardless of cost, mostly constructed around V-twin engines supplied by other British manufacturers. He made motorcycles that he personally liked to ride and was famed for competing on one nicknamed Old Bill during the 1920s. He assembled his motorcycles completely to make sure everything worked correctly, then stripped them again for painting and plating.

The SS100 was a high-performance machine that was assembled to the highest of standards. Only 384 were made. They were originally fitted with an overhead valve JAP V-twin but a Matchless-engined SS100 was announced in 1936. Smaller displacement models were the S80 and SS80 of 677cc (41.31 cu in) and 981cc (59.86 cu in) respectively.

Brough's most famous customer was T. E. Lawrence, "Lawrence of Arabia," who owned seven Broughs. He was tragically killed in 1935 in an accident on a Brough Superior. Production continued until 1940 but did not resume after World War II because Brough did not consider the engines available were suitable.

**Specifications (SS100)**
**Engine:** Four-stroke V-twin
**Displacement:** 995cc (60.96cu in)
**Horsepower:** N/A
**Wheelbase:** 59.5in (152.5cm)
**Weight:** 330lb (150kg)
**Top speed:** 100mph (161kph)

**Above:** The Brough Superior was made famous by George Brough competing on a version that he nicknamed "Old Bill." Also, T. E. Lawrence owned several machines.

**SS100**
National Motorcycle Museum
Birmingham, England

# BSA

**Founded:** 1906
**Factory location:** Birmingham, England
**Manufacturing lifespan:** 1906 - 1971

BSA stands for Birmingham Small Arms which, a long time before it manufactured motorcycles, mass-produced small arms. BSA produced its first motorcycle in 1910, a single-cylinder machine with belt drive. By 1920 there were three models in the range including a V-twin of 770cc (46.97cu in) displacement, which was seen as ideal for pulling sidecars. Harry Perry rode a 1924 model 350cc (21.35cu in) to the top of Mount Snowdon in Wales as a publicity stunt. After an embarrassment in the 1921 TT, BSA shied away from racing and preferred to concentrate on trials and reliability tests. In 1927, BSA introduced a 500cc overhead-valve single with its engine inclined forwards in the frame. With an S prefix to the bike's numerical year designation, it was generally accepted that this indicated that the model was a "sloper." The name stuck fast and the bike set a trend for inclined engines. The Sloper itself became a firm favourite and through annual upgrades remained in BSA's range until the mid-1930s.

The company concentrated on producing bikes that ordinary people would buy to ride to work and it was this philosophy which helped them to survive the Depression of the 1930s. During World War II, BSA produced over 120,000 of the M20 side-valve 500cc (30.50cu in) motorcycle for the Allied armies. In order to expand production during the war, BSA acquired Sunbeam, New Hudson and Ariel. Following the Allied victory in 1945, the factories owned by the DKW company was divided by the Iron Curtain that split Germany itself. As part of war reparations, the design of the DKW RT-125 was passed to the Allies. Harley-Davidson would later use it as the basis of the Hummer, while BSA came up with the Bantam, introduced in June 1946. Another important postwar design was the A7, which was a parallel twin with a bolted-on gearbox. By 1948 the company's range was comprehensive, from utility sidecar machines (the M-series) to sporting twins, and from 125cc (7.62cu in) motorcycles to 650cc (39.65cu in) models. ▶

**Specifications (1927 Model E)**
**Engine:** Four-stroke single
**Displacement:** 493cc (30.08cu in)
**Horsepower:** 20
**Wheelbase:** N/A
**Weight:** 337lb (153kg)
**Top speed:** 75mph (120kph) est.

**Specifications (1940 M20)**
**Engine:** Four-stroke single
**Displacement:** 469cc (30.26cu in)
**Horsepower:** 13 @ 4200rpm
**Wheelbase:** 54in (137cm)
**Weight:** 369lb (167kg)
**Top speed:** 63mph (101kph)

**Right:** The Sloper featured a hand gearchange lever for its three-speed gearbox. This lever can be seen on the side of the fuel tank where the shift gate arcs across the BSA emblem.

**Right:** In view of the lack of rear suspension, both pillion pad and saddle were sprung to give users a degree of comfort on late 1920s roads.

**Below:** The M20 was produced in vast numbers for the British Army and, like other military motorcycles of the time, was basically a militarized version of one of the company's prewar range.

**1940 M20**
National Motorcycle Museum
Birmingham, England

1927 Model E
Owner – Tony East of A.R.E. Ltd
England

**Specifications (1949 D1 Bantam)**

- **Engine:** Two-stroke single
- **Displacement:** 123cc (7.50cu in)
- **Horsepower:** 4.5 @ 5000rpm
- **Wheelbase:** 50in (127cm)
- **Weight:** 170lb (77kg)
- **Top speed:** 53mph (85kph)

**Below:** In order to make the Bantam as cheaply as possible, it was built to a very basic specification. The frame, for example, did not have rear suspension and chrome plate was kept to an absolute minimum.

**Above:** The drum brake fitted in the front hub was operated by a cable that ran back to a hand lever on the handlebars via a point on the front of the girder forks.

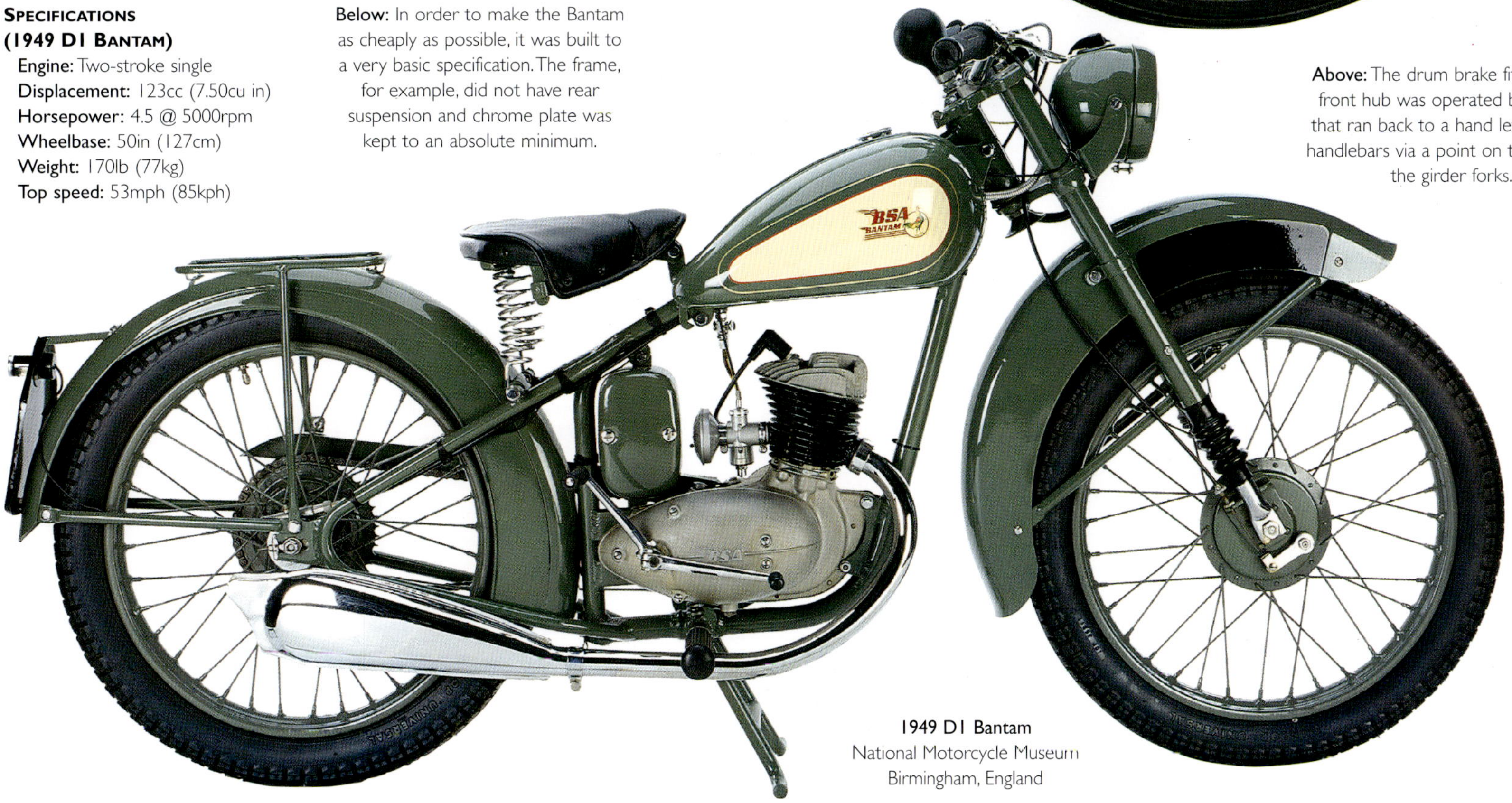


1949 D1 Bantam
National Motorcycle Museum
Birmingham, England

# BSA

Through the1950s it seemed that BSA could do no wrong. The basis of the range was solid singles such as the 350cc (21.35cu in) B31 that made its debut in 1945, followed by a 500cc (30.50cu in) B33 version in 1947, and the M33 in 1948. The M33 was intended for sidecar use and had a prewar designation and some prewar parts.

In 1948 the famous Gold Star appeared as the 350cc single B32GS, a tuned version of the 350cc B31. The first Gold Stars were supplied in a plunger frame and designated as ZB models. They became BB and CB models after the switch was made to swingarm frames in 1952, a move that anticipated a similar change to many of BSA's other motorcycles. From its introduction through the 1950s, the Gold Star came to be the stuff of legends mainly because of success in International Six Days Trials (11 trophies for the 500cc in one year, 1949) and Clubman's TT events at the Isle of Man. It was a versatile machine available in touring, trials, scrambles and racing versions, although it was necessary to alter the engine characteristics to suit the different events. Sequential upgrades were referred to by changes in designation. The CB models gave way to DB models in 1955, followed by the DBD models in 1957, this latter version surviving until the end of Gold Star production in 1963. A scrambles version of the DBD featured light alloy guards, knobbly tires, and larger diameter wheels to increase ground clearance. A smaller fuel tank was fitted while lights were not.

In September 1958 BSA launched a new series of unit-construction singles. First was the overhead-valve single-cylinder C15 247cc (15.07cu in) no-frills machine designed as a basic commuter based on the Triumph Tiger Cub. A year later there appeared trials and scrambles versions, featuring competition wheels and tires and raised exhaust systems but essentially similar to the roadgoing machine. The C15 later formed the basis of the B40, B44, and B50 and was finally superseded by the B25 Barracuda.

**Specifications (1955 B33)**
- **Engine:** Four-stroke ohv single
- **Displacement:** 499cc (30.5cu in)
- **Horsepower:** 23 @ 5500rpm
- **Wheelbase:** 54in (137cm)
- **Weight:** 340lb (154kg)
- **Top speed:** 80mph (129kph)

1955 B33
Owner – Tony East of A.R.E. Ltd
England

**Specifications (1961 Gold Star)**
- **Engine:** Four-stroke ohv single
- **Displacement:** 499cc (30.5cu in)
- **Horsepower:** 40 @ 7000rpm
- **Wheelbase:** 56in (142cm)
- **Weight:** 295lb (134kg)
- **Top speed:** Depends on gearing

**Right:** The off-road version of the Gold Star was supplied with minimal alloy fenders and knobbly off-road pattern tires.

1961 Gold Star
National Motorcycle Museum
Birmingham, England

Left: The single-cylinder B33 was a utility commuter bike built in the postwar years when the industry was shifting its emphasis to twin-cylinder engines.

1959 C15
National Motorcycle Museum
Birmingham, England

**Specifications (1959 C15)**
**Engine:** Four-stroke ohv single
**Displacement:** 247cc (15cu in)
**Horsepower:** 15bhp @ 7000rpm
**Wheelbase:** 51.5in (1308mm)
**Weight:** 143lb (65kg)
**Top speed:** 68mph (109kph)

**Above:** The C15 was one of a new range of unit-construction motorcycles made by BSA during the late 1950s. Its 247cc (15.07cu in) engine was of a simple design.

**Above:** The gearbox was a four-speed item and gearing was altered through use of sprockets with differing numbers of teeth.

**Left:** The Gold Star name was coined by BSA after they had been awarded a Brooklands Gold Star for lapping the famous circuit in excess of 100mph (160kph).

**Specifications (1962 A10)**
Engine: Four-stroke V-twin
Displacement: 646cc (39.4cu in)
Horsepower: 34 @ 5750rpm
Wheelbase: 56in (142cm)
Weight: 430lb (195kg)
Top speed: 95mph (153kph)

Right: The A10 is seen here with swingarm and shock absorber rear suspension, although at first it was also with plunger rear suspension.

1962 A10
Owner – Tony East of A. R. E. Ltd
England

The 650cc (39.65cu in) A10 in its original guise was announced in October 1949 as a 1950 model, soon followed by a 500cc A7. Through a succession of minor upgrades the remained in production until 1954. Slightly higher performance versions, Super Flash and Road Rocket, were introduced for export in 1953 and shown in the UK in 1954. By the 1960s, plans were being made to introduce a new range of twins, the A50 and A65. These were also of 500cc and 650cc (and for the first years of the 1960s were offered alongside the A10.

The next development was the 650cc Rocket A65R, a sports A65 with a slightly tuned engine and a heavy duty clutch, in October 1963. This led to a variety of sports bikes based on both 500cc and 650cc machines, including the Cyclone and Lightning as well as Wasp and Hornet for the US market. The 650cc Spitfire Hornet followed for the USA in 1964 and in 1965 was sold in the UK as the Spitfire Mk II. This was the top-of-the-range roadgoing twin, made between 1965 and 1966. Later there were Mk III and Mk IV versions, but the model was eventually dropped in favor of the triple in 1969.

In the 1960s the development of the superbike was in its infancy, but BSA/Triumph's chief designer, Bert Hopwood, knew that the company would need an engine that produced in the region of 60bhp to be competitive. Hopwood ruled out upping the capacity of an existing 650cc twin but realized that he could create a triple from Triumph's existing 493cc (30.08cu in) twin. The resultant triples were badged as both Triumphs and BSAs. The BSA engine was inclined further forward than Triumph's and the new model, known as Rocket 3, was shipped to the USA where it met with high acclaim. A number of race-prepared triples were built for Daytona, with the BSAs painted red and the Triumphs blue. Several riders dropped out with mechanical problems during the race, which Honda won, but the British teams were back for 1971 while Honda was absent. The engines were in a higher state of tune, and new frames had been built, giving a faster but easier ride. BSA took first and third, Triumph second.

At home, a Rocket 3 racer beat an MV Agusta at the 1971 Mallory Park race. The styling of the roadgoing Rocket 3 was radical for the time, but production stopped in 1971. Then, after financial difficulties, the company closed down.

**SPECIFICATIONS (1966 A65S SPITFIRE MKII)**

**Engine:** Four-stroke ohv twin
**Displacement:** 654cc (39.9cu in)
**Horsepower:** 55 @ 7000rpm
**Wheelbase:** 54.12in (137cm)
**Weight:** 382lb (173kg)
**Top speed:** 110mph (177kph)

1966 A65S Spitfire MkII
National Motorcycle Museum
Birmingham, England

**Right:** By 1966 the BSA Spitfire MkII was the top-of-the-range model in BSA's line-up of sporting parallel twins. It was superseded by the triple-cylinder-engined models.

**SPECIFICATIONS (1970 ROCKET 3)**

**Engine:** Four-stroke ohv triple
**Displacement:** 740cc (45.16cu in)
**Horsepower:** 58 @ 7250rpm
**Wheelbase:** 59in (149cm)
**Weight:** 518lb (235kg)
**Top speed:** 120mph (193kph)

**Left:** A twin-leading-shoe drum brake was considered sufficient to stop the 60bhp triple, although disc brakes would soon become the norm for sports models.

1970 Rocket 3
National Motorcycle Museum
Birmingham, England

# Buell

**Founded:** 1988
**Factory location:** East Troy, Wisconsin, USA
**Manufacturing lifespan:** 1988 - to date

Erik Buell was a roadracer, an apprentice engineer at Harley-Davidson, and a fellow who wanted to build his own motorcycles. As a senior project engineer he worked on Milwaukee's heavyweight cruisers and touring bikes, all the while hankering to put together a sport bike. Buell left Harley and scraped together the funds to build a prototype roadracer.

For six years Buell built and sold Sportster-powered sport bikes in his birdcage chassis. In 1993 Harley-Davidson bought half-interest in Buell Motorcycle Company, and became majority owner five years later. Erik Buell remains as chairman and chief engineer, and given Harley's financial horsepower and production resources, the motorcycles got both better and less expensive.

Buell has undertaken to contest experienced builders like Ducati, BMW and a growing number of specialized V-twins from Europe and Japan. Anyone who can produce a high performance motorcycle that gets faster, handles better, doesn't gain weight and costs less has recorded an achievement.

One of Buell's racing machines became a Sportster-engine Battle of the Twins bike, appropriately called the RR 1000 Battle Twin. With the advent of the Evolution engine, it developed into the RR 1200 in 1988, followed by the RS model with less bodywork.

The Lightning series, including the 1996 S1, further confirmed Buell's sporting intentions under the Harley-Davidson umbrella, with 10:1 compression, 91hp at 5800rpm, curb weight of 440lb (200kg), quarter-mile times under 12 seconds and a top speed of 130mph (209kph). The XI Lightning boasts digital fuel injection, a streamlined airbox, and a tidier exhaust system than previous Lightnings. Its frame is also new, with cast-aluminum tail section.

1990 Buell RR 1200
Owner – Otis Chandler
Ojai, California

**Specifications (1990 RR 1200)**
Engine: Four-stroke V-twin
Displacement: 1200cc (73.2cu in)
Horsepower: 68 @ 6000rpm
Wheelbase: 55.5in (141cm)
Weight: 440lb (200kg)
Top speed: N/A

**Above:** Hidden behind the full bodywork is the RR 1200's Harley-Davidson Evolution engine; the rest comes from Erik Buell's imagination.

**Below:** Erik Buell's XI Lightning shows continued determination, within the Harley-Davidson stable, to deliver high-performance sports motorcycles with innovative features but at an affordable price.

1999 Buell XI Lightning
Courtesy of Buell
Motorcycle Company
East Troy, Wisconsin

**Specifications (1999 XI Lightning)**
Engine: Ohv 45° V-twin
Displacement: 1203cc (73.41cu in)
Horsepower: 101 @ 6000rpm
Wheelbase: 55in (140cm)
Weight: 460lb (209kg)
Top speed: 140mph (225kph)

# Bultaco

**Founded:** 1958
**Factory location:** Barcelona, Spain
**Manufacturing lifespan:** 1958 – present

Former Montesa employee Francisco Bulto started this company in 1958 working from a farmhouse but soon moved to a factory based in Barcelona, Spain. Initial bikes were 124cc two-stroke road and race machines. The company is well known for building trials and motocross machines which are popular in both Europe and North America. In 1964 Sammy Miller developed the all-conquering Sherpa trail bike which achieved five straight wins in the World Trials Championship between 1975 and 1979, the first of which was taken by Martin Lampkin.

Bultaco also produced fast, if diminutive, road-racing bikes which were ridden with considerable success by Angelo Nieto. In 1976 Bultaco returned to the Grand Prix scene, winning the 50cc (3.05cu in) championship not only in that year but also in 1978 and 1981.

By 1979 Bultaco production came to an end due to industrial unrest and market pressures. Although the factory reopened in 1980 it closed again in 1983. But in 1998 Bultaco hit the motorcycle scene once again with the Sherco 250 trials bike. Even after a 20-year absence they are still making an impact, Graham Jarvis winning the Scottish Six Days Trial on his lightweight Sherco. At the beginnning of the new century more than 2000 bikes left the factory and the company now has a distributor network that covers over 40 countries.

**Specifications (1999 Sherco)**
**Engine:** Two-stroke single
**Displacement:** 249cc (15.19cu in)
**Horsepower:** N/A
**Wheelbase:** N/A
**Weight:** 154.3lb (70kg)
**Top speed:** 50mph (80kph)

1999 Bultaco Sherco
Courtesy Mirco De Cet

**Below:** Bultaco returned to the motorcycle market with the Sherco back in 1998. Competing in Trials means lightweight machinery and not many came lighter than the Sherco at 70kg.

**Above:** The compact two-stroke engine that the Sherco uses is water-cooled, has electronic ignition control and does away with starter and battery, as do most Trials bikes.

# Cagiva

**Founded:** 1978
**Factory location:** Varese, Italy
**Manufacturing lifespan:** 1978 – to date

Cagiva Motor, run by brothers Claudio and Gianfranco Castiglioni, entered the motorcycle world when they took over the Schiranna factory in Varese, once the Italian-based Aermacchi Harley-Davidson concern, in 1978. They began by producing variants of the existing models, detail upgrades, improved electrics and cast wheels, and also a new tank badge. It was enough to make the newcomer's bikes bestsellers in Italy in the 125cc (7.62cu in) class for several years. By 1979 some 40,000 bikes were being produced. Cagiva successfully sought to produce more modern and larger-capacity motorcycles and expanded by first acquiring Ducati in 1985, Husqvarna in 1986, and Moto Morini in 1987. By now Cagiva were selling bikes in over 50 countries.

Cagiva's entry into racing was back in 1980 when they were entered in the 500cc world championships. They gained their first Grand Prix points in 1982 and the first podium was gained at Spa in Belgium in 1988. They also achieved results in other competitions, including motocross, their best seasons coming between 1984 and 1988, when they successfully halted the Suzuki onslaught.

In 1990 a new factory in Varese was opened to produce both steel and aluminum frames, and the following year Cagiva acquired the famous MV Agusta name, vowing to return it to its previous glorious position in the motorcycling world. This was achieved partially in 1997 when the new MV Agusta F4 serie Oro was shown at the Milan International motorcycle show. It was a stunning machine with loads of nostalgia, and the public couldn't get enough of them. During 1996 Ducati and Moto Morini were sold off for strategic reasons, and as the new millennium approached a restructuring of the group saw MV Agusta Motor as the main brand, comprising Cagiva and Husqvarna, and soon new models were shown, the Raptor, V Raptor, and the Navigator among them.

**Cagiva Planet**
Three Cross Motorcycles
Dorset, England

**Above:** The neat little two-stroke single, water-cooled engine of the "Planet" is tucked away under the aluminum frame. The tank can be hinged back to reveal storage space.

**Above:** Exclusively designed alloy rims on the wheels help to show off this radically styled machine.

**Specifications (2000 Planet)**
**Engine:** Two-stroke single
**Displacement:** 125cc (7.62cu in)
**Horsepower:** N/A
**Wheelbase:** 54.92in (139.5cm)
**Weight:** 275.6lb (125kg)
**Top speed:** N/A

Cagiva Mito
Three Cross Motorcycles
Dorset, England

**Left:** Looking more like it has just stepped off the race circuit, the little "Mito" has fine Italian design mixed with a stunning pace from its 125cc water-cooled engine.

**Specifications (2000 Mito)**
- **Engine:** Two-stroke single
- **Displacement:** 125cc (7.62cu in)
- **Horsepower:** N/A
- **Wheelbase:** 54.13in (137.5cm)
- **Weight:** 284.4lb (129kg)
- **Top speed:** N/A

**Above:** The front suspension on the "Mito" is made up of Marzocci forks with 1.6in (40mm) legs which have 4.7in (120mm) of travel; brakes are from Brembo.

## California

| | |
|---|---|
| **Founded:** 1901 | |
| **Factory location:** San Francisco, California, USA | |
| **Manufacturing lifespan:** 1901 - 1903 | |

Roy C. Marks was one of the first California engineers to offer gasoline engine kits for bicycles, selling his first units in 1898. J. W. Leavitt and J. F. Bill owned bicycle shops in San Francisco, Oakland, and San Jose, and in 1901 they formed the California Motor Company. Marks hired on as chief engineer, and created the California Motor Bicycle.

In 1903 the California became the first motor vehicle to cross the continent. Rider George Wyman left San Francisco on 16 May and arrived in New York on 6 July with stories to tell. In 1903 the California Motor Company was sold to the Consolidated Manufacturing Company of Toledo, Ohio. These purveyors of Yale and Snell bicycles sought to expand into motorcycles, as so many other velocipede builders were doing. If people were buying engines for their bicycles, why not sell them the whole package? Thus the California became the Yale-California, and with later designs appearing in 1909, simply the Yale.

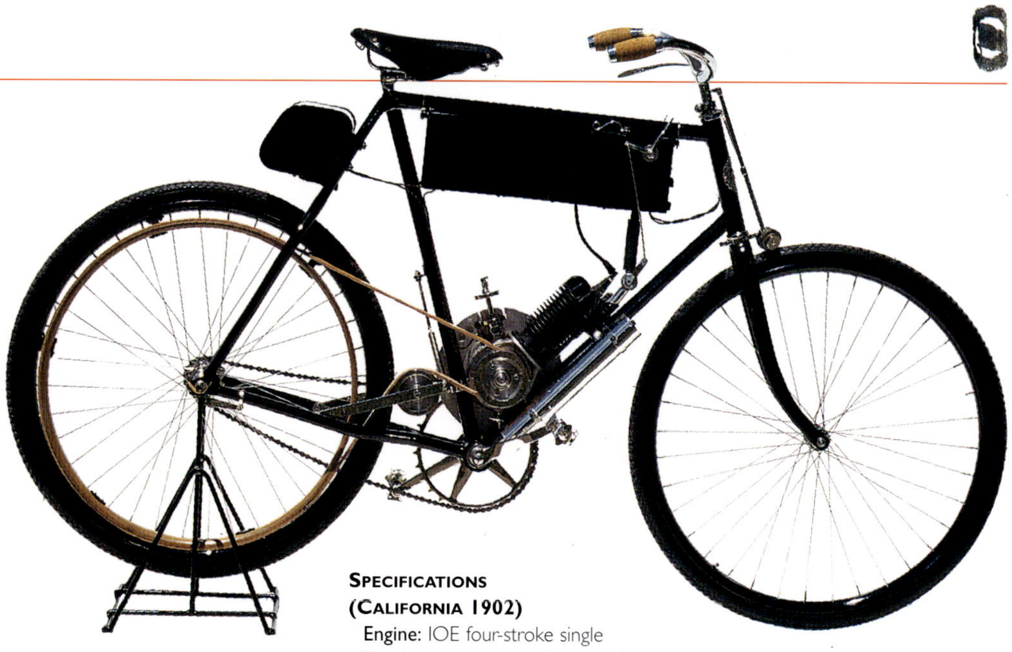

1902 California
Owner – Mark Michel
Sterling Heights, Michigan

**Specifications (California 1902)**
- **Engine:** IOE four-stroke single
- **Displacement:** 200cc (12.2cu in)
- **Horsepower:** 1.25
- **Wheelbase:** 46in (117cm)
- **Weight:** 100lb (45kg)
- **Top speed:** 25mph (40kph)

**Above:** The California was the first motor vehicle to cross the United States, in 1903. Rider George Wyman made the journey in 50 days.

## CALTHORPE

**Founded:** 1911
**Factory location:** Birmingham, England
**Manufacturing lifespan:** 1911 - 1939

George Hands founded the Calthorpe concern with 211cc (12.87cu in) two-stroke machines and then other models with Precision and JAP engines. During the early 1920s he used a variety of engines but from 1925 onwards manufactured 348cc (21.22cu in) and 498cc (30.37cu in) singles.

By the end of the 1920s the company was best known for a single model, the Ivory Calthorpe, named for its distinctive ivory paint finish which distinguished it from the many black machines of the era. By 1930 it was known as the Ivory Calthorpe II and featured a 348cc single-cylinder engine of Calthorpe's own design which was inclined forwards in the frame. The engine had the magneto positioned behind the cylinder and the dynamo positioned forward of it. Lubrication was dry-sump although the oil was carried in the forward section of the crankcase. The engine and the finish caught the motorcycling public's eye, although the rest of the bike was essentially conventional for its time.

Various upgrades followed, but the firm went into liquidation in 1938 and was sold to Bruce Douglas, nephew of the founder of Douglas Motorcycles, who moved the operation to Bristol. Here he built models with Matchless single engines, but few were finished when war broke out and Calthorpe did not return to production afterward.

1930 Ivory
National Motorcycle Museum
Birmingham, England

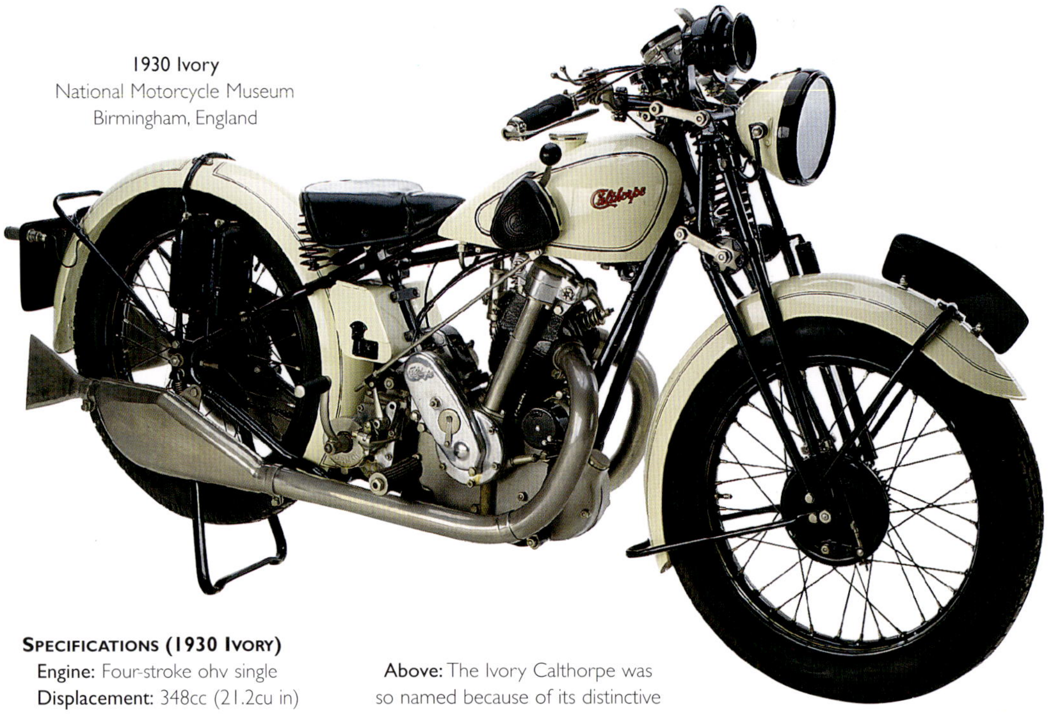

**SPECIFICATIONS (1930 IVORY)**
**Engine:** Four-stroke ohv single
**Displacement:** 348cc (21.2cu in)
**Horsepower:** N/A
**Wheelbase:** N/A
**Weight:** 267lb (121kg)
**Top speed:** 70mph (113kph)

**Above:** The Ivory Calthorpe was so named because of its distinctive paint scheme. It stood out from the crowd at a time when many motorcycles were simply finished in black.

## CLEVELAND

**Founded:** 1902
**Factory location:** Hartford, Connecticut; Cleveland, Ohio, USA
**Manufacturing lifespan:** 1902 - 1905/1915 - 1929

The first Clevelands were built by the American Cycle Manufacturing Company of Hartford, Connecticut. The more recognizable and distinct Clevelands were made by the Cleveland Motorcycle Manufacturing Company in Ohio.

The 220cc (13.43cu in) two-stroke engine was mounted transverse to the frame, with a worm drive to power the countershaft sprocket for final chain drive. The shaft exited the two-speed gearbox and extended past the rear downtube to drive the magneto, hung just forward of the rear wheel.

In 1920 the machine grew larger, adding footboards, and incorporated fuel/oil tank and wider fenders. The weight went up again the following year with a larger fuel/oil tank and seat and a battery. To offset the additional load, the engine displacement was enlarged to 270cc (16.47cu in). For 1923 the company offered a sport solo Model E, with battery and electric lights.

Although the Cleveland two-strokes appeared a little flimsy compared to some motorcycles of the period, their light weight and moderate power combined for easy riding. When heavy weather and nasty terrain slowed heavier machines, the Cleveland was more apt to plug on regardless. The two-strokes set several lightweight endurance records and routinely won their division in 100 and 200 mile (161 and 322km) races. A motorcycle of moderate power and few pretensions, the Cleveland Light served a wide market of commuters and women riders who appreciated the light weight and handling ease. ▶

**Right:** The Connecticut Clevelands shared the same configuration with the Columbia, Imperial, Crescent, Monarch, Tribune and Rambler marques.

**Below:** The Cleveland two-strokes found popularity for their light weight and simplicity. The direct-drive magneto between the engine and rear wheel was an interesting feature.

1902 Cleveland
Owner – Jim Lattin
Encinitas, California

**Below:** Despite the relatively small engine, the Cleveland was successful in many endurance contests, owing largely to its absence of weight and mechanical complexity.

**SPECIFICATIONS (1917 LIGHT)**

- **Engine:** Two-stroke single
- **Displacement:** 220cc (13.43cu in)
- **Horsepower:** 3.5
- **Wheelbase:** 53in (135cm)
- **Weight:** 150lb (68kg)
- **Top speed:** 30mph (48kph)

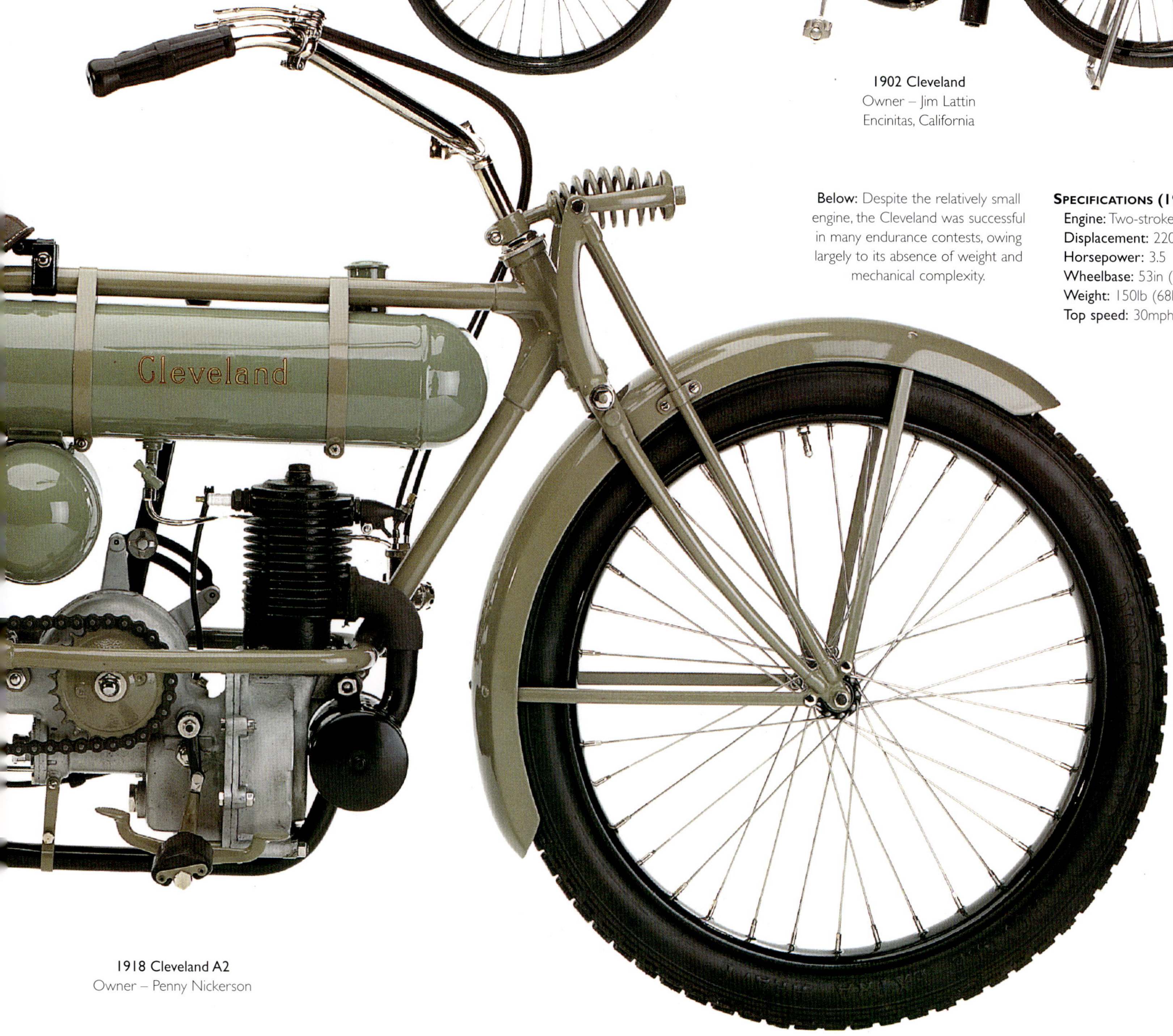


1918 Cleveland A2
Owner – Penny Nickerson

## Cleveland

The two-stroke was in production until 1925, when it was superseded by a 350cc (21.35cu in) four-stroke single designated the F-25. Also a two-speed, the F model was heavier, slower and destined for a brief production run. Then Cleveland hired automobile engineer L. E. Fowler and built a four-cylinder motorcycle. The 600cc (36.61cu in) T-head four was a side-valve, with the intake cam on the left and exhaust cam on the right. Cleveland retained the perimeter cradle frame design with the four-cylinder engine hung in the middle. Additional tubing connected the frame's mid-section to the rear axle, and a leading link spring fork graced the front end. The engine, patterned on the Pierce four, had a three-speed transmission. But the 600cc (36.61cu in) four was well off the performance pace set by Henderson and Ace, and the next engine was a 750cc (45.77cu in) F-head four designed by former Henderson engineer Everett DeLong. The engine was a four-pot monobloc casting, with the cylinder head and intake manifold in a single casting. The three-speed transmission could be removed without removing the engine. The new chassis featured a traditional split downtube cradle frame and no rear suspension.

In 1927 the displacement went to 1000cc (61.02cu in), and the Cleveland was no longer sucking wind behind the Henderson and Ace fours. The engine was rubber-mounted and the motorcycle was the first on the market with a front drum brake.

The four's finale came with the Tornado in 1929. A new frame dropped the seat by 2.5 inches (6.3cm), and light alloy pistons and more compression increased power. For 1930 Cleveland announced the Century model guaranteed good for at least 100mph (161kph), with a brass plaque to certify it had been pre-tested at that speed. But as the Century entered production the Wall Street stock market collapsed and the Cleveland Motorcycle Manufacturing Company soon followed suit.

**Below:** Development of the Cleveland four reached its peak with the Tornado model in 1929. The new frame lowered the seat height by 2.5 inches (6.35cm).

## Columbia

**Founded:** 1902
**Factory location:** Chicago, Illinois, USA
**Manufacturing lifespan:** 1902 - 1905

The Columbia was another multiple-brand motorcycle built by Chicago's American Cycle Manufacturing Company. The single had 8:1 compression, and could be spun to 2600rpm. The triangulated fuel tank held 1.5 gallons (5.7lit), reportedly good for at least 100 miles (161km). The Columbia and its brethren (American, Crescent, Imperial, Rambler) featured a rear coster brake and front tire-scrubber hand brake.

**Specifications (1902 Model)**
**Engine:** IOE single
**Displacement:** 220cc (13.43cu in)
**Horsepower:** 2.25
**Wheelbase:** 53in (135cm)
**Weight:** 125lb (57kg)
**Top speed:** 35mph (56kph)

1902 Columbia
Owner – Herb Singe
Hillside, New Jersey

**Above:** The Columbia was one of the motorcycles Pope built under various brand names.

1929 Cleveland Tornado
Owner – Otis Chandler
Ojai, California

**Specifications (1927 Four/Tornado)**
**Engine:** Inline side-valve four
**Displacement:** 1000cc (61.02cu in)
**Horsepower:** 20
**Wheelbase:** 60in (152cm)
**Weight:** 420lb (190.5kg)
**Top speed:** 90mph (145kph)

**Left:** In 1929, racer Arthur Fournier rode a stripped version of the Tornado to a speed of 108mph (174kph) at Playa Del Rey, California.

## Cotton

**Founded:** 1920
**Factory location:** Gloucester, England
**Manufacturing lifespan:** 1920 - 1980

Francis Willoughby Cotton's company was noted for a triangulated frame he had patented by Cotton before starting motorcycle production. The idea was that all the frame tubes should be straight, and therefore subject only to compression and tension forces, and triangulated so that stress was concentrated at the apex of any triangle. The steering head was supported by pairs of tubes running diagonally backwards to the rear axle. A wedge-shaped fuel tank was fitted between these tubes. This design persisted until 1939, by when the marque had enjoyed considerable Isle of Man TT success. In hard times Cotton had to offer motorcycles powered by proprietary engines from companies such as JAP and Blackburne. With the outbreak of war in 1939 the company temporarily closed its doors but in postwar years re-opened under new management, producing small-capacity, Villiers-engined two-stroke machines little better than any of their rivals. During the 1960s and 1970s Cotton concentrated on producing trials bikes and in 1980 the company was taken over by Armstrong.

**Specifications (1928 Model 7)**
**Engine:** Four-stroke single
**Displacement:** 348cc (21.2cu in)
**Horsepower:** 2.7
**Wheelbase:** 52.5in (133cm)
**Weight:** 195lb (88.5kg)
**Top speed:** 75mph (121kph)

1928 Model 7
National Motorcycle Museum
Birmingham, England

**Below:** The Model 7 used the ohv Blackburne engine, while the Model 7J used a side-valve JAP engine.

## COVENTRY-EAGLE

**Founded:** Late 1880s
**Factory location:** Coventry, England
**Manufacturing lifespan:** 1901 - 1939

Coventry-Eagle had its roots in the Victorian era of bicycling. It always used proprietary parts but through careful assembly and a high standard of finish the company survived longer than many other of their competitors. During the late 1920s its luxurious Flying 8 series was sold alongside utterly utilitarian machines. The Flying 8 machines used V-twin JAP engines and sculptured tanks and were not dissimilar to Brough Superior motorcycles in appearance, while the utility models were built with pressed-steel frames and small-displacement engines.

Only three models were listed for 1933, but for 1936 the company announced its range of three Pullman Two Seaters. These were partially enclosed and had an unusual frame consisting of a pressed-steel chassis bolted to a tubular upper section. In 1937 three machines powered by ohv Matchless engines (245cc/14.95cu in, 348cc/21.24cu in, and 497cc/30.32cu in) were offered – the N25 Flying 250, N35 Flying 350, and N50 Flying 500, respectively. Production closed at outbreak of war in 1939.

**SPECIFICATIONS (1937 N35 FLYING 350)**
**Engine:** Four-stroke ohv single
**Displacement:** 348cc (21.2cu in)
**Horsepower:** N/A
**Wheelbase:** N/A
**Weight:** N/A
**Top speed:** 60mph (97kph)

**Below:** Coventry-Eagle used proprietary ohv Matchless engines in their range of motorcycles introduced in 1937. This is the 350cc middleweight motorcycle, the N35 Flying 350.

**1937 N35 Flying 350**
National Motorcycle Museum
Birmingham, England

## CROCKER

**Founded:** 1934
**Factory location:** Los Angeles, California, USA
**Manufacturing lifespan:** 1934 - 1941

Al Crocker started as a rider/designer with Thor in the teens, and later became an Indian dealer in Denver, Colorado. His next position was the Kansas City representative for Indian, where he served with distinction for many years. In 1928 he acquired the Indian franchise for Los Angeles, California, and hired a brilliant young engineer/designer named Paul Bigsby. Together they set about building some racing machines.

The first efforts were speedway racers with Indian Scout 750cc V-twin engines. But the short-circuits were better suited to lighter, single-cylinder machines, and Crocker began building 500cc overhead-valve singles. A gear-driven magneto sat in front of the cylinder and a twin-float Amal carburetor provided the mixture, good for about 40 horsepower in a 240-pound (109kg) package. These racing bikes did quite well in the hands of speedway stars Jack and Cordy Milne, who would later be world champions. But Crocker was losing the horsepower race to the British JAP engine, and his attention turned to a sporting twin for the road.

The first batch of 1000cc V-twins were hemi-head engines with exposed valve springs, arranged at 90 degrees as the speedway engine had been. Likewise, the pushrods shared a common tube. Compression was 7.5:1 and the engine made 50 horsepower at 5800rpm. And the motorcycle weighed just 480 pounds (218kg). Crocker made liberal use of aluminum throughout; engine cases, fuel tank, generator case, footboards, instrument panel and tail light were alloy items.

The running gear was heavy duty. The gearbox was cast as an integral part of the frame, and the gears in the three-speed constant-mesh unit were oversized to deal with heaps of horsepower. Steel plates on either side of the case kept everything in alignment. ▶

**Right:** Crocker was committed to the enthusiast's credo of adding horsepower and lightness. The fuel tanks, footboards, instrument panel and taillight were aluminum.

**Below:** Both pushrods in the Crocker engine shared a common tube. The transmission was designed as an integral part of the frame.

1936 Crocker
Owner – Chuck Vernon
La Mirada, California

**Specifications (1938 Model Twin)**

- **Engine:** 45° ohv V-twin
- **Displacement:** 1000cc (61cu in)
- **Horsepower:** 40
- **Wheelbase:** 60.5in (154cm)
- **Weight:** 480lb (218kg)
- **Top speed:** 110mph (177kph)

1938 Crocker
Owner – Otis Chandler
Ojai, California

**Left:** As a hand-crafted motorcycle, the Crocker was simply too expensive to build in limited numbers. The advent of World War II effectively ended their production.

## CROCKER

But another overhead-valve hot rod appeared at the same time. Harley-Davidson debuted the 1000cc Knucklehead in 1936, and it was widely heralded in the press and on the road. The Harley may have been some 80 pounds (36kg) heavier than the Crocker, and down by about 10 horsepower, but it was a production line machine built by a veteran manufacturer. And it cost about $150 less than the custom-built California twin.

So the Crocker was no threat to Indian or Harley in the marketplace, and fewer than 100 of the V-twins were built. But it stood as sterling testament to the spirit and skill of independent builders, willing to invest their own time and talents to create a superior piece of equipment. Crocker didn't make any money on the sporting V-twins, but he showed what could be done. Between 1939 and 1943 he also built a stylish motor scooter called the Scootabout, but it was not destined for long-term production either.

None of which diminishes Albert Crocker's contribution to the American motorcycle sport, or his lifelong career as a rider, engineer, dealer, entrepreneur and designer. He had hoped that Indian would buy the manufacturing rights to the ohv twin, but the advent of World War II intervened. Crocker retired after the war and died in 1961 at the age of 79.

1940 Crocker
Owner – Dale Walksler
Mt. Vernon, Illinois

**Above:** The last batch of Crockers were built in 1940. Opinions on total production figures run between 70 and 100 machines. Minor detail changes were made during its brief run. Some engines were built to certain dimensions specified by the buyers.

## CROSLEY

| | |
|---|---|
| **Founded:** | 1939 |
| **Factory location:** | Marion, Indiana, USA |
| **Manufacturing lifespan:** | 1939 - 1952 |

Powell Crosley always hankered to build cars, and undertook production of a small car powered by a 580cc opposed twin. The first Crosley automobile appeared in 1939, in the hope that Americans were ready for a small transportation device. Nearly two years earlier, the U.S. government had begun looking for military hardware. Crosley's opposed twin was adapted to two- and three-wheeled vehicles, but neither went beyond the preliminary testing stage.

Crosley resumed car production after the war. In 1949 the Hotshot appeared, arguably the first American sports car, with a 750cc (45.75cu in) four-cylinder engine. The lightweight had 27hp and was good for 90mph (145kph).

**SPECIFICATIONS (1939 MODEL)**

**Engine:** Opposed side-valve twin
**Displacement:** 580cc (35.38cu in)
**Horsepower:** 13
**Wheelbase:** 60in (152cm)
**Weight:** 630lb (286kg)
**Top speed:** 70mph (113kph)

**Below:** The Crosley was a hybrid of motorcycle and automobile components. The engine, wheels and tires are car parts; the fuel tank was incorporated in the rear fender.

1939 Crosley
Owner – Paul Gorrell
Burlington, Iowa

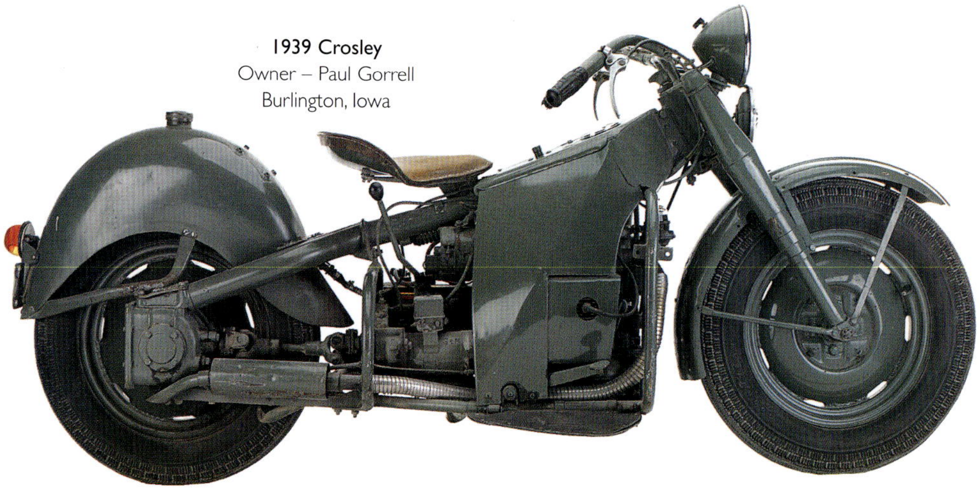

## Curtiss

| | |
|---|---|
| **Founded:** | 1901 |
| **Factory location:** | Hammondsport, New York, USA |
| **Manufacturing lifespan:** | 1901 - 1913 |

Glenn Hammond Curtiss was born in 1878 and as a young man he found employment with Western Union as a bicycle messenger, thus discovering his lust for speed. He moved to organized bicycle racing and in 1901, when E. R. Thomas began selling engine kits, Curtiss bought one for his bicycle. The creation became known as the Happy Hooligan, and inspired Curtiss's enthusiasm to build a better engine. He had settled on the engineering thesis for his entire career; more horsepower and less weight. He had his own castings made and built his first single in 1901. His products wore the trade name Hercules. The next objective was to build a V-twin and go racing. On the horse track at the Syracuse, New York, fairgrounds in 1905, Curtiss set three new records and went unchallenged in the 5-mile open race. He went on to win major dirt-track events and broke two speed records at Ormond Beach, Florida.

A California company then claimed legal right to the name Hercules, so Curtiss affixed his own name to the machines. The 5hp V-twin got the same displacement increase as the single and was rated at six horsepower, the motorcycle weighing 160lb (73kg). ▶

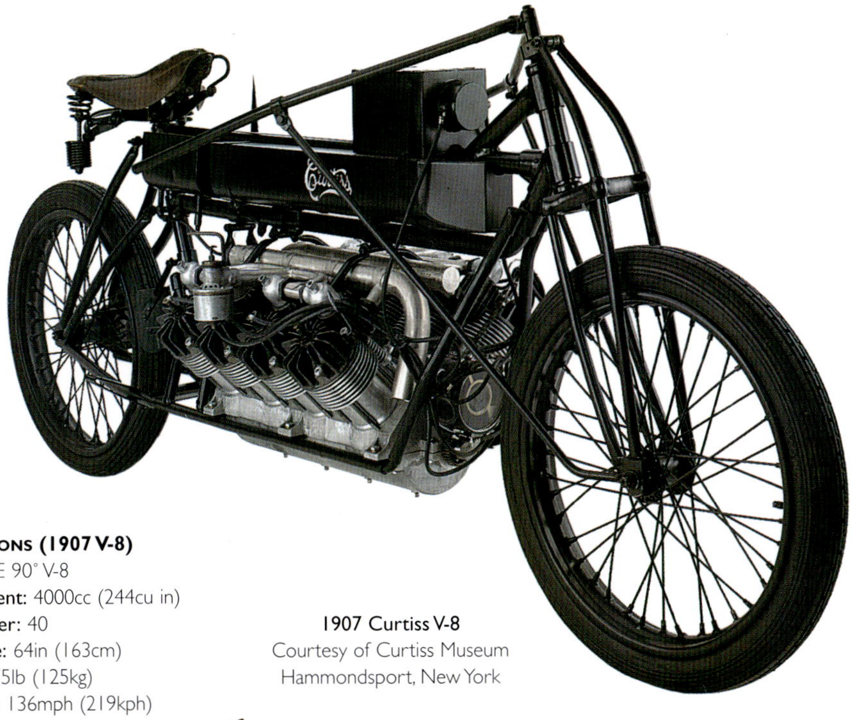

**Specifications (1907 V-8)**
- **Engine:** IOE 90° V-8
- **Displacement:** 4000cc (244cu in)
- **Horsepower:** 40
- **Wheelbase:** 64in (163cm)
- **Weight:** 275lb (125kg)
- **Top speed:** 136mph (219kph)

**1907 Curtiss V-8**
Courtesy of Curtiss Museum
Hammondsport, New York

**Above:** Curtiss developed the V-8 for aircraft use, at the request of a Dr. Silverton of Milwaukee, Wisconsin. A Curtiss carburetor on each side fed the banks of cylinders.

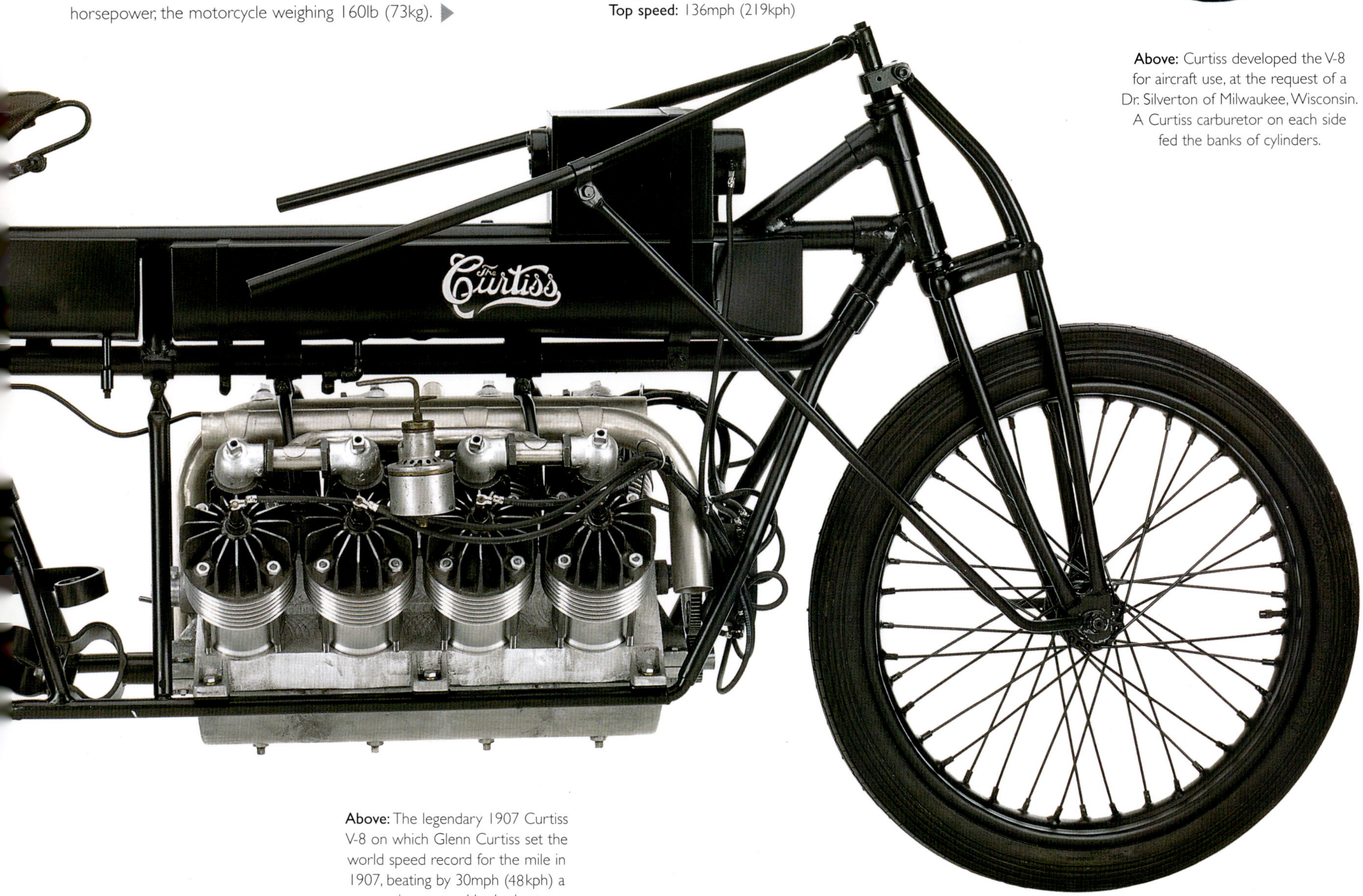


**Above:** The legendary 1907 Curtiss V-8 on which Glenn Curtiss set the world speed record for the mile in 1907, beating by 30mph (48kph) a previous record he had set.

# CURTISS

The original Hercules Double Cylinder sold for $310 in 1904, putting it in the high end of the market. By 1909 the price had dropped to $275. Curtiss remained unconvinced of the need for chain drive, and stayed with flat leather belts. A leather covering on the drive pulley minimized slippage. He later developed a 28 degree V-belt with improved grip.

If, by 1907, there were any doubters on the benefits of light weight, high horsepower and long wheelbase, Glenn Curtiss disabused their notions at Ormond Beach, Florida. On the V-twin, the New Yorker set a new world record for the mile at 76mph (122kph). When the scheduled events were over, Curtiss and two friends rolled out a seven-foot (2.1m) long motorcycle with a V-8 engine. The engine made nearly 40 horsepower at 1800rpm, with direct shaft drive to the rear wheel. The machine weighed 275 pounds (125kg). The one-quart oil tank was fitted below the seat; the fuel tank had a capacity of 2.5 gallons (9.5lit). Moments later, after a two-mile run to get up to speed, Glen Curtiss flashed by the line at 136.36mph (219.4kph) and became the fastest man on earth. "It satisfied my speed craving," he allowed. The rudimentary rear V-brake required about a mile to slow the machine.

Shortly thereafter Curtiss shifted his attention to aviation projects, for which the V-8 was originally intended. His two-wheeled creations remained in production for another six years, and came under the direction of Curtiss's old racing pal Tank Waters. Later models were sold under the Marvel name.

**SPECIFICATIONS (1908 SINGLE)**
- **Engine:** IOE single
- **Displacement:** 500cc (30.50cu in)
- **Horsepower:** 2.5/3.0
- **Wheelbase:** 58in (147cm)
- **Weight:** 130lb (59kg)
- **Top speed:** 45mph (72kph)

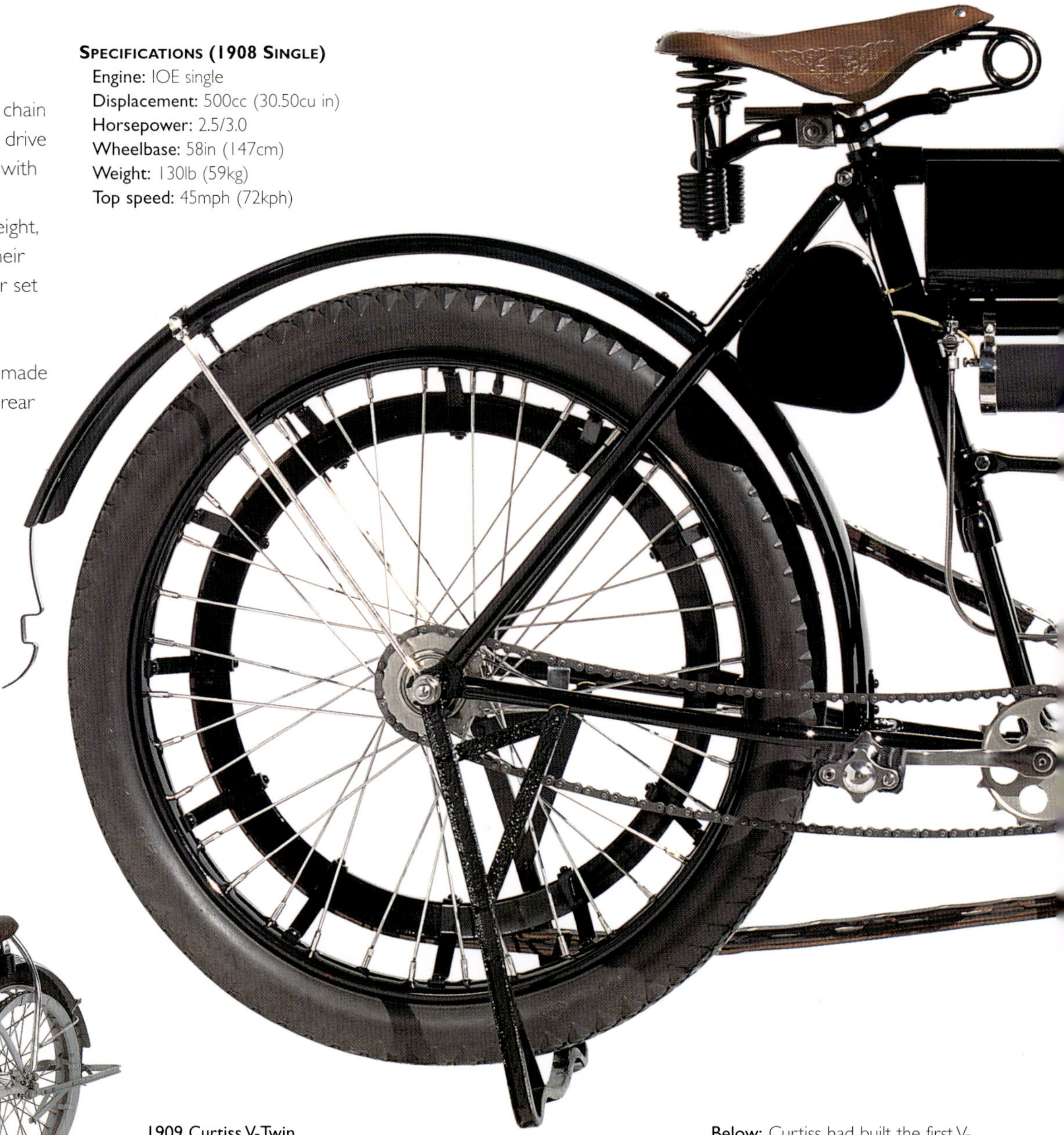

1909 Curtiss V-Twin
Owner – Charles Darling
Sodus, New York

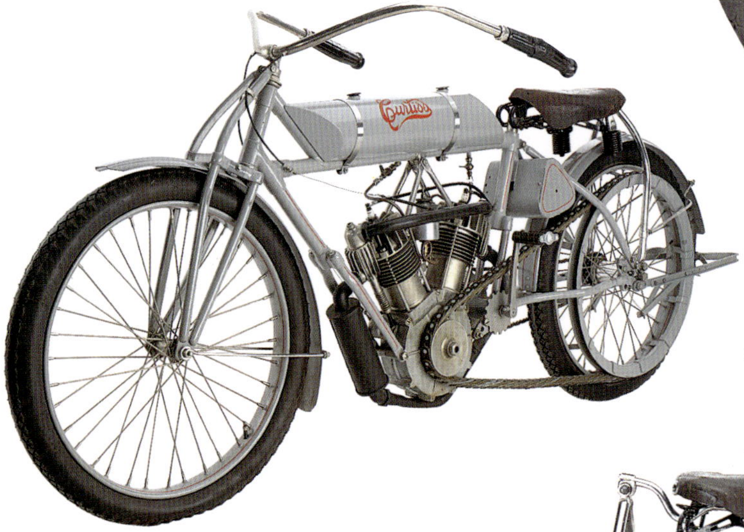


**Above:** The Curtiss V-twin was unique in the single cam operating both exhaust valves. The engine carried racers to many wins in hillclimb, dirt-track and endurance events.

**Below:** Curtiss had built the first V-twin on the American market in 1903. The engine was rated at 5 horsepower at 1500rpm, but "can be speeded to 2000." Cylinders were cast iron, the crankcase of aluminum.

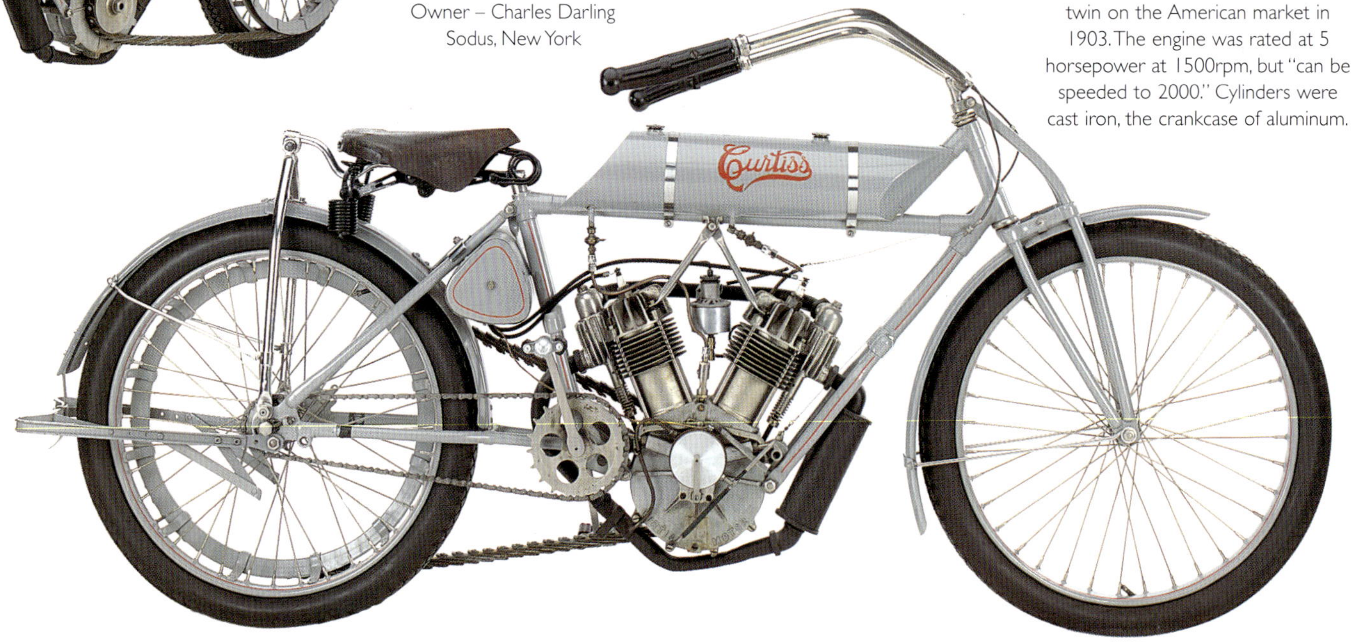


**SPECIFICATIONS (1909 V-TWIN)**
- **Engine:** IOE 50° V-twin
- **Displacement:** 1000cc (61.02cu in)
- **Horsepower:** 5.0/6.0
- **Wheelbase:** 58in (147cm)
- **Weight:** 160lb (73kg)
- **Top speed:** 60mph (97kph)

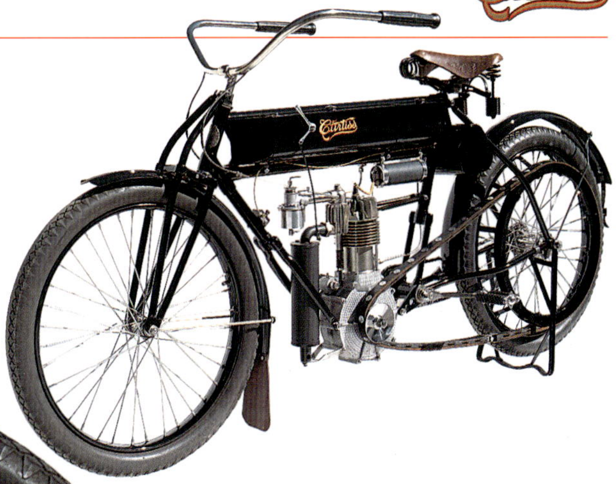

1908 Curtiss Single
Owner – Wes Allen
Yuba City, California

**Above:** The Curtiss ads claimed a top speed of 45-50mph (72-80kph) for the single. The standard gear ratio was 5:1, and 3.5:1 for racing.

**Left:** Glenn Curtiss was convinced that belt drive outweighed the disadvantages of chains. He developed a 28-degree V-belt that performed without the slippage of flat belts. The standard single made 2.5 horsepower at 1500rpm. The muffler cut-out, for country running, was operated by a lever on the tank.

## CUSHMAN

**Founded:** 1936
**Factory location:** Lincoln, Nebraska, USA
**Manufacturing lifespan:** 1936 - 1965

Cushman had been building small motors for decades when the motor scooter notion came along. It came from California's E. Foster Salsbury, who introduced a scooter designed by Austin Elmore. The Moto-Glide, from which the Cushman Auto-Glide was copied, appeared in 1935. The Cushman engine was the venerable single-horse Husky flathead, sold mostly as a water-pump motor. By 1940 the horsepower had doubled and a two-speed transmission was available.

During World War II, Cushman built several military models for non-combat use, and also continued civilian production. After the war the scooter boom blossomed worldwide, and Cushman introduced the 50 Series model, nicknamed the Turtleback, with a four-horsepower Husky engine. Cushman's later products included several other enclosed models until 1961 and the best-selling Eagle (1949-1965), designed as a "miniature Harley-Davidson," with unenclosed engines. But then the company dropped scooters.

**SPECIFICATIONS (1947 MODEL 52)**
**Engine:** Side-valve single
**Displacement:** 221cc (13.49cu in)
**Horsepower:** 4
**Wheelbase:** 54in (137cm)
**Weight:** 260lb (118kg)
**Top speed:** 40mph (64kph)

**Below:** The basic Cushman profile was unchanged since 1936. The knee action front suspension and automatic clutch meant easy riding.

1947 Cushman Model 52
Owner – Hal O'Connor
Phelps, New York

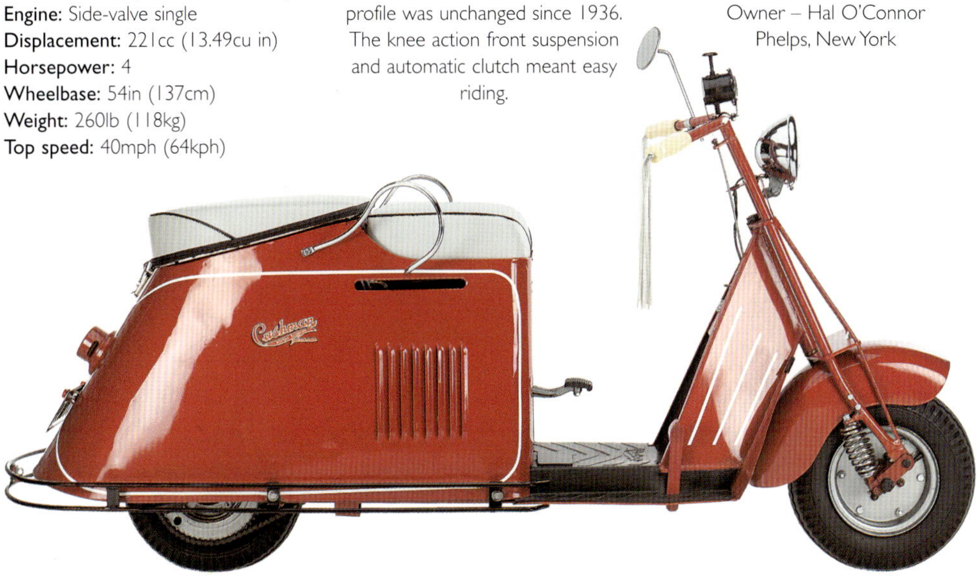

## Cyklon

**Founded:** 1900
**Factory location:** Berlin, Germany
**Manufacturing lifespan:** 1900-1905

Cyklon was one of the pioneers of the German motorcycle industry and became a leading maker for a few years. The factory assembled a variety of machines using proprietary power units. These included the popular French De Dion and Werner engines, and the Swiss Zedel (Zurcher and Luthi) engine. Cyklon eventually decided to concentrate on building a three-wheeler called the Cyklonette, but the fashion for this type of machine was short-lived.

The 1900 Cyklon was rather different from the other machines of its period. Most early motorcycle designers decided to position their engines between the two down tubes below the crossbar. In contrast, the Cyklon had its engine fitted in front of the rider and cleverly attached to the handlebars. This then led to the unusual situation where, as the engine was fitted over the front wheel, the bike had to rely on the front wheel and not the rear one as not only the steering wheel but also the driven wheel. This made the basic bicycle frame look somewhat clumsy at the front. No doubt, in emergency situations and even on the rough roads of the day, these motorized bicycles would have been a little difficult to handle.

Nevertheless, overall a very tidy design was completed. Nice finishing touches to the machine were the front and rear lights and of course a real necessity for this period would have been the bell.

In these early days of motorcycling, such contraptions as the Cyklon were not completely welcome on the roads and were often seen as rather dirty and polluting machinery, never to catch on as an everyday mode of transportation.

**Cyklon 1900 Model**
Deutsches-Zweirad Museum and NSU Museum Neckarsulm, Germany

## Cyclone

**Founded:** 1913
**Factory location:** St Paul, Minnesota, USA
**Manufacturing lifespan:** 1913 - 1916

The Cyclone was built by the Joerns Motor Manufacturing Company, which grew from the Thiem Manufacturing Company, an engine builder from 1903–1911. Professional motorcycle racing was a high-stakes game at this point; Indian were tops above Harley-Davidson. Cyclone added some spice to festivities with a 1000cc overhead-cam V-twin, ridden by a skilled racer named Don Johns. In 1914, development engineer J. A. McNeil posted a speed of 111mph (179kph) on a boardtrack.

These bevel-drive ohc twins were designed by Andrew Strand, and were the most powerful factory hot rods of their day. The crankshaft ran in four-row caged roller bearings on the drive side and self-aligning ball bearings on the other end. Lightweight connecting rods rode on three-row roller bearings, and the magneto was also driven by shaft and bevel gears. But while Johns routinely put the Cyclone in front of the Indian and Harley factory machines, reliability was another matter. By 1915 most of the mechanical problems were sorted out, but the Cyclone was plagued by minor difficulties. Sales of road models were insufficient to support the Minnesotans' underdog effort, and the Joerns company expired in 1916.

**Specifications**
**Engine:** 45° ohc V-twin
**Displacement:** 1000cc (61cu in)
**Horsepower:** 45
**Wheelbase:** 53in (135cm)
**Weight:** 260lb (118kg)
**Top speed:** 110mph (177kph)

**1914 Cyclone Racer**
Owner – Daniel Statnekov
Tesuque, New Mexico

**Below:** For a few years, the Cyclones were the fastest machines on two wheels. But reliability problems and the lack of development funding put them into the history books early.

# CYKLON

**SPECIFICATIONS (1900 MODEL)**

**Engine:** Four-stroke single
**Displacement:** 300cc (18cu in)
**Horsepower:** 1.5
**Wheelbase:** N/A
**Weight:** N/A
**Top speed:** 22mph (35kph)

**Left:** Having the engine attached to the front of the bicycle was a rather unusual set-up; most machines of the period would have had it mounted in the middle of the bicycle, below the crossbar.

**Right:** Having the engine mounted right in front of the rider was without doubt a hazard and would have made the machine a little top heavy.

## DAIMLER

| | |
|---|---|
| **Founded:** | 1883 |
| **Factory location:** | Stuttgart, Germany |
| **Manufacturing lifespan:** | 1885 – 1886 |

Gottlieb Daimler was born in Schorndorf, near Stuttgart in southern Germany, on March 17 1834. He and his good friend William Maybach worked together in Cannstatt to develop the engine that was used in the first motorcycle, the Reitwagen (riding wagon). Initially the two had to overcome ignition problems, which they did by using the "Hot Tube" system. The other problem that was overcome was the speed the engine ran at, which they controlled via the exhaust valve. Daimler patented his new engine in 1883. Fitted to a wooden "hobby horse" with stabilizer wheels, it became the first motorcycle in the world.

The single-cylinder engine was made up of two flywheels which were enclosed inside a crankcase. An inlet valve, opened by the suction from the piston, was positioned directly above the mechanically operated side-exhaust valve. This is known as IOE (inlet over exhaust). A fuel atomizer, or early type of carburetor, supplied a mixture of fuel and air. This was ignited by a platinum tube, which projected into the cylinder and was heated on the outside by a Bunsen-type burner. A primitive twistgrip control via cords worked a simple clutch and brake system.

**Below:** The wooden frame of the Daimler was in fact known as a "hobby horse" and was only used as a test bed for the engine. The two smaller wheels were to keep the machine upright.

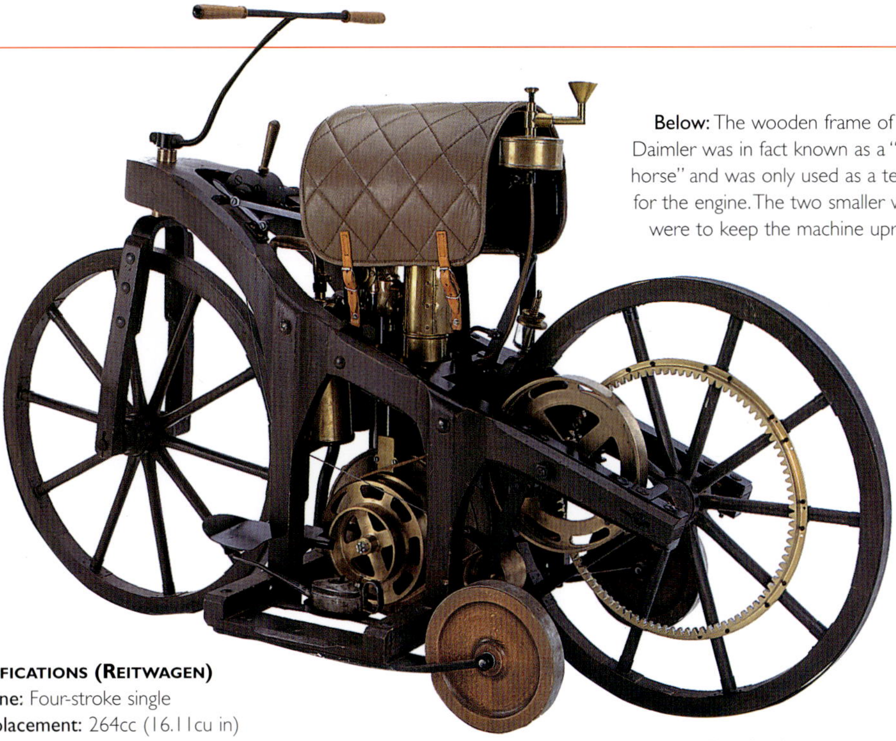

**SPECIFICATIONS (REITWAGEN)**

**Engine:** Four-stroke single
**Displacement:** 264cc (16.1cu in)
**Horsepower:** 0.49
**Wheelbase:** N/A
**Weight:** 198lb (90kg)
**Top speed:** 7mph (11.2kph)

**Daimler Reitwagen**
Deutsches-Zweirad Museum
and NSU Museum
Neckarsulm, Germany

# De Dion Bouton

**Founded:** 1895
**Factory location:** Puteaux, Paris, France
**Manufacturing lifespan:** 1895 - 1903

A Frenchman by the name of Albert Comte de Dion met another, Frenchman Georges Bouton, who had designed a steam engine, and they went into business together. The resulting company, de Dion Bouton of Paris, produced many steam-powered tricycles, one of which won the Paris to Rouen race in 1894.

Shortly after, the Comte decided he wanted to build internal combustion engines. Bouton responded and in 1895 a tricycle was fitted with the new engine. The trike went so well and was such a success it not sold only in France but abroad also. The Motor Manufacturing Company, London, England, even gained a War Department contract and the trikes were sent to the Boer War in South Africa.

Engine size increased rapidly and trikes were also used for pacing pedal cycles. Although the tricycle disappeared, the engines stayed on, initially fitted to a strengthened two-wheeler bicycle via a clip-on arrangement. Most of the bicycles using the engine were not de Dion's own make.

1900 Trike
Deutsches-Zweirad Museum
and NSU Museum
Neckarsulm, Germany

**Specifications (1900 Trike)**
**Engine:** Four-stroke single
**Displacement:** N/A
**Horsepower:** 1.75
**Wheelbase:** N/A
**Weight:** 175lb (79.6kg)
**Top speed:** 20mph (32kph)

**Above:** Probably a good testbed for their initial engine, a single-cyclinder 138cc, De Dion and Bouton decided that a tricycle would suit their purposes well. Two of these trikes were exhibited at the Paris-Bordeaux-Paris race of 1895.

# Derbi

**Founded:** 1922
**Factory location:** Barcelona, Spain
**Manufacturing lifespan:** 1922 - to date

Simeon Rabasa Singla founded his company originally as a family business that manufactured and hired out bicycles. Motorcycle production did not begin until 1950, when a range of lightweights were built, known as SRS after the founder. Soon after, the company adopted the name Derbi, did extremely well in competition, and has since concentrated on small-capacity motorcycles, including a range of off-road machines, and mopeds. The Tricampeona was a typical model, featuring a small capacity, two-stroke, single-cylinder engine in a completely traditional frame and with conventional styling.

By the end of the 1970s Derbi was the only major Spanish manufacturer to survive closure or Japanese take-over. Throughout the 1980s, it continued to launch new models and in 1984 competed in Grand Prix racing in the 80cc (4.881cu in) class. In 1987, the company became importer of Kawasaki motorcycles – a continuing arrangement. Derbi also began forging close links with Aprilia, having used an Aprilia frame for its sporty GPR race replica, and in 1991 became Spanish distributor for the Italian company, although this arrangement ceased three years later. The late 1990s saw major investment in the booming scooter market, and in 1999 Derbi returned to racing in the 125cc (7.627cu in) class. The following year it launched the Senda and Supermotard, using a Grand Prix-type perimeter frame, putting it into in a strong position for the new millennium.

**Specifications (Senda R)**
**Engine:** Two-stroke single
**Displacement:** 49.94cc (3cu in)
**Horsepower:** 8.5 @ 9250rpm
**Wheelbase:** 53in (135cm)
**Weight:** N/A
**Top speed:** N/A

# Douglas

**Founded:** 1907
**Factory location:** Bristol, England
**Manufacturing lifespan:** 1907 - 1956

The first Douglas motorcycle was designed by J. F. Barter. For many years the company produced only flat-twin models although it did manufacture models in a variety of different capacities including 384cc (23.42cu in), 498cc (30.37cu in) and 596cc (36.35cu in). During World War I Douglas received contracts to supply the British Army with motorcycles and, after the war was over, its designs were built under license in Germany by Bosch. In the late 1920s the firm built speedway bikes but in the main continued with flat-twins.

The Douglas family relinquished control in 1932 and, after some reorganization, the company attempted to offer a line of less expensive motorcycles which were to be built in larger quantities. The new range of machines stayed with longitudinally mounted flat-twin engines with the exception of the Endeavour which featured a transversely mounted flat-twin engine of 498cc (30.37cu. in.). After World War II Douglas concentrated on the 348cc (21.22cu in) flat-twins with transversely mounted overhead-valve machines including the Dragonfly. Also in the postwar years the company, which became part of Westinghouse in Bristol, England, diversified into the distribution of Vespa scooters in the UK. Production of motorcycles stopped in 1956.

**Specifications (1913 Twin)**
**Engine:** Four-stroke flat-twin
**Displacement:** 345cc (21.05cu in)
**Horsepower:** 2.75
**Wheelbase:** N/A
**Weight:** N/A
**Top speed:** N/A

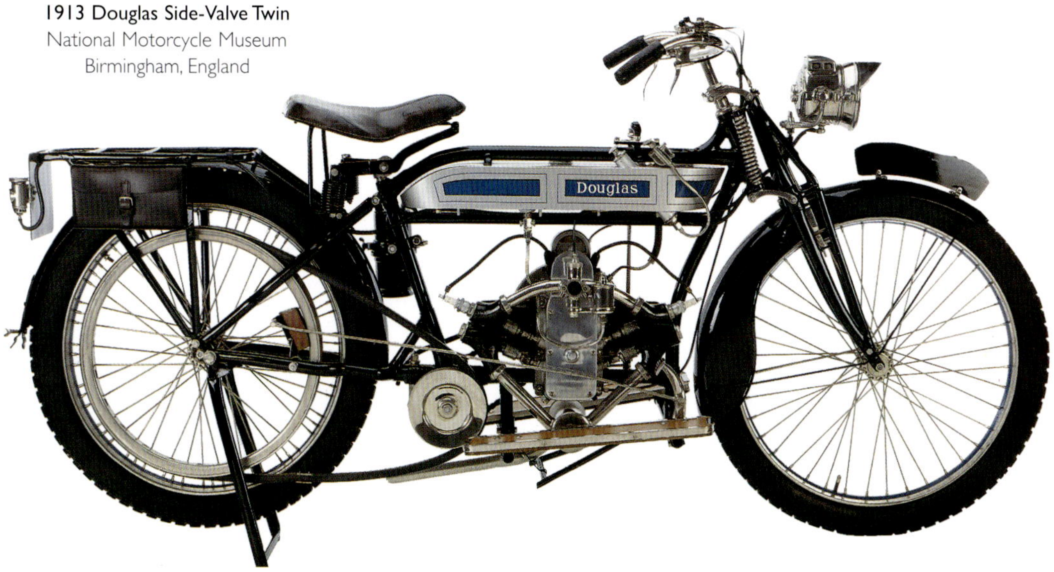


**1913 Douglas Side-Valve Twin**
National Motorcycle Museum
Birmingham, England

**Right:** Douglas was one of relatively few manufacturers worldwide to build motorcycles with a flat-twin engine arranged longitudinally in the frame.

**Left and below:** The Derbi Senda R uses a new DPF (Derbi Perimetral Frame) built in high endurance steel, lighter and with 50 percent more rigidity than the previous model. It has a swingarm with centrally controllable hydraulic 7.9in (200mm) Showa shock absorber.

**Derbi Senda R**
Powerhouse Motorcycles Ltd
Kent, England

# DKW

**Founded:** 1919
**Factory location:** Zschopau, Germany
**Manufacturing lifespan:** 1919 - 1974

The DKW concern was founded by Skafte Rasmussen, an expatriate Dane. The first machines built were simple and reliable two-stroke engines fitted to bicycle-like frames. From such humble beginnings mushroomed a company that, by the 1930s, was the world's largest motorcycle manufacturer. Its extensive racing experience gave DKW the lead in two-stroke technology, bringing fame in the Isle of Man Lightweight (250cc/15.25cu in) races. In 1936 Stanley Woods set a record lap time on a DKW before being forced to retire, while in 1938 Ewald Kluge achieved victory for the company. Success was attained through the use of supercharging and a design referred to as "split-single." This had two bores, one in front of the other, in a single casting and with a single common combustion chamber. The transfer ports were in the forward bore while the exhausts were in the rear. The pistons were articulated on different length con rods allowing maximum advantage in terms of cylinder-filling and valve-opening. The engine, which was supercharged, breathed through a rotary valve which pushed the power output up further. ▶

**SPECIFICATIONS (1922 MODEL)**
**Engine:** Two-stroke single
**Displacement:** 174cc (11cu in)
**Horsepower:** 10 @ 5000rpm
**Wheelbase:** N/A
**Weight:** 280lb (130kg)
**Top speed:** 63mph (100kph)

**1922 Reichsfaht-Mod**
Deutsches-Zweirad Museum
and NSU Museum
Neckarsulm, Germany

**Above:** From humble beginnings... DKW started with a small two-stroke engine fitted to a bicycle, and became the world's largest motorcycle manufacturer in the 1930s.

**SPECIFICATIONS (1936 250)**
**Engine:** Two-stroke single
**Displacement:** 247cc (15.07cu in)
**Horsepower:** 9
**Wheelbase:** N/A
**Weight:** 270lb (135kg)
**Top speed:** 60mph (95kph)

**1936 Sport 250**
Deutsches-Zweirad Museum
and NSU Museum
Neckarsulm, Germany

**Right:** This is the upgraded 1936 250 sport model which sold for a sum of 725RM (the currency at the time was Reichmark, not Duetschmark).

**Specifications (1936 500)**
Engine: Two-stroke twin
Displacement: 500cc (30.50cu in)
Horsepower: 18
Wheelbase:N/A
Weight: N/A
Top speed: N/A

**Right:** The 1936 500 sport model. By the late 1930s DKW were playing a large part in the prosperity seen in Germany at the period.

**Above:** DKW's racing department was the largest in the world. Production machines for the general public bore very little resemblance to those being supercharged for racing.

**1936 Sport 500**
Auto & Technic Museum
Sinsheim, Germany

**Above and left:** During the late 1930s DKW were successful in both track and off-road racing. Many of the top German riders of the day were more than happy to be on a DKW racer. This 250 sport was suitable for off road competition. By now DKW had become part of the Auto Union concern.

# DKW

World War II intervened and, although DKW manufactured a single, the RT125, it was the beginning of the end. Its factory site ended up in the Russian Occupied Zone after the end of the war and the company relocated to the West with some of the original personnel. Production of the RT125 continued after the move although two of the Allied powers, the USA and Great Britain, took the design of the RT125 and it subsequently became the basis of the BSA Bantam and the Harley-Davidson Hummer.

The 1953 DKW RT350 was one of DKWs first new postwar designs, a two-stroke twin with new engine but otherwise a completely traditional motorcycle. DKW sales declined steadily during the 1950s and the operation became absorbed into the conglomerate known as Zweirad Union. In 1966 the two-stroke engine manufacturer Fichtel & Sachs, once fierce competitors of DKW, bought Zweirad Union, at the same time adding its Hercules motorcycle factory to the group.

An unusual model appeared from DKW in 1974. This was a rotary-engined machine, the W2000. It was also widely sold as a Hercules. Unfortunately, despite the innovation that went into the design, the motorcycle was not a great success, mainly due to a combination of both its high cost and its less than pleasing appearance.

By this time the name DKW was being dropped and would soon disappear altogether, except in the occasional country where the bike was badged as a DKW.

**Specifications (1957 175)**
**Engine:** Two-stroke single
**Displacement:** 174cc (11cu in)
**Horsepower:** 10 @ 5000rpm
**Wheelbase:** N/A
**Weight:** 280lb (130kg)
**Top speed:** N/A

**Above:** Introduced in 1954 at the Frankfurt bike show, the RT175 was new but used many parts from previous models. For example, the engine was that of the RT200 but with stroke slightly changed to achieve the lower capacity.

1957 RT175
Deutsches-Zweirad Museum and NSU Museum Neckarsulm, Germany

# Dresch

**Founded:** 1923
**Factory location:** Paris, France
**Manufacturing lifespan:** 1923 -1939

Dresch was one of France's more important motorcycle manufacturers and built a large number of models. The company fitted proprietary power units from French and other European makers into its own frames, using two-stroke engines for the smaller models from 98 to 246cc (5.98 to 15.01cu in) and four-stroke engines for larger motorcycles up to 748cc (45.65cu in). Some of the more luxurious models had a very advanced specification for the time. This included a pressed-steel frame that wrapped around the fuel tank, pressed-steel forks, and shaft drive. In 1930, Dresch launched a model with a 498cc (30.389cu in) side-valve twin in line with the frame and shaft drive: a layout similar to the postwar British Sunbeam. The company also made 498cc and 748cc versions of the design.

Based in Paris, Henry Dresch used a variety of engines, such as Chaise and MAG, during the company's 16-year lifespan. Seen here is the 500cc (30.50cu in) model of 1930. The carburetor is neatly positioned between the two down pipes of the exhaust system. Two other details on the bike are worth noting also: one is the beautifully pin-striped pressed-steel frame and the other is the drive-shaft that runs from the back of the gearbox to the rear wheel. The seat is heavily sprung to compensate for the lack of suspension at the rear.

Production of Dresch motorcycles ceased with the onset of World War II.

**Specifications (1964 Violetta)**
**Engine:** Two-stroke single
**Displacement:** 48cc (3cu in)
**Horsepower:** 4 @ 6300rpm
**Wheelbase:** N/A
**Weight:** 154lb (70kg)
**Top speed:** 40mph (65kph)

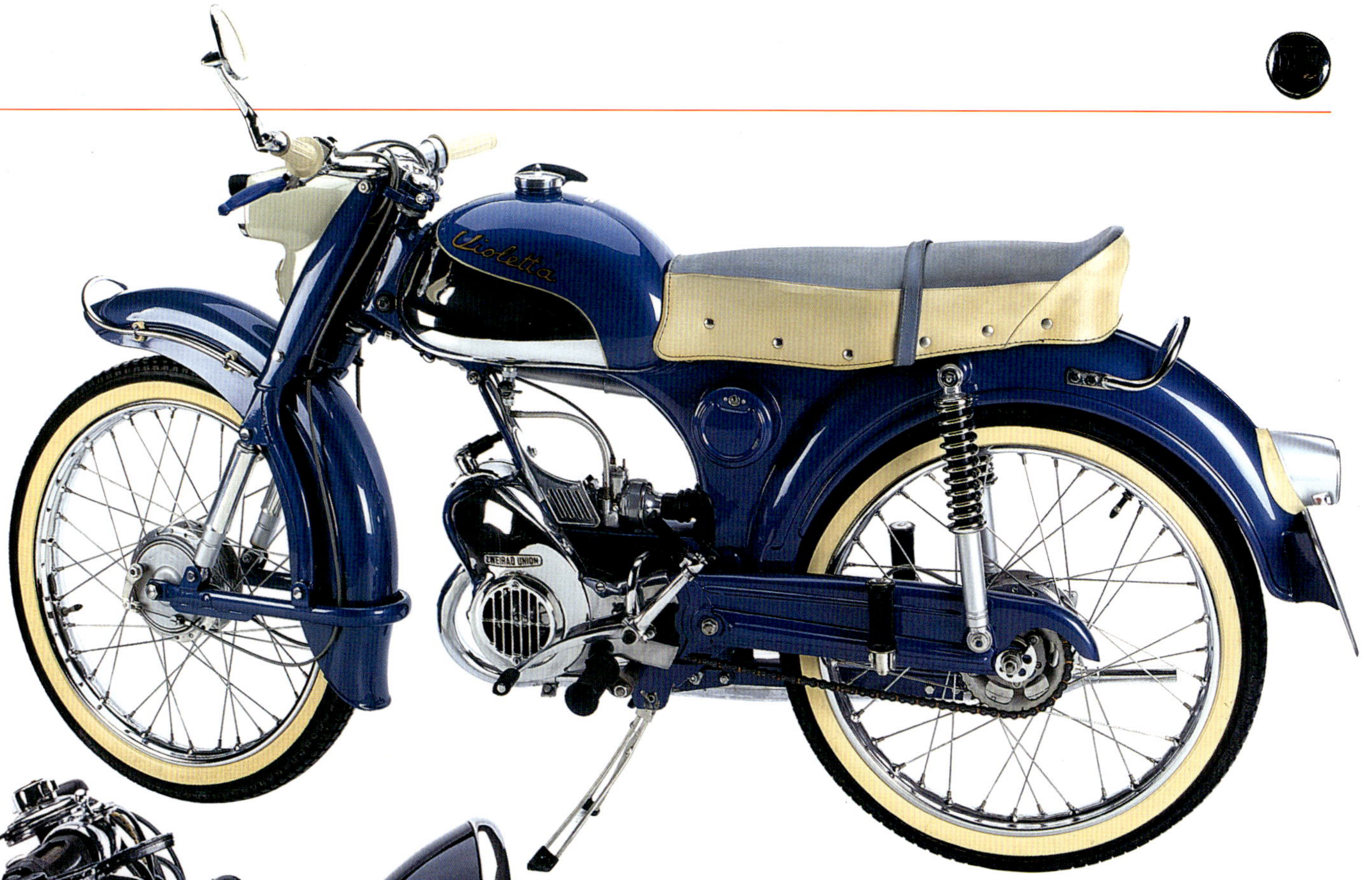


1964 Violetta
Deutsches-Zweirad Museum
and NSU Museum
Neckarsulm, Germany

**Right:** In common with many postwar German lightweight bikes, this 1964 DKW Violetta used a three-speed, fan-cooled engine from Sachs, and a kick start in place of pedals.

**Specifications (1930 500)**
**Engine:** Four-stroke twin
**Displacement:** 500cc (30.50cu in)
**Horsepower:** 16
**Wheelbase:** N/A
**Weight:** N/A
**Top speed:** N/A

Dresch 1937 500
Deutsches-Zweirad Museum
and NSU Museum
Neckarsulm, Germany

**Left:** One of the more interesting aspects of this Dresch machine is its parallel twin-cylinder 500cc engine; another is the shaft drive: not many bikes of the period had this type of set-up to the back wheel.

# DUCATI

| | |
|---|---|
| **Founded:** 1950 | |
| **Factory location:** Borgo Panigale, Bologna, Italy | |
| **Manufacturing lifespan:** 1950 – to date | |

After World War II, Ducati, a big Italian industrial company, realized there was a need for cheap and basic transportation and, through Aldo Farinelli, started to manufacture the Cucciolo, a 49cc (2.99cu in) engine designed to clip on to a normal pedal cycle. The success of this product helped the company move into small capacity motorcycles and, with the arrival of designer Fabio Taglioni, progress was steady. Taglioni designed the 100 Gran Sport which pointed the way to the superbike era.

Mike Hailwood brought good fortune Ducati's way when, in 1978, aboard a race-prepared 900SS, he won the Isle of Man TT. Ducati subsequently marketed a Mike Hailwood replica bike; it was to be Taglioni's last motorcycle design. The Pantah is acknowledged as the motorcycle that saved Ducati from closure and brought the attentions of Cagiva.

It was Taglioni who developed the unique Desmodromic valve set-up for 125cc (7.62cu. in.) race engines, allowing them to rev to 15,000rpm without harm and leading to great racing success. In the late 1960s Ducati was nationalized. It introduced legendary but costly roadgoing Desmodromic engines which displaced 250cc (15.26cu in) and 350cc (21.35cu in). These bikes were soon followed by the 750cc (45.75cu in) Ducati 750 GT, which won the 200-miler at Imola. The 900 Supersport followed hot on the heels of the successful 750 Sport. It used an existing engine, the 904cc (55.14cu in) V-twin from the Paso but without the liquid cooling of the Paso. Ducati saw the machine as an elegant café racer, which combined handcrafted motorcycle building skills with the very latest technology. This technology included an air/oil-cooled engine together with the company's Desmodromic valve system mounted in a monoshock frame. ▶

1977 900SS
Conquest Restorers
Dorset, England

**Above:** One of the Ducatis best loved by collectors, the 900SS performed well both off-road and on the track. A special package was available from Ducati for those who wanted to race their machine.

**SPECIFICATIONS (1977 900 SS)**
- **Engine:** Four-stroke 90deg V-twin
- **Displacement:** 900cc (54.92 cu in)
- **Horsepower:** N/A
- **Wheelbase:** N/A
- **Weight:** 413.6lb (188kg)
- **Top speed:** 140mph (225.3kph)

**SPECIFICATIONS (1976 DESMO)**
- **Engine:** Four-stroke single
- **Displacement:** 350cc (21.35cu in)
- **Horsepower:** 29 @ 8000rpm
- **Wheelbase:** N/A
- **Weight:** N/A
- **Top speed:** 97mph (155kph)

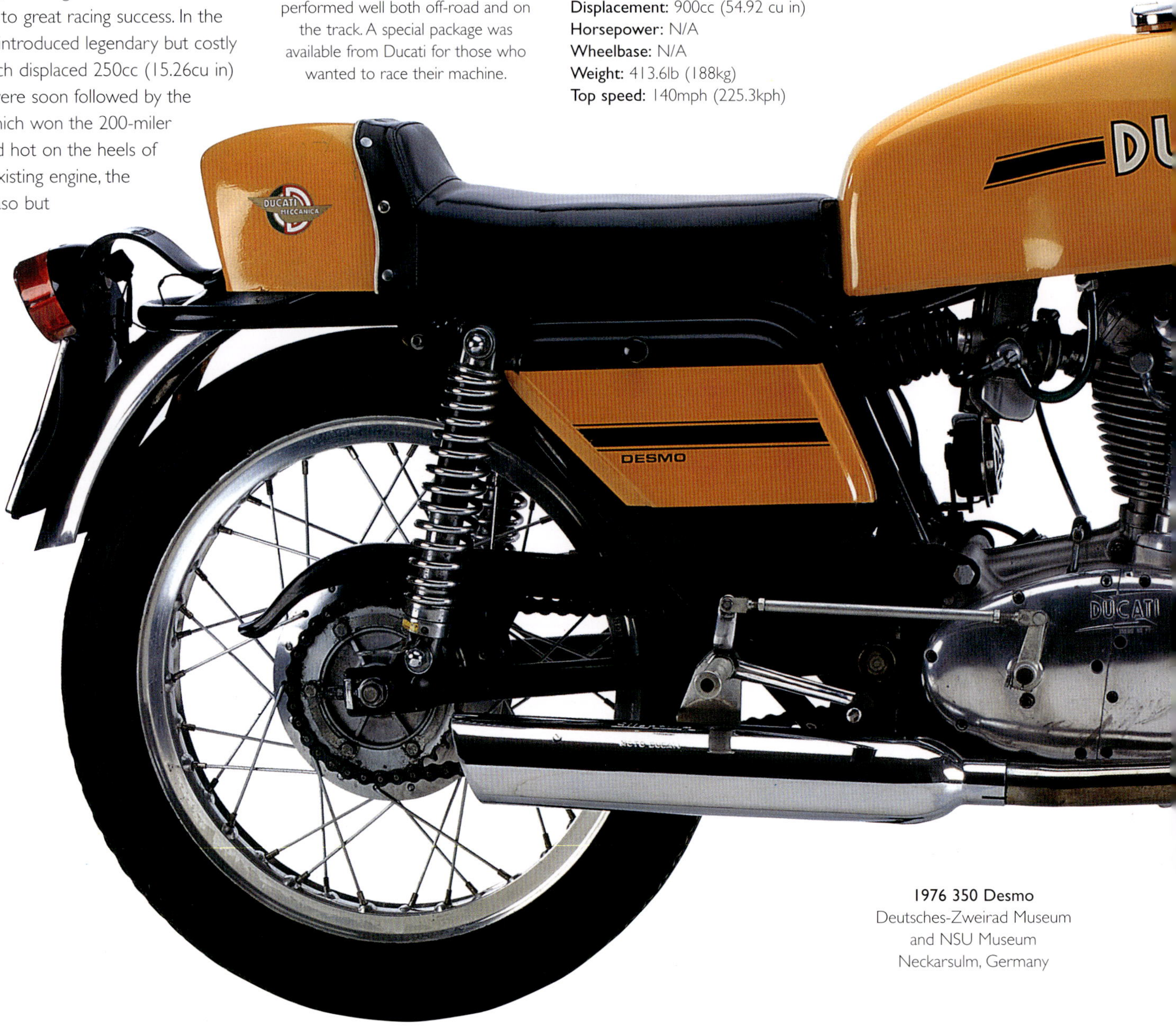


**Right:** On this model Desmo 350 everything was kept to a minimum, which suited the sporty riders of the day. Rear-set foot rests and a long gearchange lever fitted on the right side can be seen.

1976 350 Desmo
Deutsches-Zweirad Museum
and NSU Museum
Neckarsulm, Germany

**Specifications (1979 Hailwood Special)**

Engine: Four-stroke 90deg V-twin
Displacement: 973cc (59.38cu in)
Horsepower: N/A
Wheelbase: N/A
Weight: 463lb (210kg)
Top speed: 135mph (217.3kph)

**Right:** This is a replica of the bike that Mike "The Bike" Hailwood raced so successfully in the TT on the Isle of Man in 1978. Initially to have been a limited edition, it sold so well it was still around into the 1980s.

1979 Mike Hailwood Replica
Conquest Restorers,
Dorset, England

**Above:** Patriotic to the last, the MHR was painted in the colors that represented the Italian flag, which showed up beautifully on one of not too many fully faired Ducatis.

**Left:** The 350 Desmo was said to have a top speed of 100mph (160kph); with a straight-through exhaust it approached 106.3mph (170kph).

**Above:** The Desmo 350, from 1971, had a high class mechanical racing-style Veglia Borletti rev counter.

# DUCATI

In 1983 Ducati was purchased by the Castiglioni brothers and became part of the Cagiva group. Under the new management Ducati expanded its share of the motorcycle market, introducing new models and intensifying the company's commitment to racing. Racer Carl Fogerty became a legend not only with Ducati but also as a world champion on more than one occasion.

As the new millennium approached, Ducati seemed to go from strength to strength, producing some of the most mouthwatering superbikes ever seen. If you wanted speed, and good road holding, let alone a machine that looked and sounded like a real bike, then you bought a Ducati. Introduced in 1994, the 916 became a legend in its own lifetime, people drooled over it.

But, in spite of product innovation and racing success, Ducati encountered financial problems, due to some unsuccessful ventures of its sister companies.

In 1996 the company was taken over by the Texas Pacific Group and with new management and much needed cash the company began to thrive again.

A new model, the ST (Sports Tourer) series, was introduced and the company began to make profits again. Probably the best-seller and part savior for the company was the Monster Dark, starting a new era and spurring Ducati towards stock market flotation in 1999. The latest venture is the MH900e, the first bike to be sold exclusively on the internet.

**Ducati 996**
P&H Motorcycles
Crawley, England

**SPECIFICATIONS (ST2)**

**Engine:** Four-stroke L-twin
**Displacement:** 944cc (57.58cu in)
**Horsepower:** N/A
**Wheelbase:** 56in (143cm)
**Weight:** 466lb (212kg)
**Top speed:** 166mph (265kph)

**Above:** The ST (Sport Touring) 2 was launched in 1996. Its fairing promises good all-round protection for those long journeys, and the bike is also comfortable around town.

**1997 ST2**
Courtesy of Ducati
Borgo Panigale, Bologna, Italy

**Above:** The frame of the ST2 is the classic Ducati tubular steel trellis type. The single shock absorber rear suspension can be seen attached to the swingarm, and a grab handle is fitted for the passenger.

DUCATI

**Specifications (2000 996)**
**Engine:** 90° L-twin
**Displacement:** 996cc (60.78cu in)
**Horsepower:** 112 @ 8500rpm
**Wheelbase:** N/A
**Weight:** 436lb (198kg)
**Top speed:** 162mph (260kph)

**Left:** Taking over from the legendary 916, the 996 boasts an extra 80cc (4.5cu in), a new exhaust system and several other electronic upgrades to make it yet better than its smaller brother.

**Above:** The front end of the 996 makes an imposing sight; the twin headlamps give better visibility at night and wide mirrors better views to the rear.

## Emblem

**Founded:** 1907
**Factory location:** Angola, New York, USA
**Manufacturing lifespan:** 1907 - 1925

The Emblem originated in western New York state in 1907. The early singles were offered with options of direct drive or clutch, and flat or V-belt motivation. When the company introduced a twin in 1913, it was a robust 1255cc (76.58cu in) engine rated at ten horsepower. In 1916, customers could choose a 12- or 14-horsepower powerplant. The less power-hungry were offered the 800cc (48.82cu in) twin, or the venerable 600cc (36.61cu in), seven-horse single. Emblem had a brief period of professional racing effort, but soon retired to less costly enterprises.

A few Emblems were set up for racing in 1912–13, but there was never a large-scale factory effort. Belt drive was a disadvantage in the increasingly fast sport. ▶

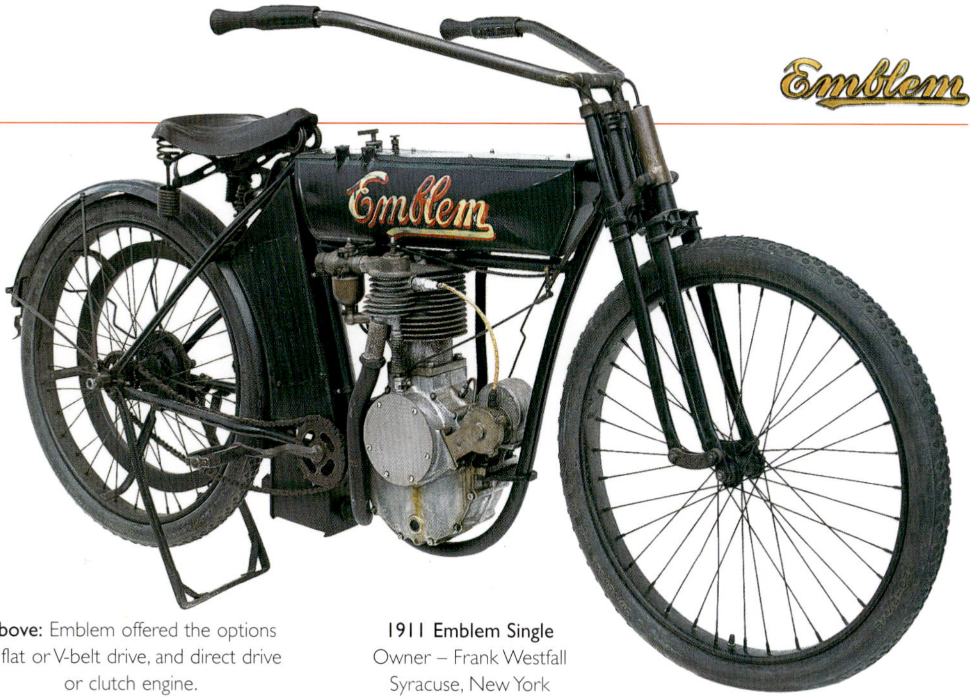

**Above:** Emblem offered the options of flat or V-belt drive, and direct drive or clutch engine.

**1911 Emblem Single**
Owner – Frank Westfall
Syracuse, New York

# EMBLEM

The big-bore trend began in 1913, when Emblem introduced a 1255cc twin rated at ten horsepower. The factory allowed as how it had even more grunt, and guaranteed a top speed of 70mph (113kph).

By 1917 the competition for motorcycle sales had narrowed the field, due largely to the motoring economics introduced a few years earlier by Henry Ford. Emblem came to market with a roster of one model that year, a V-twin of moderate displacement (530cc/32.34cu in) and performance. The lightweight twin was good for 50mph (80kph) and sold for $175, the same price their single brought the year before.

The basic model was a one-speed with an Eclipse clutch, and a three-speed version was available. The mechanical oil pump was optional. The front fork featured a triple crown cartridge spring design, which allowed 2.5 inches (6.35cm) of wheel travel. With its low seat height and center of gravity and short wheelbase (52 inches/132cm) the Emblem was a nimble machine. But American riders had cast their dollar votes for big twins, and fours, with more heaps of horsepower. The lightweight Emblem was virtually lost in the shuffle. Although it remained in production for another eight years, the Emblem was sold almost exclusively as an export model.

**Right:** A luggage rack was a popular accessory item. Emblem machines were widely used by police and postal services in the northeast USA.

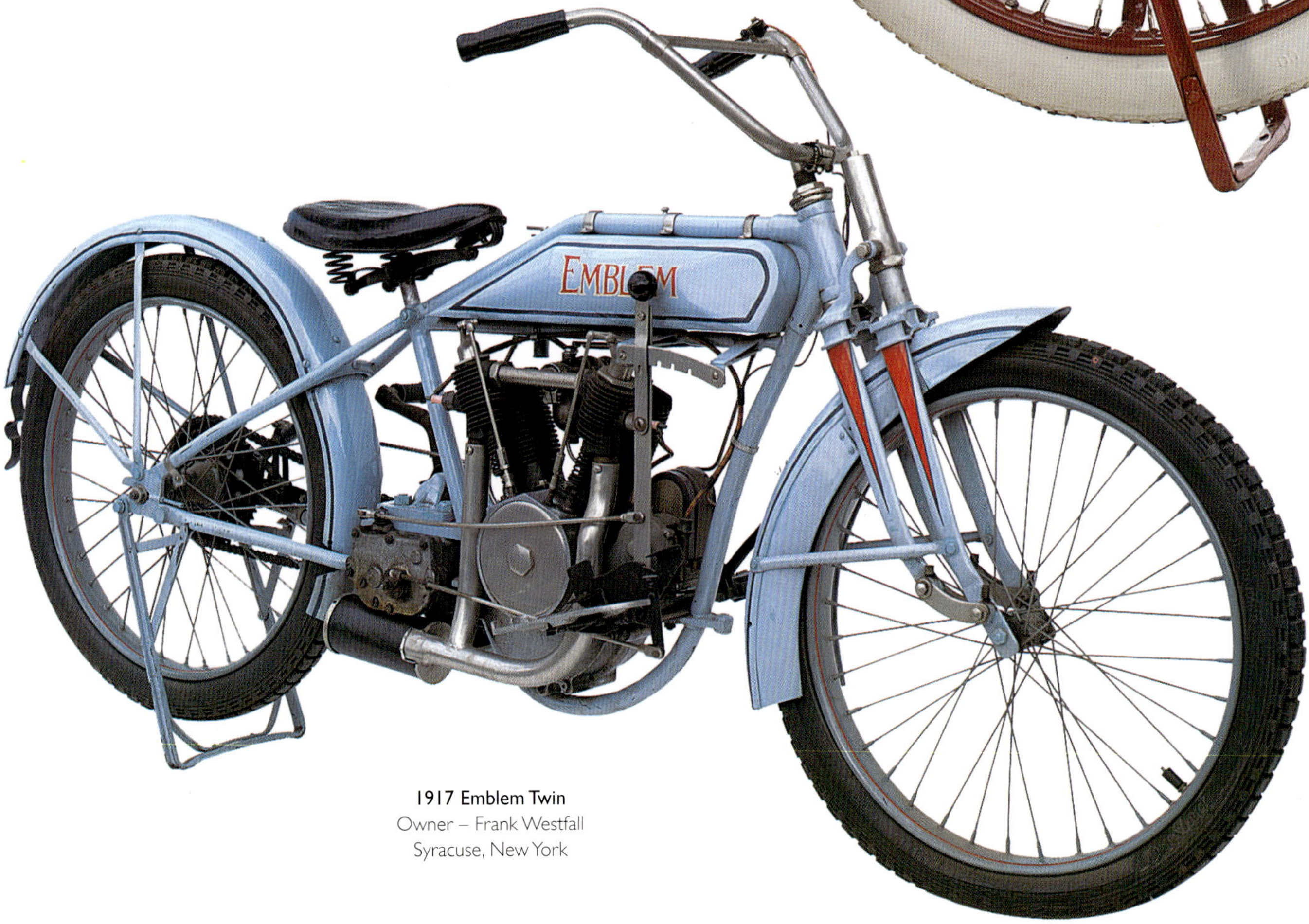


**1917 Emblem Twin**
Owner – Frank Westfall
Syracuse, New York

**SPECIFICATIONS (1917 V-TWIN)**

- **Engine:** 45° F-head V-twin
- **Displacement:** 530cc (32.33cu in)
- **Horsepower:** 7
- **Wheelbase:** 52in (132cm)
- **Weight:** 225lb (102kg)
- **Top speed:** 50mph (80kph)

**Left:** In 1917 the standard Emblem twin was available with either direct drive or, for $35 more, a three-speed transmission. The triple crown cartridge spring fork offered 2.5 inches (6.35cm) of travel, "ample to absorb all road shocks."

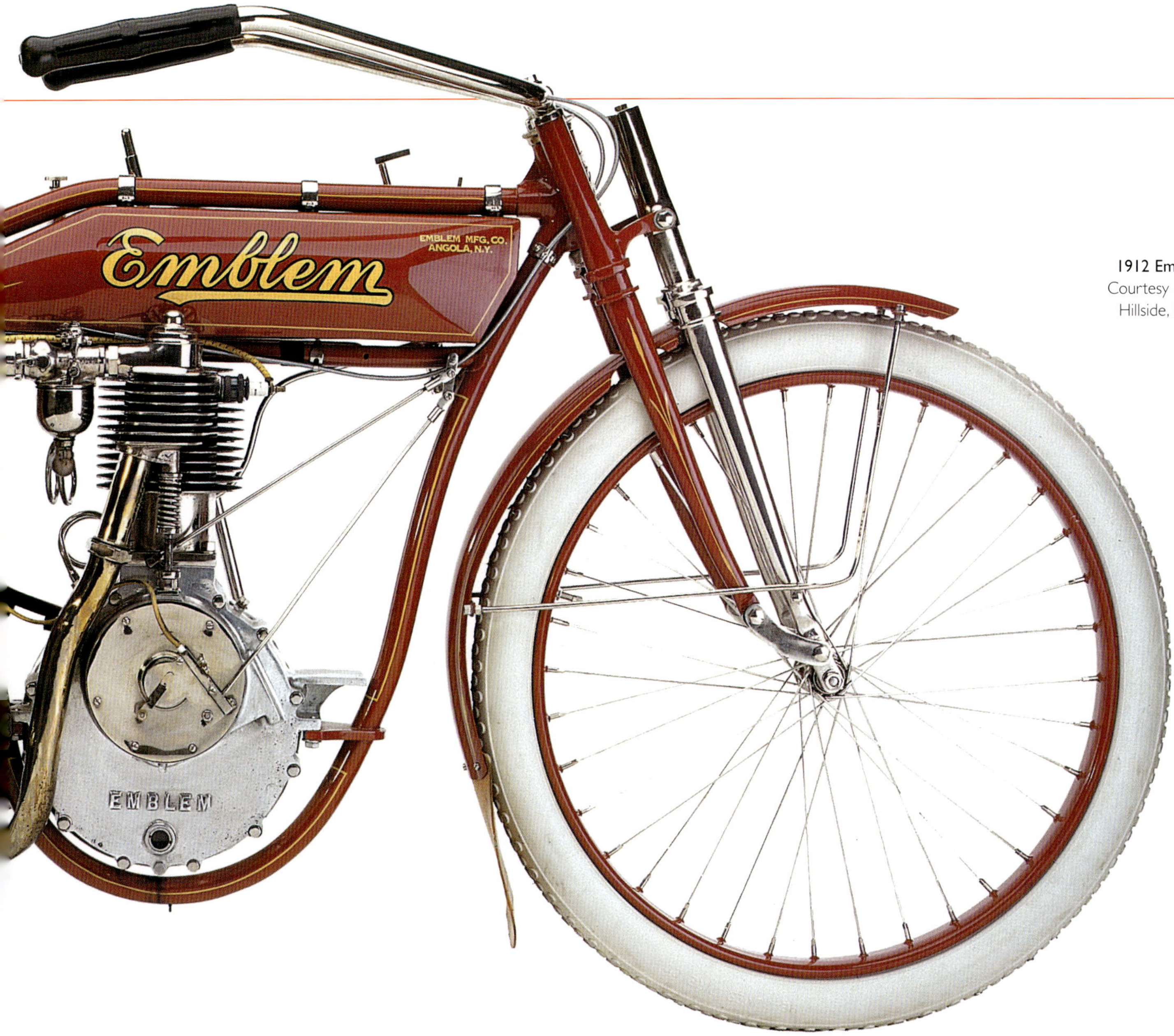


1912 Emblem Single
Courtesy of Mike Terry
Hillside, New Jersey

**Left:** The Emblem single was a stout machine, with the engine mounted quite low in the loop frame. The muffler was tucked in nicely below the rear frame section.

# EXCELSIOR

| | |
|---|---|
| **Founded:** | 1896 |
| **Factory location:** | Coventry, England |
| **Manufacturing lifespan:** | 1896 - 1964 |

In England, a company known as Bayliss, Thomas and Company built Excelsior bicycles and later offered for sale bicycles fitted with Minerva engines. By 1902 it offered a belt-drive machine with a 2.75hp single-cylinder engine fitted inclined forward under the front down-tube of the frame. The fuel and oil tanks were located within the central part of the diamond-shaped frame. The company was taken over by R. Walker & Son in 1919. Like many other manufacturers, Walker produced motorcycles with proprietary engines from companies such as Blackburne and JAP. While many of its machines were utility motorcycles, the company did build some race bikes and campaigned them at Brooklands and in the Isle of Man TT races. They won a lightweight event in 1929 and went on to debut an innovative racer at the 1933 event. This became known as the "Mechanical Marvel." Its single-cylinder engine had a displacement of 250cc (15.25cu in) and featured four radial valves in the cylinder head operated by a pair of camshafts fore and aft of the cylinder. ▶

**SPECIFICATIONS (1933 MECHANICAL MARVEL)**

- **Engine:** Four-stroke ohv single
- **Displacement:** 246cc (15cu in)
- **Horsepower:** 25
- **Wheelbase:** N/A
- **Weight:** N/A
- **Top speed:** N/A

**Above:** The Mechanical Marvel was powered by an ohv single-cylinder engine that had two exhaust ports – hence the exhaust pipe on each side of the machine.

1933 Mechanical Marvel
National Motorcycle Museum
Birmingham, England

# Excelsior

The Excelsior range was upgraded during the 1930s and given names that capitalized on the TT win. The Manxman was launched in 1935 in two versions, 246cc (15.01cu in) and 349cc (21.30cu in). Engines were single-cylinder, shaft-driven single overhead camshaft. The bevel box cover had the "Legs of Man" symbol of the Isle of Man cast into its alloy top. The motorcycle featured a 4-speed foot-change gearbox, cradle frame, and capacious fuel tank. There were sports and racing forms, the latter featuring rear-set footrests, different tanks and mudguards, as well as a slightly modified engine. But it never actually won an Isle of Man TT race.

In 1936 a 496cc (30.27cu in) version, the F14, appeared and the race models were listed as FR11 and FR12. These featured megaphone exhausts and wraparound oil tanks. By 1937, the Manxman range included the short-stroke 249cc (15.19cu in) G12 and GR12 models, similar in design to works race models of the previous year but without the radial four-valve cylinder head of the works bikes. The Manxman range ran on slightly upgraded for the next three years until the outbreak of war called a halt to production.

During the war, production of the paratrooper's mini fold-up Welbike was handed over to Excelsior. Its 98cc Villiers two-stroke engine was mounted horizontally in the frame, and the seat and handlebars folded up to fit into an airdrop container.

After the war motorcycle production continued using two-stroke engines, some from Villiers and some of the company's own. An enclosed-engine scooter-style bike, the Skutabyk, was produced in 1957, but 1964 saw the end of further production from Excelsior.

**Specifications (1937 G12 Manxman)**

**Engine:** Four-stroke single
**Displacement:** 349cc (21.3cu in)
**Horsepower:** 22 @ 6000rpm
**Wheelbase:** 54in (1372mm)
**Weight:** 335lb (152kg)
**Top speed:** 85mph (137kph)

1937 G12 Manxman
National Motorcycle Museum
Birmingham, England

**Right:** The 349cc short-stroke engine fitted to the Manxman featured a shaft-driven single ohc that operated both inlet and exhaust valves.

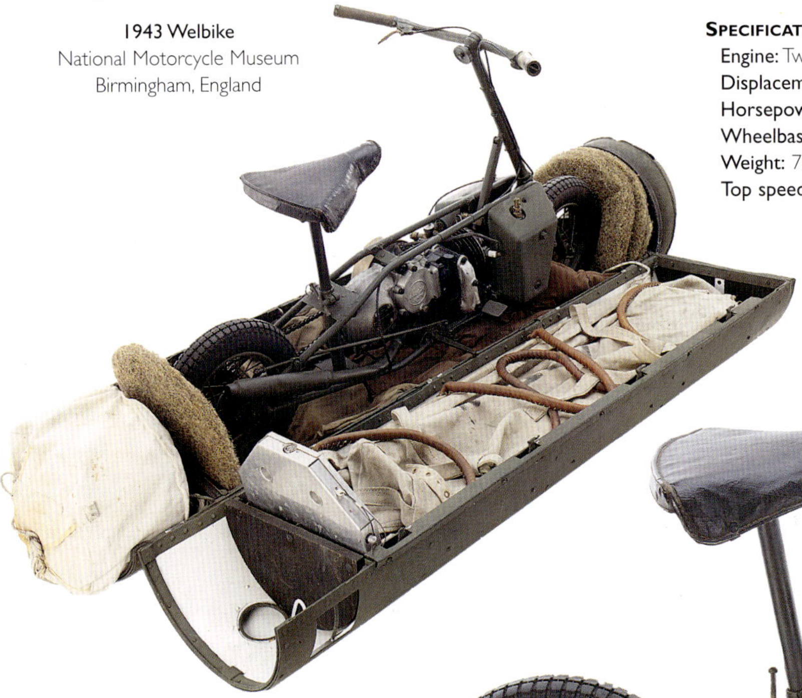

1943 Welbike
National Motorcycle Museum
Birmingham, England

**Above:** This view of the Welbike's protective canister shows the internal padding that was used to cushion the motorcycle from the effects of it being dropped from an aircraft.

**Specifications (1943 Wellbike)**

**Engine:** Two-stroke single
**Displacement:** 98cc (6cu in)
**Horsepower:** 1.5
**Wheelbase:** 39.5 (1003mm)
**Weight:** 70.5lb (32kg)
**Top speed:** 31mph (50kph)

**Below:** The Excelsior Welbike was intended for use by British paratroops and designed to be parachuted into combat with them. When it landed, the soldiers uncased it, folded up the seat and handlebars and rode away.

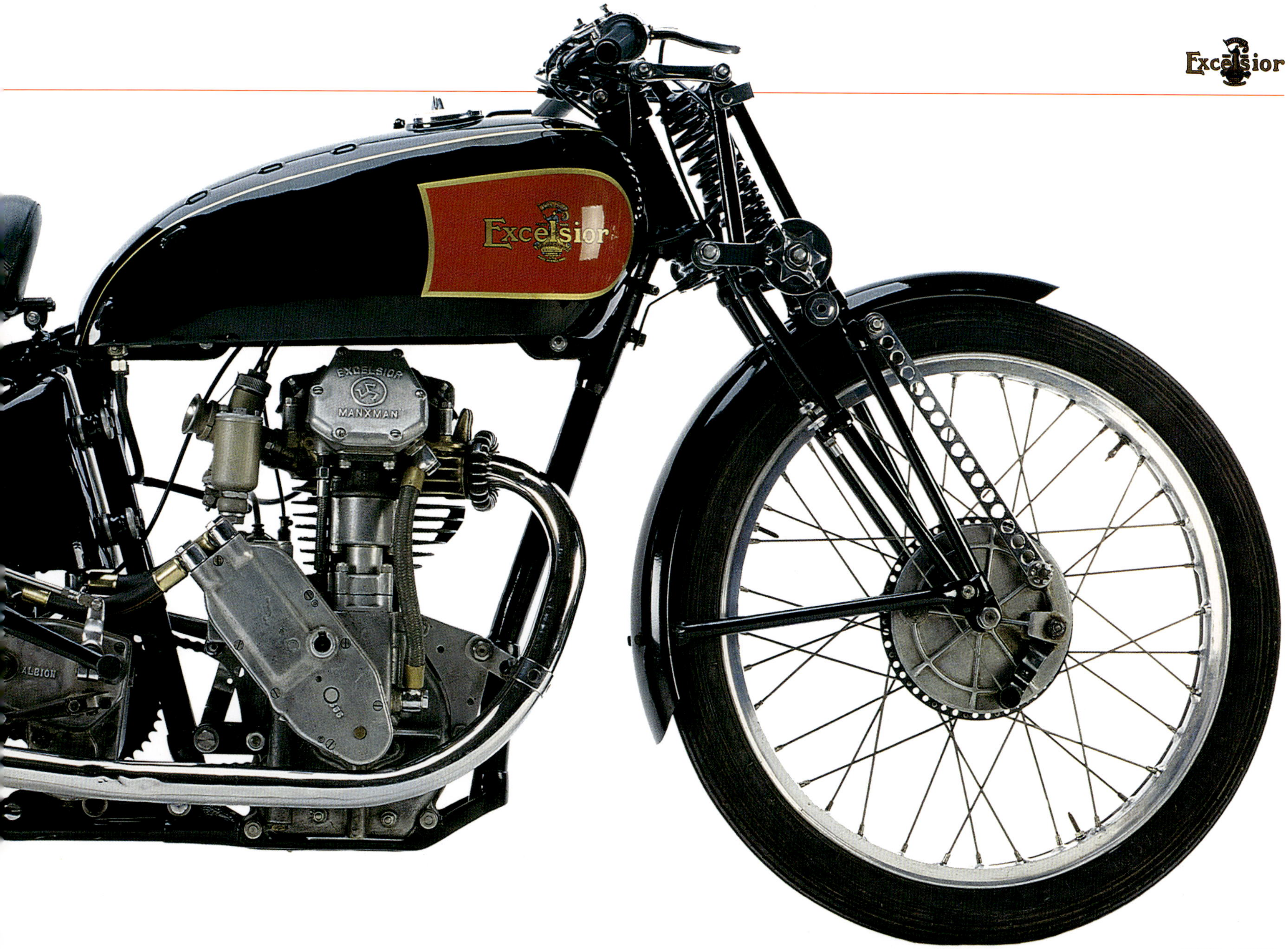


# Excelsior

| | |
|---|---|
| **Founded:** 1908 | |
| **Factory location:** Chicago, Illinois, USA | |
| **Manufacturing lifespan:** 1908 - 1931 | |

Excelsior was third of the big three in the teens and twenties of 20th century America. Indian and Harley-Davidson were the other two major players, and would become the only survivors of the Great Depression. But until its demise in 1931, Excelsior and its offspring the Super-X, insured a dynamic three-way tussle for domination of the American motorcycle market. On and off the racetrack, it was a genuine contest.

The original Excelsior Supply Company began building motorcycles in 1906. They came to market in 1908 with a well-tested belt-drive 500cc single, with the crankcase cast integral with the frame. The machine carried a leading-link dual-spring front fork and two gallons (7.6lit) of gas. Three Excelsior singles entered the Chicago-Kokomo Reliability Run, and all finished with perfect scores. Motorcycles had thus moved beyond the framework of the motorized bicycle, and become integrated entities, purpose-built machines. ▶

**Specifications (Single)**
- **Engine:** IOE single
- **Displacement:** 500cc (30.5cu in)
- **Horsepower:** 4
- **Wheelbase:** 56in (142cm)
- **Weight:** 170lb (77kg)
- **Top speed:** 45mph (72kph)

1908 Excelsior Single
Owner – Ken Smith
Philadelphia, Pennsylvania

**Above:** The first Excelsior appeared in 1908, and was thoroughly tested in advance. Powered by a 500cc single with belt drive, the new machine was built for strength and reliability. And it was easy to ride.

For many years the 500cc Excelsior single raced with success, but its production lasted only for four years. In 1910 Excelsior introduced its V-twin to the market, an 820cc (50.02cu in) engine with mechanical intake valves. A 1000cc (61cu in) model appeared the following year, then the company was acquired by the Arnold-Schwinn and Company of Chicago, a leading manufacturer of bicycles. No model changes were instituted for 1912, but a year later the company was called Excelsior Motor Manufacturing and Supply, and the single was dropped.

Against tough opposition from the Harley and Indian big two, there followed considerable racing success and record breaking by Excelsior bikes, exemplified by the first-ever 100mph (161kph) average in a board-track sanctioned competition in Los Angeles in 1913, three 100-mile event wins and the Chicago 300-miler in 1915, and Alan Bedell's 1917 ride on a Henderson Four from Los Angeles to New York in 7 days, 16 hours to beat Cannonball Baker's Indian mark by nearly four hours. In October of the same year, Ignaz Schwinn bought the Henderson Motorcycle Company.

In 1917 the company's focus was on the Henderson Four. The Ultra Power twin was rated at 15hp, with generator and electric lights, three-speed transmission and automatic compression release on the kickstarter.

Excelsior's lasting contribution to American racing came with the introduction of the Super-X in 1925. The lighter 750cc (45.75cu in) twin was immediately competitive against larger machines in hillclimb and oval racing. When Indian and Harley quickly followed with their own 750s, the pattern for national Class C racing was set in place. Excelsior would later build special over-head-valve versions of the Super-X, which came to dominate championship hillclimb events.

But with the advent of the Great Depression, and the passage of Schwinn operations to a second generation, motorcycles took a back seat to bicycle production. The Excelsior marque was terminated in 1931.

**Below:** The Super-X made its debut in 1925. Though still a traditional F-head design, the engine carried its transmission within the crankcases and had helical-gear primary drive.

**Below:** The 500cc Excelsior single was raced successfully for many years. But it would be the "Big-X" twins that pushed Indian and Harley to higher standards of performance.

**1911 Excelsior Single**
Owner – Jim Lattin
Encinitas, California

1930 Super-X
Owner – Otis Chandler
Ojai, California

**Specifications (Super-X)**
Engine: IOE V-twin
Displacement: 750cc (45.75cu in)
Horsepower: 20
Wheelbase: 61in (155cm)
Weight: 450lb (204kg) est.
Top speed: 65mph (105kph)

**Left:** The Super-X exhaust valves were enclosed in 1927, a front brake was added in 1928. The effects of the Great Depression put Excelsior out of business in 1931.

## Excelsior-Henderson

**Founded:** 1998
**Factory location:** Belle Plain, Minnesota, USA
**Manufacturing lifespan:** 1998 - to date

The contemporary revival of Excelsior-Henderson is the brainchild of the Hanlon brothers of Minnesota. Encouraged by Harley's apparent inability to keep up with the worldwide demand for cruisers in 1993, Dave and Dan Hanlon set themselves the task of building a new motorcycle with an old name. They were able to raise $100 million from investors and build a motorcycle plant.

The new Super-X hit the market in 1999. The retro-cruiser runs a 1386cc V-twin with dual overhead cams and four valves per cylinder. The rubber-mounted (Torsion Activated Vibration Absorbing System) fuel-injected motor motivates a five-speed transmission with final drive via belt. The chassis combines the rigid-look rear frame section on a single shock with the leading-link vintage-style front fork, each end getting four inches (10.2cm) of travel.

Will Excelsior-Henderson be able to compete directly with Harley-Davidson in the American cruiser market? The crystal ball remains clouded, but it's early yet.

**Specifications (1999 Super-X)**
Engine: 50° dohc V-twin
Displacement: 1386cc (84.55cu in)
Horsepower: 82
Wheelbase: 65in (165cm)
Weight: 670lb (304kg)
Top speed: 120mph (193kph)

1999 Super-X
Courtesy of Excelsior-Henderson
Belle Plain, Minnesota

**Above:** Original Super-X styling cues are reflected by the fork springs, leading-link suspension and front fender. Power is delivered by geared primary to a five-speed transmission, and by belt to the rear wheel.

# FLANDERS



**Founded:** 1911
**Factory location:** Detroit, Michigan, USA
**Manufacturing lifespan:** 1911 - 1914

The Motor Products Company of Detroit attempted, as others had, to build a comfortable and reliable machine and offer it at a reasonable price. The Flanders 4 (as in horsepower) had a 485cc (29.59cu in) single and belt drive, with a compression and rebound spring on the front fork. The single sold for $165.

The 1914 twin, with enclosed chain drive, was advertised as "The Packard of Motorcycle Value." Rated at seven to nine horsepower, the side-valve twin claimed the only direct chain drive with the "smoothness and flexibility of a belt." Flanders took some pride in offering good value at low cost, which was $210 for the twin, significantly less than the relatively rudimentary Harley-Davidson at $285. But in three years Flanders had faded into the archives.

**Below:** The Flanders fork offered a dual spring system; one worked on compression, the other on rebound.

1911 Flanders 4
Owner – Otis Chandler
Ojai, California

**SPECIFICATIONS (SINGLE)**
**Engine:** IOE single
**Displacement:** 485cc (29.59cu in)
**Horsepower:** 4
**Wheelbase:** 57in (145cm)
**Weight:** 270lb (122kg)
**Top speed:** 45mph (72kph)

# FN

**Founded:** 1901
**Factory location:** Liege, Belgium
**Manufacturing lifespan:** 1901 – 1957

A pioneering company in the motorcycle field and a major Belgian entrant, FN became famous for its shaft drive and four-cylinder models. The first machines had 225cc (13.73cu in) and 286cc (17.45cu in) single-cylinder engines and 496cc (30.27cu in) and 748cc (45.62cu in) four-cylinder inline engines. After 1924 FN used chain drive to the rear wheel due to the expense of the shaft system. In 1937 a 992cc (60.54cu in) four-cylinder bike with the engine mounted transversely was made for the Belgian army. Between two-strokes, racing ohc engines and a 498cc (30.39cu in) vertical twin that was raced by Ginger Wood, the company had a good variety of machines. After World War II it continued to produce machines that included sports models raced by Belgians with varying success.

The FN Four was designed by Paul Kelecom and sparked a generation of American four-cylinder machines, Pierce being the first, although Indian, Henderson and Cleveland fours are all reckoned to owe fealty to the Belgian marque.

**SPECIFICATIONS (FOUR)**
**Engine:** Inline four
**Displacement:** 412cc (25.24cu in)
**Horsepower:** 3.45 @ 1800rpm
**Wheelbase:** N/A
**Weight:** 165lb (75kg)
**Top speed:** 41mph (66kph)

**Below:** Paul Kelekom's Belgian design inspired American makers to develop fours.

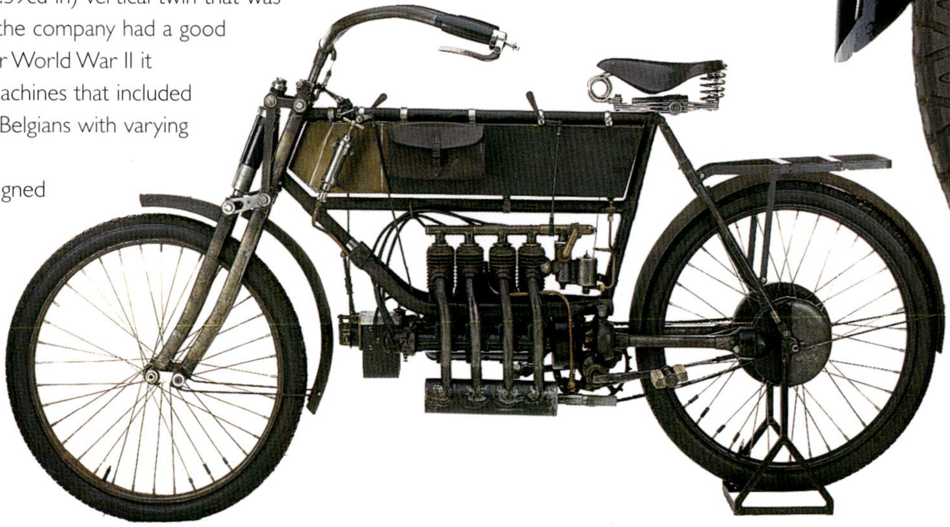

# FRANCIS-BARNETT

**Founded:** 1919
**Factory location:** Coventry, England
**Manufacturing lifespan:** 1919 -1964

This company came about in 1919 through the collaboration of Arthur Barnett and Gordon Francis. Barnett was already producing motorcycles in Coventry, England. His motorcycles were known as Invicta and used Villiers and JAP engines. The first machine from the new company, with a bolted tubular frame and a JAP engine, was introduced in 1920. Francis–Barnett manufactured machines with triangulated frames from 1923 onward and became noted for the production of lightweight machines powered by Villiers engines of 147, 172 and 196cc (8.96, 10.49 and 11.95cu in) displacement. The Model 10 Pullman was an attempt to market a luxury motorcycle, but its increased cost far outweighed the benefits of its luxury features and only average performance. The engine was constructed as a unit with the gearbox, which meant that the front and rear downtubes were considerably splayed to pass either side of the engine while the external flywheel protruded between them. Also unusual was the fuel tank, which was triangular and fitted between the frame tubes. The frame was a simple design: six pairs of straight tubes, one bent pair and a steering head were bolted together to complete it. ▶

**SPECIFICATIONS (1928 MODEL 10 PULLMAN)**
**Engine:** Two-stroke inline twin
**Displacement:** 343cc (21cu in)
**Horsepower:** N/A
**Wheelbase:** N/A
**Weight:** N/A
**Top speed:** 60mph 97kph)

**Right:** The Pullman was Francis-Barnett's attempt to market a luxury motorcycle but its average performance did not justify its cost. Sales were poor and it is likely that its triangular appearance and unusual lines did not endear it to many motorcyclists.

**Above:** Francis-Barnett made the unusual claim that their Pullman frame could be dismantled and stowed in a golf bag. However, they made no suggestion as to the stowage of the remainder of the components.

**Francis-Barnett Pullman**
National Motorcycle Museum
Birmingham, England

# FRANCIS-BARNETT

While the Pullman was discontinued in 1929, certain features of its construction survived in other Francis-Barnett products. The engine remained to power the 1930 Model 16 Dominion, whose unorthodox frame could be dismantled and stowed in a golf bag! In 1931 two 147cc (8.97cu in) models were introduced – Model 19 without lights and the otherwise identical 20 with. The following year they were renamed the 23 Merlin and 24 Kestrel as Francis-Barnett started a policy of both numbering their bikes and naming them after birds. Breaking with this tradition in 1933, the Cruiser was popular as a safe, reliable transport for Joe Public, featuring some weatherproofing and a Villiers 249cc (15.19cu in) two-stroke engine.

After the war the company offered an autocycle (Powerbike 50) and a lightweight (Model 51 Merlin), became part of the AMC group which also produced Matchless and AJS machines, and for a while little changed, with Francis-Barnet products again based around two-stroke engines of their own and Villiers designs. For 1949 the original Merlin was superseded by two new models based around the Villiers 10D engine, still called Merlins, and the Falcon in two forms using the company's 6E engine. They used the same rigid frame and had telescopic forks. The range was enlarged for 1952 with two motorcycles with swingarm rear suspension – the Villiers 10D-engined version called the Merlin 57, known as the Falcon 58 with a 6E engine. Eventually the Falcon 58 became the 67, and some models known as Kestrels were added to the range. In 1958 the Falcon was fitted with the 197cc Villiers 10E engine and became known as the 81, simply a utility commuter two-stroke.

Francis-Barnet trials bikes, including the Trials 85, were introduced and had some success in the early 1960s in spite of an unreliable and unpopular 250cc AMC engine (poor piston-ring sealing, poor electrics), but with the decline in commuter motorcycling the company stopped all production in 1966.

**SPECIFICATIONS (1958 FALCON 81)**
- **Engine:** Two-stroke single
- **Displacement:** 187cc (12cu in)
- **Horsepower:** 8 @ 4000rpm
- **Wheelbase:** 49.75in (126.4cm)
- **Weight:** 245lbs (111kg)
- **Top speed:** 55mph (88kph)

**Above:** The Falcon 81 was an unremarkable two-stroke commuter bike which remained in production after Francis-Barnett became part of the AMC group.

**SPECIFICATIONS (1962 TRIALS 85)**
- **Engine:** Two-stroke single
- **Displacement:** 249cc (15.2cu in)
- **Horsepower:** N/A
- **Wheelbase:** N/A
- **Weight:** 271lb (123kg)
- **Top speed:** Depends on sprocket/gearing

**Below:** The Trials 85 used a 249cc two stroke engine made by AMC themselves, rather than one bought in from Villiers as was normal practice.

1962 Trials 85
National Motor Museum
Beaulieu, England

**Right:** The Francis-Barnett Trials 85 was an unusual machine to be manufactured by AMC whose other marques – AJS and Matchless – already enjoyed considerable off-road competition success.

1958 Falcon 81
National Motor Museum
Beaulieu, England

**Left:** A headlamp nacelle, telescopic forks, valanced fender and blade-like number plate are all typical of 1950s British bikes.

**Above:** The 1958 Francis-Barnett Falcon was fitted with a 197cc Villiers IOE engine and simply described as the Falcon 81.

## Gas Gas

**Founded:** 1986
**Factory location:** Girona, Spain
**Manufacturing lifespan:** 1986 – to date

This Spanish company was founded in 1986 but its origins go further back, to 1982 and the Merlin marque. This latter company was founded in part by Ignacio Bulto, the son of Francisco Bulto who founded Bultaco in 1958. The Merlin Company specialized in trials bikes powered by 347cc (21.16cu in) Cagiva two-stroke engines and ceased production in 1986. From this emerged the Gas Gas operation, which also specializes in off-road machines. These are in the main for trials and enduro use and utilize their own engines as well as those from the Italian companies of Cagiva and TM.

**Specifications (1999 TXT 321)**
- **Engine:** Two-stroke single
- **Displacement:** 327.7cc (20cu in)
- **Horsepower:** N/A
- **Wheelbase:** N/A
- **Weight:** 167.6lb (76kg)
- **Top speed:** N/A

1999 TXT 321
Courtesy of Gas Gas
Spain

**Left:** Introduced in 1999, the TXT321 was the largest capacity machine in the Gas Gas range of highly specialized trials bikes.

# Geer

**Founded:** 1905
**Factory location:** St. Louis, Missouri, USA
**Manufacturing lifespan:** 1905 -1909

The Harry R. Geer Company built complete motorcycles and also sold complete engines and components to individuals and the trade. The Geer Bluebird carried a forward-mount single in a loop frame; the belt-drive, four-horsepower rig apparently weighed only 150 pounds (68kg), and sold for $200 in 1907, including the tool bag and tools. Bore and stroke were 3.5 x 4 inches (89 x 102mm). A smaller 2.5-horsepower version sold for $160.

The Green Egg, with claimed weigh-in at 165 pounds (75kg), featured a low-mount 350cc (21.35cu in) V-twin rated at five horsepower. Also a belt-drive model, the Egg was offered with either battery or magneto ignition. Fitted with a truss fork, 1.5-gallon (5.7lit) fuel tank, 1.5-quart (1.4lit) oil tank, on a 56-inch (142cm) wheelbase, the twin sold for $225. Few of either model remain extant.

**Below:** The Green Egg was offered with both single-cylinder and twin engines. The four-horsepower twin, in a different frame, sold for $225.

**Specifications (Green Egg)**
**Engine:** 60° V-twin (not shown)
**Displacement:** 350cc (21.35cu in)
**Horsepower:** 2.5
**Wheelbase:** 55in (140cm)
**Weight:** 130lb (59kg)
**Top speed:** 35mph (56kph)

1906 Geer Green Egg
Owner – Jim Lattin
Encinitas, California

# Gilera

**Founded:** 1909
**Factory location:** Arcore, Milan, Italy
**Manufacturing lifespan:** 1909 – to date

Giuseppe Gilera designed the first motorcycles (the VT317) from this company in 1909. Initially, 317cc (19.33cu in), belt-driven, overhead-valve engines were utilized in a diamond frame. The switch to side-valve engines occurred soon after and lasted until 1926 when Gilera again offered ohv-engined bikes. In 1935 Gilera bought the Rondine, a machine made by an aeronautical company which up until that time was producing a very successful supercharged four-cylinder motorcycle engine that featured inclined cylinders, double overhead camshafts and water cooling. This acquisition became the basis of Gilera's race bikes and was subsequently upgraded and refined through to the mid-1960s.

The ban on forced induction, i.e. supercharged racers, after World War II forced Gilera to redesign its racing machines. Pietro Remor designed double overhead camshaft, air-cooled, four-cylinder machines which, in developed form, went on to win numerous races with a variety of the sport's top riders.

In 1969 Gilera was taken over by the Piaggio group that manufactures Vespa scooters. Under this new ownership Gilera introduced a range of small capacity bikes including the 200T4, 125TGI, and 50TS. These designations approximated the displacement of each machine in cubic centimetres. The 200T4 was a four-stroke while the smaller machines were two-strokes. Larger capacity bikes reappeared

**Specifications (1951 Saturno)**
**Engine:** Four-stroke single
**Displacement:** 498cc (30.39)
**Horsepower:** 18 @ 4500rpm
**Wheelbase:** 57.87in (147cm)
**Weight:** 370.4lb (168kg)
**Top speed:** 85.13mph (135kph)

**Right:** After the Second World War the Saturno became well known for the victories it gained around the world's race circuits. The greatest achievement was when Nello Pagani took second place in the 500cc world championships in 1949.

during the 1980s when the company also produced a range of step-through mopeds. In 1993 came the NordWest, which had the look of the big Paris-Dakar enduro bikes but was intended to be a roadgoing machine and was fitted with road tires accordingly. It was based around Gilera's large displacement single-cylinder engine which had appeared in 1985 with a displacement of 350cc (21.35cu in) and was used in enduro machines such as the Gilera Dakota. However, the engine was later increased in capacity to 558cc (34.03cu in) and utilized in the NordWest and the Nuovo Saturno cafe racer.

Production moved in 1993 to Pontedera, and a new scooter with a sporty feel was marketed as the Runner. In 1998 a four-stroke 125 cruiser, the Cougar, was announced and in 2000 the "naked frame" DNA was made available. A year later saw Gilera announce the VX 125cc (7.62cu in) and VXR 180 (11cu in) models, building on the Runner's sport commuter personality with four-stroke, four-valve, liquid-cooled engines. More comfort, performance and low fuel consumption were also afforded by one of the most popular scooters on the road.

**Specifications (2001 VXR)**
**Engine:** Four-stroke single
**Displacement:** 182cc (11cu in)
**Horsepower:** 20 @ 8500rpm
**Wheelbase:** 53in (138cm)
**Weight:** 265lb (119kg)
**Top speed:** 75mph (120kph)

**Right:** As if the Runner range needed extra specification, Gilera's new VXR 180 comes with twin adjustable rear-mounted, shock absorbers and new hydraulic front forks. An anti-theft immobilizer is fitted as standard.

**2001 VXR 180**
Courtesy of Gilera
Italy

**1951 Saturno 500**
Deutsches-Zweirad Museum
and NSU Museum
Neckarsulm, Germany

## Gnome et Rhône

**Founded:** 1919
**Factory location:** Paris, France
**Manufacturing lifespan:** 1919 - 1959

This French concern started out as an aircraft engine manufacturer during World War I and began producing motorcycles in 1919. Its first were British-designed motorcycles rebuilt under license. From the early 1920s it produced machines to its own designs. A range of different displacement engines of both side and overhead-valve configurations were produced and then later on came a number of flat-twins mounted in pressed-steel frames. These BMW-style machines were available with both 495 and 745cc (30.19 and 45.44cu in) engines.

In the last years of the decade before World War II, Gnome et Rhône had six motorcycles in production: the Junior, Major, and Super Major, as well as the D5, CV2, and Type X. The first three were 250cc (15.25cu in) and 350cc (21.35cu in) four-speed machines while the latter three were a 500cc (30.50cu in) single, a 500cc (30.50cu in) twin, and a 750cc (45.75cu in) flat-twin. The flat-twin was enlarged to 800cc (48.80cu in) when produced for the French Army prior to World War II. The company resumed production after the war and continued making motorcycles, mostly two-strokes of less than 200cc (12.20cu in), until 1959.

**Specifications (1939 Model)**
**Engine:** Twin-cylinder boxer
**Displacement:** 749cc (45cu in)
**Horsepower:** 18
**Wheelbase:** N/A
**Weight:** N/A
**Top speed:** 82mph (130kph)

**1939 Gnome et Rhône**
Deutsches-Zweirad Museum
and NSU Museum
Neckarsulm, Germany

**Right:** Gnome et Rhône were originally aircraft engine manufacturers and diversified into motorcycles. They collaborated closely with the ABC of England and used that company's flat twins before developing their own.

## Greeves

**Founded:** 1952
**Factory location:** Surbiton, Surrey, England
**Manufacturing lifespan:** 1952 - 1977

The Trials Model 20T was one of several unconventionally built but successful off-road competition bikes produced by a company that was originally set up to produce invalid carriages. The 20Ts had minimal alloy fenders and a small fuel tank. The frame was based around the cast alloy I-section beam that ran up from the engine mounts and incorporated the headstock. The casting provided the mounting places for the swingarm pivot although the swingarm itself was tubular steel. The tubular steel section of the frame that carried the fuel-tank mounts and the rear suspension mounts was joined to the cast alloy section during the casting process, making the join permanent.

Greeves machines dominated the 250cc class in motocross for several years in the 1950s and '60s, and also built popular roadracing bikes. Production stopped in 1972 when the founder, Bert Greeves, retired.

**Below:** The Greeves Trials 20T was designed for optimum ground clearance and lightness, hence the alloy fenders and 21in (533.4mm) diameter front wheel.

**Specifications (1950 20T)**
**Engine:** Two-stroke single
**Displacement:** 197cc (12cu in)
**Horsepower:** 8.4 @ 4000rpm
**Wheelbase:** 52in (132.1cm)
**Weight:** 225lb (102kg)
**Top speed:** Depends on gearing

**1955 Trials 20T**
National Motorcycle Museum
Birmingham, England

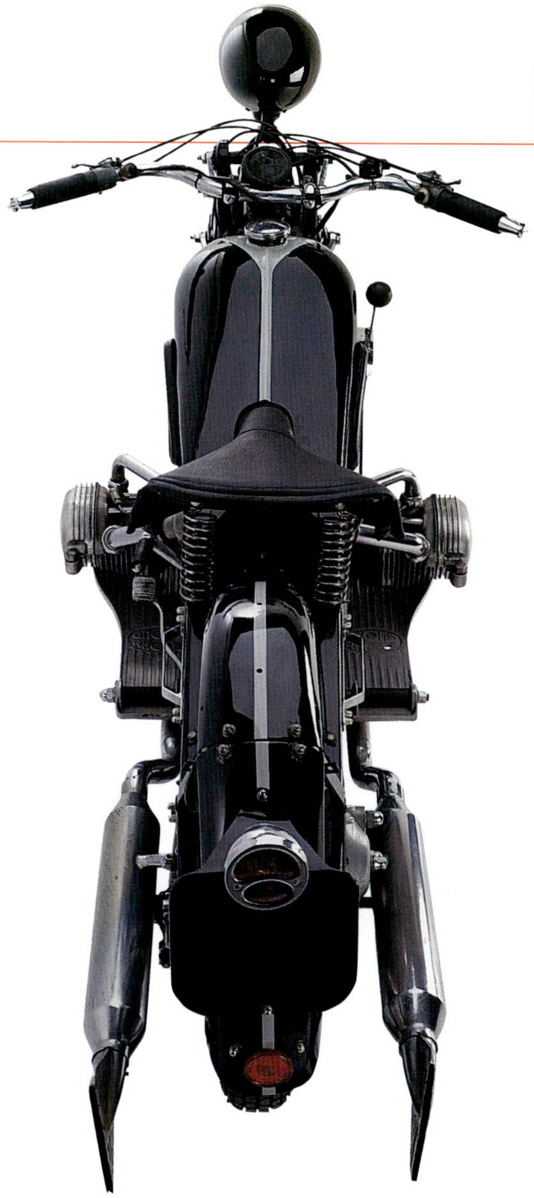

**Right:** The cylinders from the flat twin engine can be seen protruding from each side of the bike, along with the footboards.

## GREYHOUND

| | |
|---|---|
| **Founded:** 1907 | |
| **Factory location:** Detroit, Michigan, USA | |
| **Manufacturing lifespan:** 1911 - 1914 | |

The Greyhound was united hand-in-glove with the Aurora Automatic Machine Company near Chicago, Illinois. Aurora manufactured the engines for Indian motorcycles, and marketed the same engines under their Thor label. The Greyhound was fitted with the Thor engine until 1910, when Aurora was struggling to meet its own brand requirements.

The marque then switched to motors from E. R. Thomas of Buffalo, New York, and the Auto-Bi brand. The Greyhound was offered with a 494cc (30.13cu in) single or a V-twin, but by this time the market was ruled by the big three of Indian, Harley and Excelsior. Few examples of the Greyhound have survived the century.

**Below:** The single-spring girder fork was used by several motorcycle manufacturers. Torpedo-style tanks had reached their stylistic terminus.

**SPECIFICATIONS**

**Engine:** IOE single
**Displacement:** 494cc (30.13cu in)
**Horsepower:** 4
**Wheelbase:** 54in (137cm)
**Weight:** 130lb (59kg)
**Top speed:** 50mph (80kph)

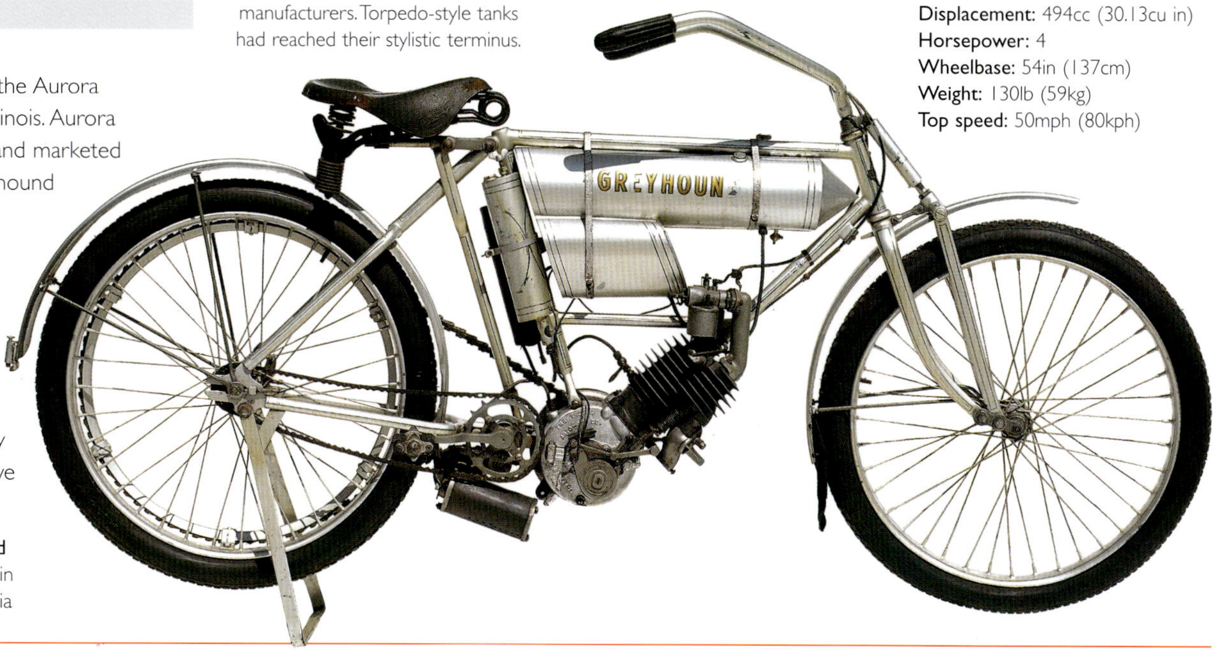

**1909 Greyhound**
Owner – Jim Lattin
Encinitas, California

# Harley-Davidson

**Founded:** 1903
**Factory location:** Milwaukee, Wisconsin, USA
**Manufacturing lifespan:** 1903 - to date

Harley-Davidson motorcycles have been produced for close on a hundred years. The company, in one form or another – family business (established by Wlliam Harley and the Davidson brothers, Arthur, Walter and William; manufacturing conglomerate; and private enterprise – has created primarily large, air-cooled, V-twin-engined, heavyweight bikes that fans and stockholders hail as the greatest two-wheel machines ever built, as well as significant single-cylinder models. Along the way, the company, its products and riders have been the pioneers in the motorcycle sport. This brief review covers highlights of outstanding machines that represent the fundamental soul of motorcycling.

Harley-Davidson had been producing successful single-engined bikes for six years by the time it offered its first V-twin in 1909. That machine, the 5D, failed to meet contemporary standards and only 27 were built; it was dropped for 1910, but it was at least a stepping stone to an altogether more satisfactory and successful 1911 7D which had mechanical intake valves and a belt tensioner that simplified operation, with the engine housed in a redesigned and reinforced frame with a straight front downtube. It faced tough competition both in the market and, when it decided to go racing, on the track and cross-country, especially from Indian.

Progressively improved models had appeared by then, the 1912 X8E featuring Harley-Davidson's first clutch, located in the rear hub, while the 1914 10F offered footboards and an internal rear brake operated by either the brake pedal or back pressure on the bicycle pedals. In 1917 the 17J production incorporated features from racing machines, such as the four-lobe cam of the 8-valve racer built in response to Indian's similar model. ▶

**Above:** Humble beginnings for a reign of twins: the unsuccessful 1909 5D. The 45-degree inline twin was built on a beefed-up bottom end, with the magneto gear-driven off the crankshaft. The 3 x 3.5 inch (76 x 89mm) bore and stroke put displacement at 49 cubic inches (810cc). Rated at 7 horsepower, the 5D was reportedly good for 65mph (105kph). Only 27 were built, and apparently just two still exist.

**1909 5D Twin**
Owner – Harley-Davidson
Milwaukee, Wisconsin
Photograph by Ron Hussey

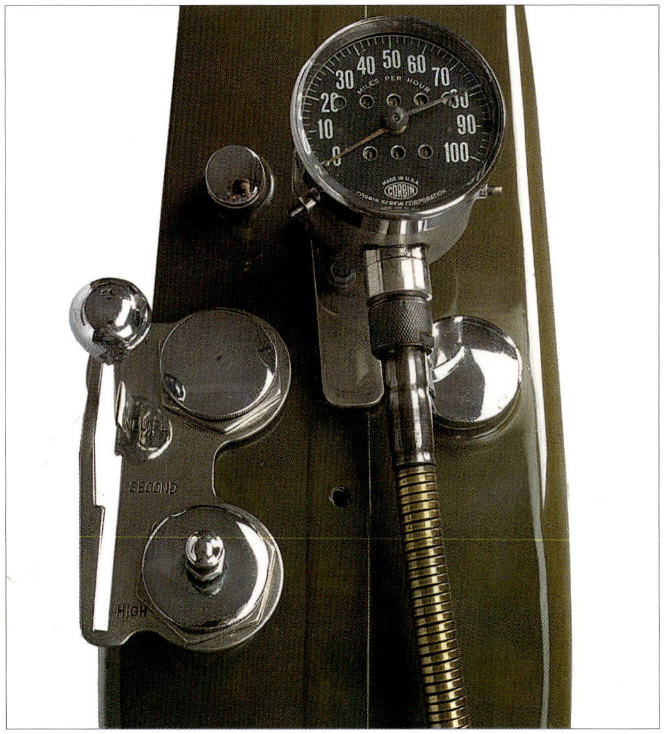


**Right:** The 17J had the four-lobe cam of the 8-valve racer, and valve springs were enclosed.

**Left:** The upper hand on the speedometer remained at the highest speed attained, in this case 79mph (126kph). The three-speed shift gate was clearly marked.

**SPECIFICATIONS (1914 10F)**
**Engine:** IOE 45° V-twin
**Displacement:** 811cc (49.47cu in)
**Horsepower:** 6.5
**Wheelbase:** 56.5in (143.5cm)
**Weight:** 310lb (141kg)
**Top speed:** 65mph (105kph)

**Right:** Production 10Fs (1914) had luggage carrier, Free Wheel Control, two-speed rear hub, Ful-Floeting seat, and the headlight's gas cannister mounted between the handlebars.

1914 10F
Owner – Bud Ekins
North Hollywood, California

**SPECIFICATIONS (1917 17J)**
**Engine:** F-head 45° V-twin
**Displacement:** 987.67cc (60.25cu in)
**Horsepower:** 16 @ 3000rpm
**Wheelbase:** 59.5in (151cm)
**Weight:** 325lb (147.4kg)
**Top speed:** 65mph (105kph)

**Below:** In 1917, with preparation for war well underway, Harley-Davidson's standard color shifted from gray to olive drab. The war also eliminated Bosch magnetos, which were replaced by Dixie units.

1917 17J
Owner – Harold Mathews
Fresno, California

During the 1910s, there was considerable interchange between American and European motorcyclists, much of it supported by the common interest in professional racing, among major manufacturers as well as racers and enthusiastic spectators. After World War I, when it was apparent that American motorcycling would be primarily recreational, Europeans were exposed to more American machines, and new lightweight bikes appeared. The Harley Model W Sport Twin, modeled on the British Douglas, came to market in 1919. It was a radical departure for Harley-Davidson in terms of design and engineering, using the engine as a stressed member in a keystone frame, and by far the smoothest running Harley ever built. But in its five-year lifespan, more were sold in England and continental Europe than at home.

Harley's signature bike was the J model, a 1000 or 1200cc (61 or 73.2cu in) V-twin with good horsepower and without extraneous weight. First sold in 1915, it became Milwaukee's top-of-the-line motorcycle, justifying Harley's decision not to follow the Indian, Henderson and Cleveland moves to four-cyclinder engines. Government contracts during the war accelerated motorcycle production, but afterward, especially during the early 1920s, demand dropped, as Henry Ford was lowering the prices on his cars.

Harley's developing racing experience was put to work on in the JDH road model introduced in 1929. Known as the Two-cam, it had dual intake valve springs, and tappets rather than roller arms, and increased compression with the use of domed alloy pistons. But it was also the finale for the J series twins in the face of bikes with side-valve engines from Indian and Excelsior.

Enter the Harley side-valve Seventy-four series, and the VLD which, along with powerplant and other changes from previous machines, also incorporated buy-me features such as streamlined fenders and Art Deco designs against a backdrop of post-Great Depression economic pressures.

1919 W Sport Twin
Owner – Otis Chandler
Ojai, California

**Specifications (1919 W Sport Twin)**
- **Engine:** F-head opposed twin
- **Displacement:** 584cc (35.62cu in)
- **Horsepower:** 6
- **Wheelbase:** 57in (145cm)
- **Weight:** 265lb (120kg)
- **Top speed:** 50mph (80kph)

**Above:** The opposed twin, based on the British Douglas, was appreciated for its lack of vibration but was not widely sold in the U.S.

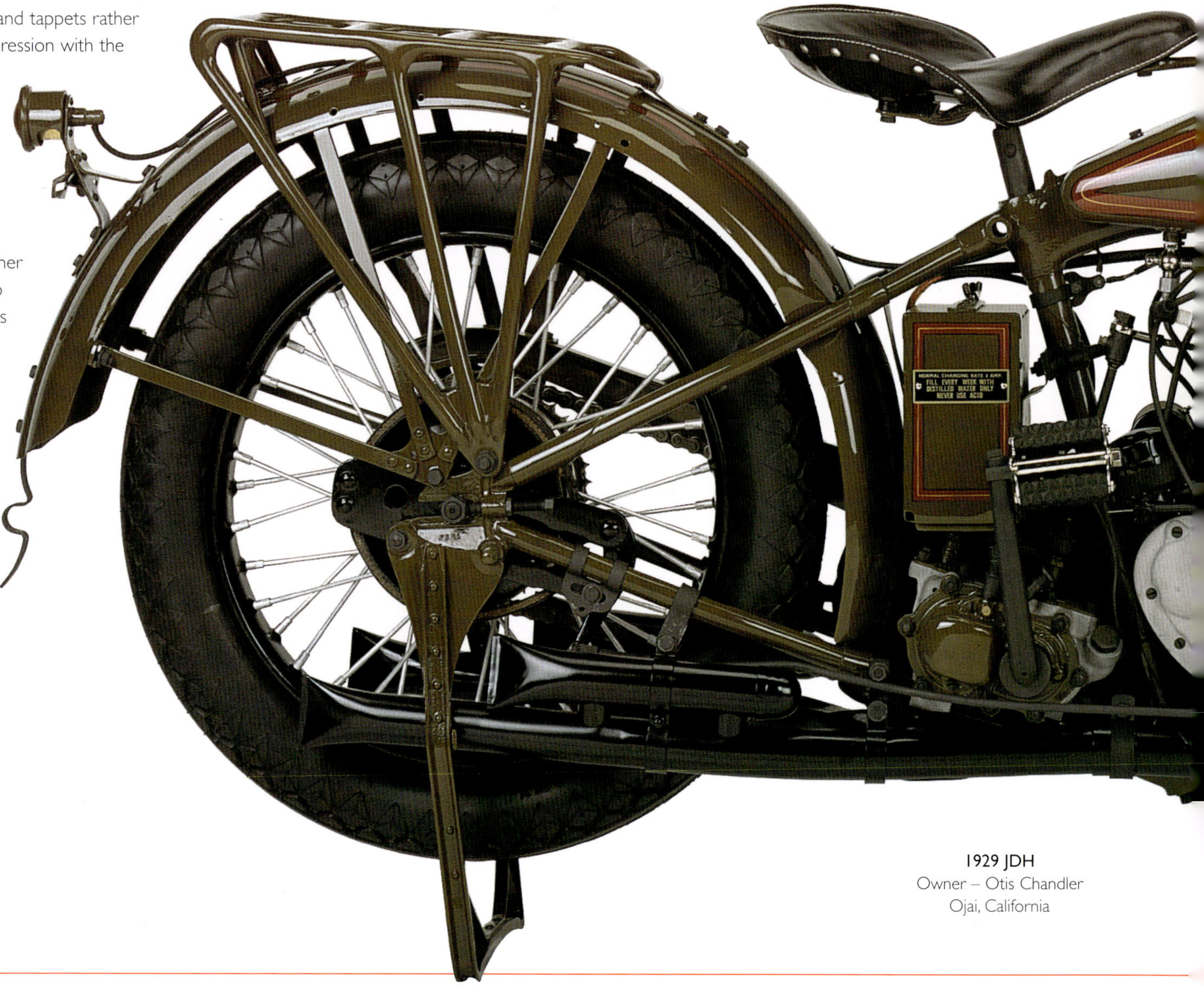

1929 JDH
Owner – Otis Chandler
Ojai, California

**Specifications (1929 JDH)**
- **Engine:** F-head 45° V-twin
- **Displacement:** 1200cc (73.2cu in)
- **Horsepower:** 29
- **Wheelbase:** 59.5in (151cm)
- **Weight:** 408lb (185kg)
- **Top speed:** 85mph (137kph)

**Right:** Style gained force in the Depression and immediately after, as Art Deco reached the motorcycle design studios in an attempt to reverse faltering sales.

1934 VLD
Owner – Mike Lady
Arroyo Grande, California

**Above:** The J series had a nine-year run, but the front brake arrived in 1928. The end of the F-head engine, and the advent of the side-valve, was at hand.

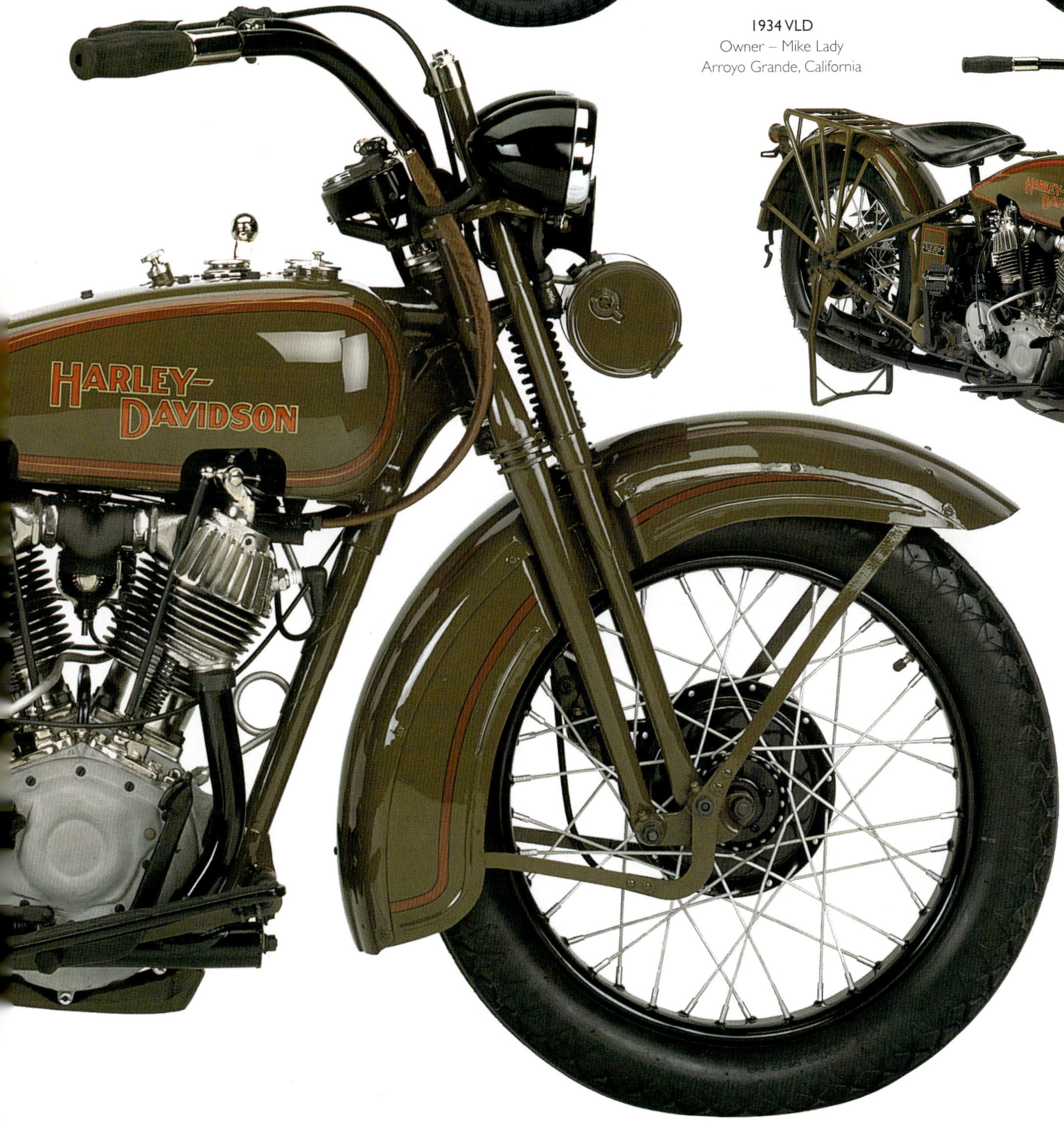


**Left:** Even the mufflers were given streamlined styling touches, and more tubes added quietness in response to public moodiness with noise, which had affected sales.

Although Harley-Davidson had demonstrated the power and strength of its side-valve engines in the early 1930s, it had been decided by 1932 that an overhead-valve, 1000cc (61cu in) V-twin would be produced. Nearly five years in development, the E 61 appeared in 1936 and quickly picked up its nickname, the Knucklehead, an allusion to the bulbous rocker boxes atop the engine. The Knucklehead combined engine design and styling in the fashion of aircraft engines, and threw in 37 horsepower in the high-compression EL, with a double-loop cradle frame and four-speed transmission. No other motorcycle had yet captured the attention of American riders in the way that the E models did.

Harley-Davidson began refining the Knucklehead from the beginning, combining constant-mesh and sliding gear systems, and in 1941 added a 1200cc (73.2cu in) version, the FL. Stainless steel strips adorned the sides of the fuel tank, but little of the Knucklehead's styling changed.

World War II postponed any further development of the motorcycles, and Milwaukee was well occupied with the production of military machines. A major evolutionary step came in 1948 with the Panhead, so-named for its inverted pan valve covers, though the engine varied little from the Knucklehead in the bottom end. In 1949-1950 the Panhead introduced the telescopic front fork, the Hydra-Glide, and there ensued further improvements such as enlarged intake ports on the ohv twins for more power, and quieter mufflers.

In 1952, to combat the growing number of English imports, Harley-Davidson introduced the middleweight K model sports machine, with four-speed transmission, shifted by foot, incorporated within the engine cases, clutch operated by hand, and both wheels hydraulically suspended. It was designated KR when trimmed as a racing bike, replacing the venerable WR in dirt-track and roadracing trim. It was ridden to some competition success, but the model's performance was generally considered disappointing.

**1941 FL**
Owner – Armando Magri
Sacramento, California

**SPECIFICATIONS (1941 FL)**
**Engine:** Ohv 45° V-twin
**Displacement:** 1208cc (73.69cu in)
**Horsepower:** 48
**Wheelbase:** 59.5in (151cm)
**Weight:** 575lb (261kg)
**Top speed:** 95mph (153kph)

**Above:** The Knucklehead added a 1200cc version in 1941, with both bore and stroke increases. The rocket-fin muffler was another styling touch.

**SPECIFICATIONS (1950 EL)**
**Engine:** Ohv 45° V-twin
**Displacement:** 989cc (60.33cu in)
**Horsepower:** 40
**Wheelbase:** 59.5in (151cm)
**Weight:** 565lb (256kg)
**Top speed:** 95mph (153kph)

**1950 EL**
Owner – Trev Deeley Museum
Vancouver, British Columbia

**Specifications (1952 K)**

**Engine:** Flathead 45° V-twin
**Displacement:** 743cc (45.32cu in)
**Horsepower:** 30
**Wheelbase:** 56.5in (143.5cm)
**Weight:** 400lb (181kg)
**Top speed:** 80mph (129kph)

1952 K
Owner – Fred Lange
Santa Maria, California

**Above:** The 1952 K model was Milwaukee's first attempt in some time at a middleweight sport model. It offered swingarm rear suspension, unit construction transmission, foot shift and choice of buckhorn or low handlebars.

**Above:** Tire options included 3.25 x 18 or 19, and potential hot-rod riders could order up a 4.00 x 18 on the rear and 3.50 x 18 front. Performance was generally disappointing, however.

**Left:** The tank nameplate designed by Brooks Stevens for 1947 models was used for the last time in 1950.

**Above:** The 1950EL's Deluxe Solo Saddle was an alternative to the Buddy Seat. It was also included in the Standard Police Group for officers of the law.

In 1958 form and function of Harley-Davidson's Panhead were enhanced with the arrival of the Duo-Glide, successor to the Hydra-Glide, boasting rear suspension, whitewall tires, hydraulic rear brake, stronger clutch and transmission, better exhaust manifolds, a new oil tank and – least popular – a plastic nameplate on the tank. The Duo-Glide yielded in turn to the Electra Glide in 1965, featuring an electric starter for the first time on one of the company's big twins. The period also saw the retirement, after 18 years, of the Panhead engine. The Electra Glide name carried on, but the engine designation became the Shovelhead, so named for its industrial rocker boxes.

In an attempt to capture some of the European cafe racer market of the 1970s, along came the XLCR. It was a modified Sportster with cast alloy wheels, small fairing and low handlebar. However, as a street-legal roadracer, it was no match for better-handling mounts from Europe four-cylinder machines from Japan, and lasted just two years.

Cruiser styling was becoming more popular each year, and none succeeded so well as Harley-Davidson's Low Rider, which set the standard for custom/cruiser looks. The company's 75th anniversary in 1978 was celebrated with special editions of the Electra Glide and Sportster.

In 1980 the FLT Tour Glide and FXWG Wide Glide were released. While the FXWG was a variation of the Super Glide, the Tour Glide had little in common with its Electra brethren: new frame, a 1340cc (81.74cu in) engine situated by a three-point rubber-mount system, and a swingarm bolted to the transmission case, which contained a five-speed gearset.

**SPECIFICATIONS**
**(1958 FLH DUO-GLIDE)**

**Engine:** Ohv 45° V-twin
**Displacement:** 1208cc (73.69cu in)
**Horsepower:** 52
**Wheelbase:** 60in (152cm)
**Weight:** 648lb (294kg)
**Top speed:** 100mph (161kph)

**Below:** What was Hydra-Glide was now Duo-Glide, with the addition of swingarm suspension behind the seat. Thus the Duo-.

**Above:** The italic numeral speedometer was introduced in 1956. Numbers were day glo green on black, with a gold center disc.

1958 Duo-Glide
Owner – Doug Stein
Los Angeles, California

Below: The Cafe Racer was an attempt to capitalize on the Euro-style street rods of the 1970s, but it lasted for only two years.

**Specifications (1977 XLCR)**
Engine: Ohv 45° V-twin
Displacement: 1000cc (61cu in)
Horsepower: 68
Wheelbase: 58.5in (148.5cm)
Weight: 515lb (234kg)
Top speed: 110mph (177kph)

Left: The Sportster engine was given a black paint job and siamesed exhaust system which bumped the horsepower by five over the standard. The bikini fairing, Morris cast wheels and Kelsey-Hayes brakes helped give the XLCR the appearance of a serious backroads scratcher.

1977 XLCR
Owner – Otis Chandler
Ojai, California

Left: Fiberglass saddlebags became quite popular in the 1950s. Hard bags were appreciated by touring riders for the all-weather protection.

**Specifications (1980 FLT)**
Engine: Ohv 45° V-twin
Displacement: 1338cc (81.62cu in)
Horsepower: 65
Wheelbase: 62.5in (159cm)
Weight: 781lb (354kg)
Top speed: 95mph (153kph)

Below: The Tour Glide incorporated a number of new approaches to the sport touring concept. The frame-mount fairing had dual headlights. Front dual disc brakes and revised frame geometry improved handling characteristics.

1980 FLT
Owner – Doug Holden
Gustine, California

Of all the Harley-Davidson developments after 1980, probably the most important was the V2 Evolution engine, which appeared in the 1984 FXST Softail. It was Harley's first all-new engine in 50 years, although still an air-cooled, big-bore V-twin. So the first of the new generation of Harley-Davidsons was, by design, traditional in appearance but far more contemporary in terms of performance. The Evolution engine did not furnish the company with instant success, necessarily, but did set the foundation for its ensuing salvation and prosperity. The Shovelhead had been shuffled off to history, and by 1985 the Evo took over as the big twin engine. The Electra Glide became the FLHTC Electra Glide Classic, with five-speed transmission, solid-mount engine and belt drive. The favored nostalgic retro look was enhanced by the 1950s-style Hydra Glide front fork, jumbo headlight and deeply valenced fenders. Other models received the same treatment, including the FLSTF Fat Boy in 1990.

And then in 1994 came one of the company's rare gambles – the VR 1000, a pure-bred racing machine, new from the ground up, with a 60-degree double-overhead cam V-twin engine, with four valves per cylinder, Weber fuel injection, liquid cooling and five-speed transmission. The development program continues.

**1993 FLHTC**
Owner – Bartels' Harley-Davidson
Marina Del Rey, California

**1994 VR 1000**
Owner – Petersen Automotive Museum
Los Angeles, California

**Above:** The Electra Glide Ultra Classic had a large trunk hinged on the left; a luggage rack was optional. Fork-mount fairing retained traditional lines, but housed modern instruments and sound systems with handlebar controls.

**SPECIFICATIONS (1994 VR 1000)**
- **Engine:** Dohc 60° V-twin
- **Displacement:** 1,000cc (61cu in)
- **Horsepower:** 135+
- **Wheelbase:** 55.5in (141cm)
- **Weight:** 390lb (177kg)
- **Top speed:** 170mph (274kph)

**Right:** The VR 1000 Superbike engine was a liquid-cooled 1,000cc (61cu in) 60deg V-twin, with dual overhead cams, fuel injection and over 135hp. Front fork was built by Ohlins; brake calipers were six-piston units from Willwood. Front wheel travel was 4.7in (12cm).

**Specifications (1993 FLHTC)**

**Engine:** Ohv 45° V-twin
**Displacement:** 1,338cc (81,62cu in)
**Horsepower:** 72
**Wheelbase:** 62.9in (160cm)
**Weight:** 774lb (351kg)
**Top speed:** 110mph (177kph)

**Left:** The height of luxury included separate controls for the stereo, while the cushy seat covering offered detachable backrest. Laid back or what!

Meanwhile, other models were upgraded, and special editions of top-selling bikes were offered to celebrate the company's 90th anniversary, one of these being the FLHTC Electra Glide Ultra Classic in anniversary trim, with a silver/gray paint scheme, new cruise control and new brake and clutch levers.

In the new millennium, Harley-Davidson continued to offer upgraded and new models, one of them being the FLHRCI. Harley emphasized the Road King's styling heritage with a huge headlamp in a highly polished nacelle on the front fork, a feature based on the 1958 FL Duo Glide. The 80 cubic inch (1,340cc) Evolution engine that originally powered the Road King was replaced by a rubber-mounted 1,450cc 88 Twin Cam engine. Standard fitment was the 40mm Keihin carburetor. Maintenance-free electronic fuel injection was an option, although on the Road King Classic it was fitted as standard, as were wire wheels.

Roll on 2003, Harley-Davidson's centenary year! One prediction is that the new century will bring a cross-cultural mix of multi-national entities, which will include economic, manufacturing, engineering and even design alliances.

**Specifications (2000 FLHRCI)**

**Engine:** 88 Twin Cam
**Displacement:** 1,450cc (88cu in)
**Horsepower:** N/A
**Wheelbase:** 63.5in (161.30cm)
**Weight:** 690lb (310kg)
**Top speed:** N/A

**Below:** The FLHRCI Road King with 88 Twin Cam engine, contoured, removable pillion duel seat and Buffalo handlebars designed to offer a relaxed, upright straight-arm riding position behind a broad plastic screen.

2000 FLHRCI
Courtesy of Harley-Davidson
Milwaukee, Wisconsin

## HEINKEL

| | |
|---|---|
| **Founded:** 1921 | |
| **Factory location:** Stuttgart, Germany | |
| **Manufacturing lifespan:** 1921 - 1954 | |

Heinkel was an aircraft manufacturer up to and through World War II but was not permitted to continue that business after the war. To keep the factory going, Heinkel turned to building mopeds, scooters and three-wheeled bubble-cars but it was 1951 before design work started. The Tourist scooter was launched in 1953, powered by a 149cc (9.093cu in) four-stroke engine. The Perle moped came a year later. It was technically advanced, with a frame cast in light alloy and effective front and rear suspension. The Tourist model grew to 174cc (10.618cu in) and gained a reputation for high quality and comfort, with very substantial bodywork protecting the rider. Its engine was also used as a power unit for the 1956 Kabinen bubble-car which was similar in design to the popular (and later) BMW Isetta.

In 1957, Heinkel launched a new 125cc (7.628cu in) scooter but it was not a success. The Tourist was updated in 1960 and was joined by the Heinkel 150 two years later. Both went out of production in 1965 as Heinkel returned to volume aircraft manufacture.

**SPECIFICATIONS (PERLE 1956)**
- **Engine:** Single
- **Displacement:** 49.9cc (3cu in)
- **Horsepower:** 1.4
- **Wheelbase:** N/A
- **Weight:** N/A
- **Top speed:** 25mph (40kph)

**Below:** The lightweight Perle had telescopic forks and a light metal enclosed chain guard, which acted as an oil bath for the chain.

**1956 Perle**
Deutsches-Zweirad Museum
and NSU Museum
Neckersulm, Germany

## HENDERSON

| | |
|---|---|
| **Founded:** 1912 | |
| **Factory Location:** Chicago, Illinois, USA | |
| **Manufacturing Lifespan:** 1912 - 1931 | |

The brothers Henderson, Tom and William, took up the manufacturing trade in 1911, the same year Ignaz Schwinn acquired Excelsior. After five years of independent manufacture, the Henderson Motorcycle Company would also be absorbed by the Chicago industrialist.

The first Henderson Four, which appeared in 1912, was long. As the ads stated: "The long wheelbase of the Henderson, 65 inches, permits the riders to sit between the wheels, reducing road shocks to the minimum." On the first seven-horsepower model in 1912, the passenger seat was fitted to the top frame tube just above the footboard. This was changed to a rear tandem the following year. The four was then up to eight horsepower and 1065cc, with a stronger front fork and new rear brake. The upper frame tube now curved down at the rear, and enclosed the new squared off fuel tank, with three-gallon (11.35lit) capacity. Tire widths went from 2.5 to 3 inches (6.35 to 7.62cm).

The contracting band rear brake appeared in 1913, operated by a pedal on the footboard. The Henderson four-cylinder engine used four individually cast iron cylinders on an aluminum crankcase, with a one-piece crankshaft on three main bearings. The engine was fitted with an Eclipse clutch, Bosch magneto and Schebler carburetor. The motor came to life car-style, with a hand crank. ▶

**SPECIFICATIONS (1913 FOUR)**
- **Engine:** IOE inline four
- **Displacement:** 965cc (58.87cu in)
- **Horsepower:** 7
- **Wheelbase:** 65in (165cm)
- **Weight:** 310lb (141kg)
- **Top speed:** 55mph (89kph)

**Right:** The Henderson Four set the standards for length and motoring excellence – the two-wheeled version of a touring car.

**Specifications (1917 Four)**
**Engine:** Inline four
**Displacement:** 990cc (60.39cu in)
**Horsepower:** 12
**Wheelbase:** 58in (147cm)
**Weight:** 310lb (141kg)
**Top speed:** 75mph (121kph)

**Right:** The three-speed Model G would be among the last Detroit-built Hendersons. Early 1918 models were released before the move to Chicago.

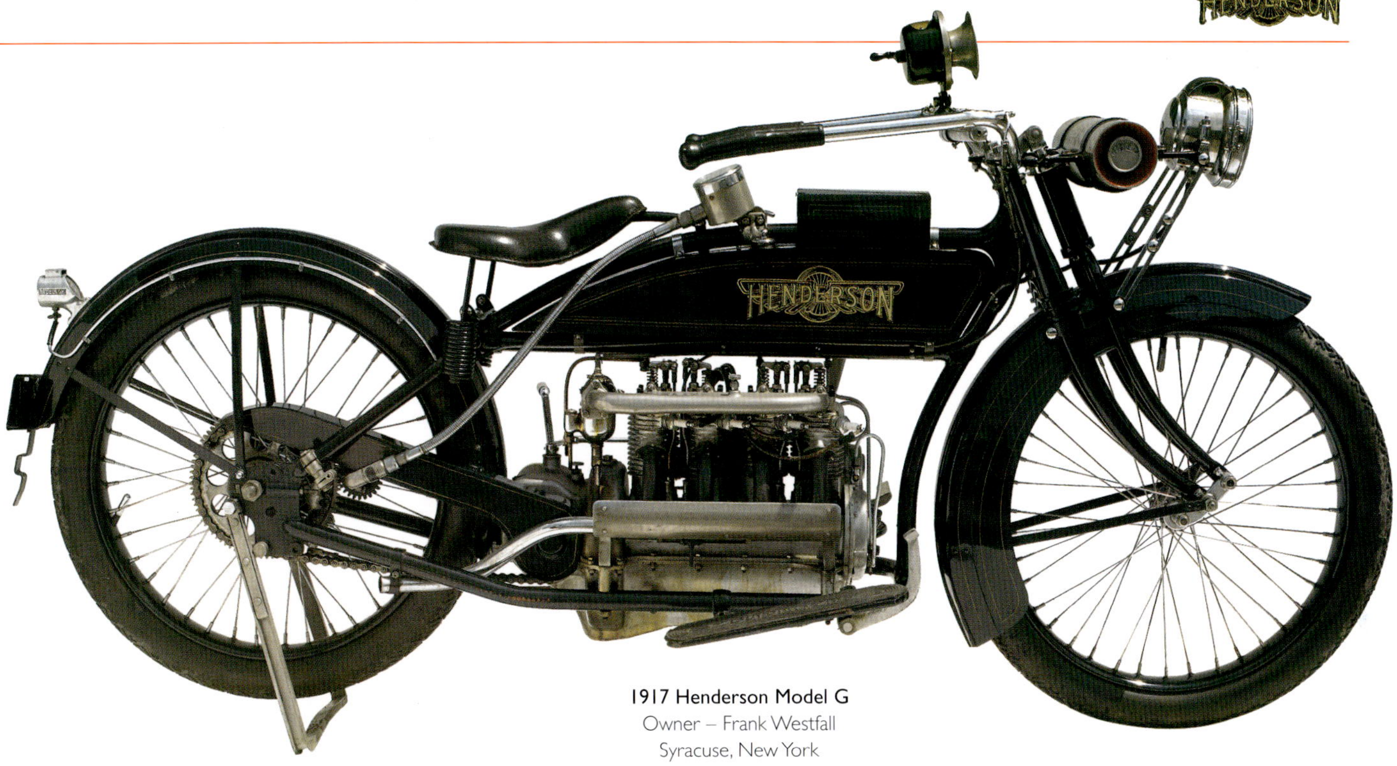


**1917 Henderson Model G**
Owner – Frank Westfall
Syracuse, New York

**Left:** Henderson's ads said the Four gave "the greatest degree of comfort to the passenger and greatly facilitating the steering and control."

**1913 Henderson**
Owner – Vince Martinico
Auburn, California

# HENDERSON

Henderson's place in two-wheeled history was assured in 1913, when young Carl Stearns Clancy became the first person to circumnavigate the planet on a motorcycle, riding a 1912 Henderson.

In 1914 Henderson introduced the Model C, with lighter pistons, two speeds and adjustable seat springs. There was no denying the smoothness of a four-cylinder engine, but likewise the motorcyclist faced added complexity, weight and cost. Work was also begun on a short-wheelbase model in 1914, in response to requests from dealers.

For 1915 the company introduced a two-speed hub of its own manufacture, improved Eclipse clutch, a stronger crankshaft, larger front fork, new seat and longer starting crank. The clevis arrangement on the intake rocker arms was replaced with a ball joint system. The short-wheelbase Model E appeared in the spring of 1915, with a reduction of seven inches (18cm) between the axles and 1.5-inch (3.8cm) lower seat height. The center footboard gave way to side footboards on the short-coupler. Both models (D long, E short) were offered in single or two-speed versions, with no change in the prices.

By 1916 only the shorter model was in production. Henderson, among other manufacturers, was now on hard times and doing everything possible to maintain the company's viability. At this low ebb, in stepped Ignaz Schwinn. With his acquisition of Excelsior five years prior, the former bicycle mechanic had become a significant force in the motorcycle industry. The 1917 model year would be the last for Henderson as an independent company. The new G model of 1917 featured a three-speed transmission, new intake manifold and improved fork.

The Excelsior connection saved Henderson, and both brothers were hired to facilitate the shift to production in the new plant. But after a year they decided to go their separate ways, Tom to sell motorcycles in Europe and William to build another motorcycle to be called the Ace.

Production of the Chicago Excelsior-Hendersons continued for another 12 years. The machines adopted heavier frames, pressurized lubrication system and side-valve cylinders. In 1920 the carburetor, now built by Zenith, moved to the middle of the manifold. The K model had larger bore and stroke for a displacement of 1310cc (79.9cu in) and 18 rated horsepower. The drive chain was fully enclosed.

In its final years (1929-1931), the Henderson gained weight and power and adopted the new streamlined styling of the era. Joe Petrali, who later became a Harley racing star, helped develop the machines. But the Depression put Excelsior out of play in 1931.

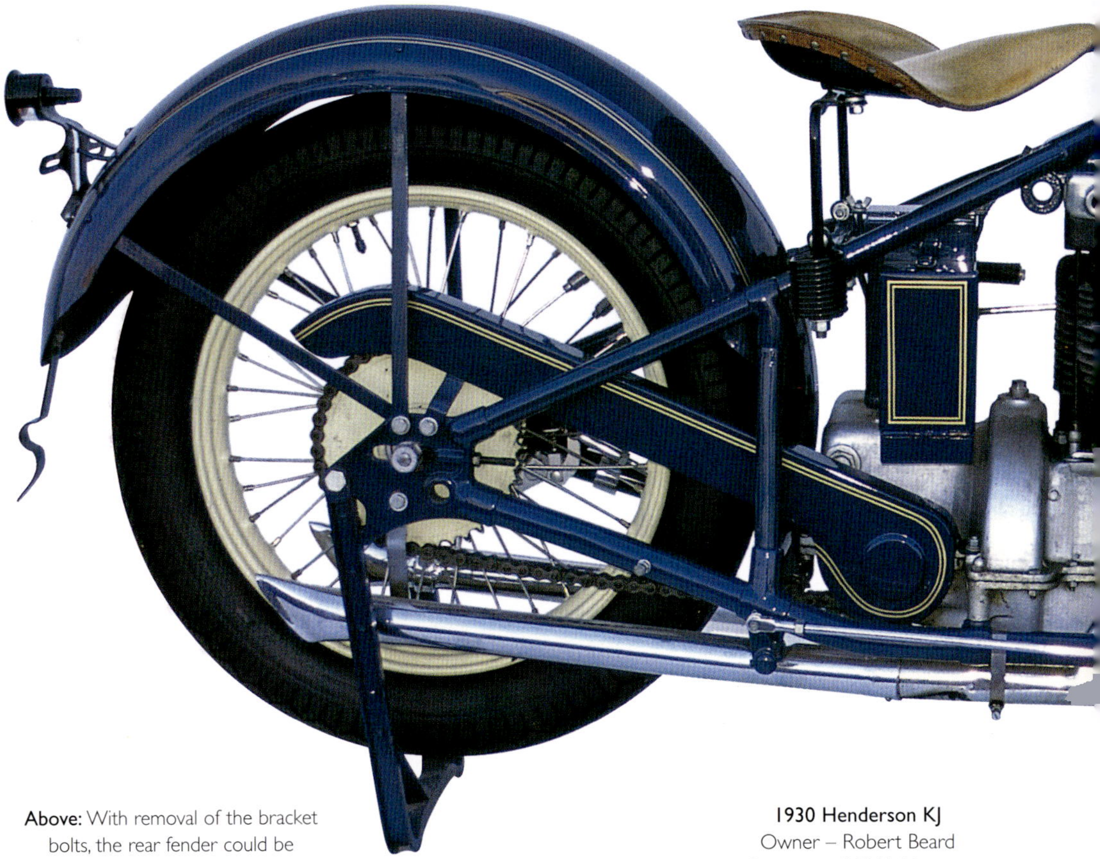

**Above:** With removal of the bracket bolts, the rear fender could be rotated upward to facilitate tire changes.

**1930 Henderson KJ**
Owner – Robert Beard
Courtesy of AMA Museum
Pickerington, Ohio

**Below:** Frank Westfall's Henderson is set up for the annual Great Race from coast-to-coast. In 1997, the engine was rained out on the last day.

**1928 Henderson**
Owner – Frank Westfall
Syracuse, New York

**Specifications (1927 Four)**
- **Engine:** Inline four
- **Displacement:** 1168cc (71.25cu in)
- **Horsepower:** 10-14
- **Wheelbase:** 58in (147cm)
- **Weight:** 325lb (147kg)
- **Top speed:** 75-90mph (121-145kph)

**Above:** On one of Chicago's wide new super-highways (four lanes wide), racer Joe Petrali ran the Henderson Special up to 116mph (187kph).

**Left:** The five-main-bearing crankshaft was introduced in 1929. And the intake valves returned to the top with the exhaust valves on the side.

## Hercules

**Founded:** 1886
**Factory location:** Nuremberg, Germany
**Manufacturing lifespan:** 1886 - to date

Hercules was a cycle manufacturer but by 1904 was offering a heavyweight bicycle with an accessory engine and direct belt drive to the rear wheel. Before World War II, the company prospered by making a wide range of motorcycles from 73 to 498cc (4.455 to 30.39cu in), in the meantime gaining a number of racing and trials wins. Motorcycle production did not restart until 1950, with a pair of lightweight two-strokes. Within two years, there were five new models on sale throughout Europe. When German motorcycle sales fell dramatically Hercules consolidated, saw out the mid-1950s and became one of the few factories to survive into the 1960s. It continued to make a range of lightweights, many of them powered by Sachs or Ilo engines.

In 1969, Hercules was taken over by Sachs but kept its own identity. The following year, it began developing the unconventional rotary-engined W2000 (sold as a DKW in some markets). The power unit used the Wankel technology owned by Sachs, developed from a snowmobile engine. The W2000 stole headlines, but sold in tiny numbers and suffered from controversy concerning what capacity class its unorthodox engine really was. Real sales were in the form of lightweights and off-road singles and the Wankel was discontinued in 1975. From then on, Hercules concentrated on making small two-strokes.

**Specifications (W2000 Rotary)**
- **Engine:** Two-stroke single rotary
- **Displacement:** 94cc (18cu in)
- **Horsepower:** 32 @ 6500rpm
- **Wheelbase:** N/A
- **Weight:** 350lb (159kg)
- **Top speed:** 100mph (160kph)

**Above:** Hercules were the first company to produce a Wankel rotary-engined motorcycle. The Fichtel & Sachs engine could take the machine to a very respectable 100mph (160kph).

**1975 W2000**
Deutsches-Zweirad Museum and NSU Museum
Neckarsulm, Germany

# HESKETH

**Founded:** 1982
**Factory location:** Northamptonshire, England
**Manufacturing lifespan:** 1982 - 1988

This motorcycle was the fruit of an ambitious but remarkably short-lived attempt to relaunch the much-lamented British bike industry by the English peer Lord Hesketh. The motorcycle was launched in 1980 but production did not get underway properly until 1982. This was a consequence of numerous engineering defects that had to be rectified in order to make the machine function properly. The complex 90-degree V-twin engine was developed by Weslake and featured four valves and two camshafts per cylinder. The 5-speed transmission was of a constant mesh design. The remainder of the bike used components and materials that were state-of-the-art at the time of its construction. The duplex cradle frame was of a tubular design that utilized the engine as a stressed member. The frame, immediately forward of the swingarm pivot point, bolted to the base of the rear cylinder casting. The V1000 featured a mini-fairing, while the Vampire models were fully faired.

Hesketh Motorcycles Ltd. went into receivership after fewer than 150 motorcycles had been built. Other companies, including Hesleydon, Mocheck, and Mick Broom Engineering, sought to continue production, but despite their efforts, it is believed that a total of fewer than 250 Heskeths were built up to 1988.

**1982 V1000**
Tony East of A.R.E. Ltd
England

**Above:** The styling of the Hesketh was acceptable for its time of manufacture and compared favorably with Japanese sports machines of the period. Indeed, a Hesketh on the road is still an imposing sight.

**SPECIFICATIONS (1982 V1000)**
**Engine:** Four-stroke V-twin
**Displacement:** 992cc (60.5cu in)
**Horsepower:** 86 @ 6500rpm
**Wheelbase:** N/A
**Weight:** 498lb (226kg)
**Top speed:** 130.5mph (210kph)

**Above:** The engine, a 90-degree V-twin, was developed by Weslake for Hesketh. It was a heavy Dohc unit and certain aspects of its styling, such as the camshaft covers, did little to enhance the bike's appearance.

## HOLLEY

**Founded:** 1899
**Factory location:** Bradfod, Pennsylvania, USA
**Manufacturing lifespan:** 1899 - 1911

George Holley began racing motorcycles as a teenager and caught the bug, which also affected his younger brother, Earl. Together they started to build motorcycles and in 1897 created a 30mph (18.7kph) single-cylinder three-wheeler, The Runabout, from plans that George, at only 19 years of age, had drawn himself. Although a racer, George's first love was building engines, and in 1899 he and Earl set up Holley Motor Co. to supply engines to the evolving motor and motorcycle trade. Demand was still, however, so they undertook the manufacture of complete motorcycles, and in 1901 they became licensed to produce and sell the French Longuemare carburetor in the United States.

In 1902 George won America's first Motorcycle Endurance Contest, and went on to set a series of world speed records for motorcycles. When Henry Ford asked them to build a carburetor for the Model T, the brothers sold the motorcycle portion of the business and shifted to the design and production of carburetors. That company remains in business today.

**SPECIFICATIONS (HOLLEY 1905)**
**Engine:** IOE single
**Displacement:** 220cc (13.42cu in)
**Horsepower:** 2.25
**Wheelbase:** 46in (117cm)
**Weight:** 110lb (50kg)
**Top speed:** 35mph (56kph)

1905 Holley
Owner – Herb Singe
Hillside, New Jersey

**Below:** The forward-mount engine and seating position indicate that the 1903 model's aft weight bias may not have offered adequate handling. In 1905 the Holley appeared with a new front fork, fuel tank and transposed frame tubes and engine.

## HONDA

**Founded:** 1948
**Factory location:** Hamamatsu, Suzuka and Kumamoto, Japan
**Manufacturing lifespan:** 1948 - to date

Honda is the world's biggest motorcycle manufacturer yet the company started after World War II from the humblest of origins. In 1948 Soichiro Honda began by fitting army surplus engines into bicycles, using a belt drive to the rear wheel. The first Honda engine was a 50cc (3.05cu in) two-stroke engine and by 1949 the company had moved to a factory in Hamamatsu, Japan. The first really successful model was the D-type, a 98cc (5.98 cu in) two-stroke. ▶

1950 Dream
Courtesy of Honda
Japan

**Below:** Although Honda was to make its reputation with four-stroke engines, the first real machine was in fact a two-stroke. It was also the first chain-driven Honda and used a pressed-steel frame with the latest telescopic forks.

**SPECIFICATIONS (1950 DREAM)**
**Engine:** Two-stroke single
**Displacement:** 98cc (6cu in)
**Horsepower:** 2.95 @ 5000rpm
**Wheelbase:** N/A
**Weight:** 180lb (80kg)
**Top speed:** N/A

# HONDA

During the 1950s the company switched to producing four-stroke engines, starting with the 148cc (9.031cu in) model E. This was a great success and was followed by several other lightweight motorcycles, including the first Benly model and a scooter. Pressed-steel was widely used for the frames and Honda invested in modern machinery to keep the factory competitive.

In 1958 Honda introduced the landmark 50cc (2.90cu in) C100 with a step-through frame. Over the years, the "Honda 50" in all its variants would go on to become the world's best-selling motorcycle ever at around the 30 million mark.

In 1959 Honda opened an American office and began to work toward penetration of the US market. It became known for its high-revving, well-engineered small twins. The 1963 4-stroke, 2-cylinder 249cc (15.18cu in) Dream Supersport, was one of Honda's first sports bikes and one of the first to make inroads into export markets. The CB72 was a road model while a street scrambler variant was tagged the CL72. Both featured the same overhead camshaft, parallel-twin engine although some of the cycle parts varied to reflect the different styles of machine.

Honda followed the success of its early models with new machines such as the 1965 CB160. The numerical designation reflected the approximate metric displacement of the parallel-twin engine. The engine itself was advanced, featuring an overhead camshaft and an electric starter which was something of a novelty in the mid-1960s. Honda claimed the frame and brakes were race-bred which made the machine safe for street riding.

The CB77, at a little over 300cc displacement, was the biggest bike in Honda's range on its introduction in 1964 and it established the company's reputation as builders of more than just small capacity mopeds. It was intended for high-speed touring and its tubular frame used the engine as a stressed member. In 1965 Honda launched its first big bike, the 100mph CB450 twin.

The company had become involved with motorcycle racing in 1960 and in the next seven years won 137 Grand Prix and 18 manufacturers' trophies. A gap in racing ensued until the mid-1970s when the company returned with endurance racing machines. Within twenty years Honda production had reached 10 million machines, including mopeds and motorcycles.

1959 Benly
Courtesy of Honda Japan

**SPECIFICATIONS (1959 BENLY)**
**Engine:** Four-stroke ohc twin
**Displacement:** 124cc (7.57cu in)
**Horsepower:** 11.3 @ 9500rpm
**Wheelbase:** N/A
**Weight:** N/A
**Top speed:** N/A

**Above:** The C92 Benly had two cylinders. Nothing unusual, but what it did was to introduce the ohc configuration to this road-going bike, normally reserved for racing machines.

**SPECIFICATIONS (1961 RC162)**
**Engine:** Four-stroke dohc four
**Displacement:** 249.37cc (15.21cu in)
**Horsepower:** Over 44.4 @14000rpm
**Wheelbase:** N/A
**Weight:** 278lb (126.5kg)
**Top speed:** 139mph (220kph)

**Above:** The RC162 of 1961 dominated its class in racing, winning all ten races it entered. In 1962 Derek Minter, Jim Redman and Tom Phillis took the first three places at the lightweight TT on the Isle of Man.

**Specifications (1966 CB450)**
**Engine:** Four-stroke twin
**Displacement:** 445cc (27cu in)
**Horsepower:** 43 @ 8500rpm
**Wheelbase:** N/A
**Weight:** 410lb (187kg)
**Top speed:** 100mph (160kph)

**Above:** Honda's first 500cc (30.50cu in) machine was the "Black Bomber": twin-cylinder engine with dohc, a tubular frame, single-unit speedometer and rev counter with warning lights built in, and the usual telescopic forks at the front and twin shocks at the rear.

**1996 CB450**
Courtesy of Honda
Japan

**Above:** Front and rear brakes were shoe/drum type, the tires 2.75 x 18in front and rear, and the engine air-cooled with chain drive to the rear wheel.

**Left:** When Kuni Mitsu Takahashi took his RC162 to victory in the 250 class West German Grand Prix, this was the first world championship win by a Japanese rider.

**1961 RC162**
National Motor Museum
Beaulieu, England

## HONDA

In 1969, Honda launched what has become known as the first superbike, the four-cylinder CB750, and started the superbike boom. The CB750 featured an inline four-cylinder, single overhead camshaft engine mounted transversely in the frame, and a 5-speed transmission. While the bike was traditionally styled, it was modern for its time with steel duplex cradle, twin disc front brakes and spoked composite-construction wheels. This development led to a variety of four-cylinder machines of different engine sizes, including the popular CB400, the so-called 400/4.

Honda led the way again in 1974 with the introduction of the heavyweight Goldwing touring bike. It was described at the time as being "a revolutionary motorcycle" and was immediately popular in the USA. Originally a 999cc (60.963cu in) water-cooled flat-four with shaft drive, the bike has remained in continuous production ever since, gaining two cylinders and growing in capacity over the years.

The immense popularity of endurance racing led to world championship being inaugurated in 1980, with Japan's Suzuka 8 hours race being included in the series. Honda immediately took this title with the RCB 1000 in-line four and the machine continued to go its winning way in both endurance racing and TT Formula 1 events. This was great promotion for the forthcoming launch of their CB900F dohc roadster in the late 1970s.

The success of the original CB750 led other manufacturers to bring out their own variations of the format and it was gradually upstaged by rivals such as the 900cc (54.921cu in) Kawasaki Z1 and Suzuki's GS750 Four, so it was periodically updated through the 1970s. Honda also countered with its own 900cc four, the CB900.

Honda's range grew to encompass all classes of machine and the company continued to innovate and experiment with different formats. As well as a range of singles, parallel twins and fours, in the middleweight field, it came up with the sophisticated CX500 of 1978, which offered a water-cooled transverse V-twin with shaft drive.

**SPECIFICATIONS (1969 CB750/4)**
**Engine:** Four-stroke four-cylinder
**Displacement:** 736cc (44.89cu in)
**Horsepower:** 70 @9000rpm
**Wheelbase:** N/A
**Weight:** N/A
**Top speed:** 124.6mph (200kph)

**Above:** Honda astonished the motorcycling world when it unveiled the CB750 Four in Tokyo in 1968. Besides the four-cylinder engine it also had a five-speed gearbox and could top 120mph (192kph). This was truly the world's first superbike.

1968 CB750 Four
Courtesy of Honda Japan

**SPECIFICATIONS (1972 750K2)**
**Engine:** Four-stroke four
**Displacement:** 736cc (45cu in)
**Horsepower:** 67
**Wheelbase:** 57in (145cm)
**Weight:** 517lb (235kg)
**Top speed:** N/A

**Right:** Although not directly apparent from the outside, as the 750 progressed through its life it was gradually improved and upgraded. Although the bike had an electric starter, in these early days a kick start was still supplied.

1972 CB750K2
Courtesy of Honda Japan

**Right:** The RCB 1000 inline fours formed an unstoppable armada at the Le Mans endurance races. They clocked up wins for three consecutive years from 1978, when the Le Mans race was inaugurated.

**SPECIFICATIONS (1978 RCB 1000)**
- **Engine:** Four-stroke dohc four
- **Displacement:** 997.48cc (60.85cu in)
- **Horsepower:** 118 @ 9000rpm
- **Wheelbase:** N/A
- **Weight:** 418lb (190kg)
- **Top speed:** N/A

**Above:** Jean-Claude Chemarin and Christian Leon took four endurance titles in a row with their RCB 1000 Honda France machines.

1976 RCB 1000
Courtesy of Honda Japan

**Left:** To cope with the speed that the CB750 could do, Honda decided to fit front disc brakes. It was a bike that outclassed all others of the period.

**Above:** The four cylinders were fed by four carburetors, positioned directly behind the main cylinder head and under the fuel tank.

# HONDA

Honda's new superbike for 1979 was the astonishing six-cylinder CBX1000, which had a 135mph (216kph) top speed from over 100bhp. Two years later, it joined the 1980s passion for turbocharging by launching the CX500 Turbo, but turbo bikes soon fell out of fashion.

The original single-overhead camshaft CB750 was replaced by a twin-overhead camshaft version, the CB750F. The older bike's natural successor became the new CB650, which offered almost the same power from a similar layout. Developed from the old CB550, it was marketed in the US as an entry-level model and beat its rivals on both power and price.

Honda's top-of-the-range fours had also gained a lead on the competition with four-valve heads from 1978. The company's four-cylinder bikes won the famous French Bol d'Or endurance race from 1976 to 1979, leading to marketing of its top superbikes in replica form with a race-styled three-quarter fairing.

In 1983 Honda changed direction to a whole new generation of superbikes that used the V-4 format, starting with the VF750F. The water-cooled engine was smooth, powerful and compact but early versions suffered from a design fault in the cam-drive mechanism. To regain its reputation, Honda reworked the 1985 VFR750F into a real masterpiece and it stayed in production with various updates until it was replaced by the VFR800 in 1998. Honda also updated the big single, both as an off-roader such as the Dominator and a sports bike such as the XBR500. Traditionally a maker of four-strokes, Honda had adopted two-stroke technology for its return to racing in the 1980s, winning the 500cc world title in 1983. ▶

1979 CB750K7
Courtesy of Honda Japan

**SPECIFICATIONS (1979 CB750K7)**
**Engine:** Four-stroke four
**Displacement:** 736 (45cu in)
**Horsepower:** 67
**Wheelbase:** 57in (145cm)
**Weight:** 517lb (235kg)
**Top speed:** N/A

**Above:** As the years went by, so the 750 accepted cosmetic and technological changes; this is the K7 model.

**SPECIFICATIONS (1982 CX TURBO)**
**Engine:** Four-stroke V-twin
**Displacement:** 497cc (30.33cu in)
**Horsepower:** 80 @ 8000rpm
**Wheelbase:** N/A
**Weight:** 520lb (239kg)
**Top speed:** 119mph (190kph)

**Right:** Honda once again surprised motorcyclists with the announcement of the CX500 Turbo, the first production turbocharged motorcycle, in 1980 at the Cologne motorcycle show in Germany.

1982 VF750S
Courtesy of Honda
Japan

**Specifications (1982 VF750S)**
**Engine:** Four-stroke V-twin
**Displacement:** 748cc (45.70cu in)
**Horsepower:** 80 @ 9500rpm
**Wheelbase:** N/A
**Weight:** 480lb (220kg)
**Top speed:** 119mph (190kph)

**Above:** First of the "V" fours and known in some countries as the "Sabre," the VF750 used anti-dive suspension on the front with the Pro-link monoshock system on the rear. It was shaft-driven, and had a liquid crystal display for the instrumentation.

1982 CX500 Turbo
Deutsches-Zweirad Museum
and NSU Museum
Neckarsulm, Germany

**Above:** The standard CX500 was a best-seller for Honda but sales for the Turbo were slow. The half fairing and integrated fuel tank were new.

**Left:** With suspension based around telescopic air-assisted anti-dive front forks and Pro-link swingarm with rising rate monoshock control, the machine also had smart looking Gold Comstar wheels.

**1990 Honda Dominator**
National Motor Museum
Beaulieu, England

**Below:** The Dominator has a five-speed gearbox and chain drive to the rear wheel. A protection plate is fitted in front of the engine to stop any damage being caused when off-road.

**SPECIFICATIONS (1990 DOMINATOR)**
**Engine:** Four-stroke single
**Displacement:** 644cc (39.28cu in)
**Horsepower:** 40 @ 6000rpm
**Wheelbase:** N/A
**Weight:** 360lb (164kg)
**Top speed:** 95mph (152kph)

By the 1990s, Honda was the major global motorcycle manufacturer, able to use its technological expertise to enhance existing designs and pioneer new ones. Having started the fashion for in-line fours over twenty years earlier, Honda set new standards with the CBR900RR FireBlade in 1992. Its engine was as powerful as an 1100 yet it weighed as little as a 600 and handled like one. Regularly updated, it kept Honda ahead of its competitors for most of the decade. For a time, the Honda Super Blackbird could claim to be the world's fastest motorcycle. The company proved it could make super-fast lightweights as well, such as the 130mph (208kph) NSR250 two-stroke V-twin.

The evergreen VFR was now established as a versatile all-rounder, delivering superbike performance as well as proving to be a civilized tourer. For those who wanted a more purpose-built tourer, the company offered something in every range from the six-cylinder heavyweight GL1500 Gold Wing, through the high-tech ST1100 Pan European with ABS and optional traction control, to the XL1000V Varadero, with off-road capability, down to the 650cc (39.665cu in) Deauville. The important new streetfighter category was contested by the X11, with an engine similar to the Super Blackbird in an unfaired chassis, and the chunky CB1300.

Honda models also covered every type of off-road riding and blanketed the important cruiser and factory custom sector. A successful racing program produced the NSR500V, the first racer that could be bought by private entrants for over ten years. This was a V-twin, a format also used for the World Superbike-winning one-liter Firestorm (and later SP-1).

**Below:** The Pan European has elegant lines and is well finished with plenty of touring equipment. It caters for two-up quite happily. The full fairing is shaped for optimal air blast protection.

1994 RVF750/RC45
Courtesy of Honda
Japan

1997 ST1100 Pan European
Courtesy of Honda
Japan

**Above:** The braking system has both the Honda CBS system and also ABS. The suspension is telescopic fork at front and monoshock single-sided swingarm with enclosed driveshaft for the rear.

**Specifications (1994 RVF750/RC45)**

- **Engine:** Four-stroke V-four
- **Displacement:** 749.2cc (45.718cu in)
- **Horsepower:** 118 @ 1200rpm
- **Wheelbase:** N/A
- **Weight:** 417lb (189kg)
- **Top speed:** 160mph (257kph)

**Above:** No stranger to the race circuit, the RVF has had many successes, such as at the Isle of Man with mountain course king Joey Dunlop, who took three Formula 1 TT wins in a row from 1985 to 1987.

**Specifications (1997 ST1100 Pan European)**

- **Engine:** Four-stroke V-four
- **Displacement:** 1084cc (66.12cu in)
- **Horsepower:** 100 @ 7500rpm
- **Wheelbase:** N/A
- **Weight:** 660lb (297kg)
- **Top speed:** 130mph (208kph)

**Below:** The Pan European's lockable and flip-open panniers are a good size with enough room to store helmets and more.

# HONDA

The CBR900RR FireBlade was Honda's super-sport sensation of the 1990s, what sports riders were waiting for, although some felt it really wasn't anything special under its semi-enclosed bodywork. It uses a normal carburated, transverse four-cylinder engine with a twin-spar aluminum alloy chassis. Honda worked on reducing weight and aerodynamics. The second generation FireBlade lost more weight and gained power, too.

Honda joined the unfaired, streetfighter, muscle-bike generation of the late 1990s with something different: the X11, with in-line four-cylinder, water-cooled engine. Scarcely hidden behind the front wheel is the radiator for cooling the water and also an oil cooler for the engine.

The SP-1 was developed by Honda to win world superbikes events. In its debut season the SP-1 did that, and also TT formula 1, Suzuka 8-hours and the gruelling Le Mans 24-hour endurance races.

Into the new millennium Honda continued to update and expand a motorcycle range with everything from 50cc (3cu in) commuters to 1500cc (91.535cu in) super-tourers. The company had also diversified into almost every form of engineering, including cars, generators, boat engines and lawn mowers, but still remained true to its motorcycling roots. Today, Honda has factories at Hamamatsu, Suzuka and Kumamoto, Japan, and exports approximately 70 percent of its annual output. It also has a number of overseas factories manufacturing a variety of machines, including the Gold Wings and Valkyries which are made in the USA.

**Above:** Rear suspension is Honda's Pro-link monoshock system. Drive is via a chain with adjustment coming via the rear wheel sprocket.

**1998 FireBlade**
P&H Motorcycles
Sussex, England

**SPECIFICATIONS (1998 FIREBLADE)**
- **Engine:** Four-stroke four
- **Displacement:** 918cc (56cu in)
- **Horsepower:** 128
- **Wheelbase:** 55in (140cm)
- **Weight:** 396lb (180kg)
- **Top speed:** N/A

**Above:** The FireBlade's fairing hides the in-line four dohc, four-stroke engine that can rush you to a dizzy 155mph (248kph). Superb stopping power, though, is provided by twin disc front brakes and four piston callipers.

**Right:** No fairing getting in the way here – and only really room for one person.

1999 X11
P&H Motorcycles
Sussex, England

**Specifications (1999 X11)**
**Engine:** Four-stroke four
**Displacement:** 1137cc (69.36cu in)
**Horsepower:** 130 @ 9000rpm
**Wheelbase:** N/A
**Weight:** 490lb (225kg)
**Top speed:** 150mph (240kph)

**Left** The large radiator at the front of the bike makes it look a little out of proportion. This houses the water and oil cooling radiators.

**Below:** The SP-1 was designed to win championships, which it has already done. Side-mounted radiators make the bike a very compact design.

**Specifications (1999 VTR1000 SP-1)**
**Engine:** Four-stroke V-twin
**Displacement:** 999cc (60.94cu in)
**Horsepower:** 135 @ 9000rpm
**Wheelbase:** N/A
**Weight:** 440lb (200kg)
**Top speed:** 170mph (272kph) road, 190mph (304kph) race

**Left:** From dual headlights to upswept exhaust, the new SP-1 is a championship contender and will take you to the heights of pleasure on the normal road.

1999 SP-1
P&H Motorcycles
Sussex, England

**Founded:** 1923
**Factory location:** Bad Homburg, Germany
**Manufacturing lifespan:** 1923 - 1958

Horex was founded in the early 1920s by the Kleeman family who were in other production businesses. The company's motorcycles used Columbus proprietary engines. Its first machine was a 246cc (15cu in) overhead-valve single. A range of larger displacement motorcycles followed and in the 1930s the designer, Hermann Reeb, came up with a pair of vertical twin engines that had chain-driven camshafts. The engines were considered technologically advanced and the motorcycles had some racing success, especially with Karl Braun riding a supercharged version.

In the years that followed World War II Horex went back to motorcycle production and the company introduced a successful 349cc (21.28cu in) machine called the Horex Regina. Later this was superseded by the Horex Imperator. Production by the company stopped in 1958.

However, the name reappeared later, when the company was owned by Zweirad Röth GmbH & Company of Odenwald, Germany. Among its products were the 1986 Horex HRD 600 and 500 based around the successful single-cylinder four-stroke Rotax engine in two capacities of 494 and 562cc (30.13 and 34.28cu in). The HRD 600 was a modern bike for its day, using a chrome molybdenum tubular frame, monoshock rear suspension, air-assisted front forks, and five-speed transmission.

**Specifications (1936 S35)**
**Engine:** Four-stroke single
**Displacement:** 341cc (21cu in)
**Horsepower:** 12.5
**Wheelbase:** N/A
**Weight:** N/A
**Top speed:** N/A

**Above:** September 1953 saw the debut of the Imperator 400cc (24.4cu in) twin at the Frankfurt motorcycle show in Germany. A prototype had been built in 1951 but was never produced. The Earls-type front forks were a design by Roland Schnell, Horex's leading rider.

**1936 S35**
Auto & Technic Museum
Sinsheim, Germany

**Left:** By the middle of the 1930s Horex was not just challenging on the race circuit but also for a leading position in the sales war. The S35 was at this time its best-seller.

1962 Imperator
Deutsches-Zweirad Museum
and NSU Museum
Neckarsulm, Germany

**Specifications (1955 Imperator)**
Engine: Four-stroke twin
Displacement: 392cc (24cu in)
Horsepower: 24 @ 6500rpm
Wheelbase: N/A
Weight: 390lb (175kg)
Top speed: 80mph (128kph)

**Below:** The Imperator's name is proudly boasted on the rear fender. The bike's capacity was held to 400cc (24.4cu in) for tax reasons; a 500cc (30.5cu in) capacity would have been more heavily taxed, making the bike 25 percent more expensive.

## Husqvarna



| | |
|---|---|
| **Founded:** 1903 | |
| **Factory location:** Huskvarna, Sweden | |
| **Manufacturing lifespan:** 1903 – to date | |

Originally, Husqvarna was a Swedish arms manufacturer that also made bicycles. In 1903 it started designing and building motorcycles and fitting them with NSU and FN engines. The company then progressed in 1920 to an engine of its own design, a 550cc (33.55cu in) side-valve V-twin. It also continued to use proprietary engines, including those from JAP, while increasing the displacement of its own engines to as much as 1000cc (61cu in).

In the mid-1930s Husqvarna made its first two-stroke, a 98cc (5.98cu in) motorcycle with a two-speed gearbox. It sold well and after World War II was over the company concentrated on such small machines. Husqvarna moved successfully into off-road motorcycles, using Albin engines in its four-strokes and its own engines in the two-strokes. Riders on Husqvarna machines had enormous success in motocross competition. The bikes had automatic transmissions and liquid-cooling. ▶

1935 Husqvarna
Deutsches-Zweirad Museum
and NSU Museum
Neckarsulm, Germany

**Below:** These racing machines, Huskies as they were known, were successful in the mid-'30s, especially with the great Stanley Woods on board. Their V-twin engines reportedly produced 44bhp.

**Specifications (1935 Racer)**
Engine: V-twin
Displacement: 496cc (30.30cu in)
Horsepower: 41 @ 6700rpm
Wheelbase: N/A
Weight: 280lb (124kg)
Top speed: 119mph (190kph)

# Husqvarna

In 1986 Husqvarna produced the multi-purpose two-stroke MC250MP for the Swedish armed forces. Its dirt-bike heritage was clearly obvious and the bike could be fitted with skis. Husqvarna also manufactured the 125WRK with a 124cc (7.56cu in) engine. Designed for motocross, it featured high ground clearance and long travel suspension through use of an alloy swinging arm and Ohlins monoshock and telescopic leading axle forks. Tall tires and wheels which were 21in and 18in (530 and 450mm) front and rear, respectively, also increased the bike's ground clearance. Fenders and fuel tank were plastic.

In 1986 the company was acquired by Cagiva, and production was transferred to Italy to deliver off-road competition bikes under the 1988 Husaberg brandname. The 1991 Husqvarna 610TE motorcycle was one of a generation of four-stroke singles used in motocross events. It featured a liquid-cooled, double overhead camshaft four-valve engine, a tube steel frame fitted with an alloy swingarm, and monoshock suspension assembly. Forks were of the upside-down type and disc brakes were fitted front and rear.

**2000 610TE**
Courtesy of Cagiva
Italy

**Specifications (2000 610TE)**
- **Engine:** Four-stroke single
- **Displacement:** 585cc (36cu in)
- **Horsepower:** c 48
- **Wheelbase:** N/A
- **Weight:** N/A
- **Top speed:** 85mph (136kph)

# Imme

**Founded:** 1948
**Factory location:** Munich, Germany
**Manufacturing lifespan:** 1948-51

During Imme's short existence after World War II, the company produced one of the most unconventional lightweight motorcycles ever made. Designed by Norbert Riedel, both the front and rear suspension were very unorthodox. The front suspension had a single leg on the right, suspended by a spring and parallelogram links similar to a conventional girder fork. The rear wheel was carried on a swinging arm, suspended by a forward-facing spring. Although this looked more conventional, it was also one-sided and the engine was connected to the suspension arm so that it pivoted with it. In fact, the tube that formed the swinging arm also formed the exhaust pipe, and extended right past the rear wheel.

The rest of the frame was minimal, consisting of a mix of tubular and pressed steel parts linking the steering head to the rear suspension pivot, plus supports for the seat and tank. The 98cc (5.98cu in) two-stroke engine also looked unconventional. It became fashionable for unit-construction engines to enclose as much as possible of the power unit and gearbox in smooth alloy castings called a "power egg." The Imme took this to extremes, with its small cylinder laid almost flat, virtually hidden by the casings.

The bike's unconventional appearance probably affected its sales, as did its low power, although Imme made small numbers of a 148cc (9.031cu in) twin-cylinder version shortly before production ceased. Riedel later used a similar pivoting engine idea for the Victoria Swing.

**Left:** Norbert Reidel initially designed and made starters for Luftwaffe jet fighters, and used the money to produce his 98cc Imme ("Bee") at Immenstadt, Germany.

**Left:** This is the Husqvarna TE model. The company is one of the most successful makers in the history of enduro and in 1993 celebrated the 90th anniversary of the brandname.

**Specifications (2000 WR125)**
- **Engine:** Two-stroke single
- **Displacement:** 125cc (7.62cu in)
- **Horsepower:** Depends on restrictions
- **Wheelbase:** N/A
- **Weight:** N/A
- **Top speed:** c 65mph (10kph)

2000 WR125
Courtesy of Cagiva
Italy

**Right:** Sitting high off the ground the WR125 uses upside down telescopic forks at the front and "soft damp" with hydraulic single shock absorber at the rear. Front tire is 21inch (53.5cm) and rear is18inch (46cm).

1948 Imme
Deutsches-Zweirad Museum
and NSU Museum
Neckarsulm, Germany

**Specifications (1948 Model)**
- **Engine:** Two-stroke single
- **Displacement:** 99cc (6cu in)
- **Horsepower:** 4.5 @ 5300rpm
- **Wheelbase:** N/A
- **Weight:** N/A
- **Top speed:** N/A

**Above:** Rather an unorthodox design, the Imme engine assembly and rear wheel were suspended together, pivoting below the seat. The connection to the rear wheel also formed the exhaust pipe. The chassis was of the pressed-steel type.

# INDIAN

**Founded:** 1901
**Factory location:** Springfield, Massachusetts, USA
**Manufacturing lifespan:** 1901 - 1953

George Hendee and Oscar Hedstrom, both former bicycle racers, met in 1900 and created the Hendee Manufacturing Company and Indian motorcycles. Hedstrom had the first Indian prototype up and running in less than five months. Hendee engaged the Aurora Automatic Machine Company of Illinois to build engines, while Hedstrom set to work on refinements to both the engine and chassis. Springfield produced 377 motorcycles in 1903, and by 1904 production was up to almost 600. And it would nearly double the following year. Horsepower was up to 2.25 from the 213cc single. Hedstrom then turned his engineering focus to development of the V-twin engine. In 1907 the V-twin arrived, with slightly larger cylinder bores it shared with the new single. The 633cc twin was rated at four horsepower and the single at 2.25. Oscar Hedstrom also produced a racing V-twin, with 698cc and seven horsepower. The front fork was given a longer cartridge spring. The smaller twin gained only about 15 pounds (7kg) on the single.

Hedstrom had been working on improvements to his carburetor, and on the conversion to mechanical intake valves. Motorcycle racing was fast becoming popular and atmospheric valves couldn't meet the high performance demands of a newly competitive racing scene. In 1907 two contests were created that have survived to this day – the Tourist Trophy event on the Isle of Man and the 1000-Mile Reliability Trial in England. The trial, which would evolve as the International Six Days Trial, was won in its inaugural event by Teddy Hastings of New York, riding a stock Indian V-twin. And in 1908 he did it again, this time with factory support. French-Canadian Jake DeRosier had apprenticed with Oscar Hedstrom, and risen to the top as a championship motorcycle racer. By 1908 he was fully sponsored by the Indian factory, and would achieve national and international fame within the next few years.

The last of the diamond-frame Indians were built in 1909, as options to the new loop frame. Boardtrack speeds were now pushing 80mph (129kph). The race was on to be first to the 100mph (161kph) mark. Between 1909 and 1912 the construction of boardtrack motor-dromes was a national growth industry in the big cities, and the banking quickly increased from 25 to 60 degrees. In 1910 Indian introduced a leaf-spring front fork that would become a lasting trademark, and also offered a two-speed transmission. Production for 1909 fell just short of 5,000 machines, and in 1910 rose to more than 6,000.

Jake DeRosier continued to set speed records on the boardtracks, and Indian riders finished 1-2-3 in the first Isle of Man TT race, and a month later at Brooklands in England, DeRosier set a new mile record at 88mph (142kph). But upon his return to Springfield, DeRosier was not granted a ride on the new 8-valve racer, so he quit and signed with Excelsior. ▶

**SPECIFICATIONS (1907 TWIN)**
**Engine:** IOE 42° V-twin
**Displacement:** 633cc (38.61cu in)
**Horsepower:** 4
**Wheelbase:** 51in (130cm)
**Weight:** 135lb (61kg)
**Top speed:** 45mph (72kph)

**Above:** The first Indian V-twin came to market in 1907. The four-horsepower engine still had atmospheric intake valves.

1907 Twin
Owner – Mike Parti
North Hollywood, California

**Specifications (1908 Racer)**
Engine: IOE 42° V-twin
Displacement: 1000cc (61cu in)
Horsepower: 7
Wheelbase: 51in (130cm)
Weight: 130lb (59kg)
Top speed: 70mph (113kph)

**Left:** The torpedo tanks were built in three different sizes, and fitted according to the different race distances. The oil tank and hand pump fit behind the engine.

1912 Big-base 8-Valve
Owner – Jim Dennie
Palmyra, New York

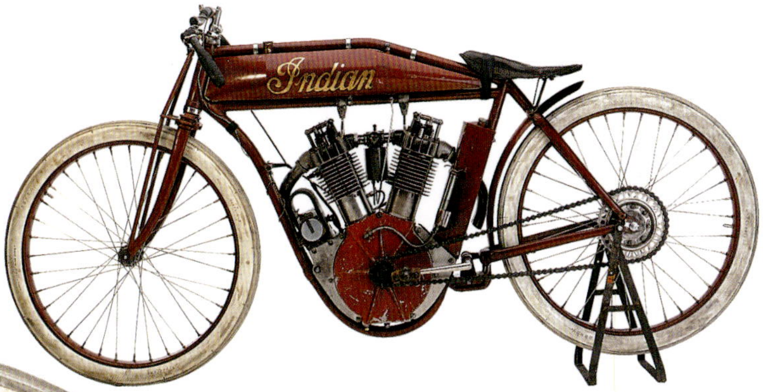


**Above:** The big-base overheads had one throttle position, wide open. Speed was controlled by a kill switch. Direct drive, no brakes, lord have mercy.

**Specifications (1911 8-Valve Racer)**
Engine: Ohv V-twin
Displacement: 1000cc (61cu in)
Horsepower: 14-17
Wheelbase: 53in (135cm)
Weight: 245lb (111kg)
Top speed: 100mph (161kph)

**Left:** Oscar Hedstrom was determined to establish Indian's domination on the racetracks. The Big-base 8-valve was a major weapon.

1908 Racer
Owner – Tony Penachio
Milwood, New York

# INDIAN

This was to be Indian's Golden Era. By 1913 Indian motorcycle production approached 32,000 machines for the year, the best figure Springfield would ever have. But Hendee and Hedstrom had come to disagree on the future of motorcycle design and marketing. Both resigned/retired within two years, and Indian came under the control of an investment group.

The 1915 Indians were the final renditions of the Hedstrom F-head engines, offered in big twin (1000cc) and little twin (700cc) versions. A three-speed transmission was offered for the first time as optional equipment, and a new kickstart mechanism was fitted. Generators were included on the electric light models, and Schebler carburetors replaced the Hedstrom units.

Ireland's Charles Franklin replaced Hedstrom as chief engineer and designed the Powerplus side-valve engine, with slightly smaller bore but longer stroke, and a bit more power than its predecessor. The bottom end, clutch and transmission were strengthened.

Most of Springfield's production for 1916 was devoted to military models ordered by the government (20,000 Indians) as courier mounts. While Indian tended to neglect its civilian dealers and customers, America's relatively short involvement in World War I proved this to be a costly mistake. Neither of the new lightweights, the Model K two-stroke or Model O opposed twin, found much success, as riders resisted small motorcycles. The Powerplus was still available in either cradle-spring or rigid frame models, and the single remained in the lineup. With the end of war the racing scene was soon revived, and Indian's Gene Walker won four of the nine dirt-track championship events in 1919.

**Specifications (1912 Boardtrack Racer)**
- **Engine:** IOE V-twin
- **Displacement:** 1000cc (62cu in)
- **Horsepower:** 12
- **Wheelbase:** 53in (135cm)
- **Weight:** 240lb (109kg)
- **Top speed:** 90mph (145kph)

**Above:** Steep-bank boardtrack racing reached its popularity peak in 1912. When eight people died at a New Jersey motordrome, the sport faded quickly.

**1912 Twin Racer**
Owner – Tony Penachio
Millwood, New York

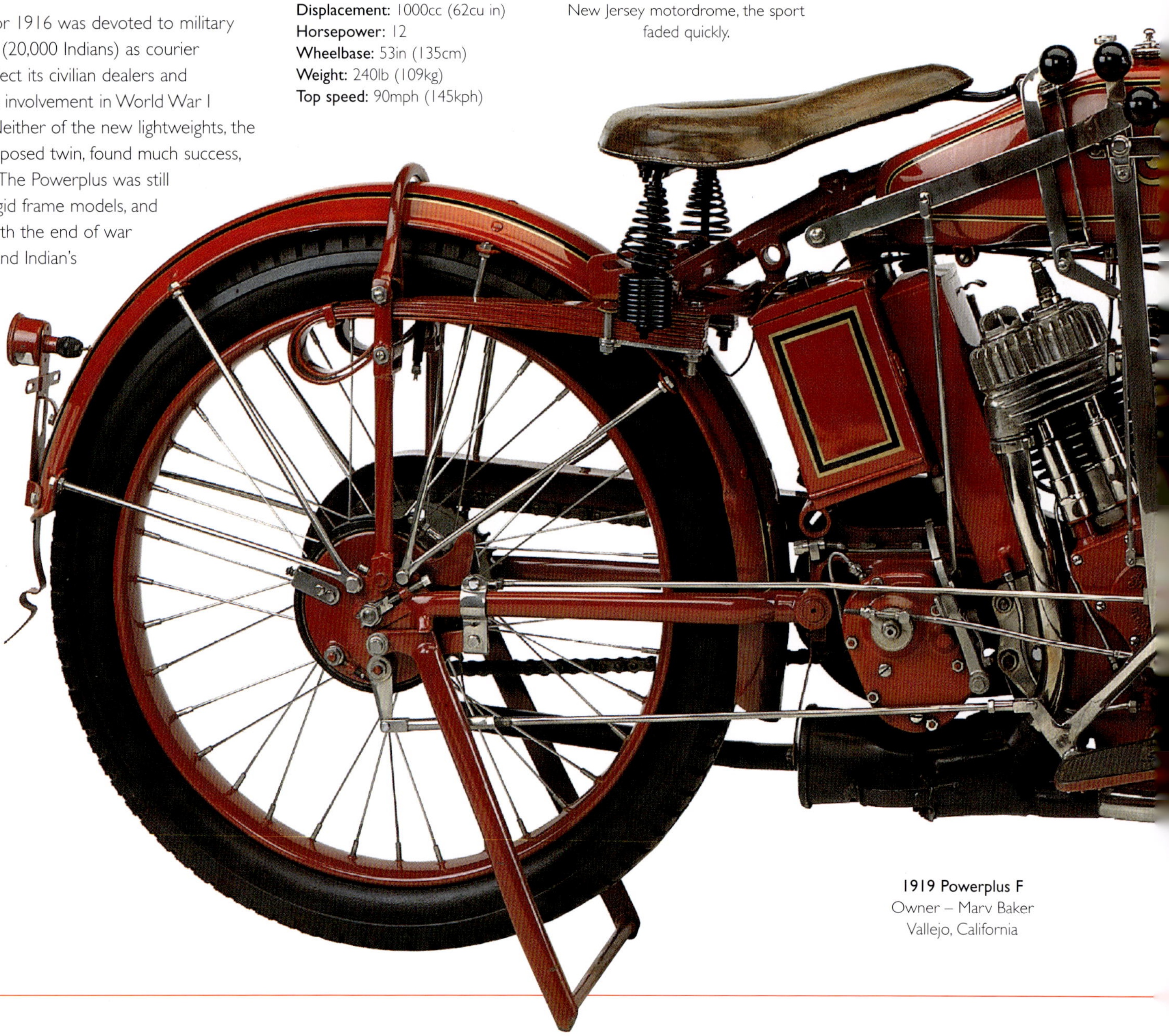

**Right:** The Powerplus V-twin was rated at 18 horsepower. Speeds were up and Cannonball Baker continued setting endurance records for Indian.

**1919 Powerplus F**
Owner – Marv Baker
Vallejo, California

**Specifications (1913 Twin)**
- **Engine:** IOE V-twin
- **Displacement:** 1000cc (62cu in)
- **Horsepower:** 7
- **Wheelbase:** 59in (150cm)
- **Weight:** 355lb (161kg)
- **Top speed:** 55mph (89kph)

**Right:** Indian was one of the first major builders to adopt rear wheel suspension. The leaf-spring system was patterned on automobile engineering. Indian suspension components were well tested during cross-country record runs by one Erwin "Cannonball" Baker.

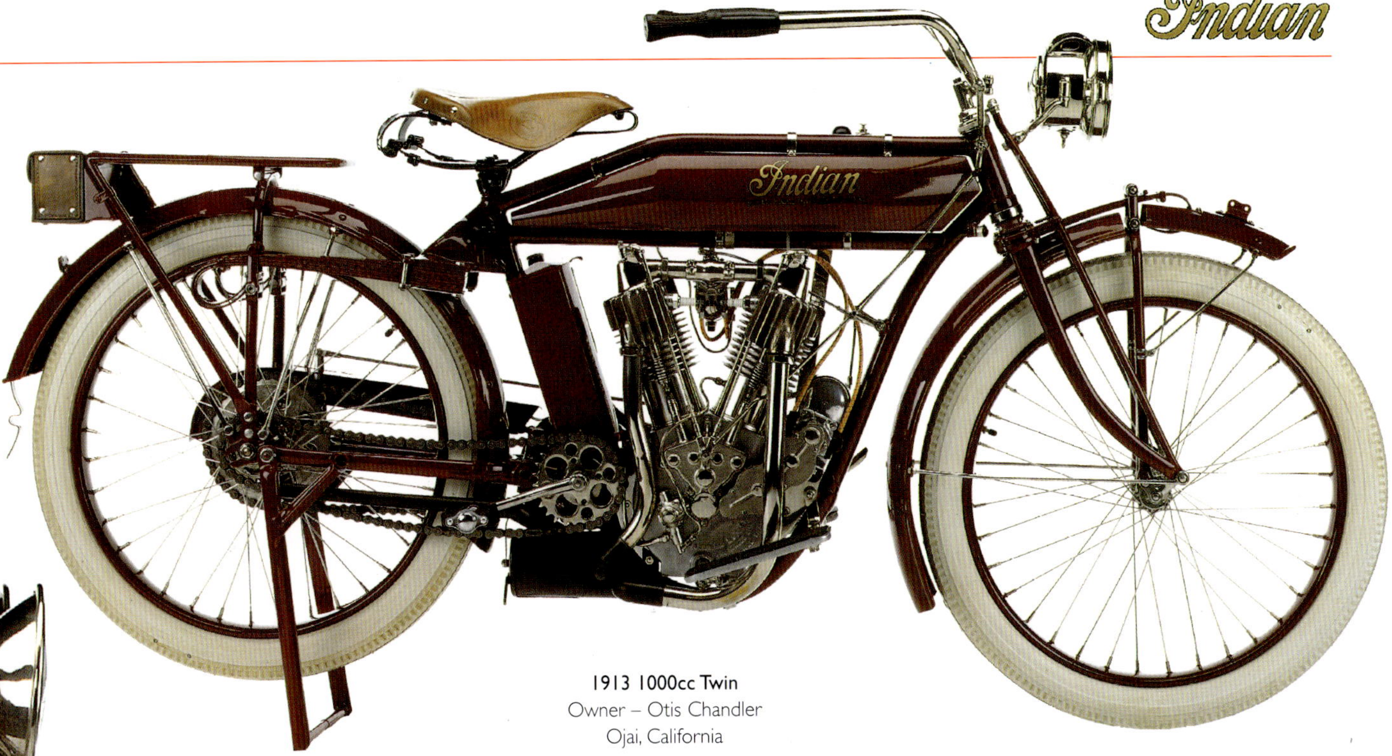


1913 1000cc Twin
Owner – Otis Chandler
Ojai, California

**Above:** The Indian leaf-spring fork was a durable system, and found application on racing and hillclimb machines as well as road models.

**Specifications (1919 Powerplus Model F)**
- **Engine:** Side-valve 42° V-twin
- **Displacement:** 1000cc (62cu in)
- **Horsepower:** 18
- **Wheelbase:** 59in (150cm)
- **Weight:** 430lb (195kg)
- **Top speed:** 60mph (97kph)

**Left:** The compression release, clutch and transmission levers juggle for space beside the fuel tank. The Powerplus had three-speed transmission, and a dry clutch.

Racing motorcycles built between 1915 and 1925 represented the leading edges of motorcycle engineering, design, style and performance. These machines, mostly Indians, Excelsiors and Harleys, were built to the optimum balance between velocity and durability. Indians captured 14 of the 17 national title events in 1920, but Harley-Davidson won the long races, and the championship. Indians were humbled the following year, when Harley riders won all the national championship events. But 1920 was also the year that Charles Franklin's engineering prowess was certified with the release of the Scout. The two-cam side-valve made about 10hp, and could be readily tweaked for more urge. With gear-drive primary and three-speed transmission, the Scout was good for about 60mph (97kph) in stock trim, and handled far better than the Powerplus, which was replaced in 1923 by the side-valve Chief. With 1000 or 1200cc (62 or 73.2cu in) engines, the Chief was derived from the Scout and built as direct competition with the Harley big twin. It was well suited to the needs of touring riders and sidecarists, but the Scout remained the popular choice among sporting riders. The 1200cc Chief featured improved carburetion and reinforcements to the frame, and soon passed the Scout in overall sales figures. In 1924 the factory went to a new front fork and larger wheels and tires. The Chief was especially popular with police departments around the country.

By the end of 1926 Indian had bought the now defunct Ace Motorcycle Company, and the Indian/Ace Four came to market in the same configuration it had under William Henderson. In succeeding years it would appear with an Indian fork, frame and fuel tank. By 1929 the Four would have a complete Springfield chassis, and extensive engine modifications. The heavier-duty Indian Four was a sophisticated sport-touring machine in 1929, but production was limited. By 1930 the economic depression had hit the Indian Motorcycle Company, which was sold to industrialist E. Paul DuPont, who had to make cuts in production. Fewer than 1,700 machines were made for 1933, but Indian showed a slight profit.

In 1936 American motorcycling entered the musclebike era, and in 1938 a new Indian Four was released – essentially the old Indian Four, still at 1265cc (77.17cu in), and once again with a Schebler carburetor, but with the casting of cylinders in pairs, to improve engine cooling. The saddle was also larger and allowed some adjustment fore and aft. The Indian head tank design was now painted in full color. No magneto model was offered in 1938. The last of the rigid-frame Fours, 1938 and '39, have become prized collectibles based on the combination of beauty, performance and rarity. Fewer than 700 were built over the two years.

**SPECIFICATIONS (1923 BIG CHIEF)**
**Engine:** Side-valve 42° V-twin
**Displacement:** 1200cc (73.2cu in)
**Horsepower:** 34
**Wheelbase:** 60.5in (154cm)
**Weight:** 440lb (200kg)
**Top speed:** 75mph (121kph)

**Above:** The Big Chief had a stronger frame and plenty of torque. The machine was well received by police riders and hillclimbers.

1923 Big Chief
Owner – Rocky Burkhart
Birdsboro, Pennsylvania

**Specifications (1928 Ace Four)**
- **Engine:** IOE inline four
- **Displacement:** 1265cc (77.2cu in)
- **Horsepower:** 35
- **Wheelbase:** 59in (150cm)
- **Weight:** 395lb (179kg)
- **Top speed:** 80mph (129kph)

1928 Indian Ace
Owner – Mort Wood
Marathon, Florida

**Above:** The purchase of the Ace inventory and tooling gave Indian the most comprehensive line of motorcycles in the industry.

1938 Four
Owner – Elmer Lower
Etters, Pennsylvania

**Specifications (1938 Four)**
- **Engine:** IOE inline four
- **Displacement:** 1265cc (77.2cu in)
- **Horsepower:** 45
- **Wheelbase:** 59in (150cm)
- **Weight:** 540lb (245kg)
- **Top speed:** 95mph (153kph)

**Left:** In 1938 the Four got a larger saddle with fore and aft adjustment. The luggage rack and saddlebags were a $13 option. No magneto ignition was offered in 1938. But the engine was right-side up again and it looked swell. Cylinders were cast in pairs.

**Above:** For 1938 only, instruments had red lettering on a gray background. This was also the first year to have a 120mph speedometer.

The best news for Indian in 1937 and a few years after was Californian racer Ed Kretz, who won the inaugural Daytona 200 on a Sport Scout, then the 100-mile national at Langhorne, Pennsylvania, and the inaugural 200-mile at Laconia, New Hampshire. He was the dominant racer in the US for five years.

World War II saw 16,000 Indians produced for the military. One development, the transverse V-twin 841 of 1944, didn't reach production but, using barrels and heads grafted from the Sport Scout, it contributed to the postwar civilian models, its hydraulic girder-spring fork being adapted to the Chief in 1946. The Chief was Indian's only production model in 1946 and 1947, after another change of ownership to Ralph Rogers in 1945. There was more financial/management reshuffling over the ensuing years, during which the Chief underwent minor changes – including revised-profile front fender, rear-tapered fuel tank, the word "Eighty" denoting number of cubic inches added to the script logo on a wing-shaped background, reshaped combustion chambers, higher compression, Western-style handlebars with external cables for throttle, choke and spark advance, and even a bench-style version of the Chum-Me seat instead of a saddle. The last model came in 1953, which also saw the end of Indian. Soon the showrooms would be filled with AJS, Royal Enfield, Norton and Matchless motorcycles from England, Honda from Japan, and even, at the risk of social ostracism, Harley-Davidsons.

**SPECIFICATIONS (1938 SPORT SCOUT)**

- **Engine:** Side-valve 42° V-twin
- **Displacement:** 750cc (45.75cu in)
- **Horsepower:** 35
- **Wheelbase:** 56.5in (144cm)
- **Weight:** 320lb (145kg)
- **Top speed:** 105mph (169kph)

1938 Sport Scout
Owner – Ed Kretz, Jr.
Monterey Park, California

**Above:** The Sport Scout of the one and only Ironman Ed Kretz. "He was so strong," said one competitor, "he could carry the bike across the line." The venerable racer was updated regularly over the years. The frame was chromed only after retirement.

1944 841
Owner – Bob Stark
Perris, California

**Above:** A modified version of the 841 fork would be adapted to the Chief after the war. This was the first Indian to have foot shift.

**Specifications (1953 Chief)**

- **Engine:** Side-valve 42° V-twin
- **Displacement:** 1300cc (79.3cu in)
- **Horsepower:** 40
- **Wheelbase:** 62in (157cm)
- **Weight:** 560lb (254kg)
- **Top speed:** 95mph (153kph)

**Left:** Final renditions of the Chief had chromed upper fork legs, and the horn was moved up near the steering head. "Eighty" indicated cubic inches. Exhaust header pipes were lengthened to circumvent the engine cover. The exhaust pipe now carried straight back.

1953 Chief
Owner – Elmer Lower
Etters, Pennsylvania

# ITALJET

**Founded:** 1966
**Factory location:** Bologna, Italy
**Manufacturing lifespan:** 1966 – to date

This Italian company has produced a number of two-stroke machines for off-road use. It has used proprietary engines from companies such as Minarelli, CZ, MZ, Yamaha and Triumph. The 646cc (39.40cu in) engines from the latter were fitted into Italjet's own frame to give a large capacity off-road machine.

Typical of early 1980s specialist trials bikes was the Italjet 350T. The designation of this motorcycle approximates to its metric displacement and other machines were similarly designated. These included the 50T, 100T and 250T. Like specialist trials bikes, the 350T featured high ground clearance, light weight and low gearing. With the new millennium came new scooters from Italjet and in today's fashion-conscious world, the scooters from Italjet set the pace. The company produces futuristic racer machines like the Dragster, through to the Velocifero, a nostalgic throwback to the early days of scooter riding.

**Specifications (Dragster D50LC)**
**Engine:** Two-stroke single
**Displacement:** 49cc (3.0cu in)
**Horsepower:** N/A
**Wheelbase:** N/A
**Weight:** 196.2lb (85kg)
**Top speed:** 48mph (77.2kph)

Dragster D50LC
Courtesy Italjet
Italy

**Below:** The Italjet Dragster is without doubt a design of the time. The thin criss-cross tubing of the frame is more reminiscent of larger Italian bikes. Its dropped handlebars and dragster-style seat give it a very racey feel.

# Iver Johnson

**Founded:** 1907
**Factory location:** Fitchburg, Massachusetts, USA
**Manufacturing lifespan:** 1907 - 1916

Iver Johnson's Arms and Cycle Works had been building bicycles for 23 years when it entered the motorcycle business, and had started manufacturing firearms many years earlier. The Iver Johnson design was unconventional in many respects. The top and middle frame tubes were bent to arch over the engine, and the front fork was an interesting leading link, leaf spring design. Customers could choose either rigid or swingarm rear suspension. This was known as a keystone frame, one that employs the engine as a stressed member.

The side-valve singles and twins had two different valve mechanisms. The belt-drive single featured a longitudinal camshaft driven by worm gears, the shaft extending forward through the case to drive the magneto. On the V-twin and chain-drive single, the cams were incorporated in a large ring gear driven by a pinion gear on the crankshaft. The magneto on these engines was chain-driven. The V-twin was designed with offset crankpins, which provided evenly spaced combustion strokes, so exhaust note sounded like a vertical twin. The engine featured both mechanical and hand oil pumps. Final versions of the twin were equipped with a planetary clutch, with either an Eclipse two-speed hub or a single speed. The twin was rated at eight horsepower, and the single at 4.5hp.

In 1916 the market for weapons began to seriously outstrip the prospects for motorcycle sales, so the company turned its attention to firearms and tools.

**Below:** The ads said, "The Iver Johson motorcycle is a wonderful example of engineering, design and construction. It has tremendous speed, very flexible control, and rides like a touring car."

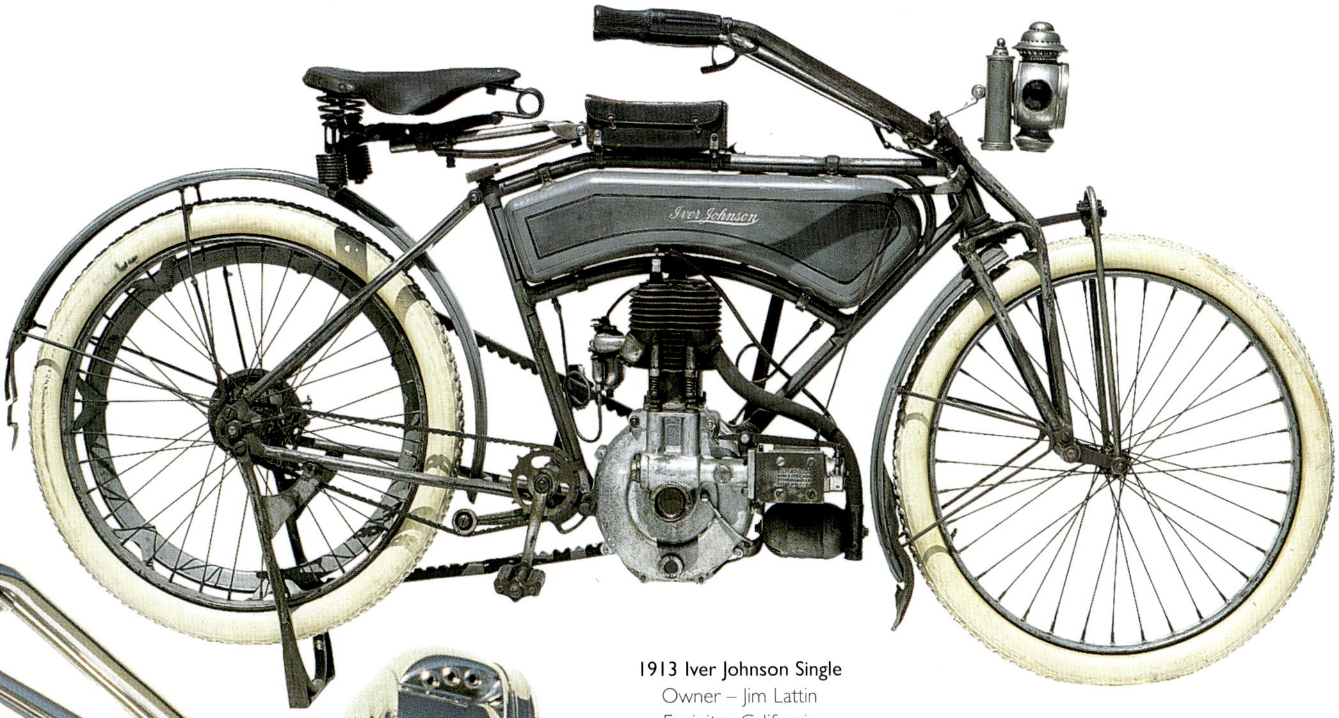

1913 Iver Johnson Single
Owner – Jim Lattin
Encinitas, California

**Above:** Iver Johnson offered a 500cc single with either chain or belt drive. The engine was rated four to five horsepower. The camshaft was fitted longitudinally, amidships. The bevel drive shaft extended forward to power the magneto.

**Specifications (V-Twin)**
- **Engine:** Side-valve V-twin
- **Displacement:** 1020cc (62.22cu in)
- **Horsepower:** 7-8
- **Wheelbase:** 58in (147cm)
- **Weight:** 265lb (120kg)
- **Top speed:** 65mph (105kph)

**Left:** The leading-link spring fork was an interesting piece of work. Iver Johnson credited the keystone frame for the machine's supple handling.

1915 Iver Johnson
Owner – Otis Chandler
Ojai, California

# JAMES

**Founded:** 1902
**Factory location:** Birmingham, England
**Manufacturing lifespan:** 1902 - 1964

Harry James's pedal-cycle manufacturing company was founded late in the nineteenth century; it produced its first motorcycle in 1902. The company had an innovative style and used engines from FN as well as those of its own design. One unorthodox machine made in 1908 featured one-sided wheel fixings, hub-center steering and drum brakes and was powered by James's own engine.

In the 1920s James produced singles and V-twins in small numbers. For the 1930s its range included both James- and Villiers-powered conventional utility motorcycles of small displacement, with rigid frames and girder forks. The Flying Ace of 1932 was derived from a range of V-twins called Models B1, B2 and B3. Only the B1 had an overhead-valve engine although all displaced 499cc and had the same bore and stroke. They featured 3-speed transmissions although a 4-speed unit was available as an extra-cost option. In 1931 the C1 and C2 models were ohv and side-valve offerings, respectively. They were also given names: the ohv machine became the Flying Ace, and the side-valve Grey Ghost. Both continued for 1932 as the D1 and D2, improved by oil-bath chain cases. The ohv V-twin was dropped for 1933 but the side-valve became the E2 Flying Ghost. By 1937 all the engines were bought in from Villiers.

During World War II 6,000 ML Military Lightweights were made for airborne soldiers, becoming the basis of a postwar civilian model. Later a new range included the Captain, Commodore, Comet, Colonel and Cadet. In the mid-1950s AMC acquired the company and a number of AMC engines appeared in the James range. Production stopped in 1964.

**SPECIFICATIONS (1932 D1 FLYING ACE)**
**Engine:** Four-stroke Ohv V-twin
**Displacement:** 499cc (30.5cu in)
**Horsepower:** N/A
**Wheelbase:** N/A
**Weight:** N/A
**Top speed:** N/A

**Below:** The D1 did not have rear suspension other than that provided in the springing of the solo saddle. Provision of rear suspension as a matter of course came postwar.

1932 D1 Flying Ace
National Motor Museum
Beaulieu, England

# JAP

**Founded:** 1904
**Factory location:** London, England
**Manufacturing lifespan:** 1904 - 1908

The initials JAP stand for J. A. Prestwich, the name of a company chiefly famous for supplying engines to other manufacturers. It was founded in 1903 and did build complete motorcycles until 1908 when a decision was made only to build engines for supply to others. After World War I the engine factory was taken over by Villiers who also supplied their engines to other manufacturers.

During the 1930s the JAP company produced its own frames designed especially for speedway use. Speedway was one area of motorcycle competition where JAP-engined machines were particularly successful. Speedway bikes are devoid of brakes and riders slow down by sliding the machines sideways into the turns while traveling anti-clockwise around the track. JAP-engined machines dominated the sport until Czechoslovakian ESO machines began to be used outside their country of origin in the late 1950s. ESO became part of Jawa in 1966 and the Czechoslovakian dominance of speedway continued until the mid-1970s.

**SPECIFICATIONS (SPEEDWAY)**
**Engine:** Single
**Displacement:** 500cc (30.5cu in)
**Horsepower:** N/A
**Wheelbase:** N/A
**Weight:** 180lb (82kg)
**Top speed:** Depends on sprocket

**Below:** The knobbly tyres used in speedway are similar to those used in off-road competition and are intended to give traction in the loose surface of the cinder track.

JAP Speedway
British Motor Museum
Beaulieu, England

**Left:** Fitted to make the Flying Ace legal for road use were horn and headlamp on the girder forks, front fender number plate, and rear light and number plate on the rear fender.

**Below:** The inlet valves of both cylinders of the V-twin engine were supplied with fuel by a single carburetor which was mounted on a manifold between the cylinder barrels.

## JAWA

**Founded:** 1929
**Factory location:** Prague, Czechoslovakia
**Manufacturing lifespan:** 1929 - to date

Originally an arms producer, in 1929 Jawa obtained a license to build German-designed Wanderer bikes and started production of a 498cc (30.37cu in) overhead-valve, single-cylinder, unit construction motorcycle that also featured a pressed-steel frame and forks. The name Jawa comes from the first two letters of Janecek, the proprietor's surname, and of Wanderer, the model name. During the 1930s the company, with English designer George-William Patchett, produced some successful racing bikes and a 173cc (10.55cu in) two-stroke that became popular.

After World War II Jawa built sophisticated 248 and 346cc (15.10 and 21.12cu in) two-strokes with automatic clutches, telescopic forks and plunger rear suspension. The company was nationalized and has produced two-stroke machines ever since, including successful speedway competition bikes, for normal surface and for ice. There is close co-operation with CZ following a 1949 merger. The 1978 634/6 is typical of Jawa's utility ride-to-work motorcycles built as basic transportation.

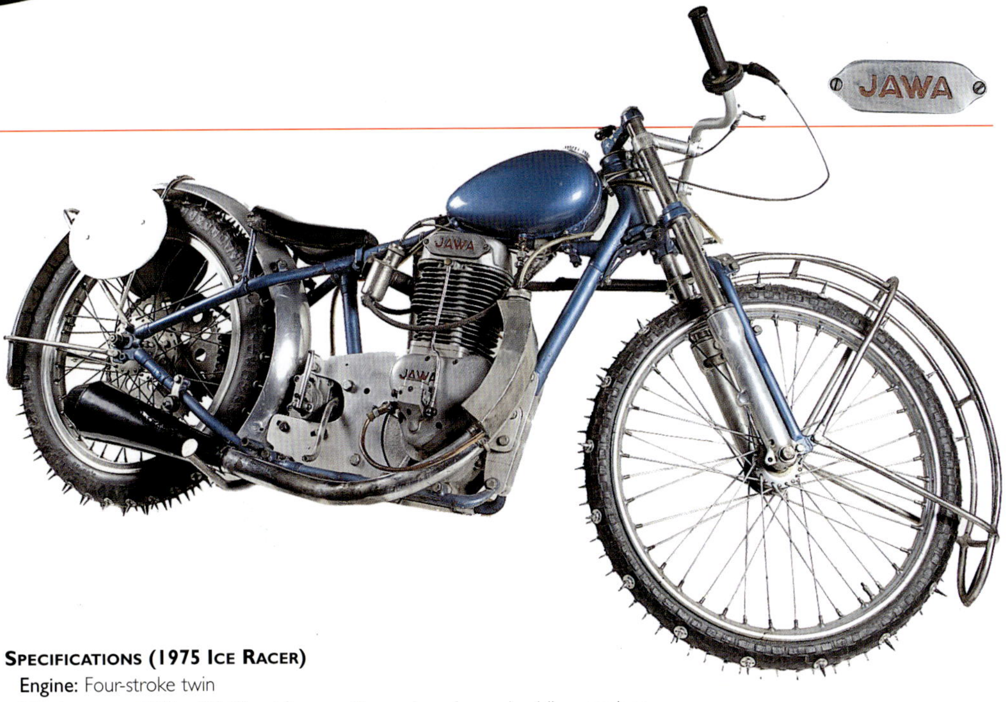


**SPECIFICATIONS (1975 ICE RACER)**
**Engine:** Four-stroke twin
**Displacement:** 500cc (30.50cu in)
**Horsepower:** 60 @ 8000rpm
**Wheelbase:** N/A
**Weight:** 280lb (120kg)
**Top speed:** 112.5mph (180kph)

**Above:** Jawa ice-racing bikes can lean at a fantastic angle and still maintain grip from the awesome spikes. You wouldn't want to have a spill with a few of these around you.

1975 Ice Racer
Deutsches-Zweirad Museum and NSU Museum
Neckarsulm, Germany

# KAWASAKI

**Founded:** 1878
**Factory location:** Akashi, Japan, Kobe, Japan
**Manufacturing lifespan:** 1949 – to date

Kawasaki Heavy Industries is an industrial conglomerate that started out building ships and has also made aircraft, trains, and industrial equipment. Kawasaki's start in motorcycle manufacture came in the years after World War II when it built its first complete machine, the 148cc (.03cu in) four-stroke KE. The company soon began supplying small-capacity two-stroke engines to a subsidiary known as Meihatsu and during the early 1960s set up an assembly plant in Kobe to manufacture small two-strokes, starting in 1961 with an 8bhp 123cc (7.5cu in) model. To expand its range, Kawasaki acquired Meguro, a Japanese manufacturer that was producing a British-styled four-stroke vertical-twin of 624cc (38.06cu in). Kawasaki added this to its range.

Meguro had originally developed a model known as the K1 but as this had reliability problems it was remodeled to become the K2. Down on power, this also had faults and attempts to sell it in the US were unsuccessful. A successor was needed and this led to the W1, a 646cc (39.42cu in) high-performance four-stroke, based on the K2. Sales of this also struggled.

Following a group reorganization in 1969, Kawasaki opted to develop a range of high-performance two-strokes. By this time Kawasaki had improved its exports of small two-strokes to the USA and at the end of the decade introduced the models that guaranteed its reputation as producers of sports bikes: its two-stroke triples. These were available as 250, 500 and 750cc (15.25, 30.50 and 45.75cu in.) models. The 250cc (15.25cu in) version was launched in 1969 and became renowned for its fantastic speed and its poor handling. Even so, the 60bhp 500cc H1 sold particularly well in the USA, as did the 750 H2. Racing versions were developed and the 750cc H2R became the most successful of the Kawasaki road racers to date. Despite their popularity, further development of all these machines was stopped when US emissions regulations made the production of oil-burning two-strokes less viable. From this point Kawasaki moved its main development effort onto four-strokes and phased out the old "strokers," although their successors would remain in production for much of the 1970s.

The S2 350 was introduced in late 1971 and went under different designations, such as the 350-SS and 350 MACH II, depending on which country it was sold in. It sold well in the US, but not in the UK where strict limitations were applied to bikes for learner-riders. Top speed was around 112mph (179kph) but fuel consumption could drop as low as 20mpg (32kpg). ▶

1966 W1
Courtesy of Kawasaki Japan

**SPECIFICATIONS (1966 W1)**
**Engine:** Four-stroke ohv twin
**Displacement:** 624cc (38.08cu in)
**Horsepower:** 49 @ 6500rpm
**Wheelbase:** 55.7in (141.5cm)
**Weight:** 399lb (181kg)
**Top speed:** 120mph (193kph)

**Above:** The W1, developed as a large, high-performance, 4-stroke based on the K2, which itself was based on the K1. These machines were initiated by Meguro prior to it getting together with Kawasaki in 1960.

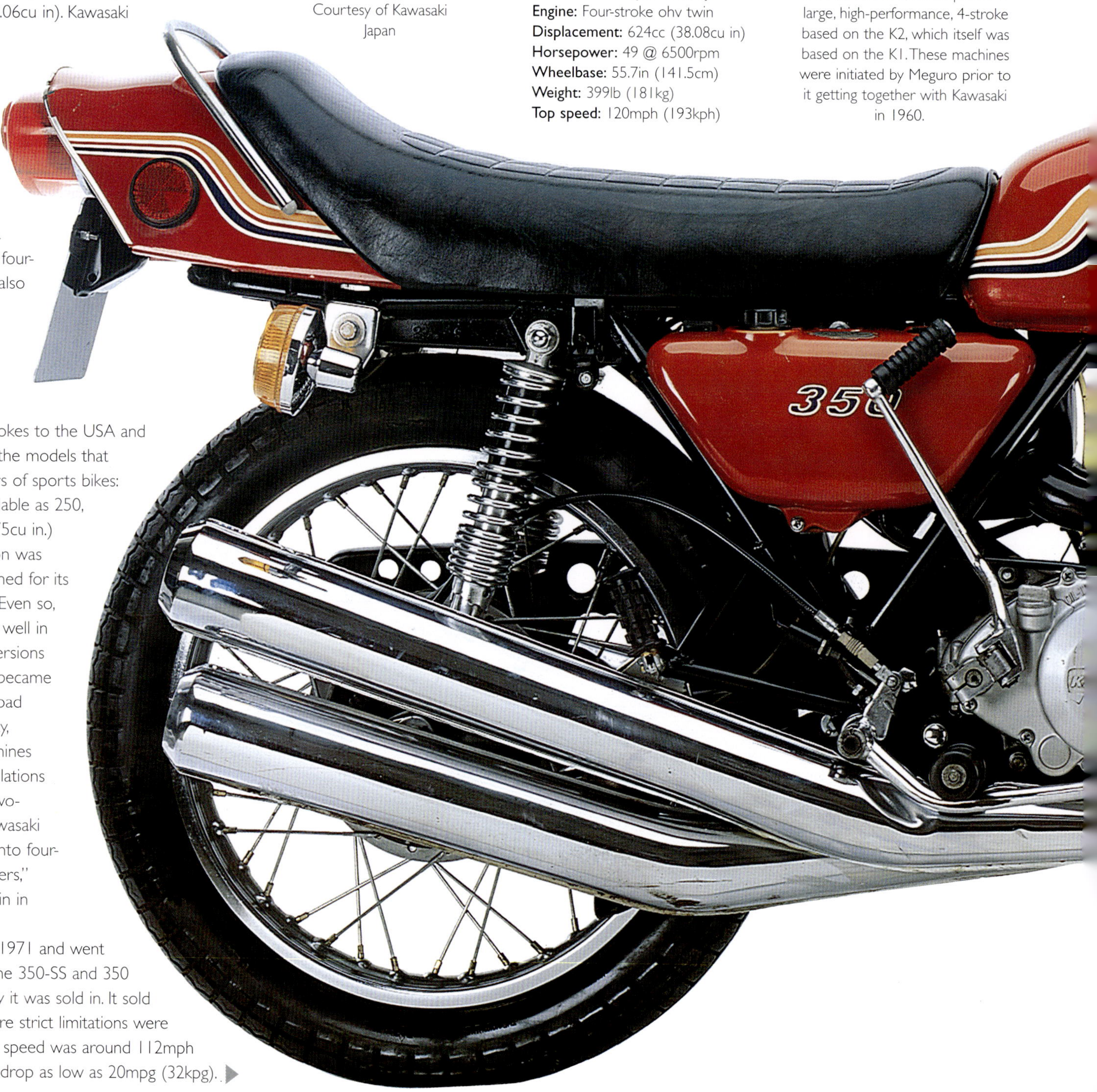

**SPECIFICATIONS (1969 H1 MACH III)**

**Engine:** Two-stroke triple
**Displacement:** 498cc (30.37cu. in.)
**Horsepower:** 60 @ 8000rpm
**Wheelbase:** N/A
**Weight:** N/A
**Top speed:** 120mph (193kph)

1971 S2
Courtesy of Kawasaki
Japan

**Above:** The initial planning phase began in July 1967 and after applying every last ounce of technical know-how Kawasaki produced the first ever MACH III in September 1968. With the sleek, luminous whiteness of its body, dark blue stripes along its tank, shining asymmetrical triple mufflers, the MACH III captured everyone's heart. This was the fastest production bike in the world.

**SPECIFICATIONS (1971 S2)**

**Engine:** Two-stroke triple
**Displacement:** 348cc (21.24cu in)
**Horsepower:** 45
**Wheelbase:** 52.4in (140cm)
**Weight:** 329lb (150kg)
**Top speed:** 111mph (177kph)

1969 H1 MACH III
Courtesy of Kawasaki
Japan

**Left:** Introduced in late 1971, the Kawasaki S2 350 replaced the A7-350 twin. The company claimed 45bhp at 8000rpm for this new model.

The early 1970s saw the birth of a superbike explosion in which all the major manufacturers offered four-stroke inline fours developing more and more horsepower. In 1972, in response to Honda's groundbreaking 750 Four of three years earlier, Kawasaki introduced the 900cc (54.92cu in) Z1. It was sensational at the time, going further than the Honda in terms of technical engineering and ultimate performance. It, too, was fitted with a transversely mounted, inline four-cylinder engine but this featured double overhead camshafts, something which Kawasaki were keen to trumpet on both the crankcases and sidepanels because the Honda was of a single overhead camshaft design.

Kawasaki had begun development of its own single-overhead cam 750 four in 1967 and had a prototype ready in 1968. When the company learned that the similar Honda was soon to appear, it stopped development and decided to launch a 1000cc (60cu in) class machine. The bike's actual capacity was 903cc (55.104cu in) and its main market was always intended to be the USA, since the Japanese market was restricted to a maximum of 750cc at the time.

The Z1's sensational engine ushered in a new era of high-performance four-strokes, although its cycle parts were still fairly conventional, with a tubular steel cradle frame, spindly telescopic forks and a twin-shock rear suspension. Liquid-cooling, electronic ignition and alloy frames and wheels were very much in the future at the time of the Z1's introduction so the machine stood at the crossroads of old and new – new in the modernity of its engine design and traditional in terms of the chassis with distinctly separate tank and seat units, wire spoke wheels and lack of any aerodynamics. The Z1's styling was fresh and managed to make the heavyweight four look much lighter than it was.

The S1 was a stunner of a bike commonly known as the "'White Swan," and available in pearl white with the striping copied from the larger H2-750. The quality and finish of the S1 put all other 250s to shame and the almost 100mph (160khp) top speed was more than adequate. The twin leading front drum brake was somewhat suspect and many a scare was had winding down from a high speed, especially in the wet. The Kawasaki triples were not the best handling bikes.

In 1973 the MC1 midi bike was introduced as an off-road fun bike for kids, although the machine could also be used on normal roads.

1972 S1
Courtesy of Kawasaki Japan

**SPECIFICATIONS (1972 S1)**
**Engine:** Two-stroke triple
**Displacement:** 249cc (15.19cu in)
**Horsepower:** 32
**Wheelbase:** 52.4in (133cm)
**Weight:** 326lb (148kg)
**Top speed:** 105mph (168kph)

**Above:** This 250 was a very quick little bike, able to reach 100mph and producing 32bhp. In the UK it was available to younger, inexperienced riders, who just were not used to this kind of power.

**Right:** Designed as an on/off-road fun bike, the 1973 90cc MC1/XM90A midi-bike featured a high-level exhaust, sump bash-plate, trials universal tires (on a 16-inch front and 14-inch rear wheel).

1973 XM90
Courtesy of Kawasaki Japan

**Specifications (1973 Z1)**

**Engine:** Four-stroke four
**Displacement:** 903cc (55.08cu in)
**Horsepower:** 82 @ 8500rpm
**Wheelbase:** N/A
**Weight:** N/A
**Top speed:** 130mph (209kph)

**Right:** The Z1 was introduced to enthusiastic American riders in September 1972, nicknamed "The New York Steak." The suggested retail price was $1,900 and the initial sales plan called for 1,500 vehicles per month, including European markets.

1973 Z1
Courtesy of Kawasaki Japan

**Right:** The Z1 style was fresh, but cool, without the look of a 900cc heavyweight machine. It had tail-up mufflers, a light tear-drop fuel tank, and a slim, flowing seat.

**Specifications 1973 MC1/XM90A**

**Engine:** Two-stroke single
**Displacement:** 90cc (5.49cu in)
**Horsepower:** 6.6 @ 6500rpm
**Wheelbase:** N/A
**Weight:** N/A
**Top speed:** N/A

**Above:** The XM90 midi bike was equipped with lighting (including indicators) front and rear on both the off-road version and the normal road version.

**Left:** Spoked front and rear wheels, kick start and drum brakes front and rear were standard. There were rear foot pegs and a one-piece double seat to accommodate a small passenger.

# Kawasaki

During the early 1970s, Kawasaki was expanding its range to include several well-regarded off-road machines and a number of smaller four-strokes from lightweight commuter bikes upwards. The smaller models were singles, joined by 247 and 338cc (15.07 and 20.62cu in) vertical twins, and the famous triples were still in production

The middle of the 1970s saw Kawasaki consolidate its position following the enormous success of the original Z1. The Z1 itself was joined by a 750cc (45.75cu in) version aimed mainly at the domestic market. Meanwhile, the company was keen to woo younger customers and commuters with roadsters in every class, including the two-stroke triples, which had become more civilized, at the expense of raw excitement.

Kawasaki's off-road range consisted of every type of machine from a 73cc (4.45cu in) minibike up through motocross and enduro singles. The company's racing program was also taking off with the development of lightweight racing twins that used an unusual tandem arrangement with two crankshafts geared together.

Introduced in 1974, the H2C was the latest in a line of 750cc two-stroke triples, resplendent in flamboyant candyflake paint and chrome. While the 750 was a little more civilized than the fire-breathing 500s, its place as a range leader had been taken by the new Z1 four.

In Britain in 1976, the "green meanie" riders, as they were called, were to become the only force capable of offering any kind of serious sustained opposition to Barry Sheen and his Suzuki. Enter Mick Grant and Barry Ditchburn and of course the 500 racer.

**1974 HW1 Triple**
Courtesy of Kawasaki Japan

**Specifications (1975 500)**
- **Engine:** Two-stroke triple
- **Displacement:** 498cc (30.39cu in)
- **Horsepower:** 59
- **Wheelbase:** 55.5in (142cm)
- **Weight:** 407lb (185kg)
- **Top speed:** 124mph (198kph)

**Right:** This is the Kawasaki racing machine used by Mick Grant: 498cc, water-cooled 3-cylinder two-stroke, capable of 145mph (232kph).

**Specifications (1974 HW1 Triple)**

**Engine:** Two-stroke triple
**Displacement:** 498cc (30.39cu in)
**Horsepower:** 59
**Wheelbase:** 55.5in (142cm)
**Weight:** 407lb (185kg)
**Top speed:** 124mph (198kph)

**Left:** The HW1 of 1975 was a late development of the long-lived air-cooled two-stroke triple, but a much tamer version of the original.

**Specifications (1974 H2C)**

**Engine:** Two-stroke triple
**Displacement:** 748cc (45.62cu in)
**Horsepower:** 71
**Wheelbase:** 57in (145cm)
**Weight:** 452lb (205.5kg)
**Top speed:** 124mph (198kph)

**Right:** High bars, chrome front and rear fenders mixed with the candy-colored tank meant it was difficult to miss this machine.

1974 H2C
Courtesy of Kawasaki
Japan

1975 500
National Motor Museum
Beaulieu, England

**Above:** The Kawasaki racing team were known as the "green meanies." Bikes and racewear were lime green and white. Green having been rejected by other teams, Kawasaki team members and their support crew decided that this would be advantageous to them as they could be picked out easily from the others.

**Above:** Mick Grant won the Senior TT on the Isle of Man in the bike's first appearance there. His average speed was 102.93mph (164.68kph).

**Left:** Stripped of its racing fairing, the triple looks somewhat bare. Weight was kept to an absolute minimum on a racing bike. No frills here.

Into the second half of the 1970s, Kawasaki developed the Z1 concept ever further. The Z1 became the Z900, then the Z1000, with a shaft-drive touring version to follow. The limited-edition sports Z1-R included Kawasaki's first factory-fitted fairing, although this was a small cockpit-type. The Z750 was joined by the even smaller Z650, which rapidly gained itself classic status and, as the decade wore on, 550, 500 and 400 fours would follow. Kawasaki's range of four-stroke twins also grew to span 248, 443 and 745cc (15.13, 27.02 and 45.45cu in) versions.

Since 1976, however, the company had been developing a new range-leader. This was designed to incorporate the latest technology and upstage the competition in the same way that the original Z1 had. The new model was to be a six-cylinder machine with shaft drive, aimed at the sport touring class that was dominated by BMW. The engine displacement was a mighty 1300cc (79cu in) but liquid-cooling helped to keep down the inevitable bulk of an across-the-frame six. The Z1300 was produced from 1978, earning itself an enthusiastic following. It gained electronic fuel injection in 1983 and was finally phased out as late as 1989.

In 1977 Kawasaki introduced a highly economical runaround – the odd but sport-looking KV75. It was a 75cc (4.58cu in) mini bike, with high bars, a comfortable seat, two shock absorbers at the rear, drum brakes and chain drive.

**Specifications (1975 Z900 A4)**

**Engine:** Four-stroke four
**Displacement:** 903cc (55cu in)
**Horsepower:** 82
**Wheelbase:** 58.7in (148cm)
**Weight:** 511lb (232kg)
**Top speed:** 125mph (200kph)

**Left:** The Z900 was a slightly more sophisticated version of the Z650, with smoother lines, a larger capacity engine and two silencers each side.

**1975 Z900 A4**
Courtesy of Kawasaki Japan

**Specifications (1976 Z650B1)**

**Engine:** Four-stroke four
**Displacement:** 652cc (39.77cu in)
**Horsepower:** 64 @ 8500rpm
**Wheelbase:** N/A
**Weight:** N/A
**Top speed:** 121mph (195kph)

**Right:** To the untrained eye the Z650 looks very much like its bigger brother, the Z1000. The handlebars are lower and it has a drum brake on the rear. A kick start is still included even though it has an electric start.

**1976 Z650B1**
Courtesy of Kawasaki Japan

**Specifications (1977 KV75)**
- **Engine:** Two-stroke single
- **Displacement:** 73cc (4.5cu in)
- **Horsepower:** 4.2
- **Wheelbase:** 38in (97cm)
- **Weight:** 121lb (55kg)
- **Top speed:** 40mph (64kph)

**Below:** The KV75 was seen mostly at Formula 1 motor racing circuits. Not that they raced! They were used as personal transportation machines –small, very nifty and easy to use.

1977 KV75
Courtesy of Kawasaki Japan

**Left:** The brakes are disc on the front and drum on the back. The wheels are 19inch (48cm) front and 18inch (46cm) at the rear. This particular machine has crash bars, not normally fitted as a standard option.

**Below:** The neatly fitted air-cooled 652cc engine is tucked up under the 3.7gallon (16.8lit) fuel tank. The clutch is a multi wet plate type and works along with a five speed gearbox.

The Z1300 was introduced in 1979 and it seems strange that it came with no fairing, since it was packed with so many other goodies. High-speed touring against the wind was made difficult because of this.

Early in the 1980s, Kawasaki knew that the Z1 concept was becoming dated and its competitors were developing a host of rival engine formats. The company developed its own new concept, which appeared as the GPZ900R in 1983. The new bike's engine was water-cooled and it had four-valve cylinder heads; the engineers kept the design astonishingly small and it was housed in an all-new diamond frame of which it formed a stressed-member. The suspension was state-of-the art with a high-tech front fork and Uni-Trak rear suspension system. Realizing that engine power was only part of the way to a high top speed, Kawasaki had developed an integral fairing that provided extremely high aerodynamic efficiency. When the bike went global in 1984 (tagged Ninja in many export markets) it was the world's fastest. It soon became the best-seller in its class and won the "Bike of the Year" accolade in many countries. Kawasaki continued to build on the Ninja concept, developing it over many years and expanding it into both larger and smaller capacity divisions.

In 1990, the company's new flagship became the ZZR1100 but Kawasaki offered supersports machines in all classes from 400cc (24.409cu in) up. Late in the decade, for the important custom cruiser sector, Kawasaki offered the 800 and 1500 Drifters, whose inspiration recalled the Indian V-twins of the postwar era. Once again, the running gear was thoroughly up-to-date and the bikes possessed every modern convenience.

1979 Z1300K2
Courtesy of Kawasaki Japan

**SPECIFICATIONS (1979 Z1300K2)**
**Engine:** Four-stroke six
**Displacement:** 1286cc (78.44cu in)
**Horsepower:** 120 @ 8000rpm
**Wheelbase:** N/A
**Weight:** N/A
**Top speed:** 137mph (220kph)

**Above:** Water-cooled, ohc six cylinders, 135mph (216kph), and shaft drive – a specification anybody would love. This is a comfort machine with grunt.

**Right:** From the big-bore, fuel-injected, V-twin engine and SOHC 8-valve heads to the front and rear disc brakes, the Drifter is a showcase of modern precision engineering in its two tone paintwork.

**Specifications (1997 ZZR1100)**
**Engine:** Four-stroke four
**Displacement:** 1052cc (64cu in)
**Horsepower:** N/A
**Wheelbase:** 59in (149cm)
**Weight:** 512.6lb (233kg)
**Top speed:** N/A

**Right:** The ZZR1100 has been revered as the ultimate supersport touring machine, powered by a mighty 145hp engine mounted in a lightweight aluminum perimeter frame.

1997 ZZR1100
Courtesy of Kawasaki
Japan

**Above:** A smart rear end has rear light cluster fixings in chrome, the stop light is teardrop shape and the two indicators are attached to chrome bars each side. The number plate fixing is positioned directly above.

2000 Drifter 1500
P&H Motorcycles
Sussex, England

**Specifications (Drifter 1500)**
**Engine:** Four-stroke twin
**Displacement:** 1470cc (90cu in)
**Horsepower:** N/A
**Wheelbase:** 65in (166cm)
**Weight:** 664.4lb (302kg)
**Top speed:** N/A

**Left:** The deeply valanced fenders, seamless fuel tank, acres of chrome and polished aluminum all combine to create a truly distinctive look for the discerning custom cruiser rider.

The original Eliminator series was launched in the mid-1980s. It was by no means the first ready-made factory custom bike – Kawasaki had been making them since the 1970s. The late-1990s ZL600 used the engine from the GPZ road bikes, featuring a peanut-shaped fuel tank, stubby handlebars, stepped seat and spoked wheels. The bike was long and low to give a drag-race feel.

As the millennium approached, Kawasaki had secured its reputation as one of the great superbike manufacturers but it remained true to its policy of offering state-of-the-art machines in every market sector. It responded to the growing interest in classic and retro machines by launching the new W650, which in styling terms looked back to the W1 of 30 years earlier although its engine used thoroughly modern technology.

The awesome Ninja ZX-12R, with an aluminum monocoque frame, was introduced for 2000. It delivers ultrasports performance, combining the stability and mind-bending engine performance of a hypersport bike with the superlative handling qualities of a supersport machine. Straight-line performance is one thing, handling is another. Until the arrival of the ZX-12R, you had to choose between the two. Most big-bore road burners do a fine job of eating up the miles, until you start flicking them back and forth up a twisty road, when their bulk (and wheelbase) begins to show. And while the repli-racers can strafe an apex like nothing else on wheels, their race-oriented egos can grow tiring when the curves straighten out. The ZX-12R is truly different.

**Below:** The ZX-12R's F1-style aluminum monocoque chassis is stiffer, stronger and narrower than many conventional frames, enhancing stability and control.

**SPECIFICATIONS**
**(1999 ZL600-B1 ELIMINATOR)**

- **Engine:** Four-stroke four
- **Displacement:** 592cc (36cu in)
- **Horsepower:** 61
- **Wheelbase:** 61in (155cm)
- **Weight:** 440lb (200kg)
- **Top speed:** N/A

**Right:** The Eliminator's four-cylinder four-stroke 592cc (36.5cu in) engine is neatly tucked into the long, sleek frame, giving the bike a hot-roddish look. The engine is water cooled, with the radiator in front of the exhaust downpipes, which flow back to a large bore but very quiet silencer.

1999 ZL600-B1 Eliminator
Courtesy of Kawasaki
Japan

ZX-12R
P&H Motorcycles
Sussex, England

**Specifications (2000 ZX-12R)**
**Engine:** Four-stroke four
**Displacement:** 1199cc (73.23cu in)
**Horsepower:** 178
**Wheelbase:** 57in (144cm)
**Weight:** 512.6lb (233kg)
**Top speed:** N/A

**Left:** On the front of the ZX-12R, powerful six-piston brakes are mounted on special fork legs with built-in high-speed wind deflectors.

**Above:** Twin projector beam headlights ensure maximum hi-profile visibility, while the air intake sucks from the still air vortex in front.

## Kokomo

KOKOMO

| | |
|---|---|
| **Founded:** | 1909 |
| **Factory location:** | Kokomo, Indiana, USA |
| **Manufacturing lifespan:** | 1909 - 1911 |

The Kokomo had a relatively short run under the name of its hometown in Indiana, but it would carry on under the Shaw imprint in 1912. The belt-drive single was housed in a loop frame with a leading-link, leaf-spring front fork. The engine was positioned mid-way between the axles, and the centerline of the crankshaft was slightly below the axles' plane. The Kokomo's gear-driven magneto was fitted at the front of the engine. The interesting muffler was positioned well away from the rider's feet. Some thought was clearly given to the design and engineering.

The company was purchased by the Shaw Manufacturing Company of Kansas, which sold the Kokomo in conjunction with their engine attachment kits for bicycles. Shaw later suspended motorcycle production to manufacture farming implements. It is not known how long the Kokomo was built in Kansas, but it's not in Kansas any more.

**Specifications**
**Engine:** IOE single
**Displacement:** 346cc (21.11cu in)
**Horsepower:** 4
**Wheelbase:** 57in (145cm)
**Weight:** 175lb (79kg)
**Top speed:** 45mph (72kph)

1910 Kokomo
Owner – Jim Lattin
Encinitas, California

**Below:** Both the drive belt and rear pulley were stout-looking items. The drive hoop was affixed to the rim by nine mounts.

# KREIDLER

**Founded:** 1950
**Factory location:** Kornwestheim, Germany
**Manufacturing lifespan:** 1950 - 1982

This German company started production in 1950 and concentrated on the manufacture of two-stroke 50cc (3.05cu in) mopeds. The machines were based around a pressed-steel frame but were otherwise conventional. Kreidler machines had some success in racing and broke world records for motorcycles of that category. One particular record-breaking machine was the all-faired-in Zigarre (so-called for obvious reasons), on ("in"?) which Rudolf Kunz set new world records for the flying kilometer and mile at Utah Salt Flats in the USA in 1965. A specially supercharged, streamlined machine, it reached a one way speed of 140.02mph (224kph) and averaged 130.88mph (209.4kph) for the "there and back" kilometer runs, and achieved 130mph (208kph) for the mile record.

In 1979 Kreidler produced the RS Florett, a sports moped with alloy wheels and a front disc brake. The two-stroke engine had a bore and stroke of 40 and 39.7mm enabling it to exceed 50mph (80kph). Its design was conventional although again based around a pressed-steel frame, much of which was hidden by the gas tank, seat and rear fender.

At one time Kreidler was Germany's largest motorcycle manufacturer but the company went into decline to the extent that it went out of business in 1982. Its last production machines were sports and step-through mopeds. Both were two-strokes.

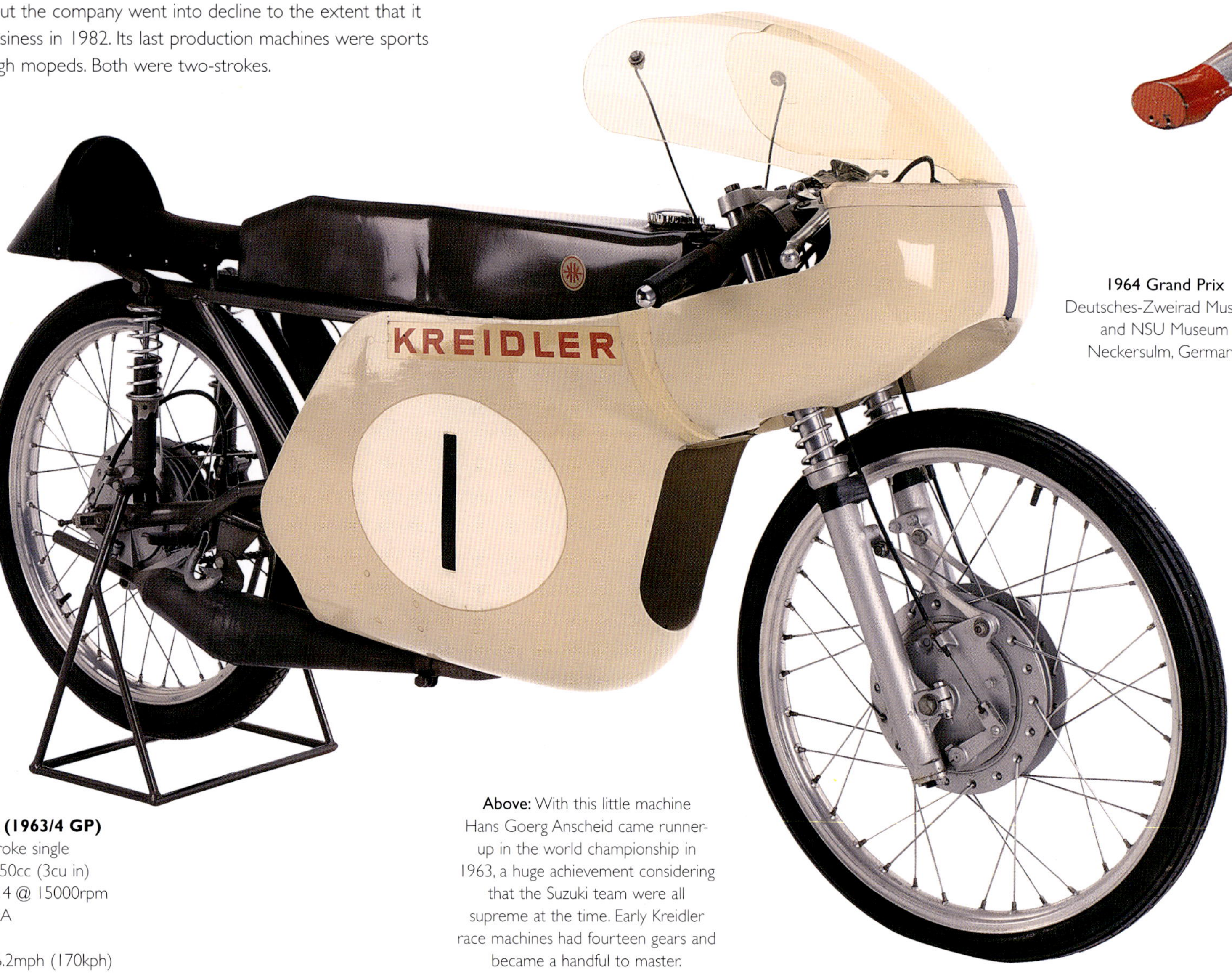


**1964 Grand Prix**
Deutsches-Zweirad Museum and NSU Museum Neckersulm, Germany

**SPECIFICATIONS (1963/4 GP)**
**Engine:** Four-stroke single
**Displacement:** 50cc (3cu in)
**Horsepower:** 14 @ 15000rpm
**Wheelbase:** N/A
**Weight:** N/A
**Top speed:** 106.2mph (170kph)

**Above:** With this little machine Hans Goerg Anscheid came runner-up in the world championship in 1963, a huge achievement considering that the Suzuki team were all supreme at the time. Early Kreidler race machines had fourteen gears and became a handful to master.

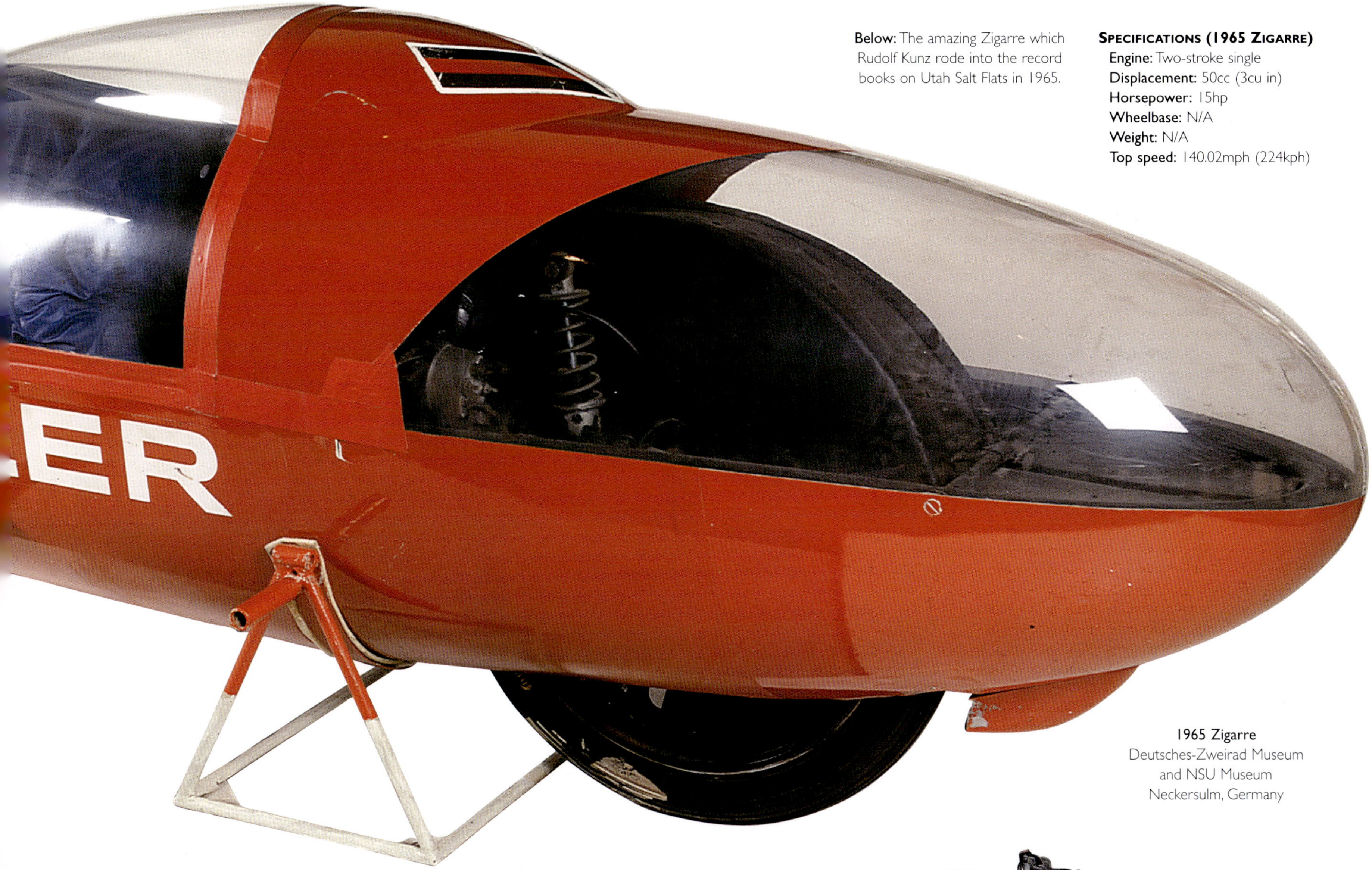


Below: The amazing Zigarre which Rudolf Kunz rode into the record books on Utah Salt Flats in 1965.

**SPECIFICATIONS (1965 ZIGARRE)**
**Engine:** Two-stroke single
**Displacement:** 50cc (3cu in)
**Horsepower:** 15hp
**Wheelbase:** N/A
**Weight:** N/A
**Top speed:** 140.02mph (224kph)

1965 Zigarre
Deutsches-Zweirad Museum
and NSU Museum
Neckersulm, Germany

## KTM

**Founded:** 1953
**Factory location:** Mattighofen, Austria
**Manufacturing lifespan:** 1953 - to date

KTM is an acronym made up of the first letters of the surnames of its two founders and the town in Austria in which the company is based: Kronreif, Trunkenpolz and Mattighofen, respectively. The partnership was started in 1953 and the duo manufactured motorcycles with Rotax, Sachs and Puch engines. The company has made road machines but has tended to specialize in off-road motorcycles like the 1977 250 G56. This off-road bike was one of several models with a similar designation dependent on the capacity of its two-stroke engine. It was a competition-proven product. The company's riders won the 250 World Moto-X Championship in 1974. The other machines of this type produced between the mid-1970s and 1980s include the 400 GS and the 350 GS.

Above: The Mini Adventure is ideal for the four-to-six-year old who wants to start early with off-roading: a well-behaved engine controlled via an automatic gearbox.

**SPECIFICATIONS (2000 MINI ADVENTURE 50)**
**Engine:** Two-stroke single
**Displacement:** 49.8cc (3cu in)
**Horsepower:** 2.5
**Wheelbase:** 36in (89.5cm)
**Weight:** 75lb (39kg)
**Top speed:** N/A

2000 Mini Adventure 50
Courtesy of KTM
Austria

## KTM

In 1991 KTM produced the 600 LC4, the largest of its enduro bikes at that time. It featured a four-stroke engine, although the smaller capacity machines which otherwise bear a close resemblance to it have two-stroke engines, namely the 300 Enduro and the 125 Enduro. Long suspension travel, high-tech forks, swingarms and disc brakes are typical of 1990s off-road competition machines.

By the end of the 1990s KTM had roared to endless championships in enduro and rally competitions. They had developed new engines and frames, such as the new generation of Z engines of 125/200cc (7.62/12.2cu in), and the company opened up new assembly works. Its 2001 motorcycle product range is impressive and, as well as for us grown-ups, caters for children with some nice off-roaders.

**Below:** The LC4-E has both kick and electric start, disc brakes front and rear and a ground clearance of 13.19in (33.5cm). The wheels are 17 inch (43cm) and the fuel tank holds approximately 3.2 gallons (12lit).

**2001 LC4-E Supermoto 640**
Courtesy of KTM
Austria

**Specifications**
**(2001 LC4-E Supermoto 640)**
**Engine:** Four-stroke single
**Displacement:** 625cc (38cu in)
**Horsepower:** N/A
**Wheelbase:** 60in (151cm)
**Weight:** 300lb (137kg)
**Top speed:** N/A

## Lambretta

| | |
|---|---|
| **Founded:** | 1946 |
| **Factory location:** | Milan, Italy |
| **Manufacturing lifespan:** | 1946 – 1972 |

Innocenti, an old-established manufacturing company in Milan, started building scooters in the years immediately following World War II. The result was the Lambretta, designed by a team headed by Pier Luigi Torre. The motorcycle took its name from the River Lambret that flowed past the factory. The early models relied on Innocenti's experience with steel tubing for industrial applications. It was later in their history that Lambrettas had enclosed engines when in 1952 the Model D was launched.

Lambretta felt pressured by the public into fitting bodywork to its rear-engined machines to compete with rival Vespa. To ensure it was heading the right way in the eyes of its customers, it offered the Model D, which was an unenclosed scooter, and the LD, which was a fully enclosed model. The enclosed model sold in such greater numbers that the company stopped making unenclosed machines after 1958.

The company intended these machines as practical utility transport and as such they were completely successful. In fact, demand outstripped supply. They also became style items, offering a futuristic look and symbolizing a new beginning for the world in the postwar era.

In the 1960s, Innocenti switched production capacity of Lambrettas to produce an Italian version of the legendary Mini car after the company had been taken over by British Leyland, the motor manufacturer. It is believed that the last Innocenti Lambretta left the factory in 1972. However, the Grand Prix 200 was still being made in India long after that, by Scooters India Ltd. in Lucknow, India, and Lambrettas were built under license by Serveta in Spain during the 1980s.

**Right:** Compared to earlier Lambrettas the 1957 LD 150 had improved silencing, better engine cooling and of course all the rear end enclosed. These panels could easily be opened via the two levers at the back.

1948 Model B
National Motor Museum
Beaulieu, England

**Specifications (1948 Model B)**
**Engine:** Two-stroke single
**Displacement:** 25cc (7.6cu in)
**Horsepower:** N/A
**Wheelbase:** N/A
**Weight:** N/A
**Top speed:** 40-44mph (65-70kph)

**Left:** One of two 1948 Lambretta Bs that were imported to the UK. These machines were developed after WWII when economical transportation was necessary. Whereas small-capacity motorcycles seemed to come from every corner of Italy, Innocenti decided to produce a scooter.

**Above:** The 148cc (9.03cu in) engine of the Lambretta LD. The scooter could reach a speed of about 50mph (80kph).

**Specifications (1957 LD1 150)**
**Engine:** Two-stroke single
**Displacement:** 148cc (9cu in)
**Horsepower:** 6hp
**Wheelbase:** 50.5in (128cm)
**Weight:** 194lb (88kg)
**Top speed:** 50-55mph (80-88kph)

1957 LD 150
National Motor Museum
Beaulieu, England

**Left:** By the time the LD was produced the little instrument cluster was fitted just under the handlebars. The footbrake is easily seen positioned on the running boards at the front.

# Laverda

**Founded:** 1949
**Factory location:** Breganze, Italy
**Manufacturing lifespan:** 1949 - to date

The family-owned industrial group that was to produce Laverda motorcycles was started in 1873 when Pietro Laverda opened an agricultural machinery factory. Moto Laverda was founded in 1949 and started motorcycle production with a 74cc (4.51cu in) overhead-valve motorcycle engine fitted into a pressed-steel frame. It was one of a series of small displacement motorcycles made by the company, which, in 1968 produced a 650cc (39.65cu in) machine along Honda lines (closely based on Honda's CB72 250cc twin), and when its displacement was increased to 750cc (45.75cu in) exports began.

In 1973 a new Laverda factory was opened and new models soon appeared. Most notable was the double overhead-camshaft triple 981cc (59.84cu in) machine which was followed by a 1200cc (73.20cu in) variant. The 1980 Laverda Jota 1000 utilized the 981cc engine and quickly became renowned as one of the superbikes of the 1970s, the fastest motorcycle available on its introduction. Its powerful engine was paired with a chassis that offered good handling. It had Brembo disc brakes front and rear, Ceriani forks, fully adjustable handlebars, cast alloy wheels and sporting lines. It was available in three forms: the 1200, the Mirage and the 1200TS. The latter model was a luxury version fitted with a fairing and partial engine enclosure, while the Mirage was a faster version capable of 137mph (220kph).

The company also produced smaller capacity motorcycles in both roadgoing and off-road trim. It stopped motorcycle production in 1988 although this was later restarted by another company known as Nuova Moto Laverda, which made the Navarro, a small capacity sports bike based around a liquid-cooled, two-stroke engine. Despite its small displacement, it featured race bike styling and components such as exhausts, disc brakes and alloy wheels. The company continues producing fast, elegant-looking sports bikes today.

**Specifications (1981 Jota 180)**
**Engine:** Four-stroke triple
**Displacement:** 981cc (59.84cu in)
**Horsepower:** 85 @ 7600rpm
**Wheelbase:** N/A
**Weight:** 475lb (215.9kg)
**Top speed:** 140mph (225kph)

**Below:** Earlier Jotas didn't have fairings. The bike could cover a standing-start quarter mile in 12.1 seconds, top 137mph (219kph) and would return about 38mpg.

**Right:** When it came on the market, the Jota was one of the fastest motorbikes on the road. It was brute power and white knuckle riding. The seat sat very high and the engine was very noisy.

**Below:** The Laverda 750 S Formula was the company's flagship when it was introduced. It was based on the twin 750S but had a higher output of 92bhp from the fuel-injected, eight-valve, twin-cylinder engine.

**Specifications (2000 750 S Formula)**
**Engine:** Four-stroke twin
**Displacement:** 747cc (45.50cu in)
**Horsepower:** N/A
**Wheelbase:** 54.13in (138cm)
**Weight:** N/A
**Top speed:** 150mph (240kph)

2000 750 S Formula
Three Cross Motorcycles
Dorset, England

1981 Jota 180
Conquest Restorers
Dorset, England

**Left:** The front suspension was telescopic forks, tire size was 18 inch (45.7cm) front and rear, and the brakes were twin disc at the front and single at the rear.

**Above:** So that you could feel just right when riding this monster, Laverda allowed you to adjust the bars to four different places. The footpegs, the left-sided foot brake (the gearchange was still on the right), the front brake lever and the gearchange could also be positioned for personal comfort. A kit could be supplied if you wanted to have the gearchange on the other more conventional side.

## Maico

**Founded:** 1926
**Factory location:** Pfäffingen, Germany
**Manufacturing lifespan:** 1926 - 1983

Otto and Wilhelm Maisch founded this company in 1926. Its first motorcycle was a 98cc (6cu in) roadgoing machine with an Ilo engine. During World War II the company moved to Pfäffingen where it manufactured parts for the Luftwaffe's warplanes. After the war the company was again producing motorcycles by 1950. The postwar range included 400cc (24.40cu in) twin and touring scooters. Later the company moved towards specializing in off-road motorcycles and its products were widely exported, especially to the USA.

In 1977 Maico produced the MD 125 supersport, a traditionally designed, small-capacity motorcycle aimed at commuters and those wanting basic motorcycling. By dint of its displacement and size, the machine was cheap to buy and cheap to run. Maico motorcycles were successful in both 250 and 500 Motocross World Championships. Production of Maicos stopped in 1983.

1969 MC 350
Deutsches-Zweirad Museum
and NSU Museum
Neckarsulm, Germany

**Specifications (1969 MC 350)**
**Engine:** Two-stroke single
**Displacement:** 352cc (22cu in)
**Horsepower:** 28 @ 6500rpm
**Wheelbase:** N/A
**Weight:** N/A
**Top speed:** N/A

**Above:** Maico has had many successes in both off-road competition, its main strength, and on the race circuits. This is the 1969 Motocross machine.

# Malaguti

**Founded:** 1937
**Factory location:** Bologna, Italy
**Manufacturing lifespan:** 1937 - to date

Malaguti is one of Italy's largest moped manufacturers. It was founded in 1937 by the Malaguti family and is based in Bologna, northern Italy. It started out by making mopeds fitted with 38cc (2.31cu in) Garelli engines, although other makes of small-capacity engines, including Franco Morini and Sachs, have been also used.

Of its recent manufacture, the 1980 Cavalcone was a small-capacity off-road style of bike fitted with a Morini engine and was one of twelve models in that year's range. One of the range was a moped designed for children and another included a model with pushbike pedals to allow its use by younger teenagers in certain countries.

By 1991 Malaguti's product line included a number of models which were all based around the same basic two-stroke engine. The RST 50 was a small sports motorcycle while the MRX 50 was an enduro-type off-roader. The Top 50 was a step-through-style moped. Although all of the engines were of the same basic type, the machines utilized different forms of frame to suit their different styles: a box section cradle for the sports model; a tubular cradle for the MRX 50; and a pressed-steel step-through for the Top 50.

**2000 RCX10**
Powerhouse Motorcycles
Kent, England

**Specifications (2000 RCX10)**
**Engine:** Two-stroke single
**Displacement:** 49.3cc (3cu in)
**Horsepower:** 1.5
**Wheelbase:** 35in (90cm)
**Weight:** 80lb (35kg)
**Top speed:** N/A

**Above:** The Grizzly RCX10 has a saddle height of about 23 inches (58cm), strong nylon fenders, and an integral plastic fuel tank with side flappers. It runs on 10 inch (25.4cm) tires. Starting is via kickstart.

# Mars

**Founded:** 1903
**Factory location:** Nuremberg, Germany
**Manufacturing lifespan:** 1903 - 1957

This German company, which was based in Nuremberg, was founded in 1903 and produced motorcycles with German Fafnir and Swiss Zedel engines until the outbreak of World War I. After this, a Herr Franzenburg designed a machine with a welded and riveted box-section frame. It was fitted with a side-valve, flat-twin Maybach engine of 956cc (58.31cu in) displacement. The bike had other unorthodox features, including a hand-starter. It sold well until the company fell on hard times and apparently closed down during the period of rampant inflation that troubled the German economy during the 1920s. ▶

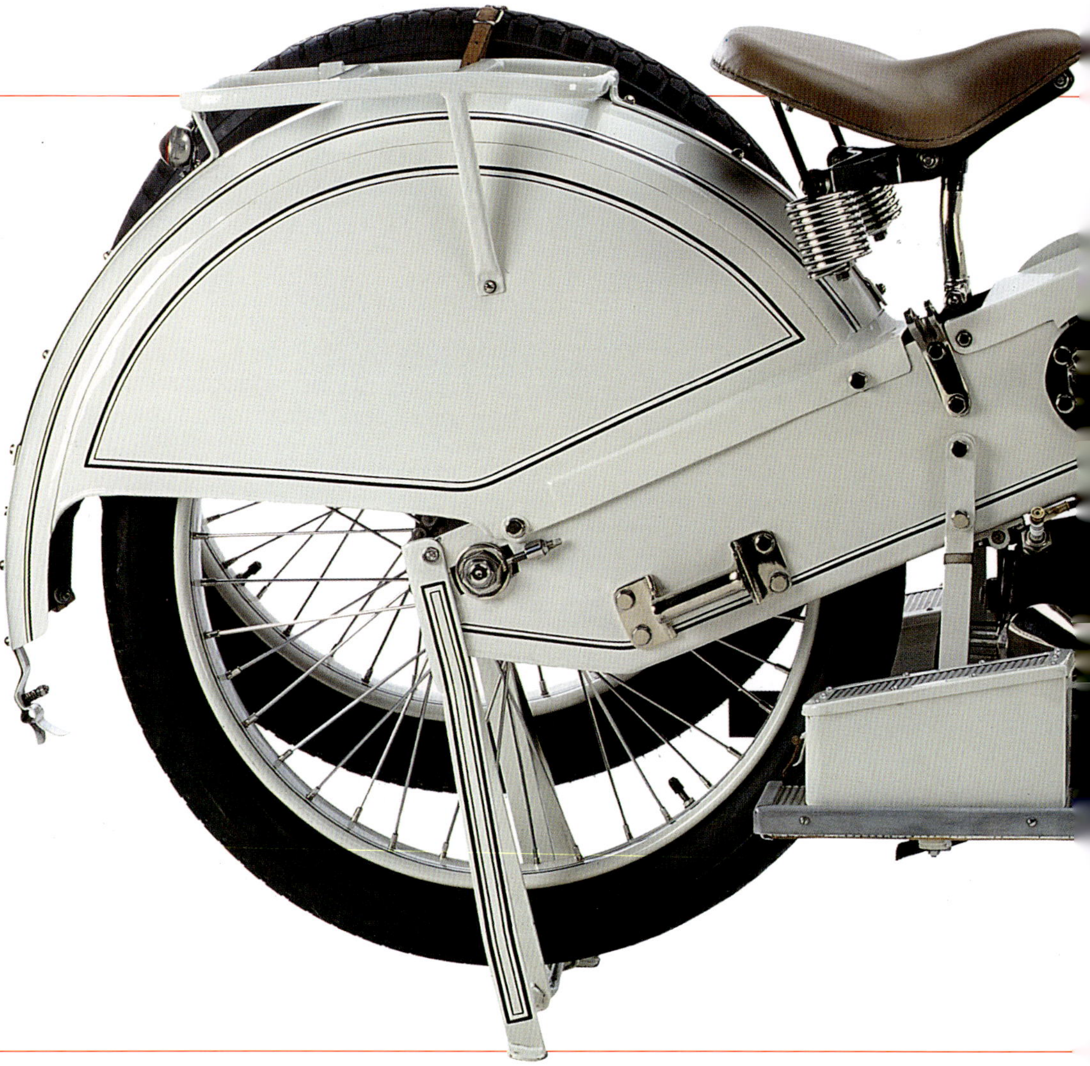

**Right:** The A20 "White Mars," as this machine was known, was designed by the then chief engineer Franzenberg. It was the best known of all the Mars machines and used an engine that was specially made for Mars by Maybach, a car and aircraft engine manufacturer of the time. The engine was a side-valve flat twin and sat in the bike facing front to back, not sideways as with the BMW.

## Malaguti

2000 RCX12
Powerhouse Motorcycles
Kent, England

**Above:** Drum brakes front and rear are used on the RCX12. Final drive is via a chain to the rear wheel.

**Left:** The RCX12 has a saddle height of 29.13 inches (74cm), the 50cc (3.05cu in) engine sits in a tubular steel frame, the front suspension uses telescopic forks, and the rear suspension is a steel swinging fork with adjustable, hydraulic, mono-shock absorber.

**Specifications (2000 RCX12)**
**Engine:** Two-stroke single
**Displacement:** 49.3cc (3cu in)
**Horsepower:** 2
**Wheelbase:** 41in (105cm)
**Weight:** 80lb (100kg)
**Top speed:** N/A

## Mars

1920 A20 "White Mars"
Auto & Technic Museum
Sinsheim, Germany

**Specifications (1920-22 A20)**
**Engine:** Four-stroke flat twin
**Displacement:** 958cc (61cu in)
**Horsepower:** 12 @ 2800rpm
**Wheelbase:** N/A
**Weight:** N/A
**Top speed:** N/A

**Left:** The large-capacity engine of the "White Mars" was somewhat against the trend of the day but the bike, with its square box-section frame, was nonetheless very popular. Note the spare wheel carried on the left side.

# MARS



With new financial backing, two employees of the company, Karl and Johann Muller, restarted production. However, they were unable to use the Mars trade name and from then on, the machines produced were known as MA. These featured a number of proprietary engines. In the years leading up to World War II the firm produced machines using Sachs 147, 174 and 198cc (8.96, 10.61 and 12.07cu in) engines.

Production ended in 1957 when the company closed down for good.

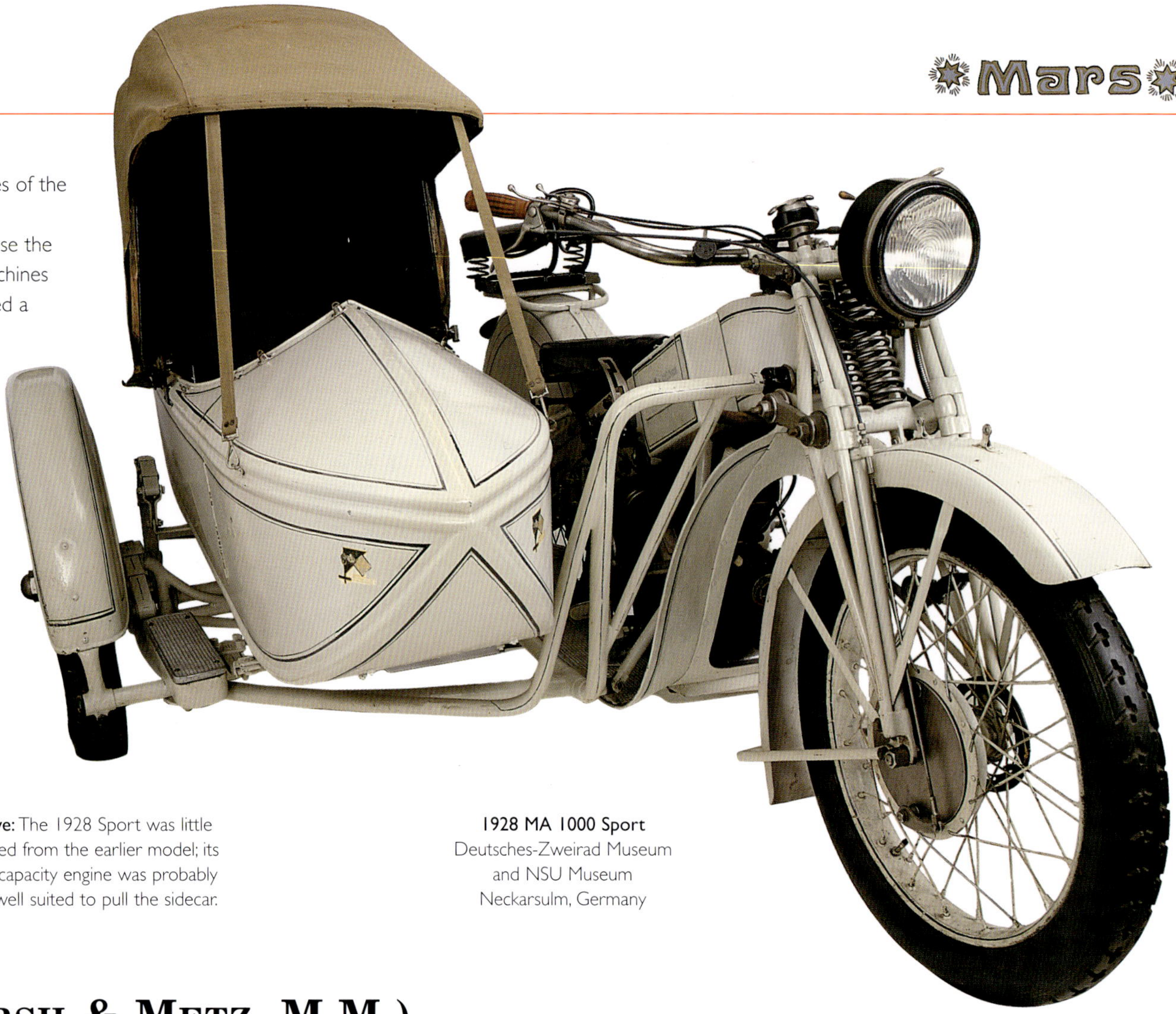

**SPECIFICATIONS (1928 MA 1000 SPORT)**

- **Engine:** Twin-cylinder boxer
- **Displacement:** 948cc (58cu in)
- **Horsepower:** 7.5 @ 3500rpm
- **Wheelbase:** N/A
- **Weight:** N/A
- **Top speed:** N/A

**Above:** The 1928 Sport was little changed from the earlier model; its large-capacity engine was probably very well suited to pull the sidecar.

**1928 MA 1000 Sport**
Deutsches-Zweirad Museum and NSU Museum Neckarsulm, Germany

# MARSH (MARSH & METZ, M.M.)

| | |
|---|---|
| **Founded:** | 1900 |
| **Factory location:** | Brockton. Massachusetts, USA |
| **Manufacturing lifespan:** | 1900 - 1913 |

The Marsh brothers (W.T. and A. R.) built their first motorized bicycle in 1899. The single horsepower single soon grew to 1.75 ponies, and the Marsh Motor Bicycle, one of the first machines built as a motorcycles rather than as adapted bicycles, was shipped to market with a one-year guarantee. The frame joints were heavier drop forgings, and the fork was beefier than most of their counterparts. The engine was fitted at first forward of the seat post, then integrated with the frame in the 1902 production model.

As early as 1902 the Marsh boys had built a short-coupled racer with a loop frame, heavy duty truss fork, lowered handlebar and seat. This was a big-base, six-horsepower single that was good for nearly 60mph (97kph); the rear belt pulley was nearly the same diameter as the wheel.

The Marshes did not continue racing efforts into the professional era that blossomed near the end of the decade. In 1905 they joined forces with Charles Metz, of Orient bicycle and motorcycle fame, to form the American Motor Company. The Marsh & Metz, or M.M., became a stronger force in the market, and developed the first 90-degree V-twin in the USA. In addition to their own models, Marsh & Metz sold engines to the trade, which appeared under other brand names such as Peerless, Arrow and Haverford. The American Motor Company, like so many of its counterparts, would not see a second decade in business and folded in 1913.

**SPECIFICATIONS (SINGLE)**

- **Engine:** IOE single
- **Displacement:** 510cc (31.11cu in)
- **Horsepower:** 3.5
- **Wheelbase:** 53in (135cm)
- **Weight:** 150lb (68kg)
- **Top speed:** 40mph (64kph)

**Right:** A forward mounted muffler helped keep heat from the rider's legs. But it was also out in harm's way. The tubular fuel tank held 1.5 gallons (5.7lit); the aft section carried two quarts (1.9lit) of oil.

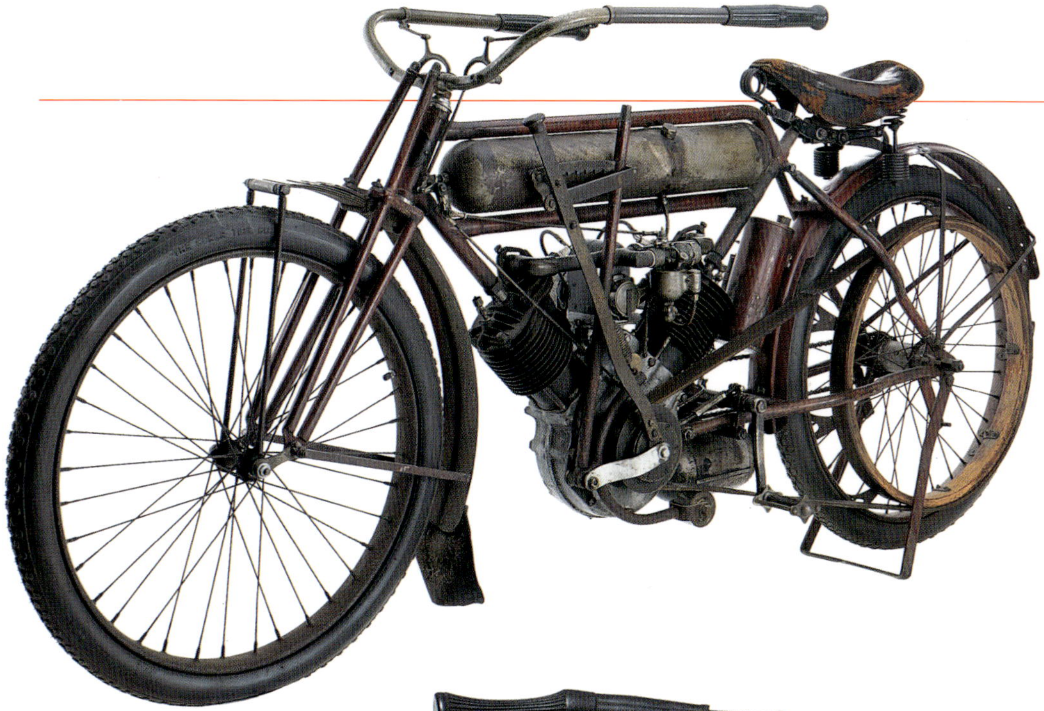

1912 M.M.V-Twin
Owner – Jim Dennie
Palmyra, New York

Left: The 90 degree V-twin first appeared in 1908. The Massachusetts company had offered a 45 degree V-twin for two years previous.

**Specifications (Twin)**
- **Engine:** IOE 90° V-twin
- **Displacement:** 1087cc (66.31cu in)
- **Horsepower:** 10
- **Wheelbase:** 58in (147cm)
- **Weight:** 230lb (104kg)
- **Top speed:** 65mph (105kph)

**Above:** M.M. built a 90 degree twin in 1909. "Forty-five degrees, the angle so generally used in motorcycle construction, is the worst possible angle, being always out of reciprocating balance."

1909 M.M. Roadster
Owner – Jim Lattin
Encinitas, California

## Marvel

**Founded:** 1910
**Factory location:** Hammondsport, New York, USA
**Manufacturing lifespan:** 1910 - 1913

The Marvel was the final iteration of the Curtiss motorcycle. By 1910, Glenn Curtiss was heavily involved in airplane projects, and had entered into partnership with Agustus Herring, who had experimented with heavier-than-air flight before the turn of the century. (For details of Curtiss's career, see *Glenn Curtiss, Pioneer of Flight* by C.R. Roseberry, Syracuse University Press.)

The Marvel was advertised as a four to five horsepower 500cc overhead-valve single with more power than most twins. "By Brake Test it shows over one horsepower more than any previous Motor of equal cylinder capacity. On hills it shows up as good as the large doubles and ahead of the smaller ones. It is not such a wonder as a racer but for ordinary road work it has not an equal in any Motor ever built." The Marvel was "guaranteed to climb a hill steeper than any other."

The Marvel employed the large frame tubes as fuel and oil containers. The engine was lubricated by a splash system, regulated by a cork float in the sight glass. The first engine had its 1⅝-inch (41mm) overhead valves disposed at 30 degrees; both intake and exhaust were controlled by a single pushrod. In 1911 the valves grew to 1¾ inches (44mm) and a more substantial front fork was fitted.

The Marvel disappeared under the weight of a grim legal battle between Agustus Herring and Glenn Curtiss. The matter was settled in 1923, in favor of Curtiss, but the decision was overturned in 1928.

**Below:** One element that distinguished the Marvel was its single pushrod operating both the intake and exhaust valves. The bike represented the end of the Curtiss motorcycle genealogy.

**1911 Marvel Single**
Owner – Wes Allen
Yuba City, California

**Specifications (1911 Single)**
**Engine:** Ohv single
**Displacement:** 500cc
**Horsepower:** 4-5
**Wheelbase:** 57in (145cm)
**Weight:** 155lb (70kg)
**Top speed:** 55mph (89kph)

## Matchless

**Founded:** 1899
**Factory location:** Plumstead, London, England
**Manufacturing lifespan:** 1899 - 1969

The Matchless company was founded by the Collier brothers, Harry and Charlie, and initially used proprietary engines from the likes of JAP and De Dion. The brothers had early Isle of Man TT successes on Matchless machines. By the 1930s Matchless produced a range of singles of varying capacities and a V-twin intended for sidecar duties, and experimented with a couple of vee-configuration engines: a V-twin and a V-four that was essentially two V-twins joined together.

The company acquired AJS in 1931 and by 1935 had introduced a model style common to both marques, the G3 Clubman. In 1937 the company acquired Sunbeam and became AMC – Associated Motor Cycles – Ltd. Postwar, Matchless and AJS models were identical although both brands were marketed separately. AMC later took over Francis-Barnett, James, Norton and the U.S. manufacturer Indian, but later joined a larger group under which the Matchless marque gradually faded into history.

The company had produced a range of singles and twins used extensively for competitive motorcycling, the singles in off-road events, and both singles and twins for road- and circuit-racing. The G9 was introduced in 1949. It was a typically British parallel twin, although it had three main bearings. Camshafts ran fore and aft and both dynamo and magneto were gear-driven. Its cycle parts were common to the sprung single. It was manufactured until 1959. ▶

**Specifications (1941 G3L)**
**Engine:** Four-stroke ohv single
**Displacement:** 347cc (21.2cu in)
**Horsepower:** 16 @ 5600rpm
**Wheelbase:** 54in (137.2cm)
**Weight:** 328lb (148kg)
**Top speed:** 65mph (105kph)

**Right:** Army dispatch riders were expected to be able to carry out numerous checks and repairs to their machines and to this end a selection of tools was carried in the asymmetric tool box fitted to the frame behind the gearbox and oil tank.

**Specifications (1953 G9)**

**Engine:** Four-stroke twin
**Displacement:** 498cc (30.4cu in)
**Horsepower:** 29 @ 6800rpm
**Wheelbase:** 55.25in (140.3cm)
**Weight:** 394lb (179kg)
**Top speed:** 84mph (135kph)

1953 G9
Tony East of A.R.E. Ltd
England

**Right:** Matchless had pioneered swinging arm rear suspension during the war years on the G3L and so used it on their postwar models.

**Left:** Although most of the motorcycles used by the British Army were military versions of civilian bikes, a number of specifically military fittings were installed, including the blackout cover over the headlamp and the military panniers and rack on the rear fender.

**Above:** The telescopic forks were called teledraulic by the G3L's maker, AMC. All other machines used by British forces were fitted with conventional sprung-girder forks.

1941 G3L
British Motorcycle Museum
Birmingham, England

# Matchless

The CSR suffix first appeared in 1958 on a slightly tuned version of the Matchless 593cc (36.14cu in) twin that had been introduced in 1956 by AMC as the G11. The new models for 1958 were the G11CS and G11CSR. The former was a street scrambler with siamesed exhaust pipes, wide section tires, a small fuel tank, alloy fenders and removable lights. The G11CSR was a sports-styled machine based around the CS engine, frame, exhaust and fuel tank but fitted with a competition dual seat and removable lights. The real racer was the new 496cc (30.27cu in) G50, the prototype of which competed in the 1958 Isle of Man TT.

Production continued with much of the Matchless range unaltered for 1959, although the twins were offered with larger displacement, 646cc (39.60cu in), as the G12, G12dl, G12CS and G12CSR. These were the standard, de luxe, CS and CSR models. The differences were minor; the standard G12 had alternator and coil ignition while the others retained their magneto. The standard model had a slightly different finish to the de luxe models, while the CS and CSR were as they had been in 1958.

Although Matchless and AJS production bikes were alike, the racers had many differences. The Matchless CSR twin was called Monarch, and Apache for export to the USA. The 650 was the basis of the bike that won the 500-mile race at Thruxton, England, in 1960. One of the last improvements to the CSR was a duplex cradle frame from 1961. The CSR tag was used on a smaller-capacity range of single-cylinder 250cc (15.26cu in) machines from 1962.

But the company's finances were in freefall and it was merged into the Norton-Villiers group.

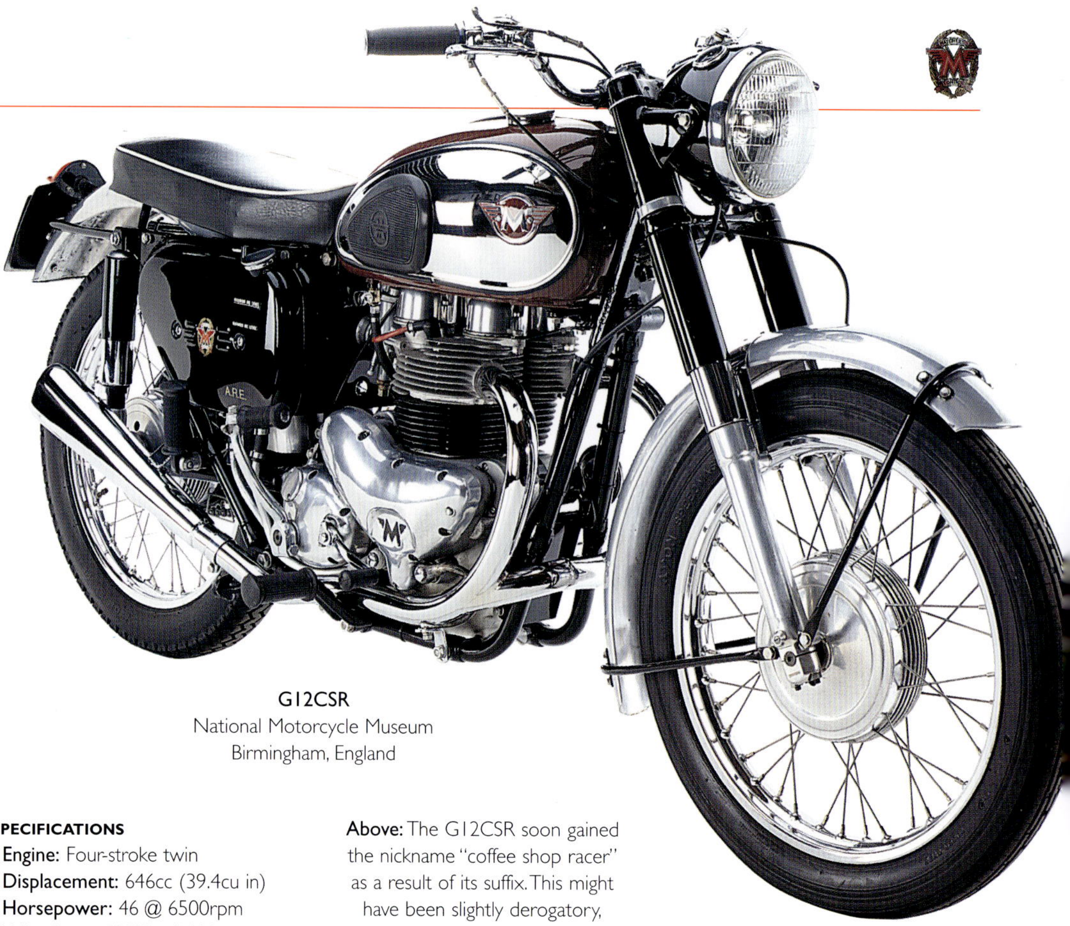

G12CSR
National Motorcycle Museum
Birmingham, England

**Specifications**
- **Engine:** Four-stroke twin
- **Displacement:** 646cc (39.4cu in)
- **Horsepower:** 46 @ 6500rpm
- **Wheelbase:** 55.25in (1403mm)
- **Weight:** 430lb (195kg)
- **Top speed:** 108mph (174kph)

**Above:** The G12CSR soon gained the nickname "coffee shop racer" as a result of its suffix. This might have been slightly derogatory, suggestive of sporting pretensions rather than actual prowess.

# Megola

**Founded:** 1921
**Factory location:** Germany
**Manufacturing lifespan:** 1921 - 1925

The name Megola was an acronym derived from the names of the three founders, Meixner, Cockerell and Landgraf, although certain latitude was taken with Cockerell's name. The short-lived German company produced around 2000 motorcycles in total, including what are generally considered to have been some of the most unorthodox motorcycles ever, with five-cylinder radial engines built into the front wheel. They were clearly based on radial aeroplane engines but did not feature components such as a clutch or a gearbox. Fritz Cockerell designed the air-cooled, side-valve engine, which was started by the rider kicking the front wheel round while the machine was on its main stand. The unusual engine application also meant that the changing of gear ratios could be accomplished only through the use of different diameter wheels. This was done for racing purposes because, although of unorthodox appearance, the Megola radial had a low center of gravity and so handled well. Front suspension was by means of semi-elliptic springs in a substantial cradle, while some models had semi-elliptic rear springs too.

There were other clever features of the design. It was possible to dismantle the engine cylinders without removing the wheel spokes. Also, the box section frame contained the main fuel tank although fuel had to be decanted into a smaller fork-mounted tank at intervals. Sports Megolas featured saddles while the roadgoing models had bucket seats.

1923-1925 Model
Deutsches-Zweirad Museum
and NSU Museum
Neckarsulm, Germany

**Specifications (1922 Radial)**
- **Engine:** Four-stroke five-cylinder
- **Displacement:** 637.2cc (38.86cu in)
- **Horsepower:** 14p @ 3600rpm
- **Wheelbase:** N/A
- **Weight:** N/A
- **Top speed:** 52mph (85kph)

**Above:** Megolas were among the most unusual motorcycles ever built, with five-cylinder, aircraft-style, radial engines built into the front wheel.

**Above:** The engine was designed by Fritz Cockerell and the bike was started by the rider kicking the front wheel round, while the wheel was on the stand. The engine cyclinders could be dismantled without removing the wheel spokes.

**Specifications (1923-1925 Model)**
- **Engine:** Four-stroke five-cylinder
- **Displacement:** 637.2cc (38.86cu in)
- **Horsepower:** 14p @ 3600rpm
- **Wheelbase:** N/A
- **Weight:** N/A
- **Top speed:** 52mph (85kph)

1921 Strassenhausfue
Deutsches-Zweirad Museum
and NSU Museum
Neckarsulm, Germany

**Left:** Megola racing mototcycles had drop-style bars and a saddle. In 1924 one of these machines clinched the German championship.

# MERKEL

**Founded:** 1902
**Factory location:** Milwaukee, Wisconsin; Pottstown, Pennsylvania; Middletown, Ohio, USA
**Manufacturing lifespan:** 1902 - 1915

The motorcycles built by Joseph Merkel set the high performance standards in the century's first decade. The engines and suspension invited high-speed exercises, and Indian soon followed suit with race-bred improvements. With the addition of Excelsior and Harley-Davidson, the American motorcycle racing scene attracted large crowds and sizable profits for promoters and riders.

A few of the 500cc (30.50cu in) belt-drive singles were built as racers at the original Merkel plant in Milwaukee. When the company was purchased by the Light Manufacturing and Foundry Company and moved to Pennsylvania in 1909, one of the bikes came to young test rider Maldwyn Jones. An inventive mechanic and racer, Jones set up the bike and defeated Cannonball Baker in a 10-mile race in Ohio. The following year he turned pro and won three of his first four races on a second-generation Pottstown leftover, which now bore the Flying Merkel logo on the tank. Jones went on to become a champion racer, and his abilities helped Merkel achieve lasting status among motorcycle performance enthusiasts. The Merkel front fork was the instrument of choice on racing bikes of other builders, and the single-shock rear suspension was an advanced concept.

When ownership shifted to the Miami Cycle and Manufacturing Company of Ohio in 1911, the factory racing team was abandoned, though Jones and several other riders were provided machines.

By 1913 the Ohio Flying Merkels had mechanical intake valves, chain drive was an option and the oil tank and seat post were integrated. The engine was steadily refined and in 1915, the final model year, it received a kickstarter. A two-speed planetary transmission was optional.

Merkel was the least conservative of the pioneer motorcycle companies. It tried more engineering innovations than most, took more chances and gave Indian and Harley fits on the racetracks. But a contracting market left them, as so many others, in the historical heyday of motorcycling.

**Above:** During the transition period in 1909, the Light Manufacturing & Foundry Company still offered machines bearing the Light brand. Singles and twins were Thor engines.

**1909 Light Single**
Owner – Herb Singe
Hillside, New Jersey

**SPECIFICATIONS (1908-09 SINGLE)**
**Engine:** IOE single
**Displacement:** 500cc (30.50cu in)
**Horsepower:** 3
**Wheelbase:** 54in (137cm)
**Weight:** 150lb (68kg)
**Top speed:** 40mph (64kph)

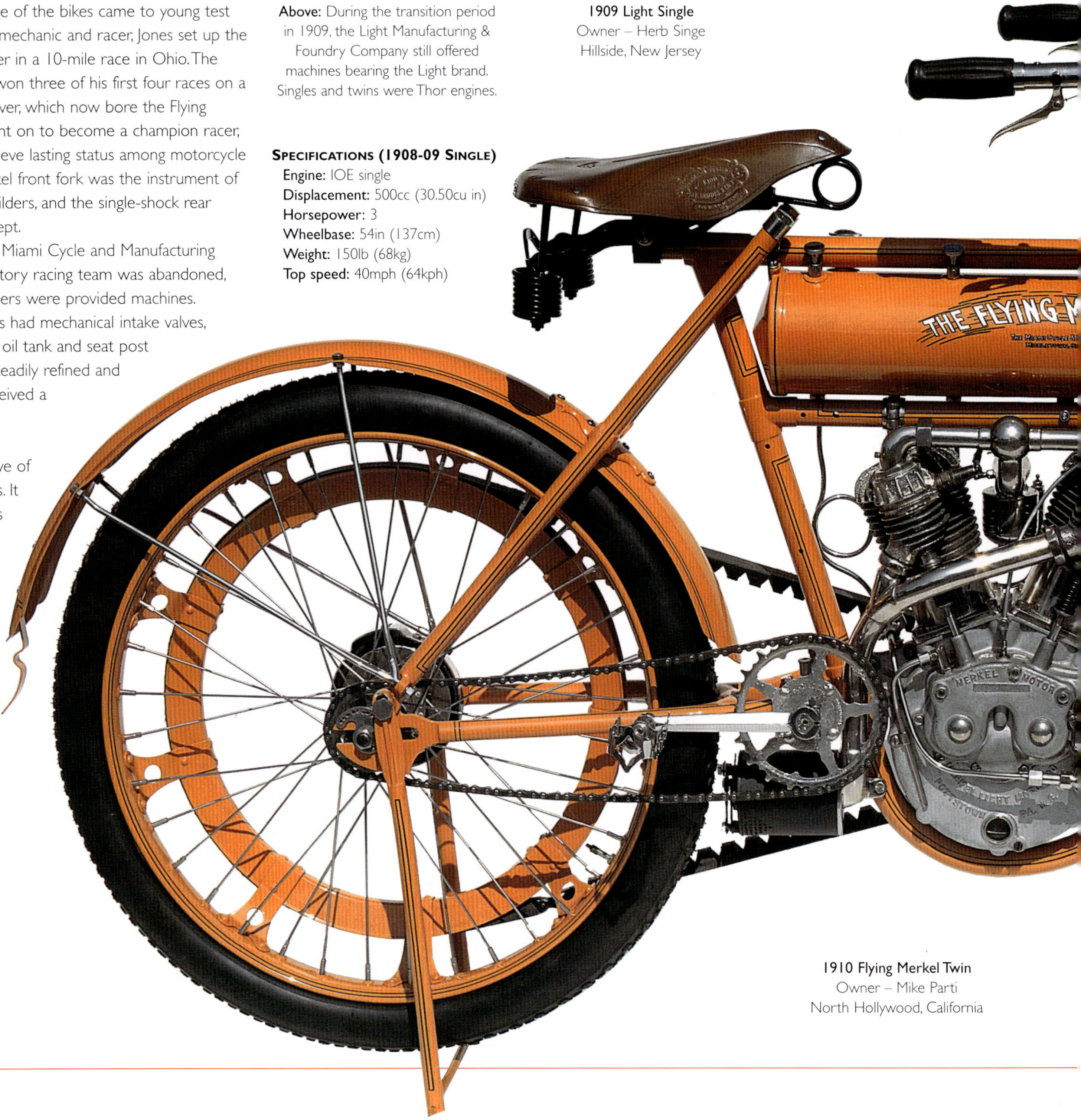

**Right:** The Flying Merkel was flashy, fast and it flew down the road. Most of the credit for Merkel's racing success goes to the innovative Maldwyn Jones, who joined the company as a mechanic in 1910. By 1910 Merkel production had been merged with the Light brand in Pottstown, Pennsylvania. This was the first year that the name Flying Merkel was used.

**1910 Flying Merkel Twin**
Owner – Mike Parti
North Hollywood, California

**1911 Flying Merkel**
Owner – Charles Petty
Jasper, Indiana

**Specifications (1915 V-Twin)**
**Engine:** IOE V- twin
**Displacement:** 1000cc (61.02cu in)
**Horsepower:** 7 - 9
**Wheelbase:** 54in (137cm)
**Weight:** 280lb (127kg)
**Top speed:** 60mph (97kph)

**Above:** The high-performance Flying Merkel was a pioneer in the use of swingarm rear suspension. Springs were housed inside the upper rear fork tubes.

**Below:** The Flying Merkel V-twin was offered in both (V) 885cc (53.99cu in) and (VS) 1000cc (61cu in) versions. The big-bore engine was rated at seven horsepower.

# Militaire

Founded: 1911
Factory location: Cleveland, Ohio; Buffalo, New York, USA
Manufacturing lifespan: 1911 - 1922

The Militaire Autocycle Company's history was plagued by financial and technical problems that dogged the owner, N. R. Sinclair, through various new-start locations (and at one time a diferent name, Militor). The company's first motorcycle departed sharply from conventional forms in design and construction, and was apparently conceived as a two-wheeled car, powered by a single-cylinder. It had hubcenter steering, a steering wheel and retractable outrigger wheels at the rear. By 1914 the single had been replaced by a four-cylinder engine, and the steering wheel was supplanted by handlebars. The automotive-style frame and rear idler wheels remained. The 1065cc (64.97cu in) engine delivered better than 11hp through a three-speed floorshift transmission and shaft drive. The wheelbase was 65 inches (165cm). The wooden artillery wheels carried 28-inch (71.1cm) Goodyears.

Militaire was surely intended as a military device from the beginning. But it was too long and heavy for a motorcycle and too unstable for a car. The U.S. Army did buy a few examples for use in France in 1918, but the machines were immobilized by mud.

As a hybrid, the Militaire was subject to numerous mechanical faults given the complex systems and overall length. Many of the motorcycles were returned for repairs, and the company would eventually fold under the burdens of warranty work and poor development.

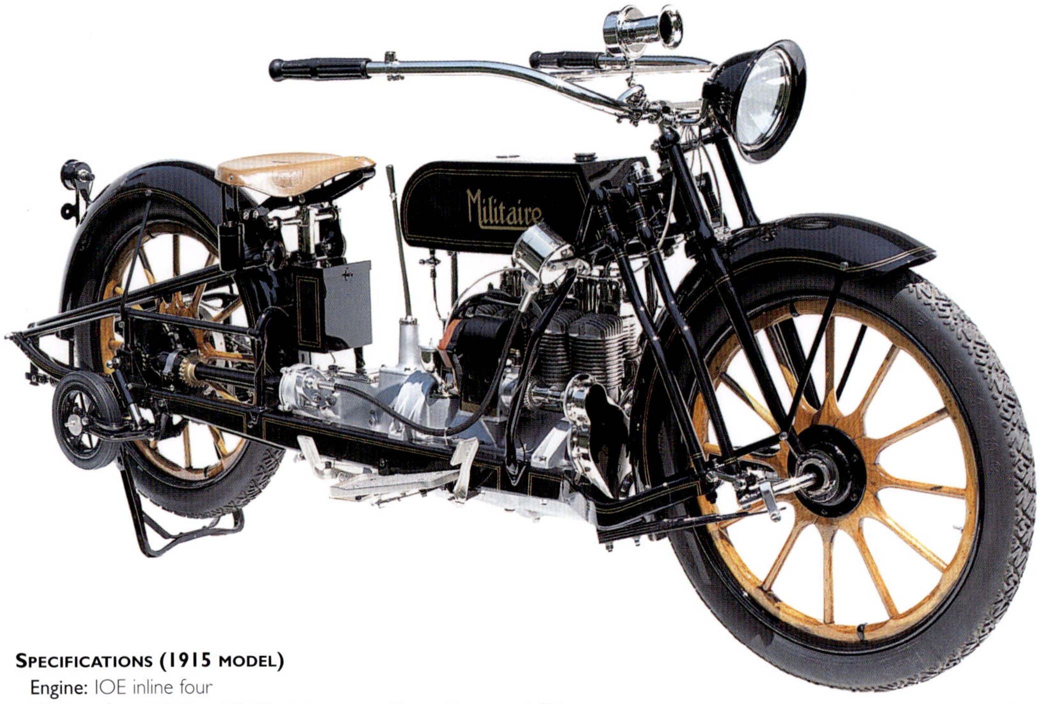


**Specifications (1915 model)**
Engine: IOE inline four
Displacement: 1145cc (69.87cu in)
Horsepower: 11 - 14
Wheelbase: 65in (165cm)
Weight: 400lb (181kg)
Top speed: 60mph (97kph)

**Above:** The gearshift lever rose directly from the three-speed transmission. As a motorcycle/automobile, the Militaire was better than neither.

1915 Militaire
Owner – Jim Dennie
Palmyra, New York

# Minneapolis

Founded: 1908
Factory location: Minneapolis, Minnesota, USA
Manufacturing lifespan: 1908 - 1914

The Minneapolis Motorcycle Company built both Minneapolis and Michaelson motorcycles. The early Minneapolis used the proprietary Aurora single engines, and were all but identical to the Thor model. In 1911 the Minneapolis had its own side-valve single and a leading link spring fork. The engine featured an internal two-speed planetary transmission.

The Mineapolis Big 5 Auto-Cycle was rated at 11.5 horsepower, with performance that was "reliable quick efficient." And the Unit Power Plant was a significant selling point. Unlike most American singles, the Minneapolis displaced its valves and exhaust pipe on the left side of the engine.

The late-series Minneapolis featured a swingarm rear suspension with an interesting monoshock system.

Toward the end of their production, the Minneapolis utilized the De Luxe engine built by the Spacke Machine Company of Indianapolis, Indiana.

**Below:** The Minneapolis employed and interesting leading-link fork. Early engines had the carburetor in front and exhaust exiting the rear of the cyclinder.

**Specifications (1910 Single)**
Engine: IOE single
Displacement: 591cc (36.07cu in)
Horsepower: 5 - 6
Wheelbase: 57in (145cm)
Weight: 190lb (86kg)
Top speed: 55mph (89kph)

1910 Minneapolis
Owner – Jim Dennie
Palmyra, New York

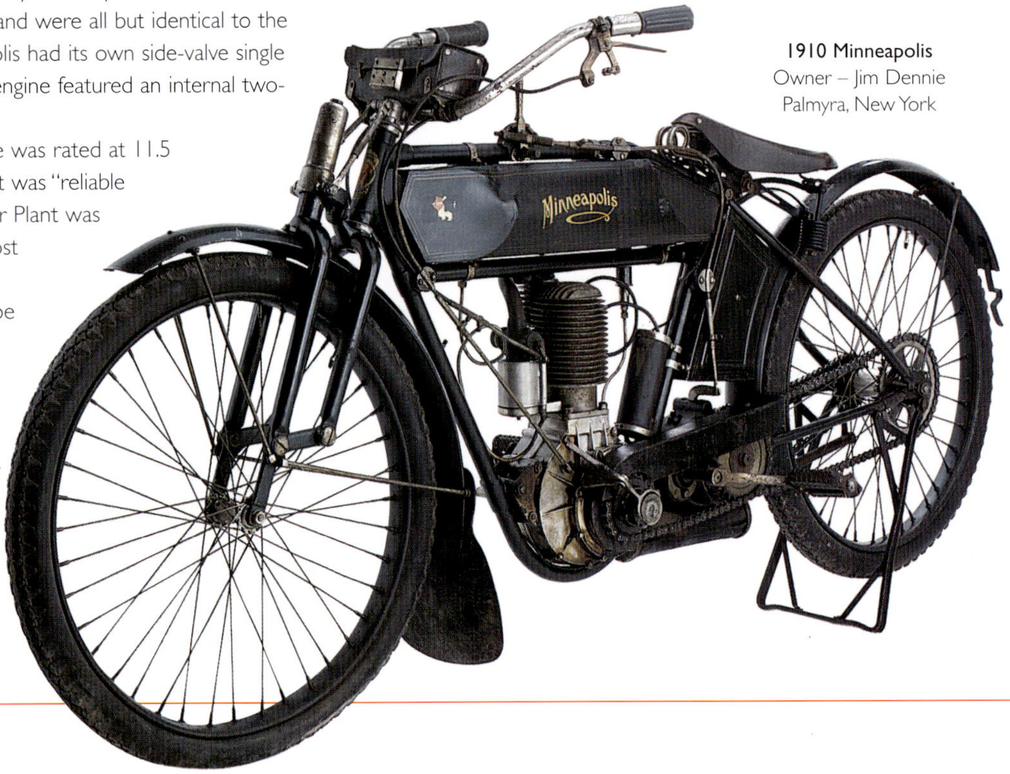

**Right:** Motorcycles figured strongly as service vehicles in the early days in the USA. Most were used for light deliveries, postal or police work.

**1911 Minneapolis Tri-car**
Owner – Otis Chandler
Ojai, California

**Below:** The Big 5 was one of the first side-valve engines in use, and was unusual in having the valve gear arranged on the left side. It was rated by the manufacturer at 11.5hp.

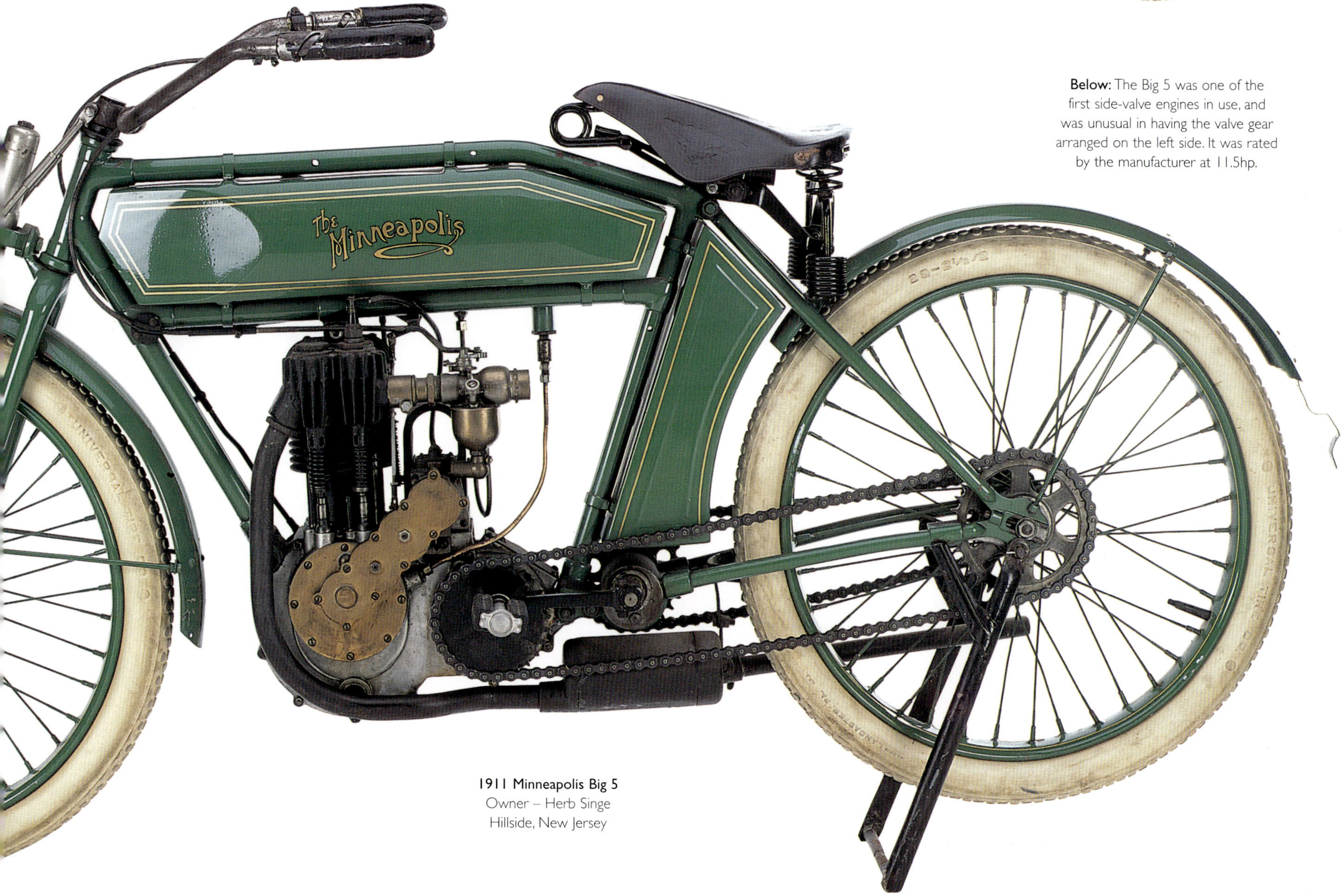


**1911 Minneapolis Big 5**
Owner – Herb Singe
Hillside, New Jersey

# Mondial

**Founded:** 1929
**Factory location:** Milan; Bologna, Italy
**Manufacturing lifespan:** 1929-1979

FB Mondial was founded in Milan in 1929 by Count Giuseppe Boselli and his three older brothers. The FB part of the company name stood for Fratelli Boselli, meaning Boselli Brothers.

They began by selling other makes but, just before World War II, Mondial began making its own three-wheel trucks, a type of vehicle that was very popular in Italy, particularly in farming communities. Components for these were made in the company's workshops in Bologna and they were powered by small two- and four-stroke engines.

Postwar, Mondial went into motorcycle racing, with a very advanced double-overhead-cam 123.5cc (7.536cu in) engine that won the first ever 125cc World Championship. The company won many more titles in the 125, 175 and 250cc classes with famous riders including Hailwood, Provini and many others. In 1957, it won both the 125 and 250cc championships.

Mondial also built a range of production roadsters from 49cc (2.99cu in) to 248cc (15.133cu in) which were very successful. However, by the end of the 1960s, the company was experiencing financial problems. It continued building small off-road bikes until 1979 when it finally closed.

Ex-Mondial racer Walter Villa and his brother Francesco attempted to relaunch Mondial in the late 1980s with a two-stroke production racer, but very few of these expensive bikes were ever made.

**Specifications (1956 Model)**
**Engine:** Four-stroke single
**Displacement:** 175cc (10.60cu in)
**Horsepower:** 13.5 @ 6700rpm
**Wheelbase:** N/A
**Weight:** 260lb (120kg)
**Top speed:** 68.5mph (110kph)

**Right:** The marque FB Mondial is well known for its racing bikes, Carlo Ubbiali, Mike Hailwood and Tarquinio Provini being some of the riders the company employed. This production 1956 model has a single-cylinder, four-stroke engine of 175cc (10.60cu in).

# Montesa

**Founded:** 1941
**Factory location:** Barcelona, Spain
**Manufacturing lifespan:** 1941 – to date

Montesa was the first motorcycle manufacturer founded in Spain. Its origins were in a workshop founded by Pedro Permanyer-Puigjaner in 1941. A new modern plant was opened in 1962 where mass-production of engines, outboard motors and motorcycles took place.

Montesa specialize in off-road motorcycles for trials and motocross and their products have an enviable international reputation. The 1977 Montesa Cota is a competent trials bike for off-road use and features a short wheelbase, high ground clearance and an engine that delivers its torque at low revs. The successful Cota series of trials motorcycles was put into production, upgraded as trial bike technology progressed.

The 1991 model moved from a swinging arm with twin shock absorbers and rear suspension assembly to a monoshock. Similarly, drum brakes were succeeded by discs, front and rear, although 21in (53cm) front and 18in (45cm) rear wheels and other features remained the same. Today, the Cota name is still a significant force and continues to win prizes.

Cota 315R/2001
Courtesy of Montesa
Barcelona, Spain

**Specifications (1999 Cota)**
**Engine:** Two-stroke single
**Displacement:** 249cc (15.19cu in)
**Horsepower:** 16 @ 5000rpm
**Wheelbase:** N/A
**Weight:** 150lb (73kg)
**Top speed:** N/A

**Above:** The Montesa Cota 315R/2001 is an improved and uprated version of the Dougie Lampkin 2000 championship bike. It has new Dell Orto carburetors, increased-size rear sprocket and frame geometry.

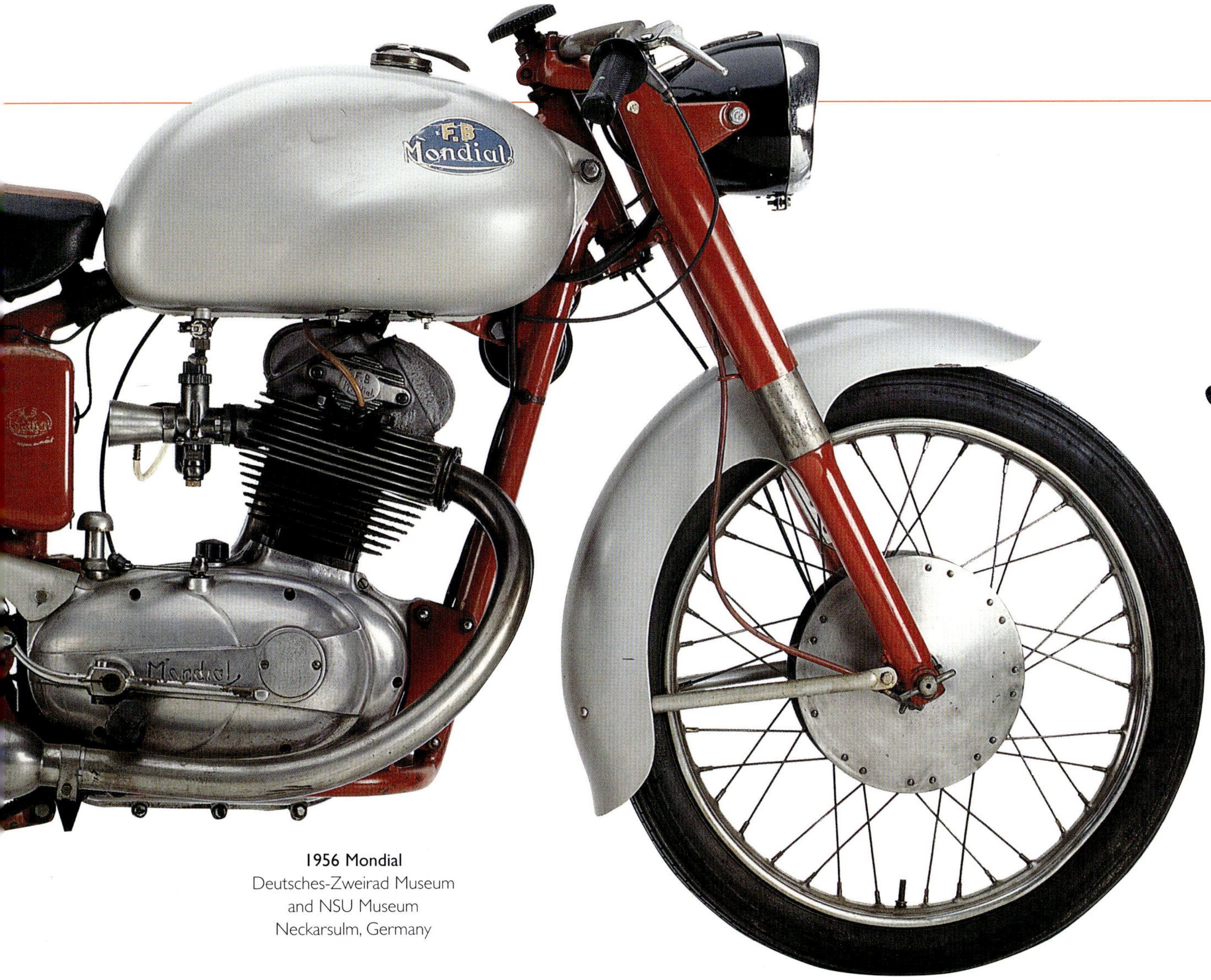


**1956 Mondial**
Deutsches-Zweirad Museum
and NSU Museum
Neckarsulm, Germany

**Below:** The sporty little 1956 model with its drop handlebars looks slim and neat from the front.

# MORBIDELLI

**Founded:** 1960
**Factory location:** Pesaro, Italy
**Manufacturing lifespan:** 1960 - to date

This Italian motorcycle was produced in only very limited numbers and was the project of Giancarlo Morbidelli, a wealthy Italian industrialist and motorcycle enthusiast. The motorcycle was truly one of the world's most exotic and expensive machines; included in the purchase price was a service contract that included airfreighting the motorcycle back to its Italian factory for servicing.

The V8 featured contemporary sports bike styling, with an integral seat, fairing and tank unit. It was designed by the noted Italian car stylist Pininfarina, whose name is normally associated with Ferrari, and featured a tubular space frame from which the V8 engine was suspended. The engine was of a water-cooled, double overhead camshaft configuration. The remainder of the motorcycle used quality proprietary components such as Marvic spoked alloy wheels and Brembo brake discs and callipers.

**SPECIFICATIONS (V8)**
**Engine:** Four-stroke V-8
**Displacement:** 847cc (51.66cu. in.)
**Horsepower:** N/A
**Wheelbase:** N/A
**Weight:** N/A
**Top speed:** 150mph (241kph)

**Below:** 32 valves, 4 camshafts, 850cc V8, 150mph. These figures would suit any sports car yet they belong to the Morbidelli motorcycle that was styled by Pininfarina.

**1999 V8**
Courtesy of Morbidelli
Italy

## Morini

**Founded:** 1937
**Factory location:** Bologna, Italy
**Manufacturing lifespan:** 1937 - to date

Alphonso Morini was a roadracer who competed on motorcycles of his own design and manufacture. In 1937 he produced motorcycles and commercial three-wheelers. Postwar, Morini manufactured 125 and 175cc (7.62 and 10.67cu in) four-strokes and had considerable racing success. One of these race motorcycles was the double overhead camshaft two-stroke Rebello built in 173 and 246cc (10.55 and 15cu in).

Alphonso died in 1969 and the company was taken over by his daughter, Gabriella. She introduced the Strada in 1971 as one of the first Moto Morini machines to become widely available outside Italy. The 344cc (20.98cu in) 72deg V-twin engine powered the machine in both Strada and Sport versions but the Sport developed four extra horsepower and had a riding position similar to that found on a sports bike.

In 1991 Morini (by now taken over by Cagiva) produced the Dart 350, a medium-capacity sports bike that featured enclosed bodywork and a wraparound front fender. The V-twin engine was completely hidden behind the bodywork, suspended from an aluminum beam frame. But sales did not match its good looks.

**Specifications (Morini 3½)**
**Engine:** Four-stroke V-twin
**Displacement:** 344cc (20.99cu in)
**Horsepower:** 39 @ 8200rpm
**Wheelbase:** N/A
**Weight:** 320lb (145.45kg)
**Top speed:** 98mph (157kph)

**Above:** The Morini 3½ came in two versions, the Sport and the Strada (touring). The two machines matched their Japanese contemporaries mechanically and at the same time retained their traditional appeal of the best Italian bikes.

Morini 3½
Courtesy of Morini Italy

## Motobecane

**Founded:** 1922
**Factory location:** Pautin, Seine, France
**Manufacturing lifespan:** 1922 - to date

Two motorcycle companies, Motobecane (founded by Charles Benoit and Abel Bardin) and Motoconfort, started in business in France during the early 1920s. In 1930 they combined and thrived and by the 1980s the company was the world's largest manufacturer of mopeds and bicycles. In the years between the two World Wars they produced 500 and 750cc (30.50 and 45.75cu in) fours but since the end of World War II they have concentrated on small capacity two-strokes.

In 1949 Motobecane launched the Mobylette, of which in excess of 11 million have been manufactured over the years. The 1970 40 VS is entirely conventional as a step-through-style of moped designed purely as a cheap, economical and basic form of transport. These attributes are the keys to its success and it has been produced in enormous numbers since its introduction. License-building has been permitted in the following countries: Spain, Iran, Zaire and Morocco.

In 1970 Motobecane commenced production of a 125cc (7.63cu in) two-stroke twin. This was followed by a 350cc (21.35cu in) triple and then, in 1977, a 500cc (30.50cu in) triple, a motorcycle which incorporated electronic fuel injection. The 350 model was named after the other company with which Motobecane had combined in 1930.

The company has a factory at Saint Quentin, France, and an engine plant in Pantin, France. The company produces its own two-stroke engine and also offers step-through designs of moped as well as a range of small-capacity motorcycles.

By 1991 Motobecane were selling their products labeled as MBK, a phonetic interpretation of Motobecane. The ZX50 Trail was a small-capacity trail bike with styling entirely typical of dirt bikes of the era.

**Right:** Even in 1923 when the founders of Motobecane, Charles Benoit and Abel Bardin, produced their first motorcycle, a belt driven 175cc (10.6cu in) machine, sales topped the one hundred thousand mark.

**Specifications (1923 Madame)**
- **Engine:** Two-stroke single
- **Displacement:** 175cc (10.7cu in)
- **Horsepower:** 1.72bhp
- **Wheelbase:** N/A
- **Weight:** N/A
- **Top speed:** N/A

**Right:** This is the 1923 version of the belt-driven Motobecane known as the Monsieur, still very much a bicycle with the engine placed neatly where the frame makes a U at the bottom end of the down tubes. This is of course a male-style frame.

1923 Monsieur
Deutsches-Zweirad Museum
and NSU Museum
Neckarsulm, Germany

**Below:** This is the female version of the 1923 machine shown above and naturally known as the Madame.

**Above:** The bike was normally started by pedaling. Once the engine caught, the belt drive would put the machine in motion. The brakes were primitive bicycle-type and although this machine has lights front and rear they were probably not too bright.

1923 Madame
Deutsches-Zweirad Museum
and NSU Museum
Neckarsulm, Germany

**Specifications (1923 Monsieur)**
- **Engine:** Two-stroke single
- **Displacement:** 175cc (10.7cu in)
- **Horsepower:** 1.72bhp
- **Wheelbase:** N/A
- **Weight:** N/A
- **Top speed:** N/A

**Left:** The Madame version of the Motobecane was a little more refined. It used a female-style frame without the crossbar and had covers each side of the top of the rear wheel to stop any clothing from getting caught in there. Lights were fitted front and rear.

# Moto Guzzi

**Founded:** 1921
**Factory location:** Mandello del Lario, Italy
**Manufacturing lifespan:** 1921 – to date

In 1917, Carlo Guzzi and Giogior Parodi met while serving with the Italian Air Force and agreed to start a motorcycle company after World War I. A third pilot in their unit, Giovanni Ravelli, was a well-known racer of the time. He would have become a Moto Guzzi partner as well, but he was killed in a plane crash. (The eagle emblem on the side of the Moto Guzzi tank was chosen as a dedication to Ravelli.) In 1920 Guzzi enlisted the help of a town blacksmith to produce the original prototype of a motorcycle powered by a four-valve overhead-cam 500cc (30.50cu in) single-cylinder engine mounted horizontally.

In 1921 Guzzi and Parodi founded the "Societa Anonima Moto Guzzi" to produce motorcycles, setting up production of the company's first bike at Mandello Del Lario, in the northern lake district of Italy, and went on to produce seventeen motorcycles in the first year. Guzzi's first machines featured a 499cc (30.43cu in) single-cylinder, inlet-over-exhaust valve engine with a horizontal, forward-facing cylinder. The same basic design was retained when the company produced overhead-valve and overhead camshaft designs of a similar capacity and later it made a 250cc (15.25cu in) version.

Carlo Guzzi saw racing as a good way of promoting the company's products and so on May 28 of the company's first year year he entered two bikes in the Milan-to-Naples race, finishing 21st and 22nd. Four months later, though, Gino Finzi finished first in the grueling Targa Florio. This was just the start of an extraordinary record of successes, with 3,329 wins in all and no fewer than 14 world championships by 1957. After the championship of Europe at the Monza Autodrome, the Secretary of the International Federation wrote: "The three Guzzis . . . dominated the event virtually from beginning to end, thus proving the importance of the Italian mortorcycle industry." ▶

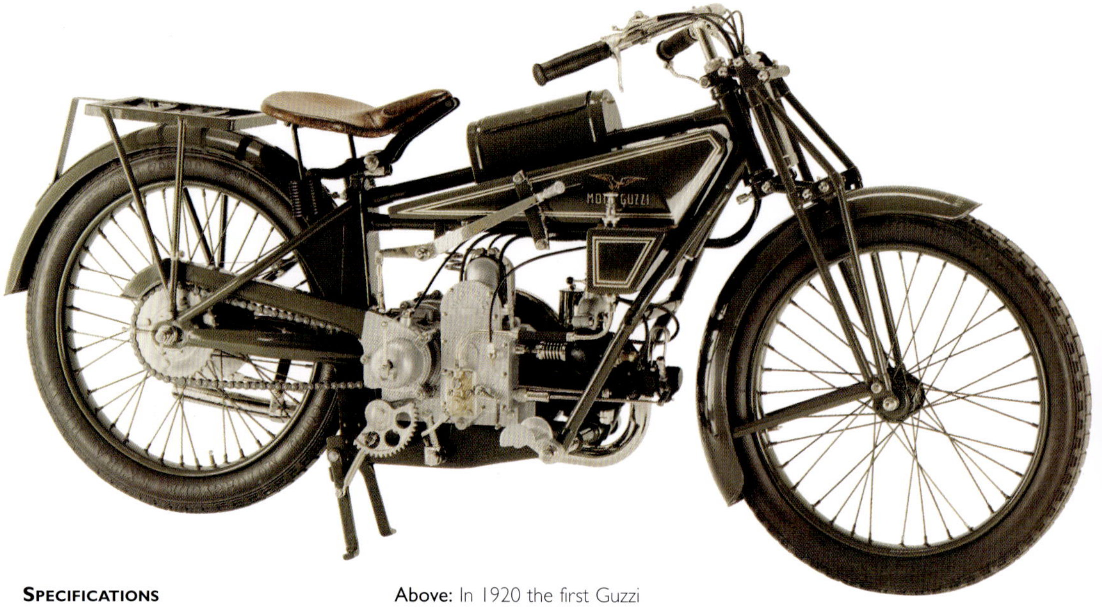


**Specifications (1921 Normale)**
**Engine:** Four-stroke flat single
**Displacement:** 498.4cc (30.414cu in)
**Horsepower:** 8 @ 3000rpm
**Wheelbase:** N/A
**Weight:** 286lb (130kg)
**Top speed:** 50mph (80kph)

**Above:** In 1920 the first Guzzi prototype was made and one year later the Normale became the first Moto Guzzi. The Normale had to be basically cheap and easy to ride. This machine used a 500cc (30.50cu in) horizontal, single-cylinder engine with external flywheel.

**1921 Normale**
Deutsches-Zweirad Museum and NSU Museum Neckarsulm, Germany

**Right:** Carlo Guzzi decided to race his machines very early on, considering it good publicity for the company and its products. Although the Guzzi's first outing was not a success, many great achievements were to follow. This is the 1928 500S.

**Specifications (1924 C4V)**
**Engine:** Four-stroke flat single
**Displacement:** 498.4cc (30.414cu in)
**Horsepower:** 22 @ 5500rpm
**Wheelbase:** N/A
**Weight:** 286lb (130kg)
**Top speed:** 94mph (150kph)

**Right:** The Guzzi C4V was the first Italian motorcycle to enter the 500cc series racing class. It was victorious in the first European championship in 1924 and was then produced in series, of which 486 were made in differing versions. Many privateers use this machine for racing, with great results.

1924 CV4
Deutsches-Zweirad Museum
and NSU Museum
Neckarsulm, Germany

**Above:** Seen clearly here on the side of the engine of the 1928 500S, flywheel was often referred to as the bacon slicer.

**Specifications (1928 500S)**
**Engine:** Four-stroke flat single
**Displacement:** 498.4cc (30.414cu in)
**Horsepower:** 13 @ 3800rpm
**Wheelbase:** N/A
**Weight:** 286lb (130kg)
**Top speed:** 63mph (100.8kph)

**Left:** A good view of the single-cylinder 500cc (30.50cu in) engine. The kick start mechanism can be seen just in front of the rear wheel. The footrests sat quite far forward on this machine.

1928 500S
Deutsches-Zweirad Museum
and NSU Museum
Neckarsulm, Germany

**Specifications (1928 GT Norge)**

- **Engine:** Four-stroke flat single
- **Displacement:** 498.4cc (30.414cu in)
- **Horsepower:** 13.2 @ 3800rpm
- **Wheelbase:** N/A
- **Weight:** 330lb (150kg)
- **Top speed:** 63mph (100.8kph)

1928 GT Norge
Courtesy of Moto Guzzi
Italy

**Right:** The initials GT were flanked by the name Norge in celebration of the Polar Circle expedition by Carlo Guzzi and his brother Giuseppe. The strong point of this bike was its comfort level, featuring Carlo Guzzi's system of housing four springs in the front part of the frame which, by working in compression, absorbed the stress coming from the oscillating fork to which they were connected. This was later adopted for the race bikes.

With the G. (Grand Tourer), Moto Guzzi introduced the sprung frame in 1928. The world was not yet ready, however, and only 78 were ever built.

By the mid-1930s, numbers of mechanics employed had grown to 700 from the original 17 employees that had started at the Mandello del Lario factory in 1921. During the decade, Guzzi produced a variety of machines, including the P175, P250 and derivations PE, PL, Egretta and Ardetta. In 1934, the racing Guzzi 500 made its debut. This bike went on to attain many wins on circuits around the world. The company won the 1935 TT on the Isle of Man, then the most prestigious race in the world, becoming the first non-British team to do so for 24 years. Irishman Stanley Woods was on board.

At around this time, the company was experimenting with multi-cylinder and supercharged racing machines, and had introduced its first V-twin, the 500cc "Bicilindrica," in 1933, but the simple, lightweight horizontal singles were already world-beaters.

**Below and right:** This 500cc (30.50cu in) 120-degree V-twin machine was very successful in racing. It was retired in 1951 when it was still at its peak. The heads and cylinders were made from aluminum alloy and the bike heralded the arrival of elastic rear suspension.

1933 Bici
Courtesy of Moto Guzzi
Italy

**Specifications (1933 Bici)**
**Engine:** Four-stroke flat single
**Displacement:** 498.4cc (30.414cu in)
**Horsepower:** 23 @ 4500rpm
**Wheelbase:** N/A
**Weight:** 374lb (170kg)
**Top speed:** 85mph (136kph)

**Left:** The "Bici" or "Bicilindrica" 500 was in service from 1933 through 1951. Part of its success was its low weight and compact overall dimensions.

**Specifications (Model PE)**
**Engine:** Four-stroke single
**Displacement:** 246cc (15.01cu in)
**Horsepower:** 9.5 @ 4800rpm
**Wheelbase:** 54in (137cm)
**Weight:** 297lb (135kg)
**Top speed:** N/A

Model PE
Auto & Technic Museum
Sinsheim, Germany

During World War II, Moto Guzzi manufactured motorcycles for the Italian Army but returned to producing racing and road bikes after the war. One of the former was the superb V8, double overhead camshaft, 498cc (30.37cu in), water-cooled works motorcycle of 1955. It was the only machine of its type ever built. but the company opted out of racing in the late 1950s on the grounds of cost.

In the 1940s and 1950s, Moto Guzzi began production of a comprehensive range of smaller-capacity machines, both scooters and motorcycles. But in the late 1960s, the company reached the verge of bankruptcy and was taken into state administration.

During the 1970s, the company became part of the group controlled by Alessandro de Tomaso which also owned Benelli and co-operated closely with Motobecane of France.

After 1969, the company became associated with the transverse V-twin-engined machines designed by Lino Tonti. Powered originally by a 700cc (42.716cu in) engine, the model range grew to 750 and then 850cc (45.767 and 51.87cu in). The earliest models were tourers, but sporting versions were also made, including the classic Le Mans of 1976, which was upgraded to the Le Mans MkII in 1979. Two years later came the 500cc V50 Monza, a machine designed to fill the gap between Guzzi's small-capacity two-stroke singles and its big four-stroke V-twins. The engine was a redesigned version of the transverse V-twin used in the larger models and the motorcycle featured electric start, shaft drive, alloy wheels and Brembo brakes.

The touring models had grown to 1000cc (61cu in). The Quota 1000 was a popular machine of the early 1990s, inspired by desert races, and featuring the proven transverse V-twin engine, protected by a bash plate but set in a frame with enhanced ground clearance, a Marzocchi monoshock rear suspension assembly, and telescopic forks. Disc brakes front and rear and shaft drive were standard features, as was a mini-fairing with twin headlamps.

The 750T, produced in 1991, was a sports bike that shared its styling with the Le Mans but featured a smaller-capacity engine denoted by its model designation. The Targa had a transverse V-twin engine, shaft drive, twin shocks rear suspension, and front and rear disc brakes. Another sporting Moto Guzzi of the early 1990s was the 1000 Daytona I. E. with fuel injection in place of conventional carburetors, but this superbike was produced in limited numbers.

A long-running line was the California, which became the California III, its name indicating where Moto Guzzi saw the market, the bike being one of several that included something of the factory custom in them but also made excellent tourers. Another range of similar bikes was produced for police use. For many years Moto Guzzi kept a single-cylinder machine in production purely in order to fill such contracts.

In the new millennium, Moto Guzzi has been bought by the Aprilia group, which no doubt provides the investment to improve and develop its products further for the future.

**1954 Bialbero**
Courtesy of Moto Guzzi
Italy

**Specifications (1954 Bialbero)**
- **Engine:** Four-stroke flat single
- **Displacement:** 249cc (15.194cu in)
- **Horsepower:** 28 @ 8000rpm
- **Wheelbase:** N/A
- **Weight:** 268lb (122kg)
- **Top speed:** 110mph (176kph)

**Above:** The 350 Bialbero was created for 350 class racing, which it dominated, winning races and championships on a regular basis between 1954 to 1957. It was a completely new design from the engine through the frame and the fairing.

**2000 California EV**
Three Cross Motorcycles
Dorset, England

1955 Otto Cilindri
Courtesy of Moto Guzzi
Italy

**SPECIFICATIONS**
**(1955 OTTO CILINDRI)**
**Engine:** Four-stroke eight
**Displacement:** 499cc (30.50cu in)
**Horsepower:** 79 @ 14000rpm
**Wheelbase:** N/A
**Weight:** 300lb (135kg)
**Top speed:** 178mph (284kph)

**Above:** The first prototypes of the V8 were assembled in 1955 and 1956 during which time much evaluation was carried out. The bike was used to break records and for racing. Unfortunately, in 1957 Moto Guzzi pulled out of racing and so the V8 never really showed its full potential.

**SPECIFICATIONS**
**(2000 CALIFORNIA)**
**Engine:** Four-stroke transverse V-twin
**Displacement:** 1064cc (64.929cu in)
**Horsepower:** 74 @ 6400rpm
**Wheelbase:** N/A
**Weight:** 545lb (247kg)
**Top speed:** N/A

**Left:** This is the flagship of the California range, the EV, with many chromed parts. The V-twin four-stroke engine is attached to a five-speed gearbox, the fuel tank capacity is 5 gallons (19 liters), and the bike has an integral braking system first introduced by Moto Guzzi.

**Above:** For the rider there is a front screen and for the passenger, to make life a little more comfortable, there is a backrest. The front wheel is 18 inches (46cm) and the rear is 17 inches (43cm).

# Motosacoche

**Founded:** 899
**Factory location:** Switzerland
**Manufacturing lifespan:** 1899-1957

The Swiss Motosacoche factory had a major influence on the early development of the motorcycle throughout Europe. Founded in 1899 by brothers Armand and Henry Dufaux, Motosacoche went on to supply engines to many important factories in England, France, Germany, Hungary and Switzerland.

The factory's first products were engines designed as bicycle attachments. Of 241 and 290cc (14.706 and 17.697cu in), these clip-on units were called the "motor-in-a-tool-bag," giving the name Motosacoche. Other early experiments included a seven-cylinder radial engine.

The proprietary power units produced through the 1920s and 1930s were also known by the MAG brand name. They ranged from 247 to 996cc (15.072 to 60.779cu in) and were fitted or made under license by dozens of companies. Motosacoche also made complete machines itself.

Racing became important to Motosacoche in the late 1920s and the company built very fast works machines for all the major road racing classes, as well as some big hill-climbers. Race engines were also supplied to a select band of customers and achieved some important wins.

Among Motosacoche's designers were the Englishmen Dougal Marchant and Bert Le Vack, who was killed testing his new V-twin tourer during the 1930s. Few new designs appeared before World War II, and when peace returned, the company produced only a small range of lightweights.

**1932 Jubilee 424**
Deutsches-Zweirad Museum and NSU Museum Neckarsulm, Germany

**Below:** The Jubilee used a MAG (Motosacoche, Acacias, Geneve) engine, the gearchange was operated via a lever that attached on the side of the fuel tank and it had a proper center stand.

**Specifications (1913 Model)**
**Engine:** Single-cylinder
**Displacement:** 290cc (18cu in)
**Horsepower:** 2
**Wheelbase:** N/A
**Weight:** 99lb (45kg)
**Top speed:** 37mph (60kph)

1913 Motosacoche 2.5hp
National Motor Musuem Beaulieu, England

**Below:** A true lightweight in every sense of the word, this is the 290cc (18cu in) side-valve Motosacoche of 1913. The engine was literally clipped into the bicycle frame.

**Below:** Shown here is the drive belt pulley on the side of the engine. The belt traveled from here to a larger pulley that ran round the outside of the rear wheel.

**Above:** This particular machine is well kitted out, with front and rear lighting, a beautifully finished red and chrome tank, and well sprung rider and passenger seats.

**Left:** Shown here is the 1932 Motosacoche Jubilee. The name Motosacoche was given by the two brothers who ran the company, Henry and Armand Dufaux. They said the concept was "Une moto sa coche," which translated would mean an "engine in a bag." In today-speak that would mean a package deal engine.

**SPECIFICATIONS (1932 JUBILEE 424)**

- **Engine:** Single-cylinder
- **Displacement:** 498cc (30.39cu in)
- **Horsepower:** N/A
- **Wheelbase:** N/A
- **Weight:** N/A
- **Top Speed:** N/A

## MÜNCH

**Founded:** 1966
**Factory location:** Ossenheim/Würzburg, Germany
**Manufacturing lifespan:** 1966 - to date

Münch motorcycles were the product of Freidel Münch, one-time racing mechanic for Horex, which closed in 1959. He developed a racing brake and a four-cylinder racing engine. Then, in 1965, Münch was asked to build the fastest, most powerful road bike possible. He installed a 996cc (60.779cu in) air-cooled NSU car engine in a special frame with forks and brakes cast in magnesium alloy for lightness. The transmission was also housed in magnesium alloy casings.

The finished bike was called the Mammut and its speed and comfort surpassed any bike of its time. Its enormous torque would even carry it from city traffic speed to over 120mph (192kph) without needing to change gear. Münch put the Mammut into small-scale production, with an increase in engine size to 1200cc (73.228cu in). Münch gained a sidecar world championship in 1971, and continued to develop exotic superbikes including a 1786cc (108.98cu in) version of the Mammut, and ultimately a 2000cc (122cu in) limited edition version in 2001, produced by Münch Motorrad Technik of Würzburg.

**SPECIFICATIONS (MAMMUT 1200)**

- **Engine:** Four-stroke four
- **Displacement:** 1177cc (72cu in)
- **Horsepower:** 88 @ 6000rpm
- **Wheelbase:** N/A
- **Weight:** 659lb (298kg)
- **Top speed:** 137mph (220kph)

1974 Mammut 1200
Deutsches-Zweirad Museum and NSU Museum Neckersulm, Germany

**Below:** The Munch 1200TTS was powered by an NSU engine with chain-driven overhead-camshaft and it was fed via two twin-choke Weber carburetors.

# MV Agusta

▶ In the mid-1950s the company developed 50cc (3.05cu in) two-stroke motorcycles, a model with a 250cc four-stroke, two-cylinder engine which brought back so many victories to MV Agusta; a 250cc single-cylinder bike with four-stroke engines (Modello Raid); prototypes for motorcycles of 250 and 300cc; a 175cc four-stroke engine; and then between 1957 and 1960 MV's most important developments were a 125cc four-stroke, two-cylinder competition machine; a six-cylinder four-stroke motor of 500cc for competitions; a light motorcycle with an 83cc (5.06cu in) four-stroke engine; the Motocarro 125cc "Centauro"; and new models of motors and motorcycles of 125 and 150cc with four-stroke four-speed erngines, called the Model 161. The latter was so well-received that a subsequent five-speed model called "Centomila" remained permanently in production, esthetically and technically improved, for several years.

Along with easy wins in almost every sporting national and international championship class there followed a two-stroke scooter (Chicco); a light motorcycle with 99cc (6.04cu in) four-stroke, four-speed engine; the two-stroke Liberty; a 600cc (36.60cu in) four-stroke, four-cyclinder, five-speed design with shaft drive and top speed of 115.6mph (185kph); a prestige 250cc two-cylinder, four-stroke, five-speed model which was the predecessor of the 350cc Turismo and Sport with brilliant characteristics including top speed of 103mph (165kph); and race-dominating three-cyclinder 350s and four-cylinder 500s. Then, in 1970, the 750 Sport was unveiled, an improved and refined version of the 600cc, with a top speed above 137.5mph (220kph).

When Count Domenico died suddenly in February 1971, his brother, Count Corrado, took control of the company, which remained a force in racing until 1975, when competition from Japan ultimately proved too strong. MV Agusta pulled out of racing after that, and the family poured its efforts into the aviation side of the business, with the motorcycle manufacturer closing down within two years.

But not before it had produced the 750S America, truly one of the most exotic motorcycles of all time. This was an exclusive sports bike designed, as the name implies, primarily for the North American market. The four-cylinder engine offered high performance (described as "scintillating" at the time of its introduction) and sports bike handling which was achieved through use of Ceriani suspension. ▶

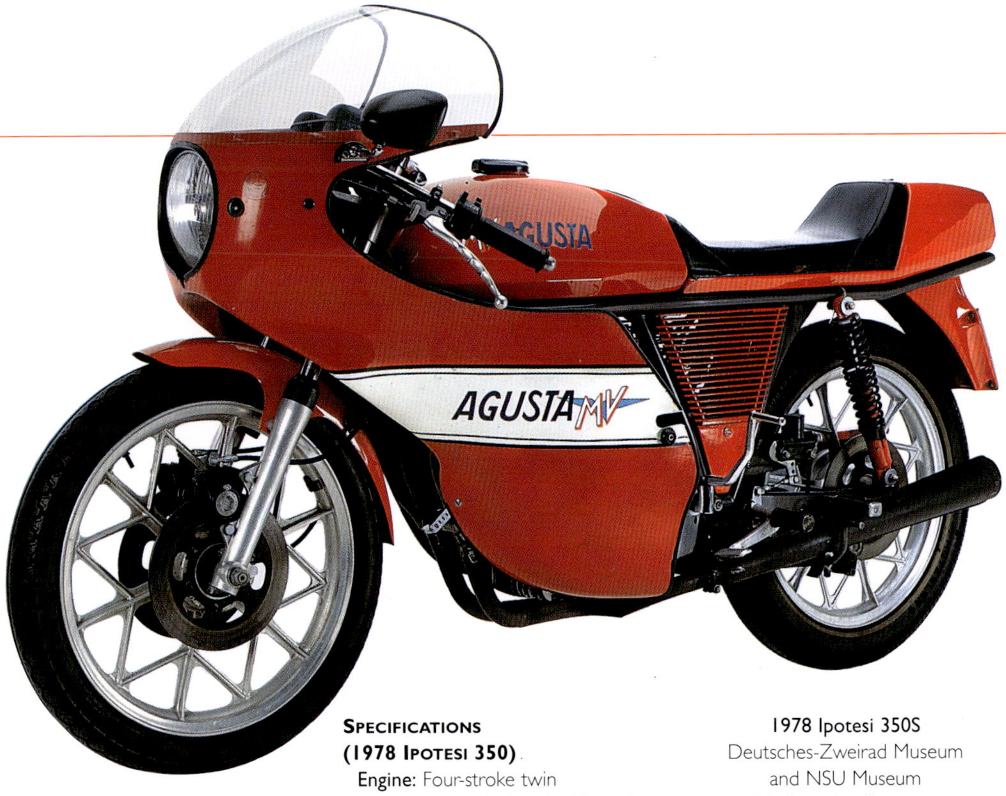


**Specifications (1978 Ipotesi 350)**
**Engine:** Four-stroke twin
**Displacement:** 350cc (21.35cu in)
**Horsepower:** 34 @ 8500rpm
**Wheelbase:** N/A
**Weight:** 330lb (150kg)
**Top speed:** 106mph (170kph)

1978 Ipotesi 350S
Deutsches-Zweirad Museum
and NSU Museum
Neckarsulm, Germany

**Specifications (America 750)**
**Engine:** Four-stroke four
**Displacement:** 790cc (48.19cu in)
**Horsepower:** 75 @ 8500rpm
**Wheelbase:** N/A
**Weight:** N/A
**Top speed:** 122mph (196kph)

1975 America 750
Deutsches-Zweirad Museum
and NSU Museum
Neckarsulm, Germany

**Left:** Until 1975 MV remained a force in racing but by then the competiion from Japan had grown too strong and the company closed its doors within a few years. The 1978 350S Ipotesi was one of the last bikes from the original company.

**SPECIFICATIONS (2000 F4)**
**Engine:** Four-stroke four
**Displacement:** 749 (45.77cu in)
**Horsepower:** 125 @ 12200rpm
**Wheelbase:** N/A
**Weight:** 400lb (181kg)
**Top speed:** 171mph (273kph)

**Below:** The four-stroke four-cylinder MV Agusta 750 America is one of the legendary machines from the 1970s.

**Right:** Unveiled to the public at the Milan motorcycle show of 1998, the MV F4 has bought back to the world one of motorcycling's legendary names. It has a four-cylinder, double overhead cam, water- and oil-cooled, four-valve, four-stroke engine.

2000 F4
Three Cross Motorcycles
Dorset, England

**Above:** In 1975 MV completely changed its range of roadgoing models, presenting three models that were sporty and used four-stroke engines. This was the new version of the 750, the America, which became one of the most exotic machines of its time.

**Right:** What the 750 America lacked in instrumentation it certainly made up for in the way of power and speed. This baby could achieve 138mph (220kph). It used a five-speed gearbox, twin front disc brakes and had drop-style sports handlebars.

## MV Agusta

Recently the MV company has been taken over and resurrected by the Cagiva company. What Cagiva did to put the name MV back in the eyes of the public was amazing to say the least. During 1998, in a blaze of publicity, they introduced the MV Agusta F4 which by any standards was a machine to be desired. Dream child of Claudio Castiglioni and Massimo Tamburini, top of the range model, the "Serie Oro" (Gold Series) came at a hefty price but soon there were to be a cheaper version and other models based on the same theme.

During 2001 MV announced the Brutale ("Beast"), which was to be a limited edition of 300 machines. It uses the F4's chassis and 750cc (45.77cu in) engine. The machine was designed in Italy and is great competition for the big Japanese four. It has a monster look about the exposed, non-faired frame, and there is an odd-looking headlamp. There is, we are told, a less expensive version to follow for those who do not have the serious kind of money needed to purchase this and the F4 – a long way from MV's 1950s philosophy, "security, durability, economy."

There is no doubt, though, that the parent company are serious about MV and its place in the market.

**Specifications (2001 Brutale)**
**Engine:** Four-stroke four
**Displacement:** 749cc (45.77cu in)
**Horsepower:** 127 @ 12000rpm
**Wheelbase:** N/A
**Weight:** 390lb (178kg)
**Top speed:** 155mph (248kph)

**2001 Brutale**
Three Cross Motorcycles
Dorset, England

**Left:** The MV Agusta Brutale is a move away from the standard, racy-looking, faired F4. It is all tubes and plates bolted together to make a brutal looking 155mph (248kph) monster.

## MZ

| | |
|---|---|
| **Founded:** | 1946 |
| **Factory location:** | Zschopau, Germany |
| **Manufacturing lifespan:** | 1946 - to date |

As the Iron Curtain descended across Germany in the years immediately after World War II, the MZ factory was created from IFA which had been established in the DKW factory at Zschopau in what became East Germany. MZ, Motorradwerk Zschopau, is the brandname of the IFA Kombinat-Zweirüder group, the nationalized East German motorcycle manufacturers.

The company became a prolific manufacturer of two-stroke machines and had considerable roadracing success against a background of Cold War politics, racer defections to the West, and East German economic shortages.

This success was due entirely to the talents of Walter Kaaden and a small group of riders. One of their greatest moments of glory was Mike Hailwood's win in the 1963 250 GP at Sachsenring, Germany. MZ also provided the bikes for the DDR entry in the ISDT.

With the reunification of Germany there came the possibility that MZ would be forced to cease motorcycle production since they now faced stiff competition from other modern European and Japanese machines without the aid of DDR state subsidy.

However, the company quickly shifted its emphasis to bring modern competitive machines into production.

The company renamed itself MuZ and sought to produce the Skorpion, which was designed by British engineers. It features a liquid-cooled, Japanese (Yamaha), single-cylinder engine and a number of Italian components. Wheels are cast from alloy and the bike looks decidedly up-to-date. In the year 2001 development of new machines continued.

**Specifications (1956 RT 125)**
**Engine:** Two-stroke single
**Displacement:** 125cc (7.62cu in)
**Horsepower:** 4.75 @ 5000rpm
**Wheelbase:** N/A
**Weight:** 190lb (85kg)
**Top speed:** 47mph (75km)

**Right:** Cars in the former East Germany were very expensive and not many people could afford them. The motorcycle was an ideal alternative. The RT 125cc (7.6cu in) was a good capacity and therefore economical. Many of these machines were exported to raise foreign currency.

**Above:** Although the RT,s seat is not sprung, the rear of the bike is. There are also covers for the drive chain, running from the rear of the engine to the back wheel, making it pretty well completely enclosed to the elements.

1973 RZ 250
Deutsches-Zweirad Museum
and NSU Museum
Neckarsulm, Germany

**Above:** This racing machine with its water-cooled, two-cylinder, two-stroke engine was the end product of a long development by Walter Kaaden in the IFA/MZ factory in 1954.

**Specifications (1973 RZ 250)**
- **Engine:** Two-stroke twin
- **Displacement:** 250cc (15.26cu in)
- **Horsepower:** 55-60 @ 11500rpm
- **Wheelbase:** N/A
- **Weight:** N/A
- **Top speed:** N/A

1956 RT 125
Deutsches-Zweirad Museum
and NSU Museum
Neckarsulm, Germany

**Above:** The RT was a popular product of MZ (Motorradwerk Zschopau), which grew out of the IFA (Industry Association of Vehicle Builders) was founded after World War II.

## NER-A-CAR

**Founded:** 1920
**Factory location:** Syracuse, USA, and London, England
**Manufacturing lifespan:** 1920 - 1927

The Ner-a-Car was designed to be "near a car" (also spelt Neracar) with a comfortable seat, protective bodywork, and the most stable steering ever seen on a motorcycle. Its name was also a pun, as the design was the brainchild of American engineer Carl Neracher.

The first Ner-a-Car was built in Syracuse, New York State, in 1921. It was based on a pressed-steel platform housing the engine, transmission and rear wheel, which had no suspension. The seat was comfortably suspended on top of the chassis and the frame splayed out to house the front wheel, which was suspended on coil springs and turned on a king-pin similar to a car's, an early example of hub-center steering.

A huge front fender and wide footboards offered excellent weather protection, improved on a later deluxe model with a windshield and instrument console. The engine was under a cowling, helping to keep the rider clean. It drove a large flywheel and the transmission consisted of a friction wheel that contacted the flywheel at different points to give different gear ratios.

The design was licensed to the British company Sheffield Simplex, which uprated the original 211cc (12.87cu in) two-stroke single to 285cc (17.39cu in). Later models used more conventional 350cc (21.35cu in) Blackburne and a three-speed gearbox.

Ner-a-Cars won several road trials and appealed to riders who wanted comfort and convenience. However, sales never reached mass-market numbers and the US company closed in 1924, with UK production ending in 1927.

## NIMBUS

**Founded:** 1919
**Factory location:** Copenhagen, Denmark
**Manufacturing lifespan:** 1919 - 1959

Denmark's most significant motorcycle, the Nimbus, was made by a company called Fisker and Nielsen, after its founders who began by making electric motors and Nilfisk vacuum cleaners. The success of the latter business frequently led to cessation of motorcycle production.

The first motorcycle stayed in production for 40 years with very few changes to a basic design that was very advanced when it was first introduced. It had a four-cylinder engine, shaft drive and front and rear suspension, as well as a pressed-steel frame. It was nicknamed the "stovepipe" because of its large tubular fuel tank.

After a gap of six years motorcycle manufacture began again in 1934 in a new vacuum cleaner factory. The new bike's layout was similar to the old but the engine was now an overhead-camshaft design and the tank had a more conventional shape. The front suspension was a Nimbus innovation, using telescopic forks even before they were pioneered by BMW. The bikes were incredibly light despite their complex power units, weighing as little as 405lb (183.7kg).

From 1936 to 1954 the Nimbus remained almost unaltered, many being supplied to the Danish Army. Then production slowed, new bikes being built only from the stockpile of spares, and stopped five years later.

**SPECIFICATIONS (1920-1927 MODEL)**
**Engine:** Four-stroke five-cylinder
**Displacement:** 746cc (45cu in)
**Horsepower:** 22 @ 4000rpm
**Wheelbase:** N/A
**Weight:** N/A
**Top speed:** N/A

**Below:** Despite upgrades, Nimbus products remained very similar over 37 years. The frame was of the pressed-steel type and the forks were originally of a trailing arm design, superseded later by a telescopic type.

1920 Nimbus
Deutsches-Zweirad Museum and NSU Museum Neckersulm, Germany

## NER-A-CAR

**Specifications (1921 Model)**
- **Engine:** Four-stroke single
- **Displacement:** 350cc(21.25cu in)
- **Horsepower:** N/A
- **Wheelbase:** 59in (150cm)
- **Weight:** 168lb (76kg)
- **Top speed:** N/A

1921 Ner-a-Car
National Motor Musuem
Beaulieu, England

**Right:** The very wide front fender stopped not only mud but any stray elements from being thrown up from the front wheel and hitting the rider.

**Left:** A Sheffield Simplex version of the Ner-a-Car, one of the most popular types of combined car/scooter/motorbike configurations for getting about town.

## NORTON

Norton

**Founded:** 1901
**Factory location:** Birmingham, England
**Manufacturing lifespan:** 1901 - to date

Norton is one of the legendary names of British motorcycling. It was founded as the Norton Manufacturing Company by James Lansdowne Norton in 1901. His first motorcycles used Swiss Moto-Reve and French Peugeot engines and were built in England under license. Aboard a V-twin Norton, Rembrandt H. "Rem" Fowler won the twin-cylinder class of the 1907 Isle of Man TT, the first running of the event. A single of 633cc (38.63cu in) was marketed in 1908 and another model of 490cc (29.9cu in) in 1911. By 1913 the company was known as Norton Motors Ltd. It produced its first overhead-valve single, the Model 18, in 1922. In 1924 Nortons won both the Sidecar TT and the Senior TT on the Isle of Man. The following year J. L. Norton passed away but the company continued in business. The racing department saw the arrival of Joe Craig as boss and he oversaw the firm's win at the 1926 Isle of Man TT with a 348cc (21.24cu in) overhead-valve single.

Walter Moore, the racing sidecar passenger, designed the first overhead-camshaft Norton before leaving to work for NSU in Germany. With the new ohc engine Norton were able to dominate the 1927 TT. ▶

**Specifications (1927 Model 18)**
- **Engine:** Four-stroke single
- **Displacement:** 490cc (29.9cu in)
- **Horsepower:** 18
- **Wheelbase:** N/A
- **Weight:** 336lb (152kg)
- **Top speed:** 80mph (129kph)

**Below:** The Norton Model 18 used a newly designed overhead-valve engine. Its antecedent, the Model 16, was a side-valve.

1927 Model 18
National Motorcycle Museum
Birmingham, England

# NORTON

Norton's roadgoing bikes looked dated by the end of the 1920s, and a revamp was not long in coming. Arthur Carroll replaced Moore in the design department and redesigned Norton's engine into a unit that would endure until 1963.

Pre-World War II Nortons were generally given numerical and alphabetical designations and in the early 1930s the range consisted of machines such as the 348cc (21.24cu in) JE and CJ, the 490cc (29.9cu in) 16H and the 588cc (35.45cu in) Model 19. The line-up was gradually updated through the 1930s; for example, Norton introduced a four-speed gearbox in 1933, and just before the war the Racing International models, also referred to as the Manx Grand Prix bikes, on which successful foundations the postwar Manx Norton was based.

The Norton 16H was a side-valve single-cylinder machine whose history stretched back to 1911. During the 1920s it had been a sporting motorcycle and it was modernized for the 1930s. The 490cc (29.9cu in) single was initially fitted with a three-speed gearbox but this was upgraded to a four-speed in 1935. The 1937 16H was considered the most suitable machine for military purposes, and 100,000 were supplied to the British Army.

During 1946 a number of road-racing machines were produced in time for the Manx Grand Prix of that year. Listed as the 348cc (21.24cu in) 40M and 498cc (30.39cu in) 30M, they were also the first to be known as Manx Nortons. Both were built around Carroll-type overhead-camshaft singles with a shaft and bevel drive to the camshaft. The frame was of the cradle type with plunger rear suspension and the forks were the Norton Roadholders.

By 1950 the much-vaunted swingarm "Featherbed" frame ("as comfortable as lying on a featherbed") was in fitted on production Manx Nortons and racers, with new gearboxes and 19 inch (48.26cm) diameter wheels, and the company was soon having competition success.

The twin-cylinder Model 88 with the Featherbed frame was superseding the popular Dominator by 1956, some models having an alloy cylinder head and Amal Monobloc carburetor. The frame included a welded-on, rather than bolted, rear subframe. Production continued until 1963 with minor improvements, notably to the clutch and gearbox.

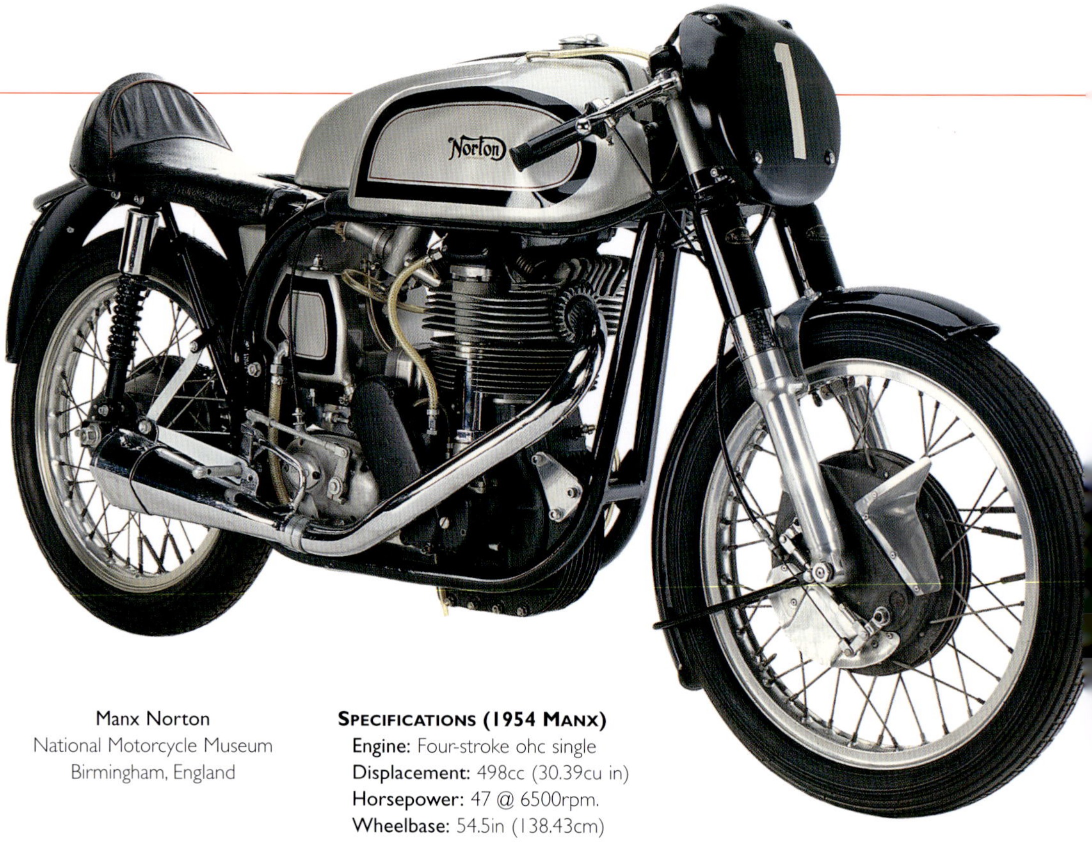


Manx Norton
National Motorcycle Museum
Birmingham, England

**SPECIFICATIONS (1954 MANX)**
- **Engine:** Four-stroke ohc single
- **Displacement:** 498cc (30.39cu in)
- **Horsepower:** 47 @ 6500rpm.
- **Wheelbase:** 54.5in (138.43cm)
- **Weight:** 309lb (140kg)
- **Top speed:** 120mph (193kph)

**SPECIFICATIONS (MODEL 16H)**
- **Engine:** Four-stroke single
- **Displacement:** 490cc (29.9cu in)
- **Horsepower:** 12 @ 4800rpm
- **Wheelbase:** 54in (137.16cm)
- **Weight:** 388lb (176kg)
- **Top speed:** 60mph (97kph)

Model 16H
National Motorcycle Museum
Birmingham, England

Left: The Manx Norton's reputation as a successful racing motorcycle was assured after the 1-2-3 victories in the Junior and Senior TTs of 1950.

Below: The 16H was manufactured in large numbers for the British Army during World War Two. It was closely based on a 1937 version of the bike.

**Model 88**
Owner – Tony East of A.R.E. Ltd
England

**Specifications (1955 Model 88)**
- **Engine:** Four-stroke twin
- **Displacement:** 497cc (30.33cu in)
- **Horsepower:** 29 @ 6000rpm
- **Wheelbase:** 55.5in (140.97cm)
- **Weight:** 380lb (172kg)
- **Top speed:** 88mph (142kph)

**Above:** The Model 88's production run lasted until 1963, albeit in an upgraded form which included a redesigned version of the frame.

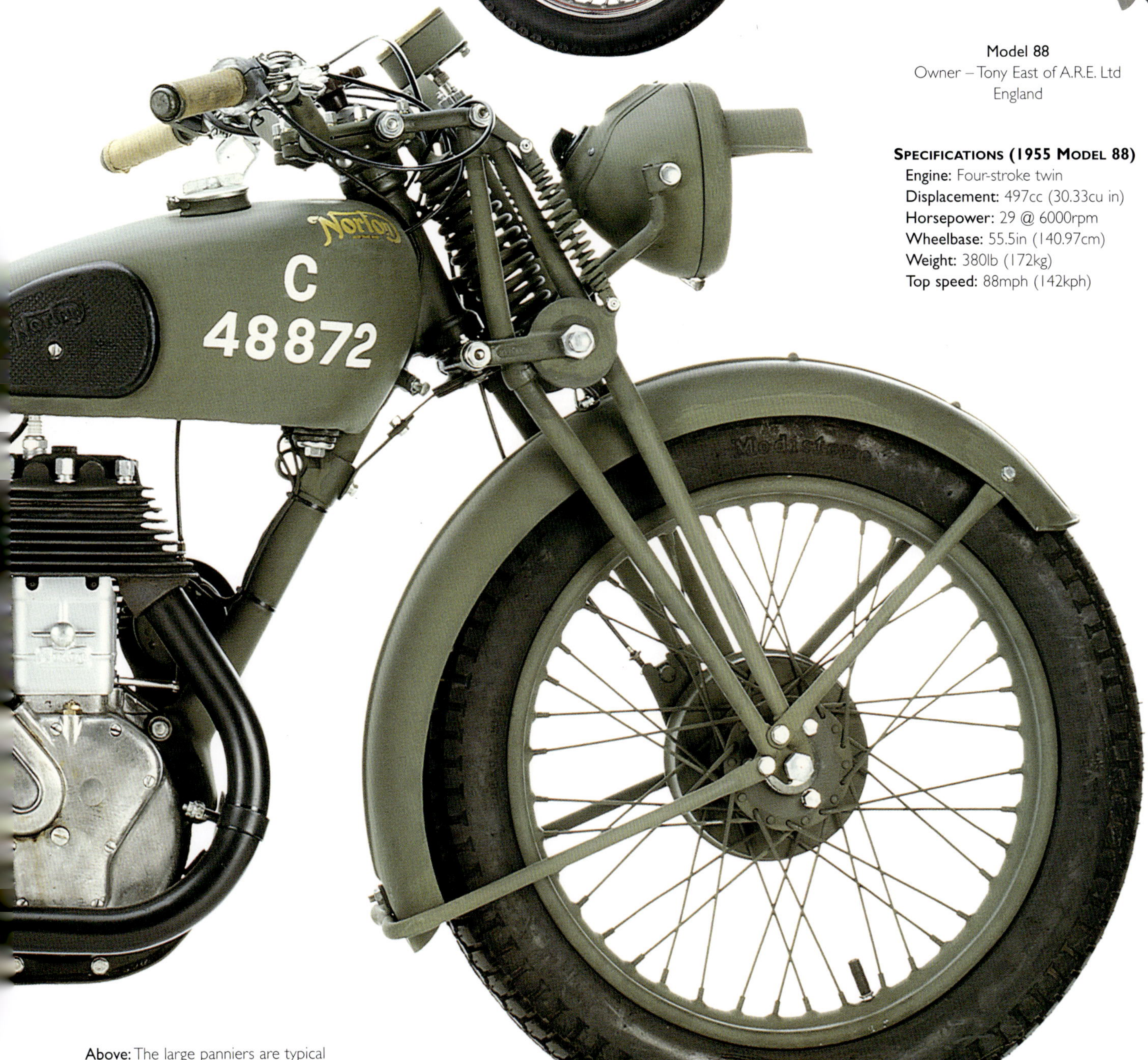


**Left:** Front suspension was by means of girder forks. The speedometer was mounted on a bracket fixed to the handlebars.

**Above:** The large panniers are typical of the equipment fitted to the 16H for military duties.

**Above:** The British War Department specified a number of military fittings, including the blackout headlamp cover designed to minimize light "scatter" from the lamp.

# NORTON

Norton was acquired by AMC in the mid-1950s; within a decade production was moved from Birmingham to London and the range rationalized. The trend was towards twin-cylinders; singles were dated. Norton, however, had a long-standing reputation for single-cylinder bikes and continued making them alongside newer twins.

When the company was upgrading its range to swingarm rear suspension, a new model was introduced, the Model 50, essentially a 350cc (21.35cu in) displacement single-cylinder engine mounted in the cycle parts of the larger-capacity singles. This was a disadvantage because the weight of these parts was greater than it needed to be for a 350. Some of the large-capacity singles were dropped through the 1950s, although the smaller-capacity Model 50 remained in production until the 1960s, by when smaller-capacity twins, such as the Norton Jubilee, overshadowed it.

The Featherbed frame was partially redesigned in 1960, and in September 1961 the 650SS made its appearance. Its engine was fitted with the race-proven downdraught cylinder head as had been used on the company's TT race bikes that year. It also featured solid skirt pistons and a flywheel, and big end journals (the part of the shaft in contact with the bearing) larger than those used on the 500cc and 600cc models. The 650SS was capable of speeds between 110 and 120mph (177 to 193kph) and economic fuel consumption was achievable. Brakes were good and handling remained as precise as ever.

The Norton twin was soon increased in capacity with an Atlas 745cc (45.40cu in) engine with increased cylinder bore but with the 89mm stroke retained. The machine was initially made for export only, and remained in production until 1970.

In 1966 AMC went into liquidation; Manganese Bronze bought the assets and moved production to the former Villiers factory in Wolverhampton. They continued production of the twins, especially the Commando, launched in 1967 for the important U.S. market. It incorporated both a race-style tailpiece, a dual seat over the rear wheel, flat race-type handlebars and a long, sleek fuel tank. The Fastback was a 1969 cafe-race-styled version featuring vibration-reducing "Isolastic" rubber mounts for the engine, gearbox, swingarm, exhaust system and rear wheel, all bolted together as a single unit and then attached to the frame by the three Isolastic mounts. The proven Atlas engine was used to power the Commando along with the four-speed AMC gearbox; the two units were connected by a triplex primary chain. The famous Roadholder forks were retained at the front and fitted with a hub that featured a large twin-leading-shoe brake.

**1959 Model 50**
Owner – Tony East of A.R.E. Ltd
England

**SPECIFICATIONS (MODEL 50)**
**Engine:** Four-stroke ohv single
**Displacement:** 348cc (21.24cu in)
**Horsepower:** 20
**Wheelbase:** 55.5in (140.97cm)
**Weight:** 360lb (163kg)
**Top speed:** 75mph (121kph)

**Above:** The Model 50 displaced 348cc (21.24cu in) and was one of Norton's attempts to exploit the middleweight commuter market. The 350cc class had long been popular in the UK.

**1969 Commando Fastback**
National Motorcycle Museum
Birmingham, England

**Specifications (1961 650SS)**
- Engine: Four-stroke twin
- Displacement: 646cc (39.4cu in)
- Horsepower: 49 @ 6800rpm
- Wheelbase: 55.5in (140.97cm)
- Weight: 398lb (180.5kg)
- Top speed: 115mph (185kph)

**Right:** The 650SS was conventionally constructed with the four-speed gearbox mounted into the tubular steel cradle frame behind the engine and under the oil tank.

1961 650SS
National Motorcycle Museum
Birmingham, England

**Below:** The Atlas engine was tilted forward in the frame. Its Isolastic mounting meant that it could be revved hard without undue vibration marring handling.

**Above:** The Fastback's seat unit tailpiece clearly owed its styling to the race bikes of the day, albeit encumbered by the addition of a rear light and number plate bracket.

**Specifications (1969 Commando Fastback)**
- Engine: Four-stroke twin
- Displacement: 745cc (45.46cu in)
- Horsepower: 56 @ 6500rpm
- Wheelbase: 56.75in (144.15cm)
- Weight: 398lb (180kg)
- Top speed: 115mph (185kph)

**Above:** The Commando Fastback of 1969 combined cafe-racer style with the proven twin-cylinder Norton engine. It had a long, sleek fuel tank that flowed into a dual seat and then into the tailpiece.

**Left:** The Commando had what Norton described as Isolastic rubber mounts for the engine and gearbox aimed at minimizing vibration.

During the 1970s and 1980s, Norton, by then part of the NVT group essentially controlled by the British government developed developed rotary engines based on German Felix Wankel's pre-World War II concept. Small numbers of the developed bike, the Interpol II, were supplied to and evaluated by British police forces and other organizations, and experience gained with these led to the production of a limited run of air-cooled rotary-engined Classics, and subsequently to the liquid-cooled Commander and F1 models, although sales remained tiny.

Meanwhile, Norton had last won the Isle of Man TT in June 1973 when monocoque-framed machines powered by Commando twin-cylinder engines held off a strong Japanese challenge. Success was to come again later, however, when in 1992 Steve Hislop was entered in the Senior TT riding a Norton rotary-powered racebike. This success had followed problems in both the handling characteristics (caused mainly by the unusual way in which the rotary engine delivered the power) and especially with the sport's governing body, FIM, which had difficulty in classifying the rotary racers, casting doubts for a time over their eligibility for Grands Prix.

Development work continued unabated, including experiments with water-cooling and new fairings. The next generation of Norton racers was the NRS588. The NRS indicates Norton Racing Services while 588 is the machine's displacement in cubic centimeters). It was first wheeled out in 1991 with performance parts including a Harris frame, WP suspension components and 17 inch (43.18cm) diameter PVM magnesium wheels. This chassis was fitted with a liquid-cooled Norton rotary engine and a six-speed gearbox connected by a Kevlar-reinforced primary drive. Final drive was by means of a chain driven through an 18-plate wet clutch. It was in almost this form that the NRS588 took Norton and Steve Hislop to their much-sought-after Isle of Man TT win in 1992.

Despite this competition success, heavily financed by sponsors, the future of the strife-torn marque was far from assured; it had changed hands several times in its history, and has continued to do so since.

**Above:** The troubled Norton marque always attracted plenty of sponsors – as evidenced by the NRS588's fairing – particularly when the bikes were winning races as this one did.

**SPECIFICATIONS (1983 INTERPOL II)**

**Engine:** Twin-chamber Wankel rotary
**Displacement:** 588cc (35.9cu in)
**Horsepower:** 85 @ 9000rpm
**Wheelbase:** 58.5in (148.59cmm)
**Weight:** 518lb (235kg)
**Top speed:** 124mph (200kph)

**Right:** The rotary engine was partially concealed by the bodywork, including the fairing and the conventional seat, tank and sidepanels, which were of an integrated design.

**1983 Interpol II**
National Motorcycle Museum
Birmingham, England

**Left:** Before Steve Hislop won the Isle of Man TT aboard this rotary-powered racer, there had been considerable development work into the viability of a rotary racing engine, and a prolonged dispute with the FIM about its displacement and therefore its eligibility for racing.

1992 NRS588
National Motorcycle Museum
Birmingham, England

**Specifications (1992 NRS588)**
**Engine:** Twin-chamber Wankel rotary
**Displacement:** 588cc (35.9cu in)
**Horsepower:** 95 @ 9500rpm
**Wheelbase:** 55.1in (139.95cm)
**Weight:** 298lb (135kg)
**Top speed:** 180mph (290kph)

**Below:** As the rotary engine is almost completely concealed behind the race fairing, there is little, at a glance, to distinguish the NRS588 from other Grands Prix motorcycles of the time, with the exception of the Norton logo.

## NSU

| | |
|---|---|
| **Founded:** | 1901 |
| **Factory location:** | Neckarsulm, Germany |
| **Manufacturing lifespan:** | 1901 - 1958 |

NSU stands for Neckarsulm Strickmaschinen Union, a German company which began making automatic knitting machines and bicycles toward the end of the 19th century. The first motorcycles produced were essentially no more than bicycles with a 1.5hp Swiss-built Zedel engine (a copy of the De Dion Bouton) clip-mounted on the downtube next to the crank assembly. Final drive was via a flat leather belt that connected a pulley on the crankshaft to a pulley on the rear wheel. The early machines were named Neckarsulm by the company's founder, Christian Schmidt, after the town where the factory was based. The bicycle subsidiary's name – Neckarsulmer Fahrradwerke – was painted on the tanks of the first motorcycles, but this was changed to just the company's initials after 1910.

As well as those from Zedel, the company used engines from Minerva of Belgium, but introduced its own singles and V-twins in 1903, and a liquid-cooled single in 1905. Orders were abundant and soon there was more demand for motorcycles than the factory could manage. ▶

**Specifications (1902 Model)**
**Engine:** Four-stroke single clip-on
**Displacement:** 211cc (13cu in)
**Horsepower:** 1.25 @ 1500rpm
**Wheelbase:** Bicycle frame
**Weight:** N/A
**Top speed:** 24mph (38.4kph)

1902 Model
Deutsches-Zweirad Museum and NSU Museum
Neckarsulm, Germany

**Above:** One of the earliest (1902) motorcycles produced by Christian Schmidt at his knitting machine factory in Neckarsulm, Germany. It is essentially a safety bicycle with a single-cylinder engine clipped on to the frame.

# NSU

As in all developed countries, demand for personal transportation in Germany was burgeoning during the first decade and a half of the twentieth century, and there was also a growing interest in motorized sports. NSU expanded rapidly, taking full advantage of the buying public's seemingly insatiable appetite, at home and abroad. Early racing success opened up export opportunities for production motorcycles, and it was possibly because of potential exports, in fact, that the abbreviated name was prompted. Anyhow, the company continued engine development, and also, in 1914, introduced a basic swing-arm rear suspension design onto its machines, which were still belt-driven at this time. It had also decided to diversify rather than stick to just one product, and so moved into car production also. These were initially license-built models of other manufacturers' products, but it wasn't long before NSU was producing automobiles of its own design.

The company was heavily involved in producing military equipment during World War I, but found that shortly afterward the demand for motorcycles had increased.

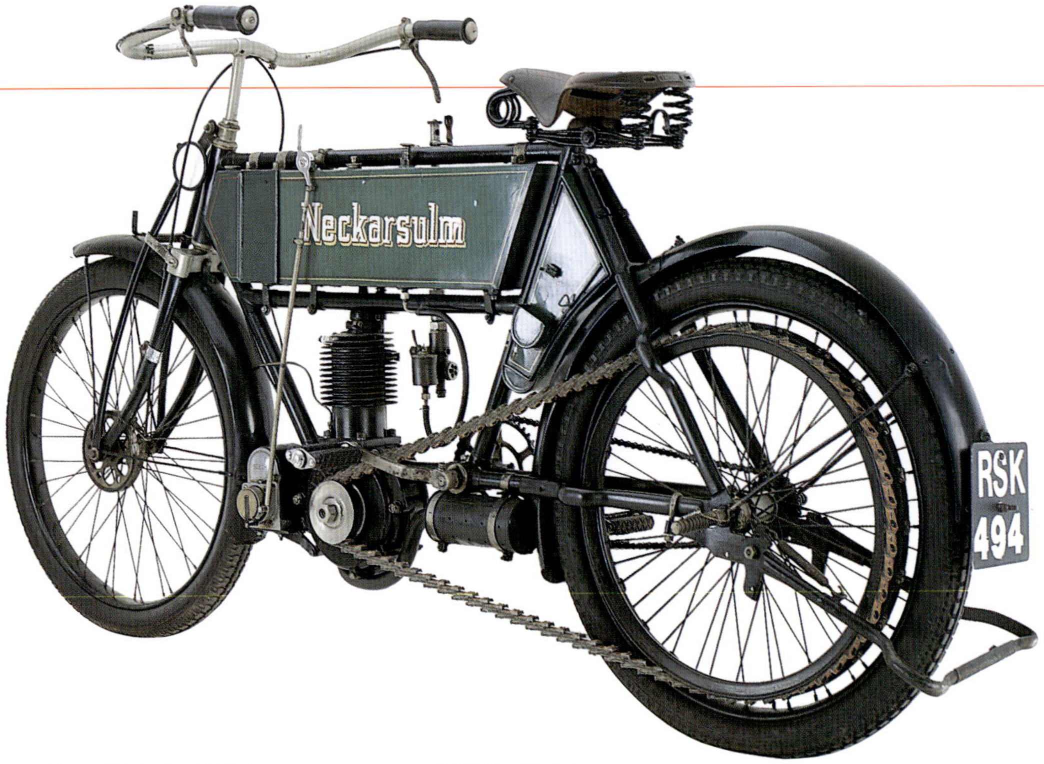


**Specifications (1906 Model)**
**Engine:** Four-stroke single
**Displacement:** 331cc (20cu in)
**Horsepower:** 2.5 @ 2000rpm
**Wheelbase:** N/A
**Weight:** 165lb (75kg)
**Top speed:** N/A

**Above:** This is the 1906 single cylinder, three and a half horsepower model of 1906. The belt drive from the engine to the rear wheel can be clearly seen in this picture.

**1906 3hp Model**
National Motor Musuem
Beaulieu, England

**Specifications (1912 350)**
**Engine:** Four-stroke twin
**Displacement:** 349cc (21.35cu in)
**Horsepower:** 7 @ 2500rpm
**Wheelbase:** N/A
**Weight:** N/A
**Top speed:** N/A

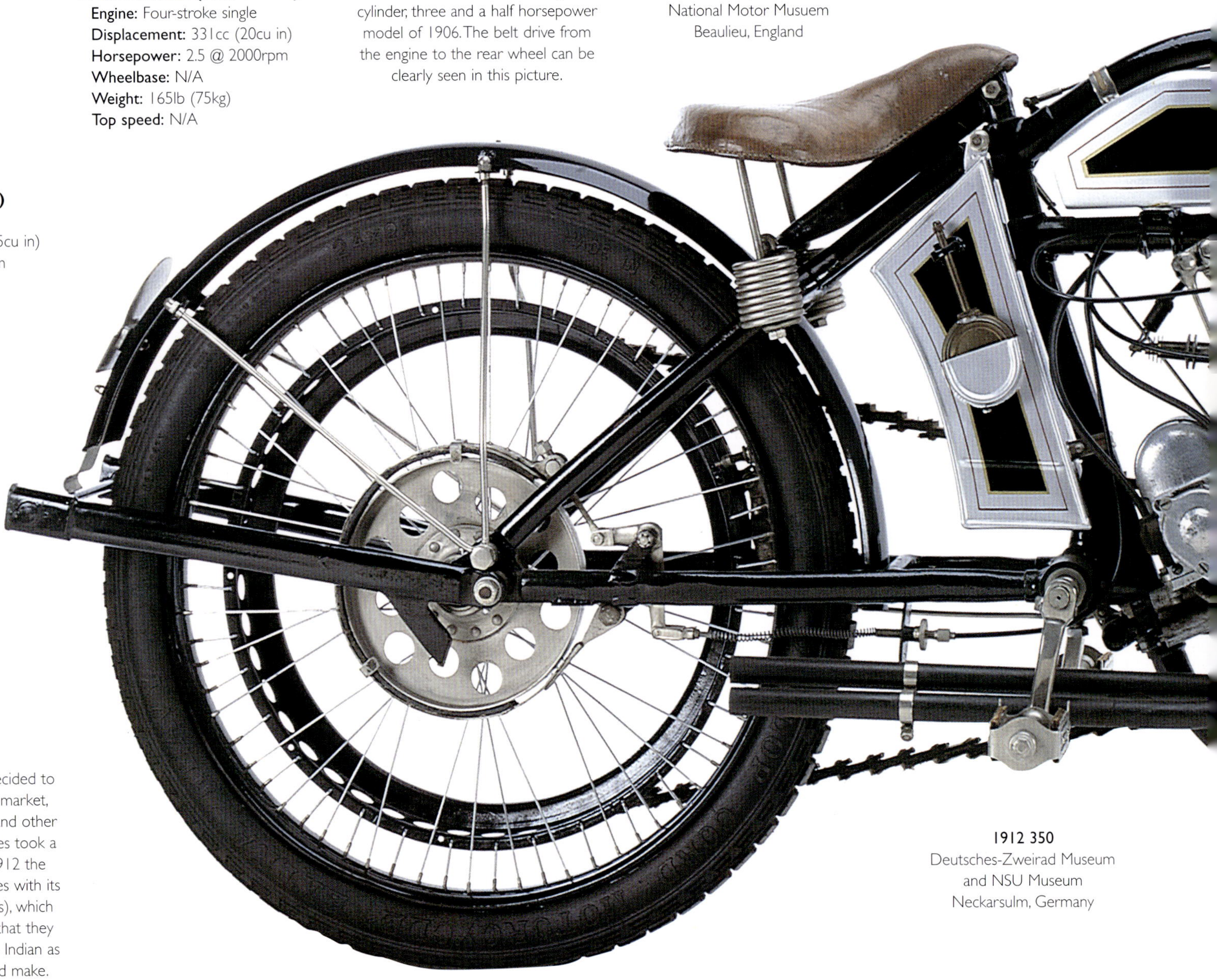

**Right:** By 1905 NSU had decided to move into the automobile market, building models of its own and other designer's makes. Motorcycles took a slightly back seat but by 1912 the company was producing bikes with its own engines (mainly V-twins), which were so popular in Britain that they were ranked second only to Indian as the most popular imported make.

**1912 350**
Deutsches-Zweirad Museum
and NSU Museum
Neckarsulm, Germany

**Right:** The NSU V-twin was entered in the Isle of Man Senior TT of 1914. With the outbreak of World War I this was a difficult year for all European companies. The TT was stopped during this period and didn't start again until 1920.

**1914 Senior TT500**
Deutsches-Zweirad Museum and NSU Museum Neckarsulm, Germany

**SPECIFICATIONS (1914 500)**
- **Engine:** Four-stroke twin
- **Displacement:** 498cc (30.39cu in)
- **Horsepower:** 10 @ 3000 rpm
- **Wheelbase:** N/A
- **Weight:** N/A
- **Top speed:** N/A

**Above:** The interest shown in Britain for NSU motorcycles was no doubt a deciding factor as to why they entered the very first TT on the Isle of Man in 1907, finishing a good fifth place in the single-cylinder class. Almost from the beginning NSU saw motorcycle sport as a marketing tool for its products. The bike shown is a 1914 TT500 model.

**Below:** The engine of the 350 of 1912 shows the exhaust down pipes exiting from the front and side of the twin cylinders. The carburetor is positioned between the two cylinders.

**Left:** This machine had belt drive to the rear wheel and sporty, slightly drop-down handlebars. The engine fitted neatly in the loop frame.

# NSU

NSU went on to make a variety of machines in the 1920s, both singles and V-twins, large and smaller capacity. From 1927 through 1929 factory race riders used 996cc (60.76cu in) ohv V-twins and the smaller 248cc (15.13cu in) machines. By 1930 the German economic gloom had arrived and, like many other companies, NSU was caught right in the middle. It had just bought a factory at Heilbronn but fortunately managed to sell it off and in 1929 the decision was made to stop any further car production.

During this time of recession the company employed the English designer Walter William Moore (formerly with Norton where he had been responsible for a towershaft-driven overhead-camshaft 500cc single), to create some new single-cylinder bikes. By 1931, NSU was producing excellent towershaft-driven ohc singles that became very popular, and as the new National Socialist regime took control both motorcycle and car sales also started to pick up. The 1930s saw NSU became one of the biggest motorcycle producers in the world. In the last years before World War II, along with a variety of other machines, the company produced supercharged vertical twins for racing. Unfortunately teething troubles prevented them from being successful and soon after that World War II intervened.

However, once again, NSU became heavily involved in war production, during which it produced the 1942 Kettenkrad half-track machine, one of motorcycling's true oddities. While three-wheeler variants of motorcycles, sidecars, forecars and trikes have been relatively common through motorcycling's history, the half-tracked machine has not. The Kettenkrad was built as a light gun tractor and personnel transporter for use in the difficult conditions experienced in war such as snow and sand, such as the German Army would encounter in the Soviet Union and North Africa, respectively. It was in effect a light armored vehicle with the front end of a motorcycle attached to the rear end of a half-track. The handlebars operated differential brakes on the tracks as well as turning the front wheel. It was powered by a 1500cc (91.50cu in) 4-cylinder Opel automobile engine.

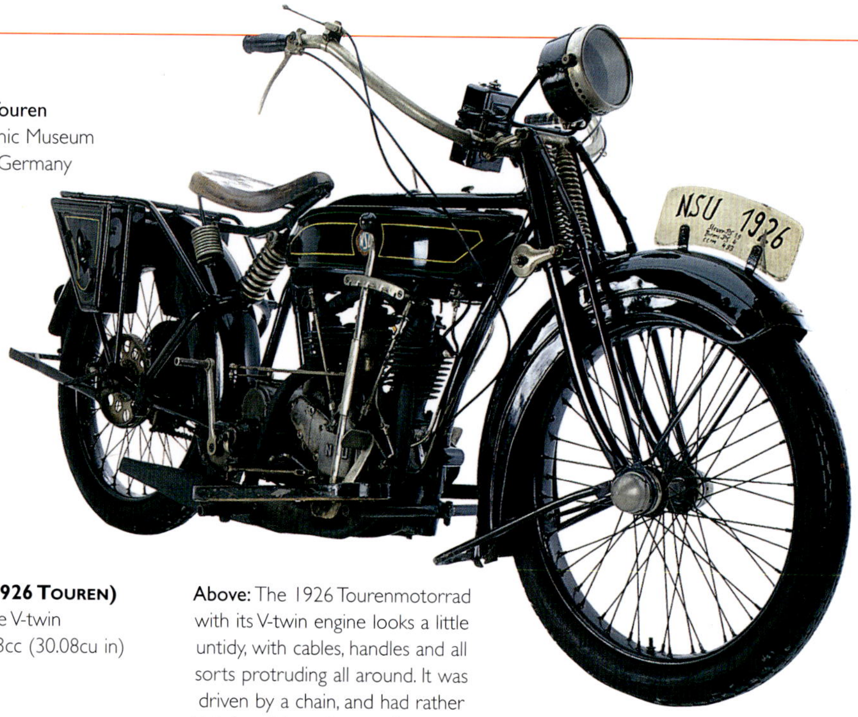


1926 Touren
Auto & Technic Museum
Sinsheim, Germany

**Specifications (1926 Touren)**
**Engine:** Four-stroke V-twin
**Displacement:** 493cc (30.08cu in)
**Horsepower:** 11
**Wheelbase:** N/A
**Weight:** N/A
**Top speed:** N/A

**Above:** The 1926 Tourenmotorrad with its V-twin engine looks a little untidy, with cables, handles and all sorts protruding all around. It was driven by a chain, and had rather high handlebars for comfort when touring.

1939 Kompressor
Deutsches-Zweirad Museum and NSU Museum
Neckarsulm, Germany

**Specifications (1939 Kompressor)**
**Engine:** Four-stroke dohc four
**Displacement:** 347cc (21cu in)
**Horsepower:** 75 @ 8000rpm
**Wheelbase:** N/A
**Weight:** 450 (200kg)
**Top speed:** 137.5mph (220kph)

**Right:** The NSU 1939 Kompressor racing machine used a two-cylinder, four-stroke double-overhead-camshaft engine. Albert Roder became NSU's chief engineer in 1947, at which point they returned to racing.

**Specifications (1935 Pony)**

Engine: Four-stroke single
Displacement: 198cc (12cu in)
Horsepower: 6.5
Wheelbase: N/A
Weight: N/A
Top speed: N/A

**Right:** This is the 1935 NSU Pony with its single-cylinder of 198cc. It was during this period that NSU concentrated on making cheap and small-displacement machines.

**1935 201 ZD Pony**
Auto & Technic Museum
Sinsheim, Germany

**Below:** Between 1951 and 1956 Wilhelm Herz broke the world speed record for motorbikes up to 350cc on this blown machine, the 1939 Kompressor.

**Above:** Wilhelm Herz had already won the German road championship with this machine in 1948.

# NSU

The company returned to civilian production in 1949, soon coming up with the speedy Fox and Max road bikes. The former was powered by a 98cc (5.97cu in) engine in a pressed-steel frame, with leading link forks and cantilever rear suspension.

The overhead-camshaft Rennmax was developed by Dr. Walter Froede out of a scrapped project. He used a sports twin crankcase and a pair of barrels from a four. The bike soon proved dominant on the racetrack in the 250 class, taking the top four places in the Lightweight 1952 Isle of Man TT. The engine was developed such that the first Rennmax delivered 27bhp at 9000rpm. Later in that same year, after further adjustment, the machine could deliver 31bhp at 10,400rpm. The bike assured its fame by claiming second place in the Italian Grand Prix, between two Moto Guzzis.

The frame was changed for a pressed-steel beam for 1953 and a fairing was fitted. Racing success continued through the year and the bike was little changed for 1954, although it now produced 39bhp at 11500rpm and the transmission was made six-speed. The Rennmax achieved swift, brief and shattering dominance of its class.

**Specifications (1952 Rennfox)**
**Engine:** Four-stroke dohc single
**Displacement:** 124cc (7.5cu in)
**Horsepower:** 14 @ 10000rpm
**Wheelbase:** N/A
**Weight:** 198lb (90kg)
**Top speed:** c94mph (150kph)

**Above:** The 1952 Rennfox on which Otto Daiker won that year's German championship. It had a single cylinder and a pressed-steel frame.

1952 Rennfox
Deutsches-Zweirad Museum
and NSU Museum
Neckarsulm, Germany

**Specifications (1953 Rennmax)**
**Engine:** Four-stroke dohc twin
**Displacement:** 248cc (15.13cu in)
**Horsepower:** 36 @ 11000rpm
**Wheelbase:** N/A
**Weight:** 270lb (117kg)
**Top speed:** 131mph (210kph)

**Above:** The machine that took the world by storm and began to eat into the domination of British and Italian racing bikes, the Rennmax of 1953 had a 248cc twin-cylinder, four-stroke, double Ohc engine.

**Specifications (1954 Fox)**
**Engine:** Four-stroke ohv single
**Displacement:** 98cc (6cu in)
**Horsepower:** 6 @ 6500rpm
**Wheelbase:** N/A
**Weight:** 190lb (87kg)
**Top speed:** 53mph (85kph)

**Below:** The 1954 Fox had a pressed-steel frame and foot-controlled gearbox. An inspiring design by NSU's Albert Roder.

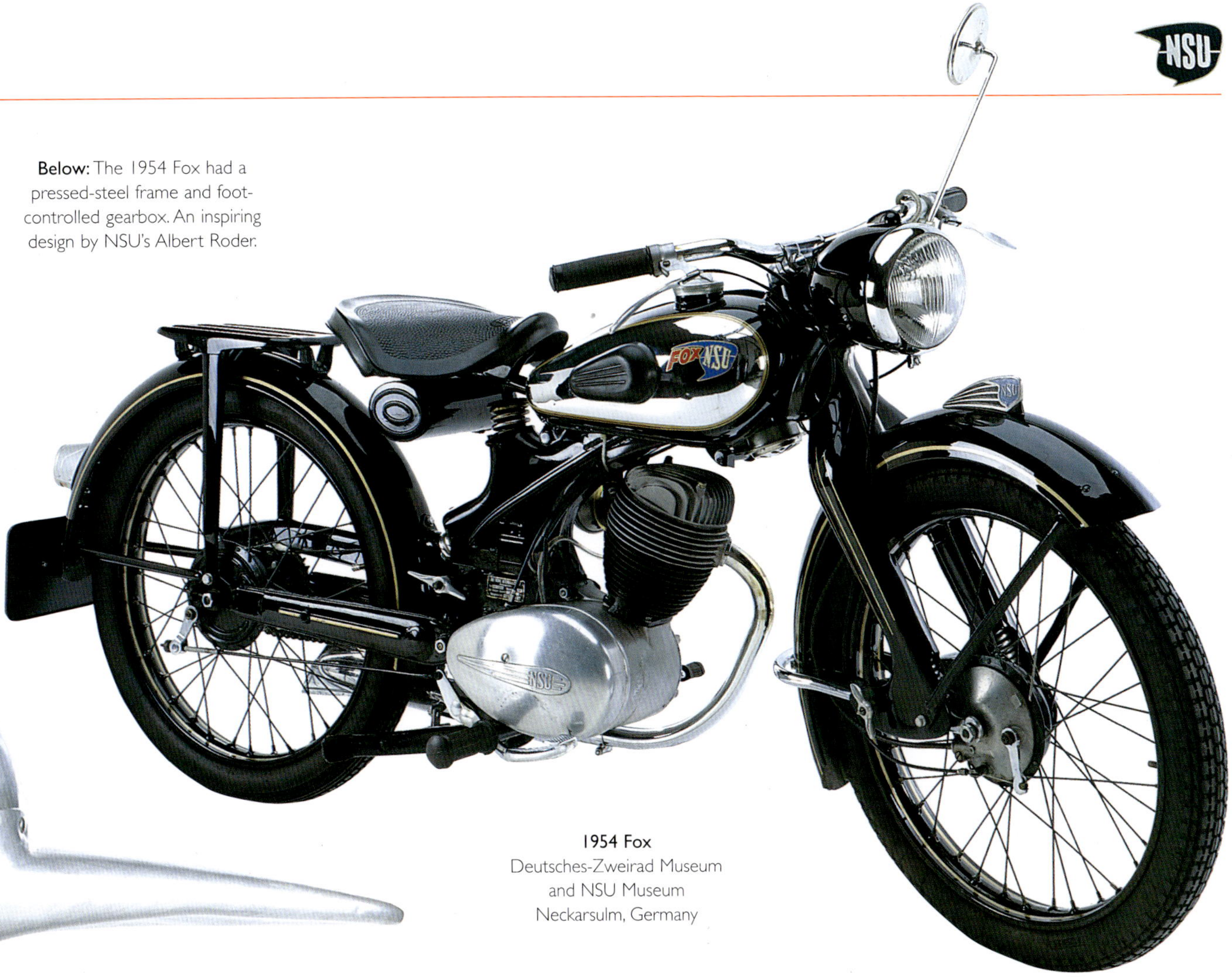

1954 Fox
Deutsches-Zweirad Museum
and NSU Museum
Neckarsulm, Germany

1953 Rennmax
Deutsches-Zweirad Museum
and NSU Museum
Neckarsulm, Germany

**Left:** The Rennmax was kitted out with a rather strange pointed front fairing. Note the drilling of holes into certain parts of the front brake operating components, obviously for weight reduction.

**Above:** The official NSU racing team for the 1953 season consisted of Lomas, Daiker, Haas and Luttenberger. This twin-cylinder machine, along with the similar 125, brought NSU the world championship on at least four occasions.

# NSU

The developed engine was installed in a Max road bike frame, fitted with aluminum bodywork and simple fairing, and given the name Sportmax. With Herman-Peter Müller (1954 250cc world champion) on board, it claimed another world championship in 1955, the only road-bike-based motorcycle to ever win a world GP title.

Tragedy struck the NSU racing team in 1956 when the leader, Werner Haas, was killed in a flying accident. Along with several other companies, NSU also pulled out of motorcycle racing shortly after Haas's death.

During the period that followed, the factory concentrated on smaller-capacity mopeds, such as the well loved Quickly. The company continued with record breaking attempts but with a variety of odd machines. One, a long, cigar-shaped contraption that was fondly known as the flying hammock, was sent to Bonneville Salt Flats in Utah, USA, where it shattered the 50cc record, reaching a speed of 121.9mph (207.84kph). Gustav Baumm must take some credit for this with his advanced aerodynamic design. Sadly, he crashed some time later and was killed.

At the same time a faired NSU machine took the absolute two-wheeler record at 210.8mph (337.28kph).

During the early 1950s Felix Wankel had started talks with NSU regarding his rotary engine concept, and after much development the idea became a reality and was used in motorcycles, such as the Hercules, and also in cars such as the NSU Ro80.

NSU automobile manufacture was to take precedence over motorcycle production. Two-wheelers were last made by NSU in 1965. The company was ultimately absorbed into the huge Audi-Volkswagen group.

**Above:** The 1954 Type Müller Fox, had a 98cc engine and foot gearchange. Many versions of the Fox were made.

**Specifications (1954 Fox-Müller)**
**Engine:** Four-stroke single
**Displacement:** 98cc (6cu in)
**Horsepower:** 6 @ 6500rpm
**Wheelbase:** N/A
**Weight:** 190lb (85kg)
**Top speed:** N/A

1954 Fox-Müller
Auto & Technic Museum
Sinsheim, Germany

**Specifications (1955 Fox-Italie)**
**Engine:** Four-stroke single
**Displacement:** 98cc (6cu in)
**Horsepower:** 6 @ 6500rpm
**Wheelbase:** N/A
**Weight:** 190lb (85kg)
**Top speed:** N/A

**Right:** The Fox Type Italie of 1955 was designed by Albert Roder. The company had always had a great relationship with Italian motorcycle manufacturers.

**Specifications (1958 Supermax)**

**Engine:** Single-cylinder
**Displacement:** 248cc (15.13cu in)
**Horsepower:** 17
**Wheelbase:** N/A
**Weight:** N/A
**Top speed:** N/A

**Left:** The final development of the Max was the Supermax. It was put on the market in 1954 and incorporated many improvements compared to the more basic machine offered.

**1958 251 OSB Supermax**
Auto & Technic Museum
Sinsheim, Germany

**Above:** The most significant advancement the Supermax had over its predesesors, was the adoption of twin shock, swinging-arm rear suspension. The Supermax gained a good reputation for a having a good finish and a long and reliable life.

**1955 NSU Fox-Italie**
Auto & Technic Museum
Sinsheim, Germany

**Left:** The 1954-built bikes from NSU were based on the prewar Konsul-type machines. New design and construction started under Albert Roder, who had interesting innovative ideas. The Fox was sold in many different countries and models would often be named after the receiving country.

# NUT

**Founded:** 1912
**Factory location:** Newcastle Upon Tyne, England
**Manufacturing lifespan:** 1912 - 1933

NUT, the initials of Newcastle Upon Tyne, was the name given to motorcycles produced in that city in the first decades of the twentieth century. Hugh Mason, a wealthy man, asked cycle dealer Jack Hall to build him a motorcycle based around an MMC engine. It was a success and over the next few years several more were built and sold under the name Bercleys.

In 1912 Hall began working with a company named after its proprietor, Sir William Angus Sanderson, with whose help, and using JAP engines specified by Mason, the NUT brand became a serious proposition. In the same year Mason designed a model which he rode to victory in the Junior TT on the Isle of Man in 1913. The surge in demand for NUT motorcycles immediately afterwards caught the company unawares and it struggled to cope. The NUT Sports machine, powered by a 50-degree JAP V-twin engine, was one of those made in that boom period.

A luxury JAP-engined V-twin was announced in 1919, but then the Sanderson company withdrew its backing to move into car production. Another backer was found and production continued, but the company was forced into liquidation.

In 1923 NUT was resurrected and a new range of machines was produced. Recurring financial problems, however, meant that NUT motorcycle production was not continuous. Another range of models was introduced in 1931 using JAP V-twins in 500cc (30.50cu in) and 700cc (42.50cu in) overhead-valve configuration as well as a 750cc (45.77cu in) side-valve. The machines were conventional in design and manufactured to a high standard. The range was for 1932 and 1933, but production was minimal and finally ceased permanently in the latter year.

# OK-Supreme

**Founded:** 1899
**Factory location:** Birmingham, England
**Manufacturing lifespan:** 1899 - 1939

OK's early motorcycles used De Dion, Minerva, Precision and Green engines, but the partners who had formed the company split up in 1926. One of them, Ernest Humphries, decided to append Supreme to the marque's name, and in 1928 a rider on an OK machine won an Isle of Man TT race. In the 1930s the company built bikes with four-stroke proprietary engines.

In 1932 the company catalogued eight different models that ranged in displacement from 148cc (9.03cu in) upwards. One, the Lighthouse, bore the nickname derived from the fact that the inclined engine, a single, had a vertical camshaft drive with a sight glass set in the top of the camshaft housing which allowed the rider to inspect the camshaft, an innovative way of producing an overhead-camshaft engine.

The firm produced a range of models in an attempt to offer something for everyone, and each year the range of both side-valve and overhead-valve models underwent slight modifications. By 1938 there were 14 models in the OK-Supreme line-up. The factory switched to military production during World War II and did not resume motorcycle production afterward.

**Specifications (OK-Supreme Lighthouse)**
**Engine:** Four-stroke ohc single
**Displacement:** 248cc (15.1cu in)
**Horsepower:** 10
**Wheelbase:** N/A
**Weight:** 270lb (122kg)
**Top speed:** 60mph (97kph)

**Below:** The OK-Supreme Lighthouse was one of a range of eight models listed by the company for 1932. They were largely conventional mechanically with the exception of the Lighthouse's overhead camshaft engine.

**1932 OK-Supreme Lighthouse**
National Motorcycle Museum
Birmingham, England

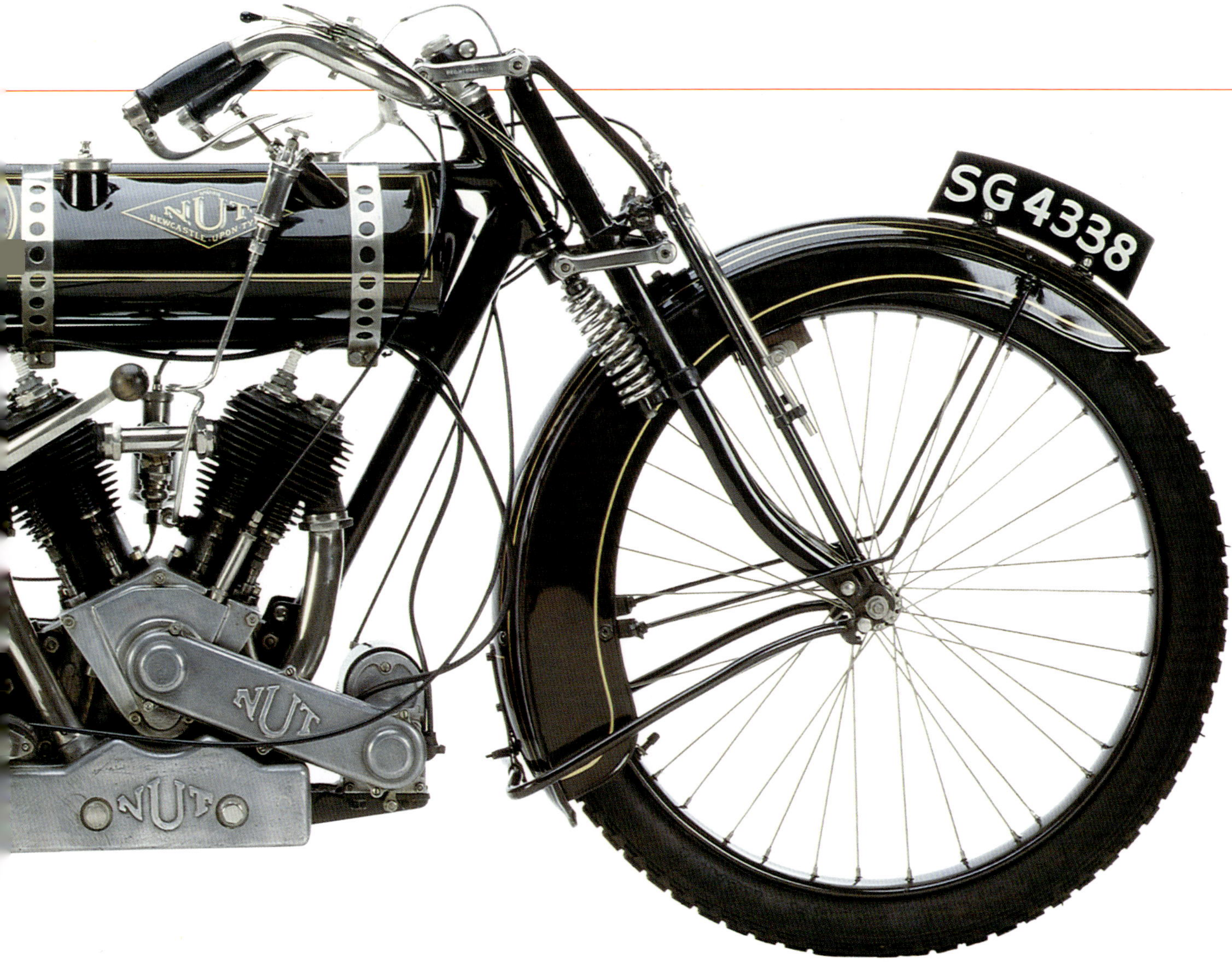


**SPECIFICATIONS (NUT SPORTS)**
- **Engine:** Four-stroke V-twin
- **Displacement:** 678cc (41.4cu in)
- **Horsepower:** 5
- **Wheelbase:** 56in (142.2cm)
- **Weight:** 275lb (125kg)
- **Top speed:** 60mph (97kph)

NUT Sports
National Motorcycle Museum
Birmingham, England

**Left:** the NUT had an unusual design of girder forks to provide front suspension, but was reliant on rear-wheel braking only.

## PEUGEOT

**Founded:** 1899
**Factory location:** Beaulieu, France
**Manufacturing lifespan:** 1899 - 1939

This French company was among the pioneers of the automobile and motorcycle industries. Peugeot built both single- and twin-cylinder engines for other motorcycle factories including Britain's Norton and Dot. A Peugeot V-twin-engined Norton ridden by H. R. Fowler won the first-ever Isle of Man TT in 1907.

Cycles Peugeot was founded in 1926 to concentrate on motorcycle production. Its model range was redesigned at the end of the 1920s and the new models in various forms continued in production until the outbreak of World War II.

Many Peugeot racing bikes were designed by Jean Antoinescu and these featured gear-driven overhead camshafts and a displacement of 494cc (30.13cu in ). These machines had not inconsiderable success during the 1920s and were finally retired in 1927.

Peugeot's first successful production model was a 334cc (20.30cu in) single. After World War II Peugeot produced V-twins of 295, 344, 738 and 746cc (17.99, 20.98, 45.01 and 45.50cu in, respectively). The firm also produced singles of 173, 269 and 346cc (10.51, 16.40 and 21.10cu in). ▶

1932 Model
Deutsches-Zweirad Museum
and NSU Museum
Neckarsulm, Germany

**SPECIFICATIONS (1932 MODEL)**
- **Engine:** Four-stroke single
- **Displacement:** 242cc (15cu in)
- **Horsepower:** 10.5 @ 5200rpm
- **Wheelbase:** N/A
- **Weight:** N/A
- **Top speed:** N/A

**Above:** Peugeot were pioneers of the car and motorcycle world, supplying engines to many different motorcycle companies. This single-cylinder 1932 model was one of the company's own designs.

In the postwar years the Peugeot operation concentrated on small capacity mopeds and motorcycles following a slump in the sales of larger machines in the mid-1950s.

The TSE, produced in 1980, was a diminutive trail bike produced at the plant in Montbeliard in France. It featured trials-type tires and off-road styling and was an enduro version of the Peugeot TSAL Roadster. Other similar machines made by Peugeot at the time include the SX8T and SX5C.

This same year saw the 103SP, a completely orthodox step-through design of moped intended as basic transportation and based around a small and economical two-stroke engine.

Twenty years later, Peugeot is one of the top scooter producing companies. It offers a good range of machines including a plug-in-and-go type electric model, which literally plugs into your mains to recharge its battery and will do up to 38 miles (61km) on a single charge.

The Speedflight model was voted best scooter for three years and today the Speedflight 2 is an attractively restyled version of that commuter two-wheeler.

**Left:** The front end of the Speedflight reveals a sleek profile with powerful headlamps.

**Right:** One-piece stepped seat and chunky rear wheel give the Speedflight a mean but good looking rear end. Disc brakes are used all round.

**PECIFICATIONS**
**(2000 SPEEDFLIGHT)**
- **Engine:** Two-stroke single
- **Displacement:** 50cc (3cu in)
- **Horsepower:** N/A
- **Wheelbase:** N/A
- **Weight:** 198lb (90kg)
- **Top speed:** 35mph (56kph)

**Below:** The Speedflight has single arm front fork with hydraulic shock absorber, allowing good road holding and control. The instrumentation is positioned neatly and clearly on top of the handlebars.

**2000 Speedflight 2**
Powerhouse Motorcycles
Kent, England

## Piaggio

| | |
|---|---|
| **Founded:** 1946 | |
| **Factory location:** Genova, Italy | |
| **Manufacturing lifespan:** 1946 – to date | |

Rinaldo Piaggio set up a company in 1884 to manufacture components for ships, and then diversified into the aeronautical industry in 1915. Soon after World War II Piaggio became a producer of motorized two-wheelers. Piaggio manufactured the famous Vespa range before taking over Gilera in 1969.

In the 1990s the company introduced a new range of scooters. The 1991 Cosa 200 had similarities with the earlier scooters for which Piaggio was famous but with an updated design. The Cosa 200 used a two-stroke, rotary-valve, single-cylinder engine concealed behind the composite bodywork. The bodywork was so designed as to provide storage for the rider's helmet when the machine was parked. Another similar 1991 machine from Piaggio was the PX 50XL Plurimatic scooter of 49.28cc (3cu in). Today the company is owned by a private equity fund which has a majority stake in the shares. The year 2000 saw Piaggio produce the first four-stroke 50cc scooter, alongside many other run-abouts it has to offer.

**Specifications (1987 Vespa PX 125 T5)**
- **Engine:** Two-stroke single
- **Displacement:** 125cc (7.62cu in)
- **Horsepower:** 12
- **Wheelbase:** 49in (125cm)
- **Weight:** 246lb (112kg)
- **Top speed:** 62mph (99kph)

**Below:** The PX series of Vespas was born in 1978, spawning 125, 150 and 200cc versions. This is a T5 model of 1987. Vespa has become possibly the world's most famous scooter.

1987 Vespa PX125 T5
National Motor Musuem
Beaulieu, England

## Pierce

| | |
|---|---|
| **Founded:** 1909 | |
| **Factory location:** Buffalo, New York, USA | |
| **Manufacturing lifespan:** 1909 - 1913 | |

George Pierce founded the Pierce Great Arrow Motor Car Company and the Pierce Cycle Company to build cars and bicycles to high standards and command premium prices. When Pierce put his son Percy in charge of the bicycle division in 1908, the young man added motorcycles to the roster. He had recently returned from Europe with an FN Four. Pierce did not copy the FN, but its influence on the first American four-cylinder motorcycle was apparent. While the FN was an IOE design, the Pierce employed a side-valve arrangement, with intake valves on one side of the engine and exhausts on the other. This two-cam system was called a T-head engine. And rather than suspend the engine in a loop frame, Pierce adopted the keystone system with the engine as part of the frame. Like the FN, the Pierce used enclosed shaft drive to the rear wheel, and was the first American motorcyle to fit the automotive-style final drive mechanism.

The other distinctive aspect of the Pierce was the use of the frame tubes to carry fuel and oil. The tubes were 3.5-inch (8.9cm) 18-gauge steel, copper plated on the inside. The upper and rear frame tubes held seven quarts (6.6lit) of gasoline, while the front downtube carried five pints (2.36lit) of oil. ▶

**Specifications (1910 Four)**
- **Engine:** In-line T-head
- **Displacement:** 696cc (42.47cu in)
- **Horsepower:** 7
- **Wheelbase:** 65in (165cm)
- **Weight:** 275lb (125kg)
- **Top speed:** 55mph (89kph)

**Below:** Pierce based its own Four on that of FN, but departed with regard to frame construction and the engine's valve mechanism.

1910 Pierce Four
Owner – Otis Chandler
Ojai, California

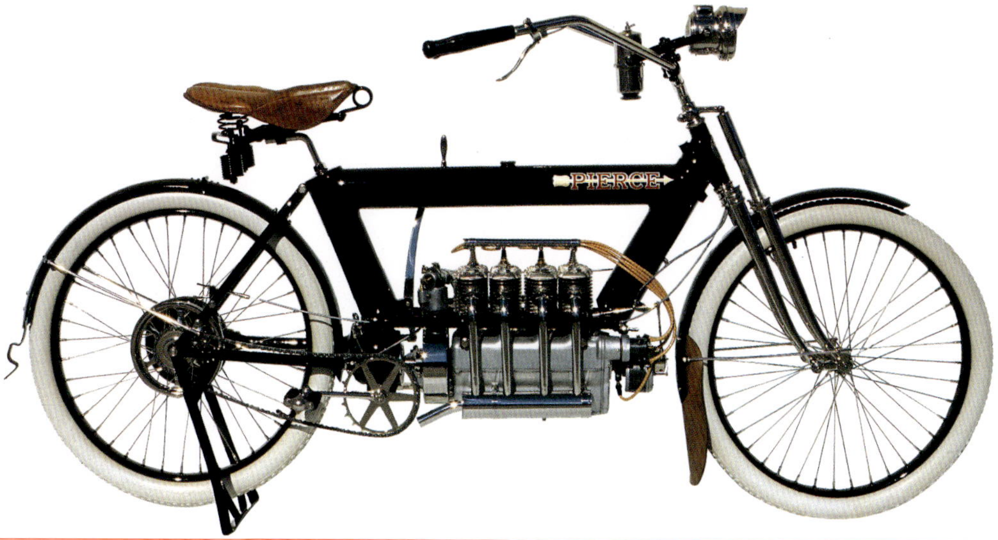

## PIERCE

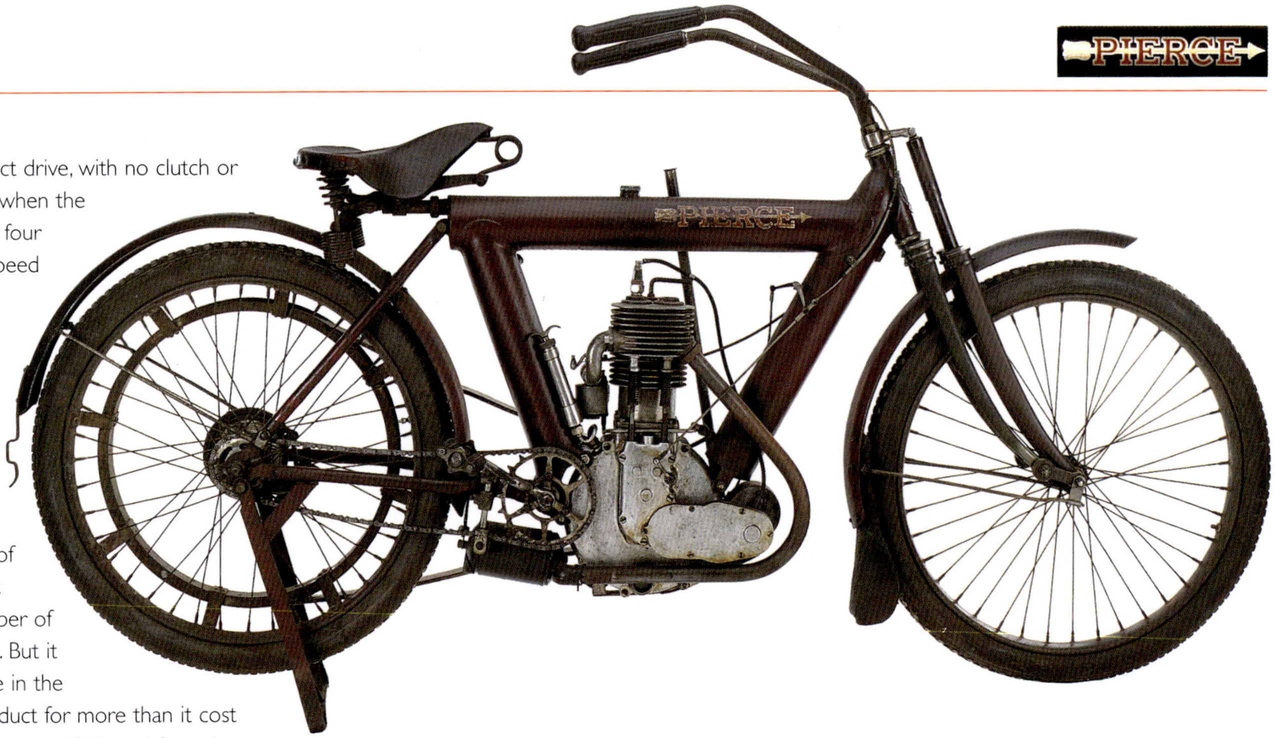


The original 1909 model was genuine direct drive, with no clutch or gearbox; so the rider had to be ready to go when the engine fired up. In its second model year the four was fitted with a multi-disc clutch and two-speed transmission.

The Pierce "vibrationless motorcycle" would give "motor car comfort and travel comfortably from a mere walking pace up to the speed of the motor car."

Percy Pierce obviously traded on the good reputation of his father's automobiles, but the connection was not undeserved. The motorcycle featured some of the most sophisticated engineering of its day. And the machine took top honors in a number of serious endurance contests around the USA. But it was soon apparent that in order to compete in the motorcycle business, one had to sell the product for more than it cost to produce. This necessity caught up with Pierce in 1913, and forced the enterprise into submission. But the Pierce stood as the original American four, a design that would be continued by William Henderson.

With war on the horizon, the Buffalo assembly plant was converted to production of Pierce-Arrow trucks intended for military use in Europe.

**SPECIFICATIONS (1913 SINGLE)**
**Engine:** Side-valve single
**Displacement:** 592cc (36.13cu in)
**Horsepower:** 5
**Wheelbase:** 57in (145cm)
**Weight:** 235lb (107kg)
**Top speed:** 55mph (89kph)

**Above:** The five-horsepower Pierce single claimed the "efficiency of a twin with the simplicity of single-cylinder construction."

**1911 Pierce Single**
Owner – Herb Singe
Hillside, New Jersey

## POPE

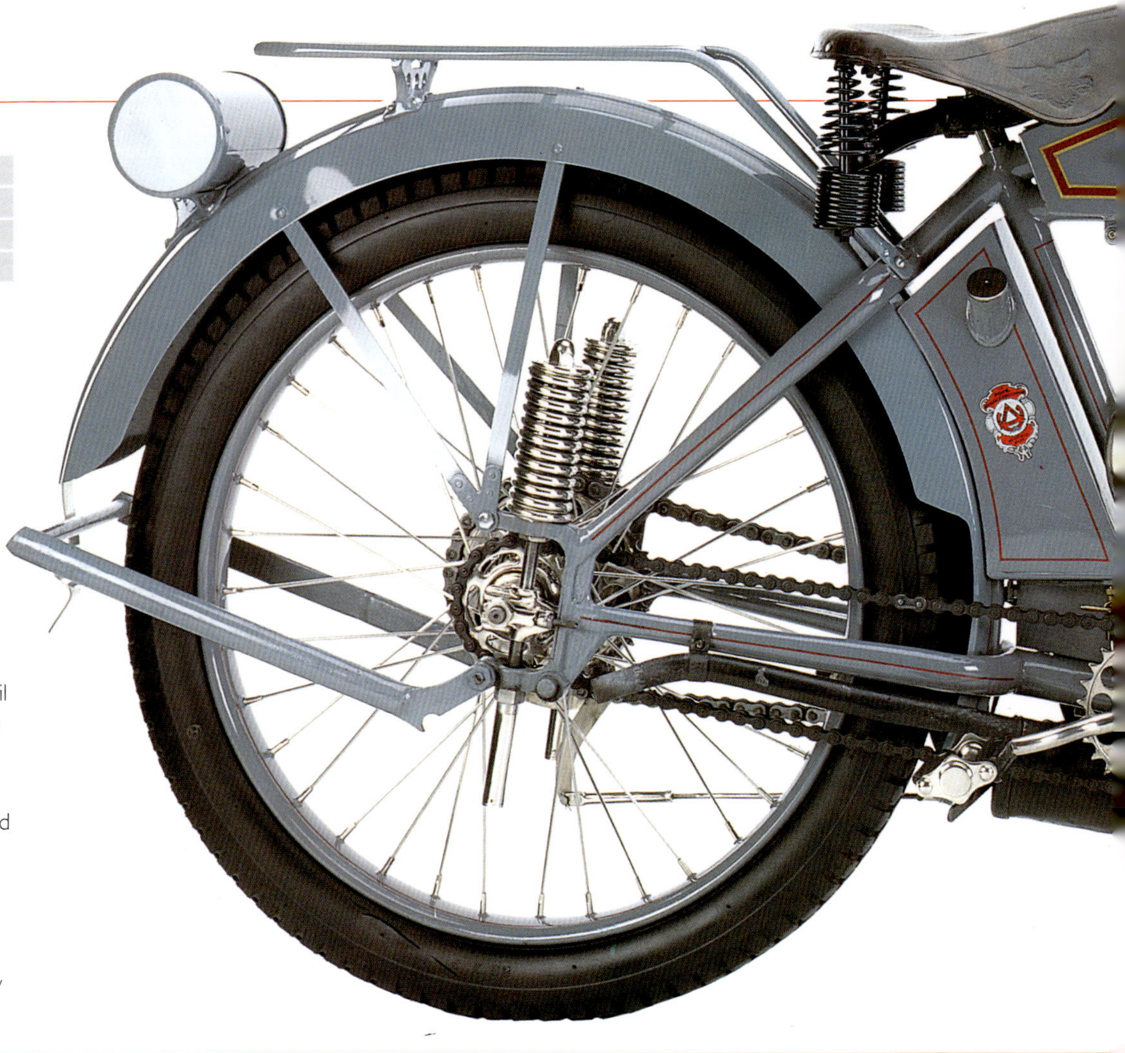

| | |
|---|---|
| Founded: 1911 | |
| **Factory location:** | Hartfield, Connecticut; Westfield, Massachusetts, USA |
| **Manufacturing lifespan:** | 1911 - 1918 |

Lieutenant Colonel Albert Augustus Pope (Union Army, Civil War) was one of the American transportation pioneers. He began importing then manufacturing bicycles in the 1870s, and undertook building automobiles in 1896. Pope bicycles were sold under the Columbia brand, and also as Cleveland, American, Imperial, Crescent, Monarch and Tribune. The same names were attached to motorcycles built by the American Cycle Manufacturing Company.

Pope had factories in Connecticut, Indiana, Illinois and Ohio. He founded *Wheelman* magazine and was instrumental in the promotion of paved roads, but by 1908 his financial situation had seriously deteriorated. Pope's own name wasn't applied to the motorcycles until 1911, two years after his death. Motorcycle production was moved to Westfield, Massachusetts.

The second generation of Pope machines showed a number of engineering advances compared to the competition (Indian, Harley and Excelsior). The single of 1911 was a conventional F-head engine with belt drive, a four-horsepower workhorse with a long production run. But the Pope engineers knew that to compete up-market with the heavyweights they needed something faster. The singles were adapted for racing with overhead valves, and in 1912 the 1000cc (61cu in) ohv V-twin was on the market. ▶

**Specifications (1913 Single)**

**Engine:** Ohv single
**Displacement:** 623cc (38cu in)
**Horsepower:** 5-8
**Wheelbase:** 56.5in (143.5cm)
**Weight:** 255lb (116kg)
**Top speed:** 50mph (80kph)

**Right:** The Pope overhead-valve single for 1913 was a stately machine with chain drive, rear suspension and front leaf-spring fork. A Bosch magneto was also available.

1913 Pope Single
Owner – Shorty Tomkins
Sacramento, California

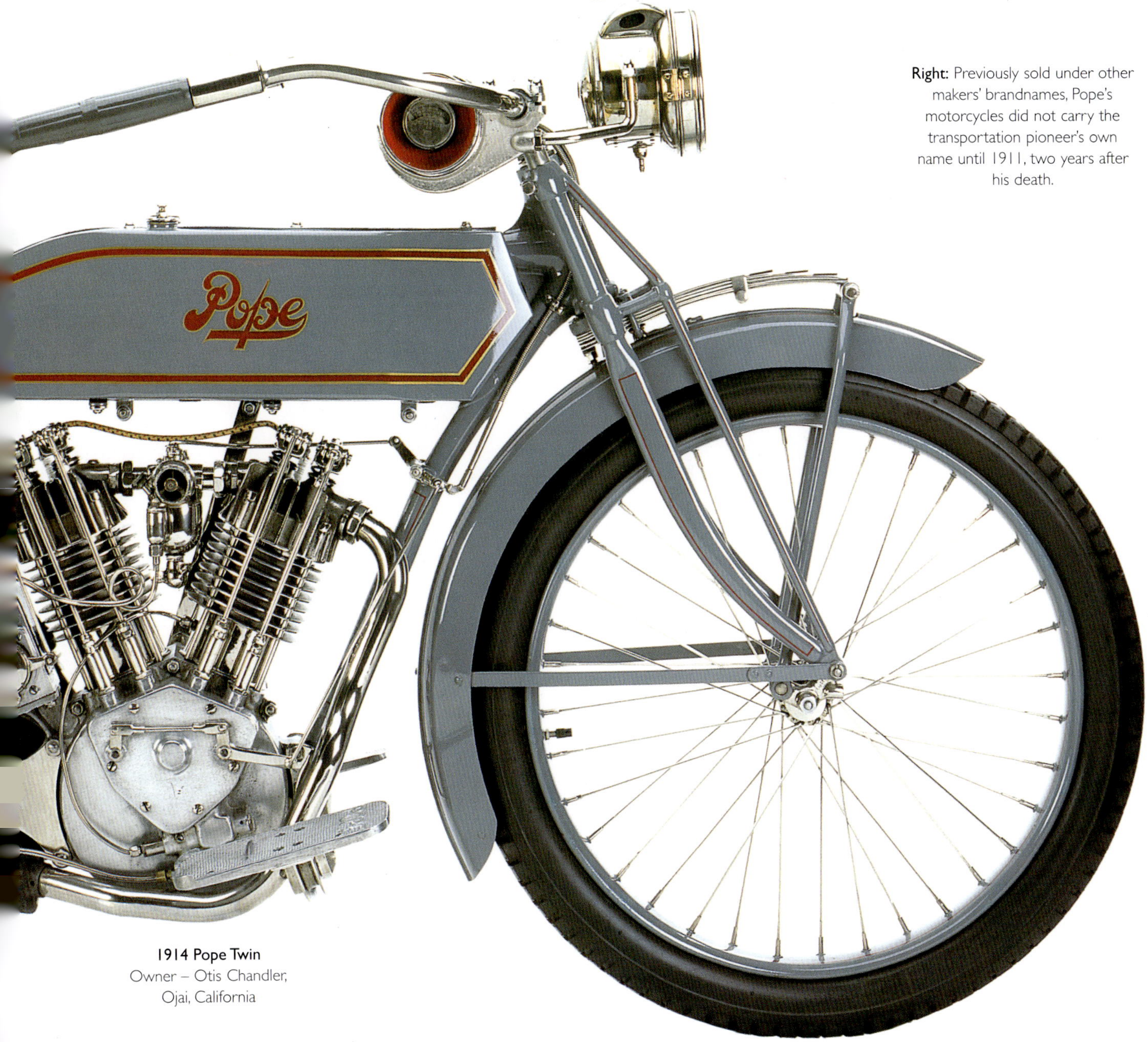


**Right:** Previously sold under other makers' brandnames, Pope's motorcycles did not carry the transportation pioneer's own name until 1911, two years after his death.

**Specifications (1914 Twin)**

**Engine:** Ohv twin
**Displacement:** 1000cc (61.02cu in)
**Horsepower:** 12-18
**Wheelbase:** 56.5/58.5in (143.5/148.5cm)
**Weight:** 305lb (138kg)
**Top speed:** 65mph (105kph)

**Left:** The overhead-valve Pope twins were built from 1912 to 1918. The two-speed transmission and rear suspension were strong selling points.

1914 Pope Twin
Owner – Otis Chandler,
Ojai, California

## POPE

Pope didn't enjoy huge success on the racetracks, but the firm gave it a good try. In 1914 the twin was offered as a single- or two-speed, for $265 and $300, respectively. The eight-horsepower engine used roller bearings for the connecting rods, Eclipse multi-disc clutch and Corbin-Duplex brake. The big Pope twin had a leaf-spring fork in front and plunger rear suspension, decades ahead of other manufacturers. The rear suspension allowed tuning to match the rider's weight.

The belt-drive single expired in 1916, and the big twin was offered with a three-speed transmission at the reduced price of $275. The same engine was available in the "short-coupled frame for speed work" at $260.

By 1918 Pope was down from seven models to two, the three-speed and single-speed twin. With a new Schebler one-inch (25.4mm) carburetor, the twin was good for "over eighteen horsepower". But by now the company's financial woes had put it beyond recovery, and motorcycle production was abandoned.

**SPECIFICATIONS (1915 TWIN)**

**Engine:** Ohv twin
**Displacement:** 1000cc (61.02cu in)
**Horsepower:** 12-18
**Wheelbase:** 56.5/58.5in (143.5/148.5cm)
**Weight:** 305lb (138kg)
**Top speed:** 65mph (105kph)

1915 Pope Twin
Courtesy of Mike Terry
Union, New Jersey

**Right:** In 1915 the Pope rear suspension was upgraded with twin shafts. Spring tension could be adjusted to match the rider's weight.

## PUCH

**Founded:** 1903
**Factory location:** Graz, Austria
**Manufacturing lifespan:** 1903 - 1987

Puch began motorcycle production with a range of singles and V-twins incorporating its own engines. After 1923 the major product line was of double-piston two-stroke machines in as many as six capacities. Puch had some racing success with two-stroke machines, including victory in the German Grand Prix of 1931 and although the road bikes were not of the same design, the two-stroke technology was efficiently applied. In 1934 Puch amalgamated with Steyr and Daimler to form the group known as Steyr, Daimler, Puch.

The S4 was a popular sports bike built between 1934 and 1938. It used a two-stroke, single-cylinder engine and was quite conventional for its day. Toward the end of the 1930s the company produced some side-valve flat-fours of 792cc (48.31cu in), mainly for military customers. After World War II the company manufactured a range of two-stroke motorcycles with single-piston engines and pressed-steel frames, and also updated some of the larger-displacement two-piston designs, such as the 248cc (15.12cu in) SGS in a pressed-steel frame which stayed in production until the early 1970s. Then production concentrated on 49, 123 and 173cc (2.98, 7.50 and 10.55cu in) machines including a range of trials and motocross bikes, in addition to a line of more basic mopeds. The 1977 M50 Cross was one of three machines with the designation M50, the others being the M50 Jet and M50 Grand Prix. The Jet and Grand Prix were roadgoing models while the Cross was an off-road, enduro-style motorcycle. All had 48.8cc (2.97cu in) engines. The 1980 Maxi S was intended as basic transportation for the shopper market. It was a step-through design available in three versions: the S, which had a single-speed transmission; the D with a dual seat; and the N with a rigid frame.

Production in Austria ceased in 1987 when the two-wheeler department of Steyr, Daimler, Puch was acquired by Piaggio.

**1916 Pope Single**
Owner – Dale Walksler
Mt. Vernon, Illinois

**Below:** 1916 was the final year for the belt-drive single. The economy model had changed little in six years of continuous production.

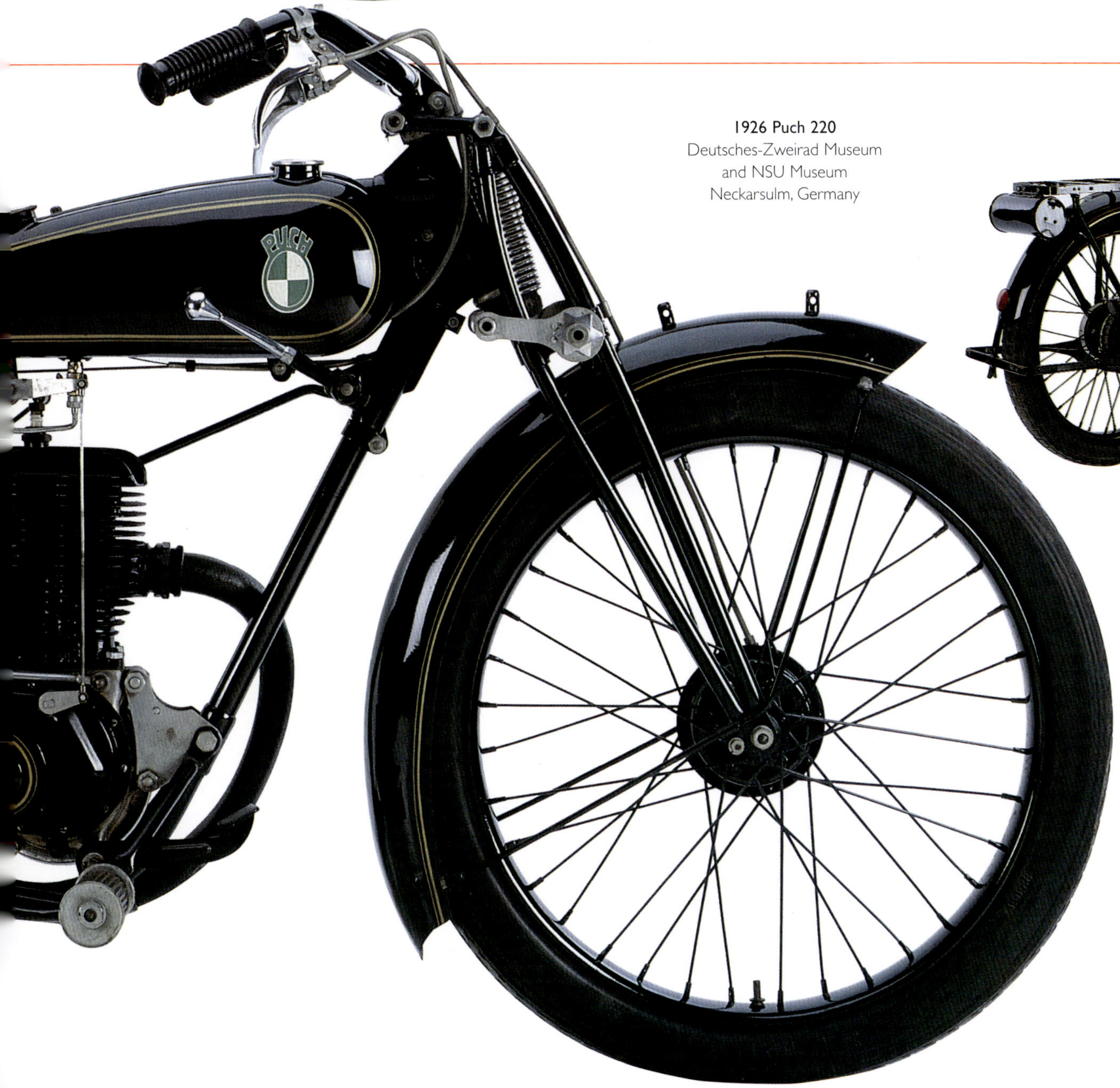

**1926 Puch 220**
Deutsches-Zweirad Museum
and NSU Museum
Neckarsulm, Germany

**Above:** The rear stand clipped to the rear fender. Once unclipped it acted as the main stand and would be folded down as far as the ground, after which the bike could be pulled backwards and onto the stand.

**Specifications (1926 220)**

**Engine:** Two-stroke single
**Displacement:** 223cc (14cu in)
**Horsepower:** 4.5
**Wheelbase:** N/A
**Weight:** N/A
**Top speed:** N/A

**Left:** Puch started making motorcycles in 1903, using its own single or V-twin engines. This is a 1926 single 220 model.

# Racycle

**Founded:** 1905
**Factory location:** Middletown, Ohio, USA
**Manufacturing lifespan:** 1905 - 1911

The first Racycle, from the Miami Cycle & Manufacturing Company of Ohio, was a re-labeled Indian. The Thor engine was used by several other manufacturers until 1908, when the Aurora Automatic Machinery Company brought to market a complete machine under the Thor brand.

The second generation of Racycle singles lasted until 1911, when Miami bought out the Merkel-Light company. Still an intake-over-exhaust engine with atmospheric intake valve, the new single was a larger engine set vertically in a keystone frame. The new chassis featured a leading-link, parallel-strut fork with a single cartridge spring, quite similar in design and construction to the New Era front suspension.

In its final rendition, the Racycle engine had the carburetor fitted aft of the cylinder and the spark plug in front. The frame was also modified, with a second rear downtube and seatpost suspension. Production was discontinued when Miami switched to the Merkel design.

**Specifications (1910 Single)**
**Engine:** IOE single
**Displacement:** 475cc (28.88cu in)
**Horsepower:** 4
**Wheelbase:** 60in (152cm)
**Weight:** 175lb (79kg)
**Top speed:** 40mph (64kph)

1910 Racycle
Owner – Herb Singe
Hillside, New Jersey

**Below:** The 1910 Racycle used the Thor engine. The next year's model retained the rear exit exhaust, but the carburetor moved aft of the cyclinder.

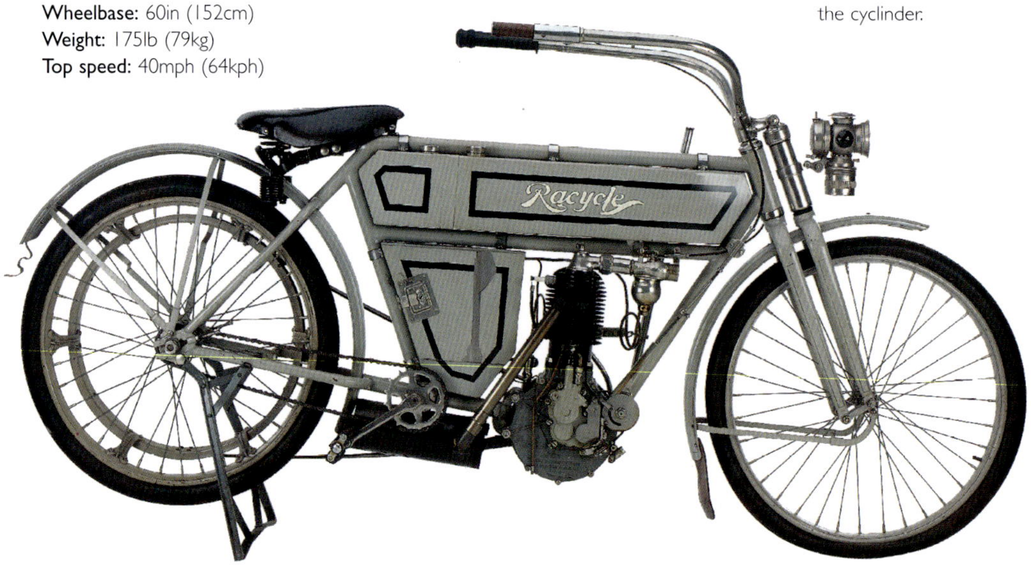


# Reading-Standard

**Founded:** 1903
**Factory location:** Reading, Pennsylvania, USA
**Manufacturing lifespan:** 1903 - 1922

The early Reading-Standards were also Indian replicas using the Thor engine, but the Pennsylvania company soon made its own modifications. The first change was a spring fork of its own design, and the fuel tank moved to the upper frame tube. The most significant revision came in 1906, when Reading-Standard released the first side-valve engine produced in the United States. Designed by engineer Charles Gustafson, the three-horsepower engine disposed the intake and exhaust ports 180 degrees apart in the cylinder head. The R-S, as it was called, also had a new oil tank on the rear fork just below the seat. Turning the lever one way released a measure of oil into the engine and shut off the tank; turned the other way, the valve refilled the oil cup.

R-S produced their first twin in 1908, but it did not employ the single's side-valve configuration. The F-head twin was rated at six horsepower, and had the unusual feature of the valve gear on the left side of the front cylinder and the right side of the rear. The twin was raced with some success in the early teens, most notably by Paul "Daredevil" Derkum of Los Angeles. But it was soon outpaced by the larger manufacturers. Charley Gustafson, Reading-Standard's top engineer, went to work for Indian.

By the mid-teens R-S had reduced its output to three models: two twins (with or without electrics) and a single, all with side-valve engines. All had three-speed transmissions; the twin was rated at twelve horsepower and the single at six. These were larger engines, a 557cc (33.98cu in) single and 1100cc (67.1cu in) twin. But R-S faltered in the early 1920s, and was sold to the Cleveland Motorcycle Manufacturing Company. The final editions in 1924 had a 1180cc (71.98cu in) twin with sixteen horsepower, no match for the big Indian and Harley twins.

1906 Reading-Standard
Owner – Mike Parti
North Hollywood, California

**Specifications (1906 Single)**
**Engine:** Side-valve single
**Displacement:** 361cc (22.03cu in)
**Horsepower:** 3
**Wheelbase:** 51in (130cm)
**Weight:** 150lb (68kg)
**Top speed:** 30mph (48kph)

**Right:** Reading-Standard produced the first side-valve engine in an American motorcycle. The model debuted in 1906.

# REX

**Founded:** 1900
**Factory location:** Birmingham, England
**Manufacturing lifespan:** 1900 - 1933

Rex produced comfortable singles and V-twins, first with its own engines and then Blackburnes. Early models had a variety of innovative features. One 372cc (22.75cu in) machine incorporated a silencer cast in one piece with the cylinder barrel. The Light Rex, as the 1907 3.5 horsepower model was called, had belt-drive transmission, and a total-loss lubrication system dependent on the rider pumping oil from the tank into the engine. Both brakes operated on the rear wheel; the foot pedal operated the brake on the inside of the belt-drive rim while the hand lever operated the internal expanding band brake.

After World War I Rex made a 550cc (33.55cu in) side-valve single, but it was also dropped in favor of models with Blackburne engines. Rex machines came in two wheelbases, depending on whether or not a sidecar was to be attached.

In 1922 Rex amalgamated with Acme to form Rex-Acme, which had some racing success before the factory was taken over in 1932 by a sidecar manufacturer, Mills-Fulford, which halted motorcycle production in the following year.

**SPECIFICATIONS (1907 LIGHT REX)**
**Engine:** Four-stroke single
**Displacement:** 453cc (27.6cu in)
**Horsepower:** 3.5
**Wheelbase:** N/A
**Weight:** 135lb (61kg)
**Top speed:** N/A

1907 Light Rex
National Motorcycle Museum
Birmingham, England

**Below:** The Rex 1907 was clearly derived from a bicycle with a diamond type frame and a single cylinder engine installed into it. Drive was direct as there was no gearbox.

**Right:** Early carbide headlamps retained the ornate craftsmanship developed for carriage lamps of the late 19th century. Their glow was minimal.

# Rokon

**Founded:** 1962
**Factory location:** Keene, New Hampshire, USA
**Manufacturing lifespan:** 1962 – to date

The Rokon Trail-Breaker is a work-horse motorcycle of an entirely different order. The two-wheel drive machine was designed to go where other motorcycles, or even animals, could not. With chain drive to both wheels, the Rokon will ascend very steep slopes at walking speeds and plow through mud. When added traction is required, the aluminum wheels can be filled with water for more weight, or used as supplementary fuel tanks. With wheels empty, the machine will float.

The Trail-Breaker is powered by a single-cylinder Chrysler two-stroke engine. In the mid-1970s the power was bumped from eight to ten horsepower, and a power take-off added. Popular with farmers, hunters, firefighters and mountaineers, the Trail-Breaker is still in production.

More conventional but still unusual was the Rokon RT-340, powered by a Sachs engine with automatic transmission. Developed as an enduro bike, the RT was also offered as a motocrosser and dual-purpose motorcycle. Other uncommon features were disc brakes and optional magnesium wheels. The Rokon Automatic went out of production in 1979.

1969 Rokon Trail-Breaker
Owner – Robert Sinclair

**Specifications (1969 Trail-Breaker)**
**Engine:** Two-stroke single
**Displacement:** 134cc (8.17cu in)
**Horsepower:** 8
**Wheelbase:** 49in (124cm)
**Weight:** 185lb (84kg)
**Top speed:** 25mph (40kph)

**Above:** Bumpers protect the Trail-Breaker's eight-horsepower two-stroke from rocks and brush. The three-speed transmission is hooked to an automatic clutch.

# Royal Enfield

**Founded:** 1898
**Factory location:** Worcestershire, England
**Manufacturing lifespan:** 1898 - 1971

The New Enfield Cycle Company was formed to embrace the bicycle portions of the two companies, Eadie Manufacturing and the Enfield Manufacturing Company. The Enfield name had been adopted when the company won contracts to supply the Royal Small Arms factory at Enfield in Middlesex. The Royal prefix was added in 1893, and by 1897 the company had dropped the "New" prefix.

Enfield manufactured its first motorcycle in 1900, with a 211cc (12.87cu in) Minerva engine mounted over the front wheel, followed by more conventional motorcycles, including a MAG V-twin-engined machine, and a 770cc (47cu in) JAP-engined V-twin. After World War I the company built a large displacement V-twin of 976cc (60cu in) specifically for sidecar use. A medium-weight four-stroke was introduced in 1924 with a JAP engine although the company later installed an engine of its own design. Later in the 1920s a 996cc (60.76cu in) V-twin sidecar outfit ridden by E. Magner, a Swede, broke the One Mile World Record.

In 1928 the Royal Enfield firm adopted saddle tanks and center-spring girder forks for its range of motorcycles. Vertical singles appeared in 1936, of which one was the Model JF Bullet, a name that had already been used for other models. The engine was of 499cc (30.44cu in) with a four-valve cylinder head. The machine was fitted with a new style of silencer. The range was altered for 1937, although the JF continued unchanged. ▶

**Specifications (1922 V-Twin)**
**Engine:** Four-stroke V-twin
**Displacement:** 976cc (59.6cu in)
**Horsepower:** 6-8
**Wheelbase:** N/A
**Weight:** 320lb (145kg)
**Top speed:** N/A

1922 V-Twin
National Motorcycle Museum
Birmingham, England

**Right:** The V-twin still retained many bicycle-type features, including the rigid diamond frame, dummy rim brakes front and back, and a sprung saddle.

**SPECIFICATIONS (1937 BULLET)**

**Engine:** Four-stroke ohv single
**Displacement:** 499cc (30.5cu in)
**Horsepower:** 19 @ 5000rpm
**Wheelbase:** 54in (1372mm)
**Weight:** 364lb (165kg)
**Top speed:** 80mph (129kph)

**Right:** The 499cc single-cylinder Bullet had a speedometer in front of the handlebars while the ammeter and ignition switch were mounted in a panel on top of the fuel tank which was finished in chrome with painted panels.

1937 Bullet
National Motorcycle Museum
Birmingham, England

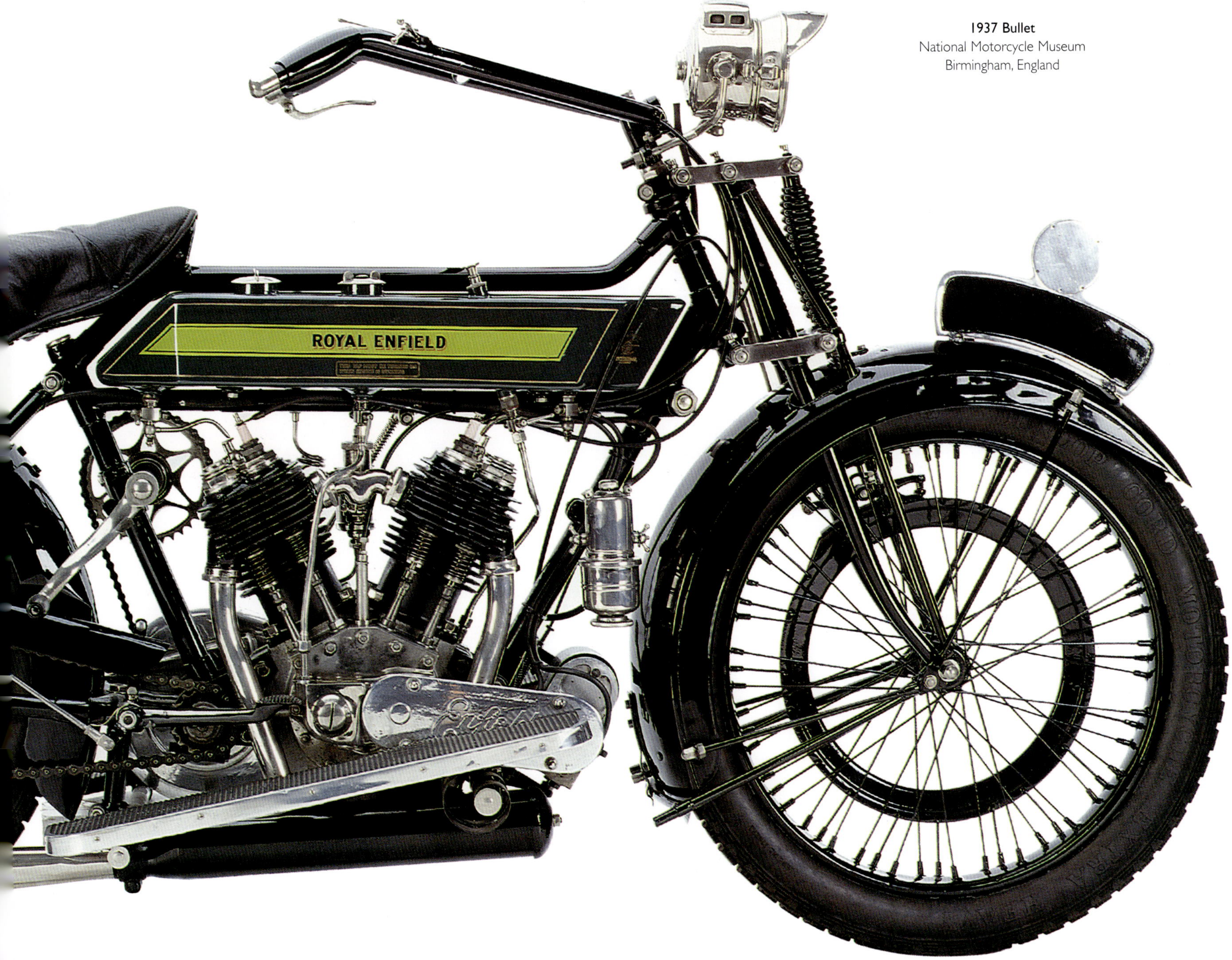

# Royal Enfield

By 1938 there were 20 different models in the range. When World War II intervened, Royal Enfield built motorcycles for the military, including the 125cc (7.62cu in) two-stroke Flying Flea for airborne troops, which postwar was sold in civilian colors, and the 346cc (21.06cu in) Model C and CO singles.

In 1948 the company introduced a completely new engine, a 495cc (30.21cu in) overhead-valve vertical twin constructed around a single alloy-iron cast crankshaft mounted in ball and roller main bearings. The big ends were of the plain type. The engine had two camshafts which were chain-driven. The dynamo was also chain-driven but from the forward camshaft. It had a skew-gear drive to the distributor which housed the points for the coil ignition system. The cylinder barrels were made from alloy while the cylinder heads were cast in iron. The oil pumps were the standard Enfield items and, in line with Enfield practice, the lubricant was carried in a crankcase sump. The gearbox was bolted to the rear of the engine crankcase and the whole unit fitted in to cycle parts that were almost identical to the single-cylinder Bullets of the time, including the girder forks.

Royal Enfield also introduced a new model, again called Bullet, in 1948. The internals of the engine were carried over from the prewar Model G, although the crankcase was different. The bike caused a sensation on its first outing as it was the first time a swingarm frame had been used in trials competition. The road version officially appeared in 1949. Gradually the power crept up to 350cc (21.35cu in) producing 21bhp @ 6500rpm as a result of increased compression ratio. The larger 500cc (30.50cu in) displacement Bullet appeared for 1953 and used mostly the same cycle parts as the 350cc (21.35cu in). The Bullet was available in trials, scrambles and roadgoing trim, and the bike had some success in International Six Days Trial events.

The Bullet model was discontinued after the appearance of the 1962 versions. The name, however, would be used again, this time on a unit-construction 350cc (21.35cu in) machine.

In 1966 Royal Enfield presented the Continental GT became popular as a cafe racer because of its sleek lines and racetrack-inspired features. It was basically a stripped-down version of the Crusader Sports using the 250cc (15.29cu in) Crusader engine and 5-speed gearbox. Race-style parts included sweptback exhaust, bell mouth on the carburetor in place of an air cleaner, a plastic tube crankcase breather, rear-set footrests and levers, clip-on handlebars, fly screen, cooling discs on the front brake hub, humped-back dual seat and fiberglass fuel tank with quick-release filler cap.

The bike was expensive to make, and the company had to restrict its range of other models before being taken over by Norton-Villiers in 1967.

1951 500 Twin
National Motorcycle Museum
Birmingham, England

**Specifications (500 Twin)**
**Engine:** Four-stroke ohv twin
**Displacement:** 495cc (30.2cu in)
**Horsepower:** 25 @ 5500rpm
**Wheelbase:** 54in (137.2cm)
**Weight:** 390lb (177kg)
**Top speed:** 78mph (125kph)

**Above:** Because other British manufacturers were offering twins in their ranges, Royal Enfield also felt it needed one. The new engine, a 495cc ohv twin, was introduced in 1948 and lasted a decade.

**Right:** The Continental was a genuine attempt to offer a motorcycle with race-style features that Royal Enfield decided that younger customers really wanted.

1966 Continental GT
National Motorcycle Museum
Birmingham, England

Left: The Bullet featured swingarm rear suspension – a fork pivoted behind the gearbox – and was damped by a pair of hydraulic rear shocks. The rear wheel could therefore move up and down over bumps.

**Specifications (1954 Bullet)**

- **Engine:** Four-stroke ohv single
- **Displacement:** 346cc (21.1cu in)
- **Horsepower:** 18 @ 5750rpm
- **Wheelbase:** 54in (137.2cm)
- **Weight:** 350lb (159kg)
- **Top speed:** 68mph (109kph)

1954 Bullet
Owner – Tony East of A.R.E. Ltd
England

**Below:** The Bullet in its roadgoing trim, although there were also trials and scrambles versions.

**Specifications (Continental GT)**

- **Engine:** Four-stroke single
- **Displacement:** 248cc (15.1cu in)
- **Horsepower:** 26 @ 7500rpm
- **Wheelbase:** 52in (132.1cm)
- **Weight:** 300lb (136kg)
- **Top speed:** 86mph (142kph)

**Left:** Cafe racer styling touches applied to the Continental included the front brake drum trims intended to replicate race-style brake cooling devices.

**Above:** Befitting its cafe racer image, the five-speed Continental GT was genuinely nippy – it could reach 86mph (138kph) and handled well.

## Royal Enfield

During the 1950s the Indian Government made arrangements with Royal Enfield to manufacture the Bullet, and in 1956 the company set up a subsidiary in Madras to produce the 350cc Bullet under license. This led to the formation of Enfield India Ltd. The Indian factory reproduced the 1955 specification Bullet and continued doing so long after the British-built Bullets were discontinued. The Indian-produced motorcycles are now exported around the world, and they are bought, apart from the Indian Army and police forces, by bikers who desire a modern classic bike, who want simple and inexpensive transport, or those who find it an intriguing curiosity. Exports have at times been affected by such diverse factors as labor disputes, tidal waves and floods in India.

The current Bullets have changed slightly from the original 1955 specification. Refinements have been introduced sparingly or when required by law. The motorcycles now feature 12-volt electrics instituted in 1987, an alternator in place of a dynamo, a distributor in place of a magneto and indicator lights.

Subsequently 500cc Bullets have been built in India and exported; these models optionally feature a single disc brake on the front wheel. The Indian-manufactured Bullets are available in three specifications: Standard, Deluxe and Superstar. The latter two feature minor improvements such as chromed panels on the fuel tank.

In the two decades since the Indian-built Bullets started to be exported to Britain through various concessionaires, changes have been made to the design of the fenders as well as to smaller components. The type of hubs, footpegs, kickstarter and side-stands fitted have all been changed, but overall the motorcycles are still effectively mid-1950s British bikes powered by a single-cylinder engine with an iron barrel and an alloy cylinder head and featuring a swinging-arm frame and telescopic forks. The forks bear the headlamp "casquette," as it was termed by Royal Enfield, which also houses the instruments and switches.

## Rub and Hab

**Founded:** 1894
**Factory location:** Munich, Germany
**Manufacturing lifespan:** Unknown

In 1892 a talented shoemaker who lived in Ulm and whose name was Ludwig Rub decided to move to Munich, Bavaria, in southern Germany. While there he met with Alois Wolfmuller, who along with his partner Henry Hilderbrand is reported to have produced the world's first ever mass-produced motorcycle in 1894. Wolfmuller commissioned Rub to help with the new motorcycle but Rub soon became disenchanted with the situation and left. Moving on, he met up with Hab, who was a lathe operator and worked at the Krauss & Co. locomotive factory in Munich. Together they designed and constructed a motorcycle with many of their own new ideas, one of the features being the Bosch electric ignition.

**Specifications (1898 Model)**
**Engine:** Four-stroke single
**Displacement:** 235cc (14cu in)
**Horsepower:** c 0.6
**Wheelbase:** N/A
**Weight:** N/A
**Top speed:** N/A

1898 Rub and Hab
Deutsches-Zweirad Museum
and NSU Museum
Neckarsulm, Germany

**Left:** The innovative machine designed and constructed by Rub and his partner Hab had a four-stroke engine layd flat on the up tube at the front of the frame, and a belt drive with a pulley mechanism to help keep it taut.

1997 Bullet 500
Bavanar Products Ltd
England

**Left:** Although the 500cc (30.50cu in) version of the Enfield-India Bullet is fitted with the traditional drum brake hub, a disc front brake is now available as an extra-cost option.

**Above:** The Indian factory still produces both 350 and 500cc displacement versions of the Bullet, just as the British factory did many years ago, but with minor amendments.

**Specifications**
**(Enfield India Bullet)**

- **Engine:** Four-stroke ohv single
- **Displacement:** 499cc (30.45cu in)
- **Horsepower:** 22 @ 5400rpm
- **Wheelbase:** 54in (137.2cm)
- **Weight:** 370lb (168kg)
- **Top speed:** 78mph (125kph)

## Rudge

**Founded:** 1911
**Factory location:** Coventry, England
**Manufacturing lifespan:** 1911 - 1940

The Rudge-Whitworth bicycle factory in Coventry, England, started producing motorcycles in 1911, was later bought by EMI and moved to Hayes, in the south of England, and then acquired by Raleigh, the bicycle makers.

Along the way, it first produced a 499cc (30.43cu in) IOE-configuration machine; developed the multi-gear which was a variable gear that gave up to 21 positions; enjoyed competition success including the 1928 Ulster Grand Prix which led to a 499cc sports model being called the Rudge Ulster; offered engines and gearboxes to other manufacturers under the Python name; and built the notable Rudge Special, which was in fact a standard machine powered by an overhead-valve single-cylinder engine. The Special had a four-valve cylinder head in which the valves were arranged in parallel pairs rather than in the radial configuration of the Ulster models. This difference helped make the Special a more docile motorcycle and one requiring less frequent adjustment of valve clearances.

**Specifications**
**(1937 Rudge Special)**

- **Engine:** Four-stroke ohv single
- **Displacement:** 493cc (30.1cu in)
- **Horsepower:** N/A
- **Wheelbase:** N/A
- **Weight:** N/A
- **Top speed:** 70mph (113kph)

**Below:** The Rudge Special was powered by an overhead-valve 493cc (30.08cu in) single-cylinder engine with a bore and stroke of 84.5 x 88mm.

1947 Rudge Special
National Motorcycle Museum
Birmingham, England

# SCHICKEL

| | |
|---|---|
| **Founded:** 1912 | |
| **Factory location:** Stamford, Connecticut, USA | |
| **Manufacturing lifespan:** 1912 - 1924 | |

The Schickel Motor Company was another pioneer in two-stroke technology. The Connecticut firm offered a choice of two engines, with chain or belt drive. The 695cc (42.41cu in) Big Six (horsepower) model with chain drive sold for $240 in 1914. The five-horsepower belt version was $20 less.

The Schickel magneto was enclosed in the crankcase. By 1916 the machine had added an Eclipse clutch and the price had dropped to $210. The belt-drive model sold for $200, and the Lightweight (290cc/17.7cu in) version was offered at $109. At the end of Schickel production in 1924, only the Lightweight model remained on the roster.

1912 Schickel Big Six
Owner – Bud Ekins
North Hollywood, California

**Below:** The Schickel's crankshaft, crankpin and flywheel were cast in one piece.

**SPECIFICATIONS (1912 BIG SIX)**
**Engine:** Two-stroke single
**Displacement:** 495cc/695cc (30.26/42.41cu in)
**Horsepower:** 5/6
**Wheelbase:** 53in (135cm)
**Weight:** 190lb (86kg)
**Top speed:** 50mph (80kph)

# SCOTT

| | |
|---|---|
| **Founded:** 1909 | |
| **Factory location:** Shipley, Yorkshire, England | |
| **Manufacturing lifespan:** 1909 - 1958 | |

This company's founder, Alfred A. Scott, was among the pioneers of the two-stroke motorcycle, employing rotary inlet valves, water-cooling and the 180-degree parallel twin two-stroke long before Japanese manufacturers did. He used the engine as a stressed member in his duplex, triangulated tube frames to enhance handling and he pioneered all-chain-drive and countershaft gears.

A. A. Scott parted with the company in 1915 and died in 1923 but production of his basic designs continued. The water-cooled two-stroke engine used in the Flying Squirrel was unusual in its design; the flywheel was centrally positioned with twin inboard main bearings, overhung crankpins and crankcase doors to allow access to the engine. The whole was located in a large alloy casting on which sat the block with non-detachable cylinder heads. The engine was made in 499cc and 598cc (30.44 and 36.48cu in) through using cylinders with a common stroke but a change in bore diameter.

**SPECIFICATIONS (1949 FLYING SQUIRREL)**
**Engine:** Two-stroke twin
**Displacement:** 598cc (36.5cu in)
**Horsepower:** 30 @ 5000rpm
**Wheelbase:** 57in (1448mm)
**Weight:** 395lb (179kg)
**Top speed:** 84mph (135kph)

**Below:** The fuel tank was positioned atop the triangulated frame and was oval in shape. A number of variants, including sprint and TT replica models, were offered.

1949 Flying Squirrel
National Motorcycle Museum
Birmingham, England

# SEARS

**Founded:** 1910
**Factory location:** Chicago, Illinois, USA
**Manufacturing lifespan:** 1910 - 1916

The Sears Auto-Cycle was built for Sears, Roebuck and Company of Chicago by The Aurora Automatic Machine Company. This had the redesigned Thor engine, following the Illinois company's production of Indian engines. The Brown and Barlow carburetor was controlled by the left twistgrip, while the right regulated the spark. The keystone frame was fitted with a twin leading-link fork. In 1912 Sears switched suppliers, employing the Excelsior Cycle Company of Chicago, and offered the DeLuxe Big Five, called "The Big Single With Nearly Twin Power," and the DeLuxe twin in seven- and nine-horsepower versions. Sears, Roebuck joined many other retailers in abandoning motorcycles with the advent of World War I.

**Right:** The DeLuxe engine employed an interesting longitudinal camshaft with worm-gear drive to the magneto. The V-twin version displaced an impressive 1157cc (70.58cu in).

**Below:** Second generation Sears featured the new Musselman air-cooled rear brake, and the seat post incorporated a double spring.

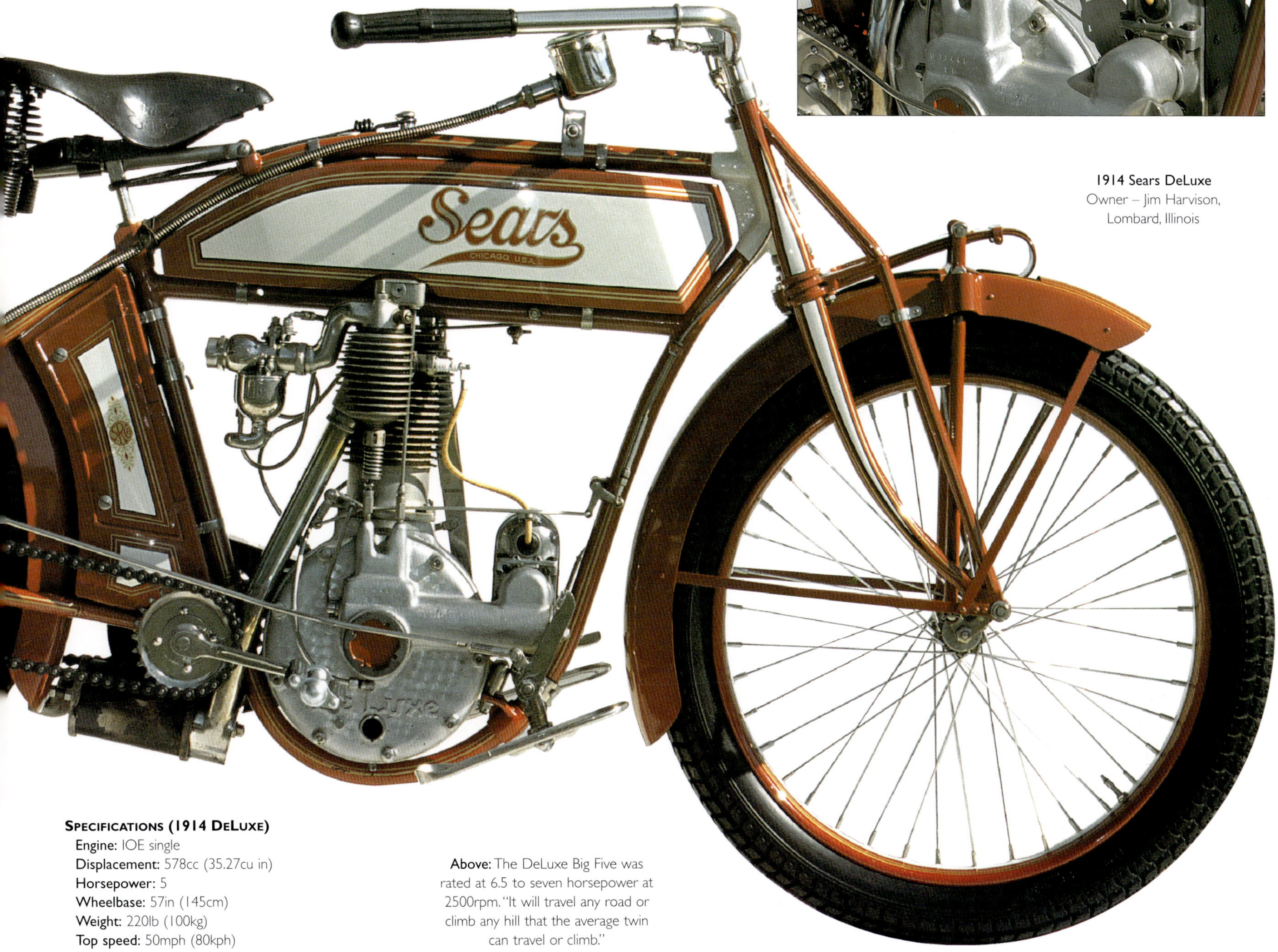


**1914 Sears DeLuxe**
Owner – Jim Harvison, Lombard, Illinois

**Above:** The DeLuxe Big Five was rated at 6.5 to seven horsepower at 2500rpm. "It will travel any road or climb any hill that the average twin can travel or climb."

**SPECIFICATIONS (1914 DELUXE)**

**Engine:** IOE single
**Displacement:** 578cc (35.27cu in)
**Horsepower:** 5
**Wheelbase:** 57in (145cm)
**Weight:** 220lb (100kg)
**Top speed:** 50mph (80kph)

# Shaw

**Founded:** 1903
**Factory location:** Galesburg, Kansas, USA
**Manufacturing lifespan:** 1903 - 1917

Stanley Shaw wasn't the first to offer engine kits for bicycles, but his company lasted longer than most of the other manufacturers. The Shaw Motorcycle Attachment was widely advertised and sold throughout the United States for twelve years. The Shaw 240cc (14.65cu in) single fastened to the bicycle downtube, with belt drive to the rear wheel.

Shaw later produced a complete motorbike for the market, and continued to offer the engine in kit form. In its last years the machine had chain drive and magneto ignition, but remained an example of functional simplicity. Shaw suspended production in 1914, and later manufactured tractors.

**Specifications (1909 Model)**
**Engine:** IOE single
**Displacement:** 240cc (14.65cu in)
**Horsepower:** 2.5
**Wheelbase:** 48in (122cm)
**Weight:** 85lb (39kg)
**Top speed:** 35mph (56kph)

**Above:** Shaw said, "Everything is complete and we send it to you all ready to attach to your bicycle in just a few minutes without the aid of an expert mechanic."

**1909 Shaw**
Owner – John Hasty
Galesburg, Kansas

# Standard

**Founded:** 1925
**Factory location:** Germany and Switzerland
**Manufacturing lifespan:** 1925-1951

When the Klotz factory foundered in 1925, Wilhelm Gutbrod started his own company, calling it Standard. Early models used British JAP engines but Gutbrod started fitting Swiss MAG engines in the late 1920s, ranging from small singles to large V-twins. For 1929, the factory produced 350 and 500cc (21.358 and 30.511cu in) racing models with MAG overhead-cam engines. Many models appeared with the same forks as Brough Superiors: these were built under license from the British factory.

Standard machines gained a reputation for good design and top quality. From 1930, Standard began making its own engines for some models and ventured into building small cars and a range of lightweight two-strokes later in the decade. The company also acquired the Swiss Zehnder factory and continued making these well regarded lightweights in Switzerland. Swiss-built versions of the popular German Standard models also appeared during the 1930s.

Gutbrod died soon after World War II and although there were several attempts to relaunch Standard motorcycles, few of these went further than the prototype stage. The founder's sons chose instead to concentrate on making light cars and agricultural machinery, including lawnmowers.

**Right:** The CS500 came from a very popular and successful motorcycle stable. Standard designed its own engines, but also bought in engines, and had works racers for 1939 with Marchant-designed MAG powerplants.

1930 CS500
Auto & Technic Museum
Sinsheim, Germany

**SPECIFICATIONS (1927 500)**
- **Engine:** Single
- **Displacement:** 500cc (30.50cu in)
- **Horsepower:** 16
- **Wheelbase:** N/A
- **Weight:** N/A
- **Top speed:** N/A

**Below:** The early Standard bikes were fitted with JAP engines but not for long. Wilhelm Gutbrod, founder of the factory, decided to change to the Swiss MAG units. This is a 16 horsepower 1927 model.

**SPECIFICATIONS (1930 CS500)**
- **Engine:** Single
- **Displacement:** 493cc (30.08cu in)
- **Horsepower:** 16
- **Wheelbase:** N/A
- **Weight:** 320lb (145kg)
- **Top speed:** N/A

**Above:** The combination of Swiss engines and Standard's Black Forest precision workmanship contributed to the success of the 350, 500, and 750cc models, not forgetting also the 1000cc series.

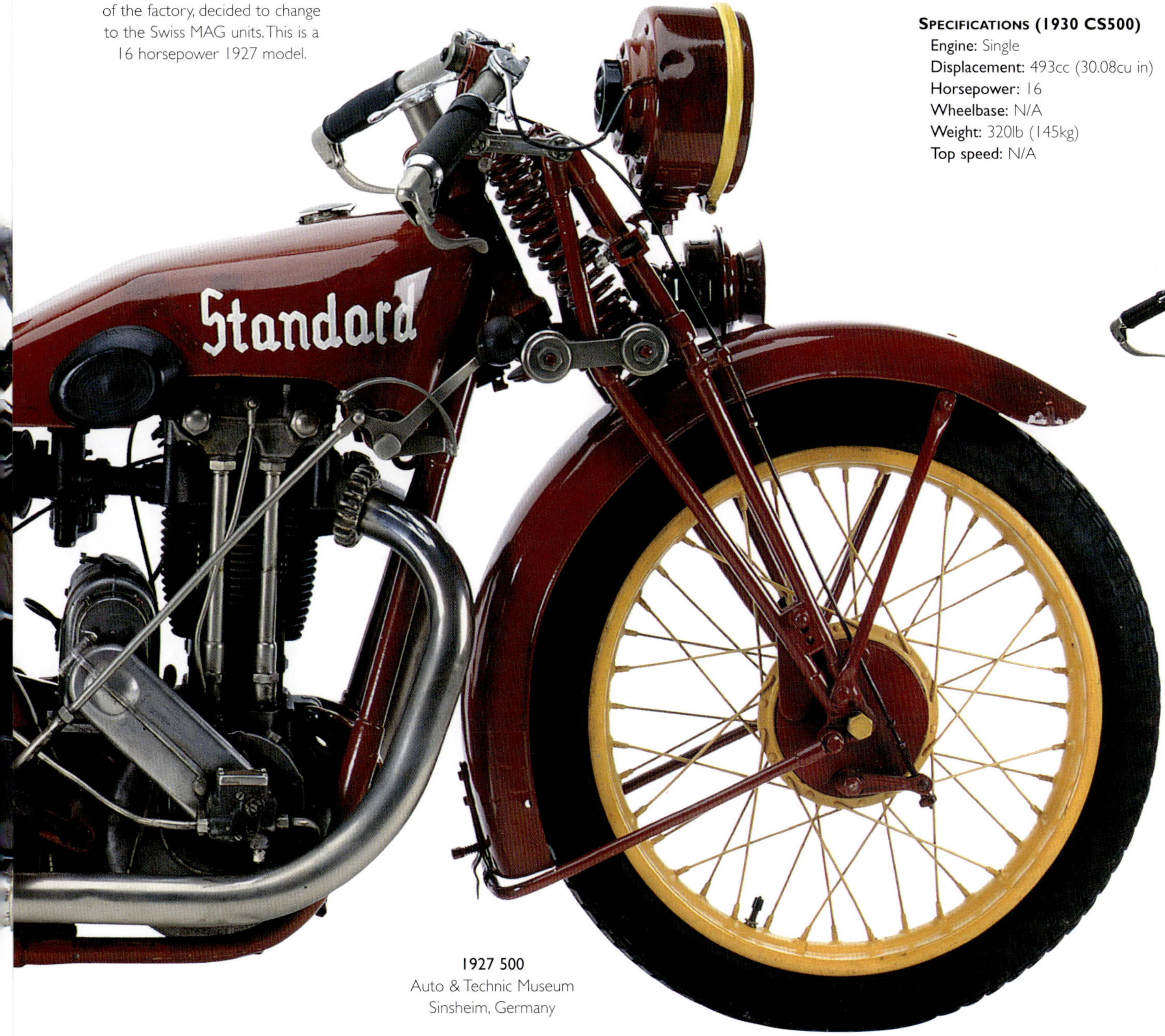


1927 500
Auto & Technic Museum
Sinsheim, Germany

**Left and above:** Red framework and yellow wheel trims made the 1927 500cc an exciting-looking machine when most others were black.

# Suzuki

**-Founded:** 1909
**Factory location:** Hamamatsu, Japan
**Manufacturing lifespan:** 1952 - to date

Suzuki was originally a textile engineering company that had been founded in 1909 by Michio Suzuki. The company started its production of motorcycles in 1952 when it built the 36cc (2.19cu in) "Power Free" motorized bicycle. The company changed its name to Suzuki Motor Company Limited in 1954 and then entered a period of phenomenal growth. Its motorcycle division initially concentrated on two-stroke production but was forced to add four-strokes to its range due to the increasingly stringent emissions regulations in the USA, one of Suzuki's largest export markets.

The GT 750 was launched in 1971 as a water-cooled, two-stroke, inline triple-cylinder motorcycle. It was relatively sophisticated for its time and updated throughout its production run. The twin-disc front brakes on the 1977 model, for example, were instituted in 1974 to replace the four leading shoe drum originally fitted. Due to its water-cooling, the GT 750 was nicknamed the "Kettle" in Britain and the "Water Buffalo" in the USA. Emission regulations outlawed it in the USA after 1977.

This year was also the last in production for the RE5, which had only been introduced in 1974. It featured a Wankel rotary engine and was innovative for its time. Unusual features included a cylindrical instrument binnacle which rotated open when the ignition was switched on. In many other ways it was conventional, being based on a tubular steel swinging-arm frame and telescopic forks. A later variant, the RE5A, used a number of GT 750 cycle parts.

The company started racing in Europe in 1960 in the smaller classes but by 1970 it was racing full works teams. The RG500 two-stroke race bike took Barry Sheene to world championships in 1976 and 1977. It also saw numerous Isle of Man TT wins: John Williams in 1976, as well as other victories from Mick Grant, Mike Hailwood and Phil Read. The engine was a square four which fired in diagonal pairs every 180 degrees. Suzuki had gained considerable knowledge of two-strokes when Ernst Degner, MZ's leading rider, had defected from East Germany taking many of Walter Kaaden's secrets with him. In the late 1970s Suzuki won the manufacturers world 500cc championship four times in a row. ▶

**Specifications (1966 Model)**
**Engine:** Two-stroke twin
**Displacement:** 125cc (7.62cu in)
**Horsepower:** 32 @ 14500rpm
**Wheelbase:** N/A
**Weight:** 210lb (96kg)
**Top speed:** 131mph (210kph)

1966-67 "Dieter Braun" Model
Deutsches-Zweirad Museum
and NSU Museum
Neckersulm, Germany

**Below:** The 125cc 1966/67 Model on which Dieter Braun had private (non-company) championship success.

**Right:** The first rotary-engined motorcycle to see mass production, this is the Suzuki RE5. The engine used to run hot and so Suzuki opted for a complex cooling system, which unfortunately added to the intricacies of the machine.

**Specifications (1973 GT 750K)**
**Engine:** Two-stroke triple
**Displacement:** 738cc (45cu in)
**Horsepower:** 67 @ 6500rpm
**Wheelbase:** 57.8in (146cm)
**Weight:** 482lb (219kg)
**Top speed:** 115-120mph (184-192kph)

**Below:** The GT 750 Suzuki was known as the "Kettle" (UK) and "Water Buffalo" (USA), because of its liquid cooling system.

1973 GT 750K
Courtesy of Suzuki Japan

1975 RE5
Deutsches-Zweirad Museum and NSU Museum Neckersulm, Germany

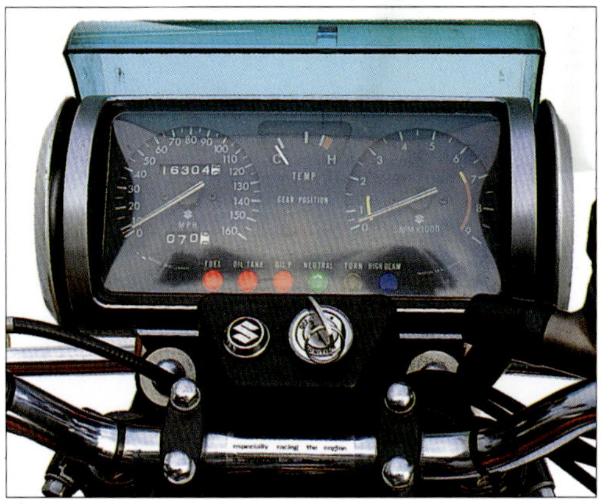

**Above:** The instruments of the RE5 are inside a cylindrical housing, mounted on top of the headlight. It has a translucent rolltop lid and reflectors either side.

**Left:** The front braking was performed via twin stainless steel discs, the rear via drum. Front suspension was a telescopic fork system; the rear was swingarm with two shock absorbers, one each side.

**Specifications (1975 RE5)**
**Engine:** Wankel rotary
**Displacement:** N/A
**Horsepower:** 61.2 @ 5200rpm
**Wheelbase:** N/A
**Weight:** 480lb (230kg)
**Top speed:** 104mph (166kph)

The four-stroke range introduced to ensure export success were given the GS designation while the figures approximated to the metric displacement. Suzuki produced GS1000, 850, 750, 500 and 400cc (61, 52, 46, 30 and 22cu in) models over a number of years. They had similar conventional styling and were upgraded during production. One change was from wire-spoked to cast alloy wheels, for example. The GS750 was the fastest 750 on the market in 1976. Another designation from Suzuki was GSX. This identified a double-overhead-camshaft, sixteen-valve, four-stroke engine and was produced in various capacities. The GSX 1100 was the largest when it was introduced and featured cast alloy wheels, disc brakes back and front, and high performance. The designation was retained for an altogether uprated motorcycle, the 1982 Katana range featuring angular styling of both fuel tank and fairing. The GSX1100S was the 1986 variant, available in various displacements including 997cc and 1074cc (60.81 and 65.51cu in). It included anti-dive forks, disc brakes and alloy wheels and was intended as a high performance sports bike.

A new designation was also derived from the GSX – the GSX-R, launched in 1986, heralding the start of the true race-replica era from the big Japanese manufacturers. The GSX-R1100 was fast, with full fairing and race-type frame.

Suzuki began building US custom-styled motorcycles, including, in 1991, the Intruder range in a variety of displacements including the 750cc (45.77cu in) and the 1360cc (84cu in) variant, the VS1400GL. It featured a V-twin engine, shaft drive and an upright riding position as well as custom styling that included a teardrop fuel tank, pullback bars and a two-level seat.

1978 GS550
Courtesy of Suzuki
Japan

**Specifications (1978 GS550)**
**Engine:** Four-stroke four
**Displacement:** 549cc (37.5cu in)
**Horsepower:** 48 @ 9000rpm
**Wheelbase:** 56.5in (143cm)
**Weight:** 432lb (196kg)
**Top speed:** N/A

**Above:** The Suzuki GS550 came with front and rear disc brakes neither vented or drilled. The engine was matched to a six-speed gearbox.

**Specifications (2000 GSX-R600)**
**Engine:** Four-stroke four
**Displacement:** 599cc (36.6cu in)
**Horsepower:** 113.3 @ 14000rpm
**Wheelbase:** N/A
**Weight:** 370lb (163kg)
**Top speed:** 164mph (262kph)

**Right:** The Suzuki GSX-R range was introduced in the mid-1980s. From the early 750cc bike up to today's GSX-R600 the machines benefited from and used race technology gained by their experiences on the race circuits of the world.

2000 GSX-R600
P&H Motorcycles
Sussex, England

**Specifications (1979 X7)**
**Engine:** Two-stroke twin
**Displacement:** 247cc (15.07cu in)
**Horsepower:** 30 @ 8000rpm
**Wheelbase:** N/A
**Weight:** 282lb (128kg)
**Top speed:** 99.50mph (159.2kph)

**Right:** The standard GT250 X7 was introduced in 1978 as a direct descendant of the Super Six. Like its predecessor, the X7 was extremely fast but could handle well also. On the racing model shown the front discs are drilled for weight and ventilation. The fairing and spoked wheels are non-standard.

1979 X7
Deutsches-Zweirad Museum
and NSU Museum
Neckarsulm, Germany

**Left:** The front suspension of the GSX-R600 is telescopic while the rear is the link type, both being fully adjustable.

**Above:** From the front end the GSX-R600 looks pretty mean, showing off its large headlamp fitted neatly into the aerodynamic fairing.

Suzuki has had considerable success in off-road competition such as motocross since 1970, with, typically, the 1990s 216lb (98kg) RM250 bike supplied race-ready and with a water-cooled 250cc (15.26cu in) engine combined with what is described as "Automatic Exhaust Timing Control" in a tubular steel frame with long travel suspension.

The RGV250, introduced in 1993 took Suzuki two-stroke race technology on to the street in a modern sports bike form. It had a full fairing behind which was a liquid-cooled, two-stroke V-twin engine. The frame and attached components were equally modern: upside-down forks, alloy wheels, twin disc brakes and at the rear an alloy banana swingarm with disc brake alloy rear wheel.

The little Japanese company that some ninety years previous had been producing weaving looms and deciding to diversify due to a cotton recession is today not only one of the big four Japanese motorcycle manufacturers but one of the world's leading producers of motorcycles. Its range of machines is more than impressive, from the fastest production GSX1300R Hayabusa, through a range of V-engined models, the cult classic Bandits of 600cc (37cu in) and 1200cc (73.23cu in), the custom bikes, commuters, dual-purpose on- and off-road machines and of course the extensive scooter range, a must for today's motorcycling market.

On the racing scene, where Suzuki has always done so well, the company is still ever present. It has committed to road racing and off-road events around the circuits of the world. For example, in April of 2001 the awesome new Suzuki GSX-R1000 took top spot in the world endurance event at Le Mans in France. And Team Corona Suzuki's Mickael Pichon climbed to the top of the podium at Broadford, Australia, clinching his third successive Grand Prix victory at the third round of the World Motocross Championships.

**2000 Bandit S**
P&H Motorcycles
Sussex, England

**Below:** In 2000 the Bandit received a full model change that enhanced and advanced every feature while retaining the award-winning, essential styling and performance.

**SPECIFICATIONS (2000 BANDIT 600)**

- **Engine:** Four-stroke four
- **Displacement:** 599cc (36.6cu in)
- **Horsepower:** 79 @ 10500rpm
- **Wheelbase:** N/A
- **Weight:** 450lb (198kg)
- **Top speed:** 128mph (205kph)

**Below:** Extending the wheelbase of the Bandit the rake angle to be reduced from 25.6° to 25.4° and the trail from 103.6mm to 100mm to make steering lighter and more responsive.

**Below:** The year 2000 Bandit saw several new engine features. New Keihin CVR32 carburetors are fitted with TPS (throttle position sensor) for better control.

2000 GSX-R1000
Courtesy of Suzuki
Japan

**Left:** The faired Bandit has a new aerodynamic half-fairing design offering greatly improved rider protection and comfort. The new, sharper-looking package adopts dual projector headlamps, fairing mounted mirrors and a scoop at the bottom of the windscreen for reduced turbulence.

**Specifications**
**(2001 GSX-R1000)**
**Engine:** Four-stroke dohc four
**Displacement:** 988cc (60cu in)
**Horsepower:** N/A
**Wheelbase:** 55.5in (141cm)
**Weight:** 375lb (170kg)
**Top speed:** N/A

**Above:** The GSX-R1000 is an open class interpretation of the world-beating GSX-R750. The all important weight factor is helped by the use of stainless steel and aluminum, and new, lighter six-piston front calipers are fitted.

## Terrot

**Founded:** 1901
**Factory location:** Dijon, France
**Manufacturing lifespan:** 1901 - 1961

Charles Terrot founded his motorcycle production company in Dijon, France, in 1901 and saw it grow rapidly into a major motorcycle manufacturer in pace with demand for personal transportation during the early part of the twentieth century. At various times the company fitted proprietary engines from Bruneaux, Dufaux, JAP, MAG and Zedel to its motorcycles.

During the 1920s, Terrot took full advantage of the accommodating French taxation on motor vehicles, that made small-capacity machines popular. The 1924 175cc (11cu in) model was typical of its time with the fuel tank between the two top tubes of the diamond frame. It was clearly bicycle-inspired. Although conventional in its overall design, it featured unusual cooling fins on the inclined cylinder barrel. During the 1920s Terrot also acquired Magnat Debon, another French manufacturer, but themselves became part of Peugeot in the 1950s. Production ceased in 1961.

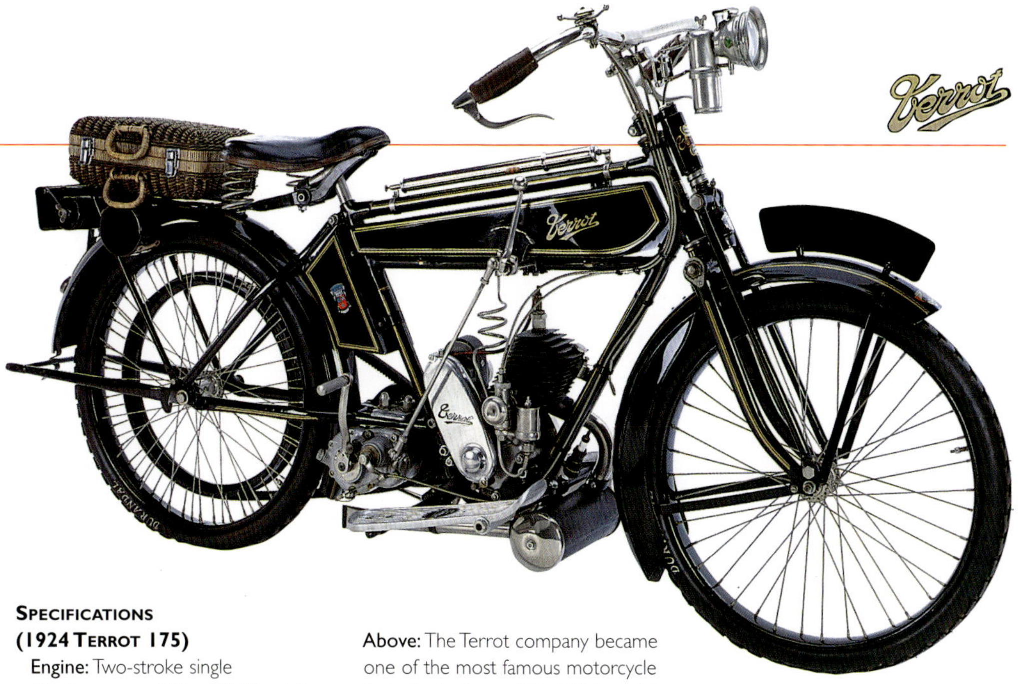

**Specifications**
**(1924 Terrot 175)**
**Engine:** Two-stroke single
**Displacement:** 173cc (10.53cu in)
**Horsepower:** 3
**Wheelbase:** N/A
**Weight:** N/A
**Top speed:** 30mph (50kph)

**Above:** The Terrot company became one of the most famous motorcycle factories in France. This 1924 model came equipped with belt drive, front and rear lights and a pump, just in case of any flat tires, fitted to the top cross bar of the frame.

1924 Terrot 175 L
Deutsches-Zweirad Museum
and NSU Museum
Neckarsulm, Germany

# Thor

**Founded:** 1902
**Factory location:** Aurora, Illinois, USA
**Manufacturing lifespan:** 1902 - 1917

The Aurora Automatic Machinery Company entered the motorcycle game in 1902, as a supplier of engines for Indian. With the end of that contract in 1907, the Illinois firm brought to market its own machine under the Thor brand. It continued to market proprietary engines to other motorcycle companies such as Reading-Standard, Manson, Racycle and others.

Given its engine-building experience, Thor was emboldened to participate in the racing game. While Thor bikes did not enjoy broad success against veterans like Indian and Harley, Thor riders often did well. In 1915 Bill Briers on a Thor twin came second to Indian ace Glenn Boyd in the prestigious Dodge City 300. This race was a harsh test for man and machine.

The early Thor singles used the Indian-design engine, but by 1910 the company introduced its own motor. A new V-twin featured mechanical intake valves, and the next generation motor was enlarged to 1190cc (76cu in).

The Thor set several speed records on dirt tracks. By 1914 the roster included choices of single- or two-speed seven- or nine-horsepower V-twin, and a four- or five-horsepower single.

In its last model year, 1917, Thor offered a 12- and 15-horsepower three-speed twin, with or without electrical equipment, a six-horse three-speed single and a four-horsepower two-speed Supersingle. The latter was $200. The top of the line twin sold for $285. The big twin was said to be good for 18 horsepower, but as civilized fellows the makers rated it at 15.

The intake valve springs were now enclosed in the head, and a front wheel stand was added. The lifter pivoted at the footboard mounts. The Lightweight twin, with smaller bore and stroke, displaced 633cc (38.63cu in) and still had exposed intake valve springs. Wheelbase on the smaller version was 57 inches (145cm) compared to 59 (150cm) on the big twin.

In late 1916, Aurora sold all of its motorcycle inventory to the Standard Salvage Company of Detroit, and concentrated on air- and electric-powered tools.

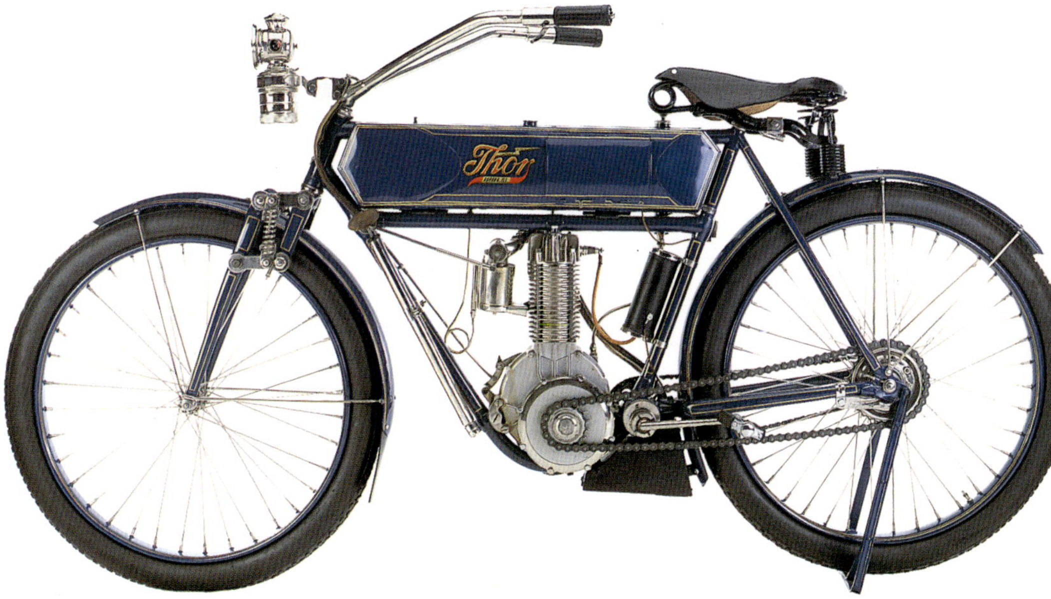


**Specifications (1908 Single)**
**Engine:** IOE single
**Displacement:** 243cc (14.83cu in)
**Horsepower:** 3
**Wheelbase:** 56in (142cm)
**Weight:** 165lb (75kg)
**Top speed:** 40mph (64kph)

**Above:** The first Thor engines were identical to the Indian powerplant designed by Oscar Hedstrom. Thor chose the vertical position.

1908 Thor Single
Owner – Marv Baker
Vallejo, California

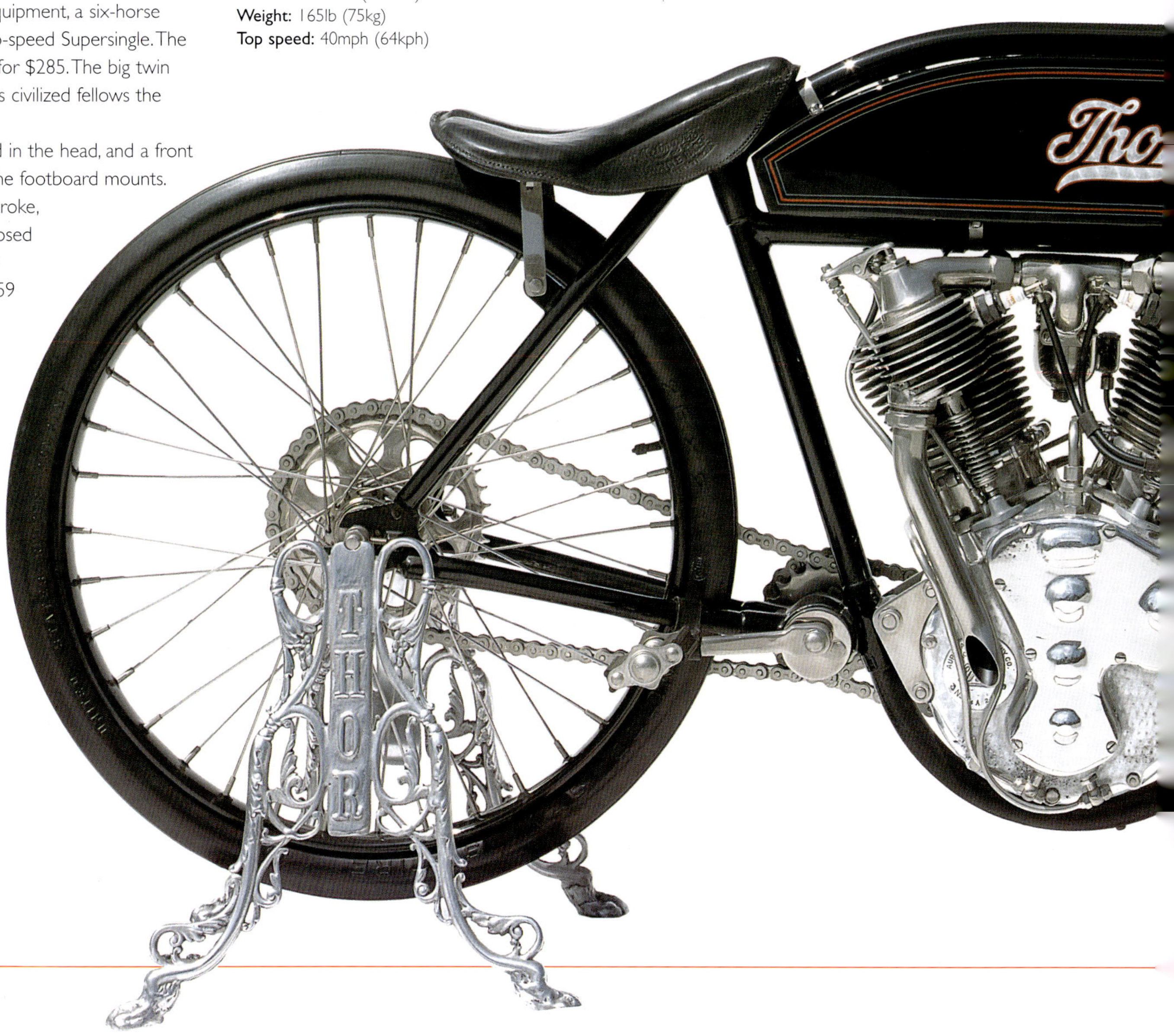


**Right:** The Thor V-twin was developed by racing engineer William Ottaway, who left Aurora to join Harley-Davidson, where his success is a matter of record.

1908 Thor Twin
Owner – Jim Lattin
Encinitas, California

1914 Thor Twin
Owner – Jim Lattin
Encinitas, California

**Specifications (1914 Twin)**
**Engine:** IOE 50 V-twin
**Displacement:** 1000cc (61.02cu in)
**Horsepower:** 9
**Wheelbase:** 58in (147cm)
**Weight:** 250lb (113kg)
**Top speed:** 90mph (145kph)

**Above:** The V-twin appeared in 1908 as a double of the single. Thor left the carburetor aft of the rear cylinder, creating a long intake manifold joined between the jugs.

**Left:** Thor racers enjoyed competition success, but by 1915 the Aurora company got out of the motorcycle business to concentrate on home appliances.

**Above:** In 1914, the nine-horsepower V-twin was offered with a two-speed transmission or direct drive. A seven-horse twin and a five-horse single were available.

# TRIUMPH

**Founded:** 1885
**Factory location:** Coventry, England
**Manufacturing lifespan:** 1885 - to date

Initially a bicycle manufacturer destined to become one of Britain's most famous motorcycle makers, Triumph experimented with motorized bicycles in 1897 and by 1902 had made a motorcycle powered by a 220cc (13.43cu in) Minerva engine. The first Triumph engine was made in 1905. It was of a side-valve design in 499cc (30.40cu in) and 547cc (37.50cu in) and developed 3.5hp.

Triumph made 250 motorcycles in 1905 and 3,000 in 1909. Sales were boosted by racing in the 1907 Isle of Man TT, the first ever, and by registering a win in the following year's TT.

By 1908 Triumph was using its own design of twin-barrel carburetor and was experimenting with various types of transmission to give more than a single speed, although it would be a number of years before Triumph could offer a functional gearbox and clutch.

A sports TT motorcycle was introduced in 1910, intended for racing with a short wheelbase and no pedals. The tourer was more sedate with pedals and a long wheelbase. The Triumph motorcycle then stayed almost unchanged until 1914 when a 225cc (13.50cu in) single with a two-speed gearbox but no clutch was introduced. The Model H came the same year, a 500cc (30.50cu in) machine with a three-speed gearbox, clutch and kickstarter. Around 30,000 were supplied to the British Army for World War I and earned the accolade of "Trusty". It also sold well in the postwar boom for motorcycles and formed the basis for an expanded Triumph range.

The first parallel vertical twin from Triumph was announced in 1933 and manufactured until 1936. Then Ariel bought the Triumph motorcycle business. Soon came the overhead-valve parallel twin of 499cc (30.45) which appeared in the Speed Twin of 1937. This engine would form the basis of many Triumph motorcycles right up until the 1980s, powering bikes such as the Daytona, Bonneville, Tiger and Thunderbird.

The Tiger 100 was the sports version, announced in 1939. The compression ratio had been raised and a few changes were made to the internals. The appearance closely matched that of the single-cylinder Tiger 70, 80 and 90 models of various displacements. The numerical designation approximated to the machine's top speed. Few changes were needed or made for the following year's production. ▶

**SPECIFICATIONS (1908 500)**
**Engine:** Four-stroke side-valve single
**Displacement:** 476cc (29.05cu in)
**Horsepower:** 3 @ 1500rpm
**Wheelbase:** 49in (124.5cm)
**Weight:** 250lb (113kg)
**Top speed:** 40mph (64kph)

**Below:** Early motorcycle manufacturers tried numerous layouts for the various hand and foot controls. Triumph used long levers mounted into the handlebar ends.

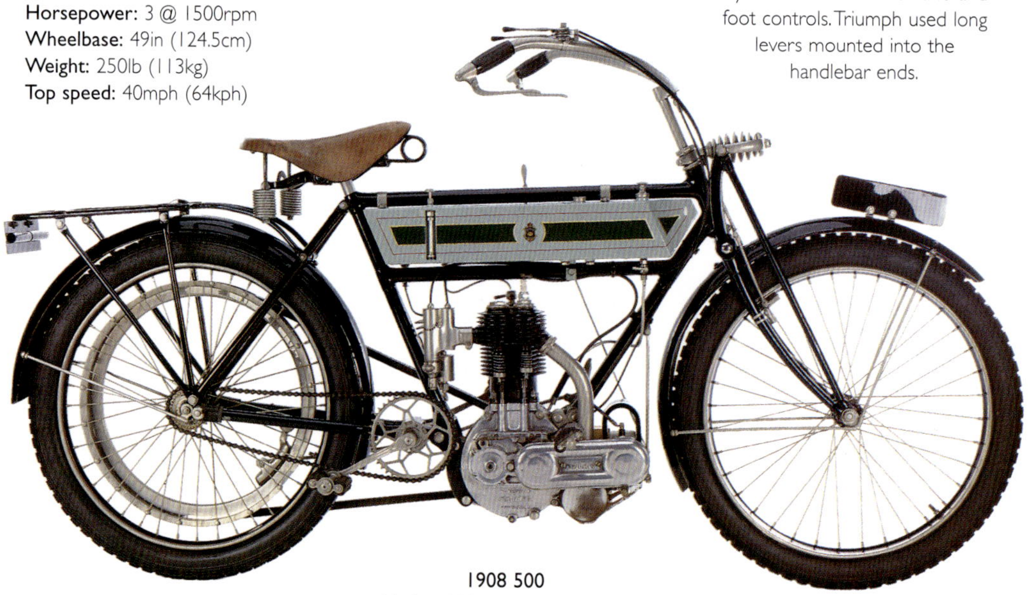

**1908 500**
National Motorcycle Museum
Birmingham, England

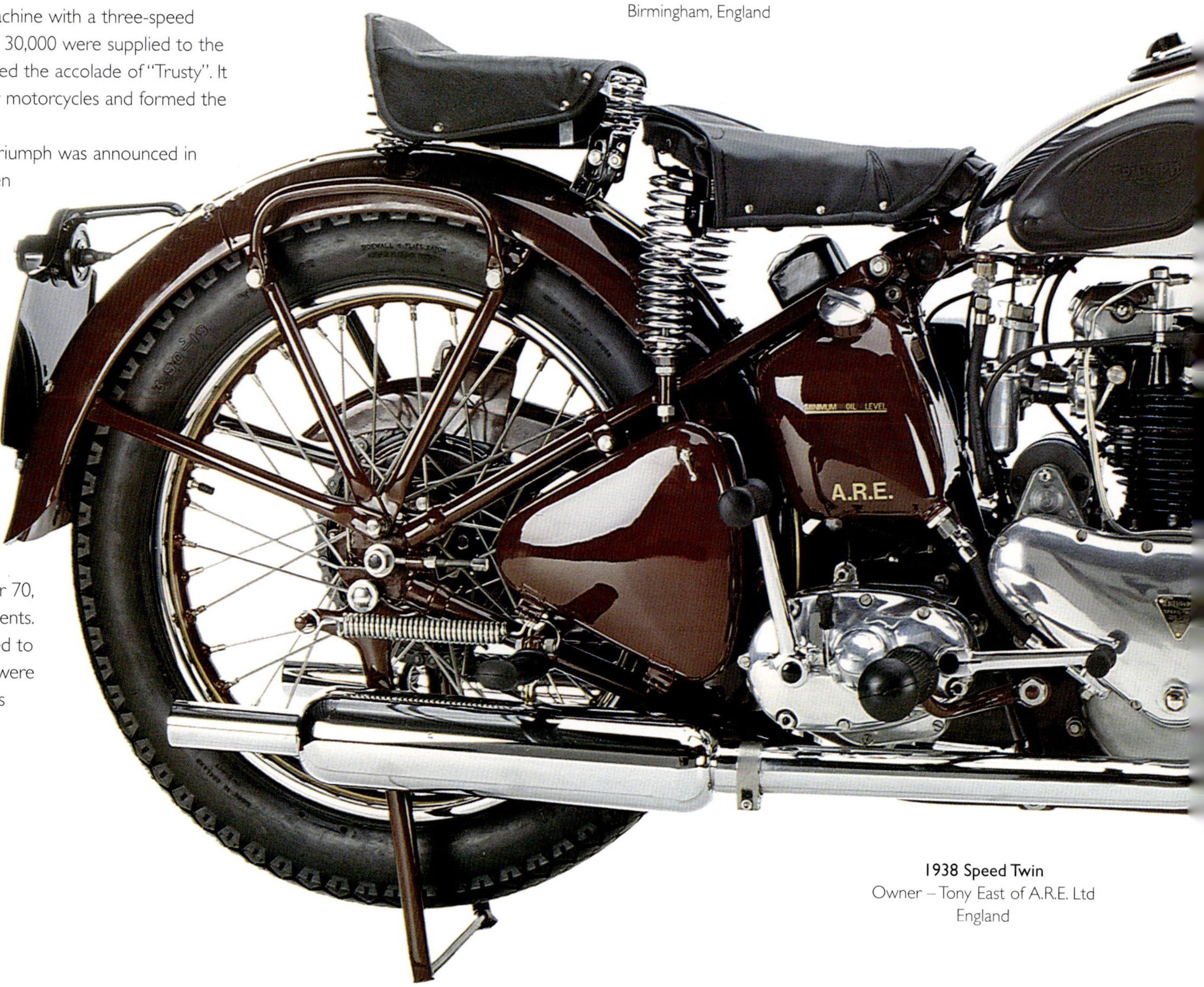


**1938 Speed Twin**
Owner – Tony East of A.R.E. Ltd
England

**SPECIFICATIONS (1938 SPEED TWIN)**
**Engine:** Four-stroke twin
**Displacement:** 499cc (30.45cu in)
**Horsepower:** 26 @ 6000rpm
**Wheelbase:** 54in (137.2cm)
**Weight:** 353lb (160kg)
**Top speed:** 93mph (150kph)

**Specifications (1939 Tiger 100)**
- **Engine:** Four-stroke ohv twin
- **Displacement:** 499cc (30.45cu in)
- **Horsepower:** 34 @ 7000rpm
- **Wheelbase:** 54in (137.2cm)
- **Weight:** 365lb (166kg)
- **Top speed:** 100mph (161kph)

**Right:** Triumph increased the compression ratio of the Speed Twin engine to make it suitable for use in the sporting Tiger 100 model, and made detail engineering changes.

1939 Tiger 100
National Motorcycle Museum
Birmingham, England

**Left:** The Speed Twin used the first incarnation of the twin-cylinder engine that was to become so famous for Triumph and would endure into the 1980s.

**Above:** Sprung girder forks were the norm before World War II, but afterward they would be quickly replaced by hydraulic telescopic units.

**Above:** The numerical designation approximated to the machine's top speed. The speedometer extended to 120mph (193kph), but Triumph expected to achieve only 100mph (161kph). The speedometer was driven from the front wheel hub. The cable can be clearly seen extending up from the hub in front of the girder forks to the speedo.

During World War II (when the Coventry factory was destroyed in the blitz, and the company moved to Meriden), Triumph supplied the 3HW, a military version of the Tiger 80 single, to the British Army, and began design work on the 3TW based on a shelved 350cc twin Tiger 85, and the design reappeared postwar as the 3TW. The Speed Twin and Tiger 100 also reappeared, with telescopic front forks.

At the end of the 1940s a new model based on the 500cc twin was announced to supplement the range. It was the TR5 Trophy, so called because three works riders had competed in the 1948 International Six Days Trial and won individual Gold Medals and the Team award. The Trophy was based on the parallel-twin engine but featured the alloy cylinder barrel and cylinder head spawned from a wartime Triumph-engined electricity generator. The Trophy engine was fitted with standard camshafts, low compression pistons and a single carburetor which combined to produce 25bhp at 6000rpm. The Trophy was an instant success as club riders could commute aboard the bike and then compete on it at weekends.

The lucrative American market was demanding a larger-capacity twin and in September 1949 Triumph unveiled the 650cc (39.65cu in) Thunderbird. The engine was derived from the 500cc powerplant, and in a motorcycle otherwise made up of Speed Twin parts, it was demonstrated at a race circuit outside Paris. On this circuit three Thunderbirds were ridden 500 miles (805km) at over 90mph (145kph). The Speed Twins for 1950 were altered slightly and due to shortages of nickel were marketed with painted fuel tanks and partially redesigned gearboxes. Both the Thunderbird and the Speed Twin would remain in production with Triumph through most of the 1950s.

The 6T Thunderbird survived until 1966 as part of the history of the 649cc (39.65cu in) Triumph Twin, although this production run was divided into three distinct periods; 1949-1954, 1955-1962 and 1962-1966 because of the way the machine was progressively upgraded.

**1954 TR5 Trophy**
Owner – Tony East of A.R.E. Ltd
England

**Specifications (1954 TR5 Trophy)**
- **Engine:** Four-stroke twin
- **Displacement:** 499cc (30.5cu in)
- **Horsepower:** 25 @ 6000rpm
- **Wheelbase:** 53in (134.6cm)
- **Weight:** 304lb (138kg)
- **Top speed:** 95mph (153kph)

**Above:** The Trophy was so called because a British team on Triumph twins won the 1948 International Six Days Trial.

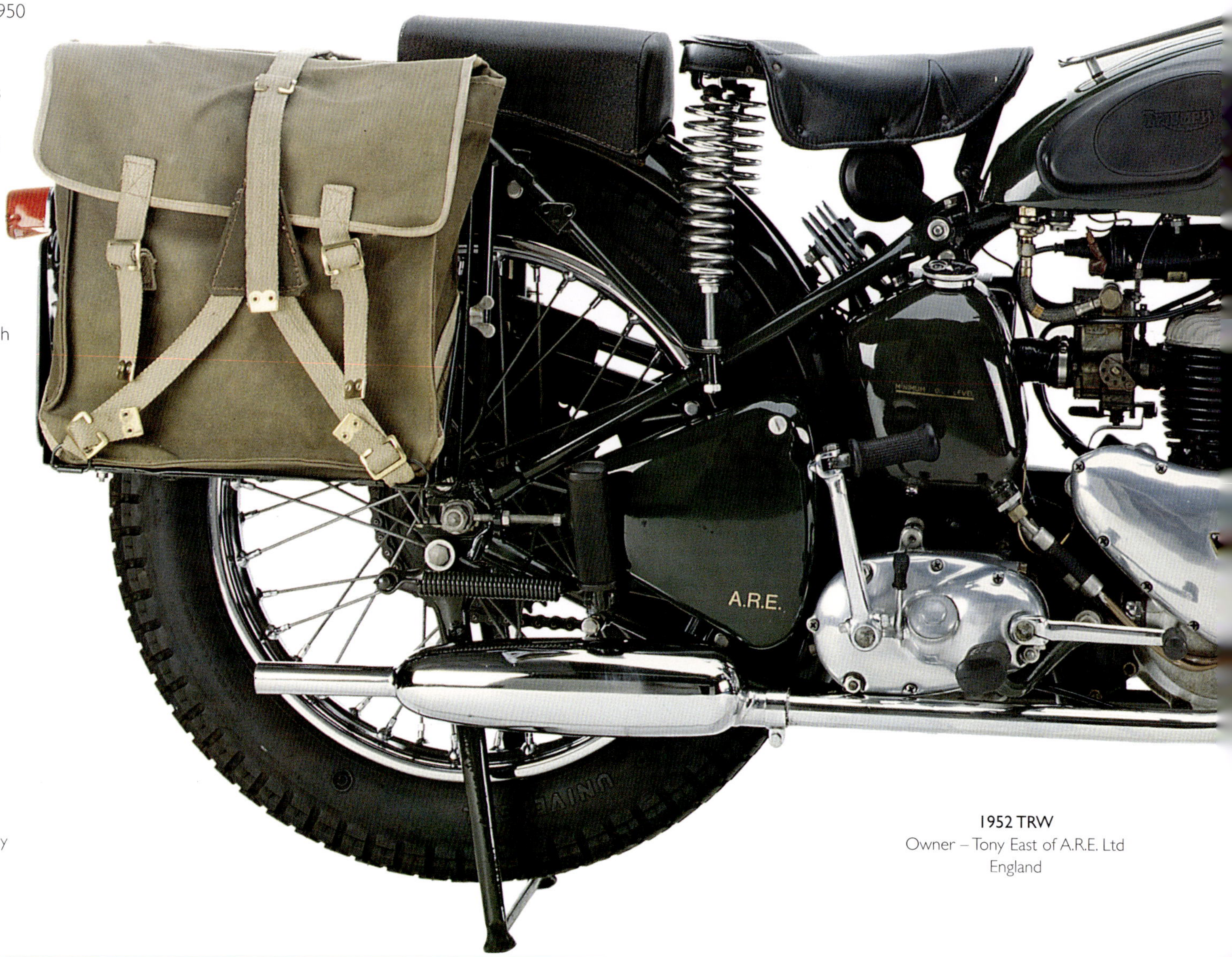


**Specifications (1952 TRW)**
- **Engine:** Four-stroke twin
- **Displacement:** 499cc (30.45cu in)
- **Horsepower:** 18 @ 5000rpm
- **Wheelbase:** 53in (134.6cm)
- **Weight:** 340lb (154kg)
- **Top speed:** c.70mph (113kph)

**Right:** The Triumph TRW was an unusual machine built by the company for military evaluation. It used a twin-cylinder engine.

**1952 TRW**
Owner – Tony East of A.R.E. Ltd
England

**Right:** The Thunderbirds made from 1955 onwards featured a swingarm and shock absorbers, which provided better rear suspension than the earlier optional sprung-hub device.

1955 6T Thunderbird
National Motorcycle Museum
Birmingham, England

**SPECIFICATIONS (1955 6T THUNDERBIRD)**

- **Engine:** Four-stroke twin
- **Displacement:** 649cc (39.6cu in)
- **Horsepower:** 34 @ 6300rpm
- **Wheelbase:** 55.75in (141.6cm)
- **Weight:** 385lb (175kg)
- **Top speed:** 96mph (154.5kph)

**Above:** The 650cc displacement parallel-twin engine was later to be engineered in unit form, meaning that early models such as this are referred to as pre-unit Triumphs.

**Above:** The military background of the TRW engine meant that ease of maintenance and reliability took precedence over out-and-out performance.

In 1952 Triumph aimed a new lightweight, the T15 Terrier, at younger buyers who it was hoped would in time move up to a larger displacement twin. It had a four-stroke ohv engine, four-speed unit gearbox, telescopic forks and a plunger frame. It was a success and for 1954 Triumph introduced a larger displacement version, the 200cc (12.2cu in) T20 Tiger Cub with a number of detail improvements, notably to the electrics. Its sprung-plunger frame was changed to a swingarm and shock absorbers for 1957, and the machine stayed in production until 1968, meanwhile having considerable competition success, particularly in trials.

The Speed Twin had had various modifications since 1952 (crankshaft-mounted alternator leading to changes to both the crankshaft and chaincase, new wiring, and, along with all Triumph's twin-cylinder motorcycles, the introduction of frames with swingarm rear suspension in 1955, plus a full-width hub front brake in 1957). But it was being overshadowed by other, more sporting models in the range, such as the Tiger 100 and T110, and in 1958 it and the TR5 Trophy were dropped in favor of the unit-construction machines (that is, the engine crankcase and gearbox were both integral parts of a pair of castings divided vertically).

One of these was the four-stroke 1958 3TA with a displacement which put it in the 350cc (21.35cu in) class, an engine size largely ignored by Triumph since the 1940s. The motorcycle in which this new engine was fitted was called the Twenty-One. The engine was was supplied with fuel and air mixture by a single Amal Monobloc carburetor, while two exhaust pipes were fitted in the manner of the larger displacement twins.

The styling was a radical departure from Triumph's norm. While at the front a headlamp and switches mounted in a nacelle could be found, the rear was almost fully enclosed. Two panels were supported by the frame tube and acted both as a seat base and as a large, wide fender that covered the top of the shock absorbers. This styling was soon nicknamed the "bathtub" design but it was sufficiently popular for Triumph to introduce a 500cc version in 1958 which was known as the 5TA.

**Below:** The Tiger Cub was to all intents and purposes a small "big bike" and it promoted brand loyalty to Triumph by getting youngsters started on machines of that marque.

**SPECIFICATIONS (1955 T20 TIGER CUB)**
- **Engine:** Four-stroke ohv single
- **Displacement:** 199.5cc (12.17cu in)
- **Horsepower:** 10 @ 6000rpm
- **Wheelbase:** 49in (124.5cm)
- **Weight:** 218lb (99kg)
- **Top speed:** 70mph (113kph)

**1955 T20 Tiger Cub**
Owner – Tony East of A.R.E. Ltd
England

**SPECIFICATIONS (1956 5T SPEED TWIN)**
- **Engine:** Four-stroke twin
- **Displacement:** 499cc (30.5cu in)
- **Horsepower:** 27 @ 6300rpm
- **Wheelbase:** 55.75in (142cm)
- **Weight:** 380lb (172kg)
- **Top speed:** 92mph (148kph)

**Right:** The Speed Twin was what has subsequently been described as a pre-unit twin, in that the engine and gearbox were separate items.

**Above:** Triumph's range of twin-cylinder machines were redesigned in 1955 to accommodate swingarm rear suspension.

**Specifications (1958 3TA)**
**Engine:** Four-stroke twin
**Displacement:** 349cc (21.3cu in)
**Horsepower:** 18.5 @ 6500rpm
**Wheelbase:** 52.75in (134cm)
**Weight:** 340lb (154kg)
**Top speed:** 80mph (129kph)

**Right:** The 3TA engine was constructed around a new design, the unit-construction type. The gearbox and crankcase were largely cast as one, meaning that the primary drive centers were fixed.

1958 3TA
National Motorcycle Museum
Birmingham, England

**Right:** The battery and tools were stored under the side-hinged duel seat. The top edges of the "bathtub" finished at the edge of the metal seat base.

**1956 5T Speed Twin**
Owner – Tony East of A.R.E. Ltd
England

**Above:** Styling of the Speed Twin included the headlamp nacelle for which Triumph was noted, as well as a fuel tank rack.

In 1959 Triumph introduced the bike that was to become a legend, the T120 Bonneville, named in recognition of Triumph's high-performance successes on the Bonneville Salt Flats, Utah, in 1956 and 1958. It was basically a tuned T110 with a higher performance alloy head that featured twin splayed ports and twin Amal carburetors. A one-piece forged crankshaft and cast-iron flywheel was used. The styling was typical of Triumphs of the time, including such elements as the one-year-only headlamp nacelle and valanced fenders. Less typical was the tangerine and pearl gray finish. With various modifications, including a single larger-diameter frame tube and more sporting looks, the model range would endure until the absolute end of Triumph parallel-twin production in the 1980s.

Meanwhile, Triumph had won the Daytona 200 race in Florida in 1962 but lost to Harley-Davidson in 1963, 1964 and 1965, so the company was eager to reclaim the honors in 1966. Race T100/R motorcycles were shipped from England and, despite many problems, won the 53-lap race, settng a new average speed record of 96.582mph (155.43kph), and then took first and second places the following year. The 1966 win had given the Triumph Daytona its name. This was introduced in 1967, and the 500cc version on 1969 was to become one of the most powerful 500cc motorcycles ever produced in Britain, capable of 68mph (109kph) in second gear, 88mph (142kph) in third gear and with a top speed in excess of 110mph (177kph) in fourth gear.

To compete in the "Easy Rider" market in the U.S. Triumph introduced the American-designed "factory-custom," chopper-styled X75 Hurricane, based on a BSA triple-cylinder engine mounted in the Trident frame fitted with slightly overlength forks and with three exhaust pipes curving out and down the right side of the machine. Only limited numbers were produced, due to financial and labor problems in the UK.

**Specifications (1959 T120 Bonneville)**
- **Engine:** Four-stroke twin
- **Displacement:** 649cc (39.6cu in)
- **Horsepower:** 46 @ 6500rpm
- **Wheelbase:** 55.75in (141.6cm)
- **Weight:** 404lb (183kg)
- **Top speed:** 110mph (177kph)

**Right:** The Triumph Bonneville created a sensation when introduced for 1959, not least because of its unusual tangerine and pearl gray paint finish.

**Below:** The 1959 Bonneville used a type of headlamp nacelle which contained the instruments on the top.

**Specifications (1969 T100T Daytona)**
- **Engine:** Four-stroke ohv twin
- **Displacement:** 490cc (29.9cu in)
- **Horsepower:** 39 @ 7400rpm
- **Wheelbase:** 54.5in (138.4cm)
- **Weight:** 338lb (153kg)
- **Top speed:** 113mph (182kph)

**Left:** The T100T Daytona was powered by a unit-construction 490cc version of essentially the Trophy parallel-twin-cylinder engine that was fitted with twin Amal carburetors.

1969 T100T Daytona
National Motorcycle Museum
Birmingham, England

**1959 T120 Bonneville**
National Motorcycle Museum
Birmingham, England

**Specifications (1973 X75 Hurricane)**

- **Engine:** Four-stroke triple
- **Displacement:** 740cc (45.16cu in)
- **Horsepower:** 58 @ 7250rpm
- **Wheelbase:** 60in (152.4cm)
- **Weight:** 444lb (201kg)
- **Top speed:** 105mph (169kph)

**Below:** The Hurricane's fuel tank was a steel canister hidden within the fiberglass molding that ran from the headstock back into the sidepanels on each side of the dual seat.

**Below:** The Hurricane had a 3.25 × 19in (8.26 × 48.26cm) front tire fitted to a rim that was laced to the standard twin-leading-shoe front brake hub.

**1973 X75 Hurricane**
National Motorcycle Museum
Birmingham, England

While the roadgoing Triumph (and BSA) triples had an enviable racing pedigree, there were initial problems with the design of the triple engine, which was derived from the 500cc twin with, basically, another half an engine grafted on to it, which made it relatively complex and costly to produce. Problems were ironed out, and the final version of the triple was the T160 of 1974. This was produced until 1976. It would have undoubtedly been manufactured for longer but for the industrial unrest affecting the Triumph-producing factories (and the rest of Britain at the time), and the eventual collapse of then-parent company Norton-Villiers-Triumph.

The T160 was longer, lower and sleeker than its predecessors and the frame was derived from the production TT-winning Slippery Sam racers. The T160 incorporated all the features of the T150 and boasted an electric starter before this was commonly available. A classic design of sports bike, the T160 had swept-back handlebars that followed the line of a long sleek tank which reached back into a long low seat. Vibration was reputed to be minimal although the handlebars were rubber-mounted to reduce any vibration being transmitted to the rider's hands. The cylinders were inclined forwards to increase weight distribution and the redesigned frame meant that the seat was lower than before, while the engine was an inch (25mm) higher for improved ground clearance. The bike was fitted with a U.S.-style left foot gear change, unlike the T150, because of the importance of American sales. The transmission, the same unit as used in 650 (39.65cu in) and 750 (45.77cu in) Triumph twins, was five-speed. The T160 was capable of 48mph (77kph) in first, 67.5 (109kph) in second, 88.5 (142kph) in third, 104 (167kph) in fourth and 120 (193kph) in top.

Meanwhile, the Triumph Bonneville series bikes were upgraded and given increased capacity in 1973, the company having already redesigned the frame to act as the oil tank. These bikes, the T140 series, are referred to as oil-in-frame Bonnevilles to differentiate them from the earlier models. The machine was available in European and American specifications. In the American specification, the new model was greeted in the motorcycle press as "the best Bonneville to date." It featured a disc front brake and conical rear hub drum.

**SPECIFICATIONS (1975 T160 TRIDENT)**
**Engine:** Four-stroke vertical ohv triple
**Capacity:** 740cc (45.16cu in)
**Horsepower:** 58 @ 7250rpm
**Wheelbase:** 59in (149.9cm)
**Weight:** 518lb (235kg)
**Top speed:** 119.5mph (191kph)

**Above:** Trident was a clever name for a three-cylinder motorcycle and Norton-Villiers-Triumph put it on the sidepanels of the triples, both the T150 and T160 (seen here).

**1975 T160 Trident**
National Motorcycle Museum
Birmingham, England

**Right:** The commonality of parts across U.S. and European Bonnevilles as well as single carburetor Tigers and twin carburetor Bonnevilles made production somewhat easier in British plants suffering from industrial unrest.

**Below:** So that the Triumph motorcycles would conform to the emissions regulations of some US states, Triumph switched to the use of a pair of Amal Mark II concentric carburetors fitted, as normal, behind the cylinder barrels.

1977 T140V Jubilee Bonneville
National Motorcycle Museum
Birmingham, England

**SPECIFICATIONS (1977 T140V JUBILEE BONNEVILLE)**
- **Engine:** Four-stroke twin
- **Displacement:** 744cc (45.4cu in)
- **Horsepower:** 50 @ 7000rpm
- **Wheelbase:** 56in (142cm)
- **Weight:** 443lb (201kg)
- **Top speed:** 111mph (179kph)

**Above:** The "Jubilee Bonnie" was a sensible marketing ploy by the British cooperative plants as it attempted to get over the effects of industrial strife and exploit the American market with a machine specifically revised for it.

**Above:** Triumph Bonnevilles featured the logo on the vinyl of the dual seat, but the limited edition Silver Jubilee models also carried additional identification.

**SPECIFICATIONS (1979 T140D BONNEVILLE)**
- **Engine:** Four-stroke twin
- **Displacement:** 744cc (45cu in)
- **Horsepower:** 51
- **Wheelbase:** 56in (142cm)
- **Weight:** 413lb (187kg)
- **Top speed:** 96mph (154kph)

**Left:** The cast alloy wheels were of a seven-spoke design, while the integral cast hub facilitated the mounting of a disc brake.

1979 T140D Bonneville
National Motorcycle Museum
Birmingham, England

**SPECIFICATIONS (1981 BONNEVILLE ROYAL)**

- **Engine:** Four-stroke twin
- **Displacement:** 744cc (45.4cu in)
- **Horsepower:** 50 @ 7000rpm
- **Wheelbase:** 56in (142cm)
- **Weight:** 443lb (201kg)
- **Top speed:** 111mph (179kph)

1981 Bonneville Royal
National Motorcycle Museum
Birmingham, England

**Right:** The Bonneville Royal of 1981 celebrated the wedding of Prince Charles and Lady Diana Spencer. The limited edition motorcycle had a chromed petrol tank but otherwise was largely a stock 1981 Bonneville.

Triumph continued to sell its Bonneville series successfully, grabbing at marketing possibilities that came along. One such was when an estimated 700 million TV viewers worldwide watched the wedding of England's Prince Charles and Lady Diana Spencer in July 1981. To celebrate the occasion, Triumph issued a limited edition Bonneville, the Royal.

The popularity of desert "raids" such as the legendary Paris-Dakar race led to the development of a new style of motorcycle, usually based around large-displacement engines and combining aspects of racing with some off-road competition bikes. They had to compete in long-distance races over roads, tracks and deserts, so they had large fuel tanks, long-travel suspension, off-road tires and high ground clearance. Triumph introduced its version in 1994, choosing a name from the past. The Tiger had already had considerable competition success and was a name with a connection to the wilder parts of the globe. Design started in 1991 with the intention of making the new Tiger very different from the other motorcycles in the range. It included a large-capacity nylon fuel tank that extended forward into the twin headlamp fairing to replicate the desert-race styling and keep the weight forwards. Fairing and fuel tank flowed into the seat and sidepanels from which the high-level exhaust pipe appeared to emerge below a luggage rack. To ensure good ground clearance, long-travel suspension components were fitted to the steel frame in which the liquid-cooled, three-cylinder engine was fitted.

Through the 1990s the trend for sportsbikes was increasingly towards higher performance and enhanced handling. The range of liquid-cooled triple-cylinder Triumphs initially introduced in 1990 were well-engineered, but not cutting-edge sportsbikes. Then, in 1997, came the T595, designed to compete with the likes of the Honda FireBlade and Ducati 916. It was liquid-cooled triple-cylinder-engined with fuel injection to enhance performance while meeting increasingly stringent emission regulations. Weight was kept as low as possible. The frame was of oval-section alloy tube in a twin-spar design. The suspension, rising-rate monoshock rear and telescopic forks at front, was fully adjustable. Brakes and forks were Japanese-developed items. The geometry of the frame and forks was such that the rake and trail (24 degrees/86mm) meant that the T595 was fast-steering but balanced by a long wheelbase. Fairing and bodywork were distinctive.

1996 Tiger
Carl Rosner
London, England

Right: The liquid-cooled, double-overhead-camshaft triple engine was fitted to the tubular steel cradle frame and protected during off-road use by a steel bash plate.

**Specifications (1996 Tiger)**

- **Engine:** Four-stroke triple
- **Displacement:** 885cc (54cu in)
- **Horsepower:** 84 @ 8000rpm
- **Wheelbase:** 61in (155cm)
- **Weight:** 460lb (209kg)
- **Top speed:** 130mph (209kph)

Left: The Triumph Tiger had a small fairing (in which the dual headlamps were mounted) that flowed into the lines of the large-capacity fuel tank. The model name was writ large on the sides of the fairing of this unique motorcycle.

**Specifications (1997 T595 Daytona)**

- **Engine:** Four-stroke triple
- **Displacement:** 956cc (58.28cu in)
- **Horsepower:** 112 @ 9200rpm
- **Wheelbase:** 56.7in (144cm)
- **Weight:** 436.5lb (198kg)
- **Top speed:** 160mph (275kph)

Below: Many of the components associated with liquid cooling were hidden behind the fairing. Other components, such as the lights, became an important element in the overall shape.

1997 T595 Daytona
National Motorcycle Museum
Birmingham, England

Left: In the 1990s tires, in particular rear ones, were considerably developed and became much wider in order to enhance the handling performance of a superbike.

## TRIUMPH

A trend that became particularly popular during the 1990s was that for "retro" machines, modern bikes that took their styling cues from the motorcycles of twenty and thirty years earlier. The "new" Thunderbird conjured up images of the old parallel-twin-powered machine. It actually used a version of the three-cylinder water-cooled Triumph engine. The old-time styling can be recognized in the rounded fuel tank with nostalgic tank badges, a traditional dual seat over a rear fender, old-style lights and traditional paint colors.

The Thunderbird's name followed Triumph's policy of using old model names on brand new motorcycles. It was introduced to immediate acclaim from the press and public in 1994.

Triumph built on the success of its nostalgic Thunderbird with another machine in similar style, the Adventurer 900. This was more of a cruiser-styled motorcycle, even though it was based around the same liquid-cooled triple and monoshock frame. The Adventurer had high pullback handlebars, nostalgic tank badges and a solo seat over a custom-styled rear fender. Many of the engine parts were chromed and the exhaust pipes were typically English megaphones. Both the Thunderbird and Adventurer were partially designed to appeal to important export markets including America. Production at the firm's Hinckley, Leicestershire, factory was increased dramatically as the machines went on sale in the USA.

**SPECIFICATIONS (1997 THUNDERBIRD)**
- **Engine:** Four-stroke dohc triple
- **Displacement:** 885cc (54cu in)
- **Horsepower:** 70 @ 8000rpm
- **Wheelbase:** 61in (155cm)
- **Weight:** 485lb (220kg)
- **Top speed:** N/A

1997 Thunderbird
National Motorcycle Museum
Birmingham, England

**Above:** There is a distinctive retro look about the Thunderbird's tank, seat and fenders that many bikers were attracted to. The new model appealed to lovers of the Triumph tradition but now they had the modern technology to go with it.

## TS

| | |
|---|---|
| **Founded:** | 1927 |
| **Factory location:** | Daarmstadt, Germany |
| **Manufacturing lifespan:** | 1927 - 1929 |

From 1927 through 1929, a talented student by the name of Theodor Scherf, who studied at the Technische Universitat of Darmstadt in Germany, worked on a new design for a motorcycle. Very little information is available for the one-off design, but it is known that it was a motorcycle that he would construct at the university and which would have several new and innovative ideas for the period. These included patented front wheel suspension and handling designs. It had a three-speed gearbox with hand and foot gearshift, hand and foot clutch and fresh oil lubrication.

**SPECIFICATIONS (1929 TS 500)**
- **Engine:** Four-stroke single
- **Displacement:** 498cc (30.39cu in)
- **Horsepower:** N/A
- **Wheelbase:** N/A
- **Weight:** 418lb (190kg)
- **Top speed:** 71.2mph (114kph)

**Below:** The TS took two years to come to build. It had a patented front wheel suspension, hand and foot gearchange, hand and foot clutch and the frame was bolted together with a mass of tubes and struts.

1929 TS 500
Deutsches-Zweirad Museum
and NSU Museum
Neckarsulm, Germany

# VELOCETTE

**Founded:** 1904
**Factory location:** Birmingham, England
**Manufacturing lifespan:** 1904 - 1968

This famous marque came from what was initially cycle builder Taylor-Gue, which began manufacturing motorcycle frames for another company. The latter folded, Taylor-Gue bought out its interests, and started production of motorcycles under the Veloce name in 1905. By 1910 a 276cc (16.50cu in) four-stroke motorcycle was in production. It was advanced for its day, featuring wet-sump lubrication and a unit-construction engine and two-speed gearbox. In 1913 a two-stroke model of 206cc (12.30cu in) displacement was introduced and christened the Velocette, the name that would be used on all subsequent machines.

The Model K appeared in 1925 and was the first Velocette with an engine designed by one of the Goodman family, three generations of which ran the company. It was also the first four-stroke offered by the company since 1916 when the company had switched to making components for Rolls-Royce armored cars for the remainder of World War I. The Model K engine had a cast-iron cylinder barrel and head with a lapped joint constructed without a head gasket.

Through the late 1920s a number of Isle of Man TT victories went to Velocettes using the Goodman ohc engine. This 348cc (21.30cu in) unit was developed into a range of models, namely the KSS, KTT and KTP. These in slightly modified form were the basis of Velocette's range, along with the 248cc (15.20cu in) MOV, for several years. The MSS, a 495cc (30.20cu in) model, was introduced in June 1935. ▶

**SPECIFICATIONS (1925 MODEL K)**
**Engine:** Four-stroke ohc single
**Displacement:** 348cc (21.23cu in)
**Horsepower:** N/A
**Wheelbase:** N/A
**Weight:** 260lb (118kg)
**Top speed:** 65mph (105kph)

**Right:** The Model K used a four-stroke, overhead-valve 348cc (21.23cu in) engine. It had exposed valve springs and rockers that were operated by a pushrod contained in a metal tube. Ignition was by magneto, and the carburetor was a B&B.

**1925 Model K**
National Motorcycle Museum
Birmingham, England

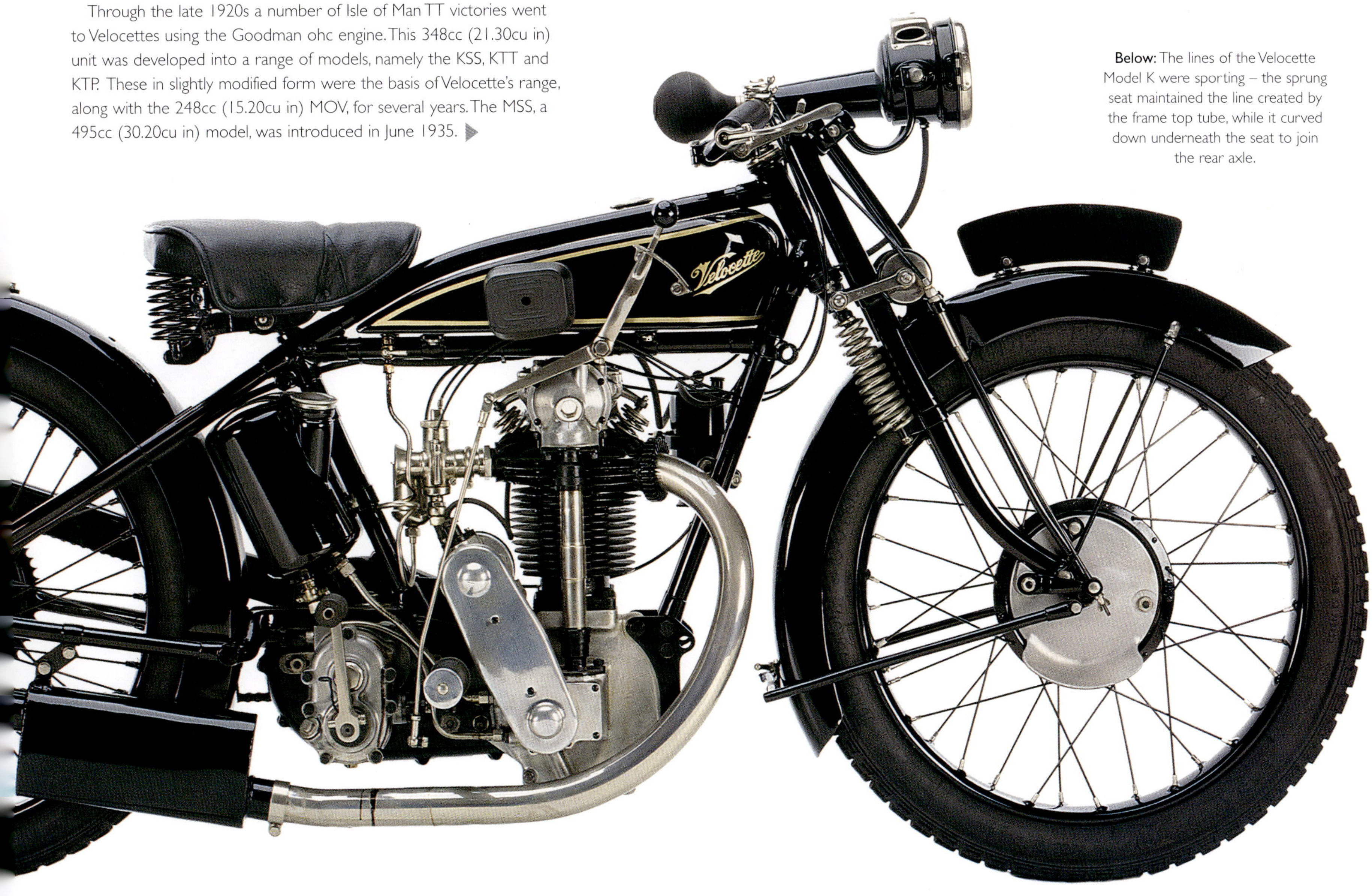


**Below:** The lines of the Velocette Model K were sporting – the sprung seat maintained the line created by the frame top tube, while it curved down underneath the seat to join the rear axle.

**SPECIFICATIONS (1936 KTT MK VI)**

**Engine:** Four-stroke ohc single
**Displacement:** 348cc (21.2cu in)
**Horsepower:** 34
**Wheelbase:** N/A
**Weight:** 320lb (145kg)
**Top speed:** 70mph (113kph)

1936 KTT Mk VI
National Motorcycle Museum
Birmingham, England

**Right:** A KTT Mk VI such as this won the Manx Grand Prix of 1936. The war interrupted Velocette's racer production.

The KTT model was one of a range of three machines based on the works race model of 1928. The Mark I KTT, a production racer on sale to the public, was closest to the race bike; the KSS was marketed as a sports roadbike; the KTP featured coil ignition and a dynamo in place of the magneto. All used a 348cc (21.24cu in) ohc engine. Any year's improvements were signified by a different suffix. By 1936 the KTT had developed into the Mk VI, which had essentially a KSS cylinder head fitted to the race-bred Mk V engine, with race-type carburetor, magneto ignition, open exhaust pipe and a left-side oil filler cap to suit Isle of Man TT pits. Fewer than ten of these machines were built for racing. One was victorious at the Manx Grand Prix of that year in a frame that was to become the basis of the Mk VII. The 1939 Mk VIII was the final version and featured a swingarm rear suspension set-up based on air suspension and oil damping.

During World War II the company sold some motorcycles to the military. Production of the company's black and gold machines resumed after the war with a range similar to that of 1939. There had been an MSS of 1938 derived from the racing 350 MAC. The first postwar MSS appeared in 1946 as an ohv single-cylinder motorcycle of 495cc (30.20cu in) with a rigid frame and girder forks. It was popular for use with a sidecar. Production was discontinued during 1948 and the company turned its attention to the innovative LE models. The second postwar MSS was unveiled in 1954 in a redesigned form with a new single-cylinder 499cc (30.50cu in) engine. It was considerably faster than its predecessor. Pretty dated, the MSS stayed in production for 1955, when there was a scrambles version. Later came a fiberglass enclosure around much of the engine, gearbox and sides of the machine. In this form the range of four Velocette singles continued into the 1960s.

But in 1949 Velocette had sprung a real surprise with the introduction of the LE model, featuring monocoque frame, adjustable pivoted-fork rear suspension, hand-lever starting, a 149cc (9cu in) horizontally opposed side-valve twin engine with water-cooling, three-speed hand-change gearbox and extensive weather protection. It was an attempt to capture a segment of the mass-market for basic transportation, but was somewhat ahead of its time and never really caught on. By 1952 its displacement had been improved by increased to 192cc (12.2cu in). With various slight modifications the LE ran on to 1958 when the Mk III appeared, with a four-speed gearbox, foot gearshift and kickstart. ▶

**Below:** The Velocette MSS of 1954 was the second version of the ohv single-cylinder motorcycle to be made in the postwar years.

**Specifications (1954 MSS)**

**Engine:** Four-stroke ohv single
**Displacement:** 499cc (30.45cu in)
**Horsepower:** 25
**Wheelbase:** 53.75in (136.5cm)
**Weight:** 385lb (175kg)
**Top speed:** 80mph (129kph)

**Specifications (LE Mark III)**

**Engine:** Four-stroke twin
**Displacement:** 192cc (11.7cu in)
**Horsepower:** 8 @ 6000rpm
**Wheelbase:** 51.25 (130cm)
**Weight:** 250lb (113kg)
**Top speed:** 55mph (89kph)

**Below:** The advent of widespread use of rear suspension allowed for the fitment of unsprung dual seats to motorcycles as here.

**Right:** The Velocette LE was an unusual machine based around a shaft-driven water-cooled flat-twin engine of 192cc displacement and a monocoque frame.

LE Mark III
Owner – Tony East of A.R.E. Ltd
England

**Above:** The Mark III LE featured a kickstart in place of a hand-lever.

1954 MSS
Owner – Tony East of A.R.E. Ltd
England

**Above:** The transmission was a separate assembly, in this case a four-speed gearbox with, as was the norm for the time, a foot-pedal kickstarter.

## Velocette

In the middle of the 1950s Velocette introduced the Viper and Venom models, of 349 and 499cc (21.35 and 30.50cu in) displacement, respectively. Both were high-performance sports bikes and were followed by other derivatives including the Viper and Venom Clubman, and later still the Thruxton Venom. The Venom Clubman was derived from the MSS; the Thruxton Venom was named after the famous southern England race circuit on which a series of production-machine marathons were run. It was introduced in 1965, when Velocette machines were dominating the 500cc class.

The Thruxton Venom featured as standard a number of race-type components that had to be purchased separately in order to make the Clubman Venom a competitive racer. These included an Amal GP carburetor, a 10:1 compression piston, hairpin valve springs, close-ratio gears, a racing-style seat, clip-on bars and alloy wheel rims. The GP carburettor was angled steeply upwards and to provide sufficient clearance for it the rear corner of the fuel tank had to be cut away. The cycle parts comprised a strengthened version of Velocette's motocross forks and a steel cradle frame. In 1967, a Thruxton Venom was ridden to an Isle of Man TT victory. But the company closed in 1971, having ceased production of the Thruxton Venom in 1970.

**Specifications (1967 Thruxton Venom)**
**Engine:** Four-stroke ohv single
**Displacement:** 499cc (30.5cu in)
**Horsepower:** 41 @ 6200rpm
**Wheelbase:** 53.75in (136.5cm)
**Weight:** 375lb (170kg)
**Top speed:** 105mph (169kph)

1967 Thruxton Venom
National Motorcycle Museum
Birmingham, England

**Above:** The Thruxton Venom was powered by an overhead-valve 499cc single-cylinder engine with an Amal carburetor. It was capable of exceeding the magic 100mph (161kph).

## Victory

**Founded:** 1998
**Factory location:** Osceola, Wisconsin, USA
**Manufacturing lifespan:** 1998 - to date

**Specifications (1999 Model)**
**Engine:** Ohc 50 V-twin
**Displacement:** 1507cc (91.96cu in)
**Horsepower:** 75 @ 5700rpm
**Wheelbase:** 63in (160cm)
**Weight:** 665lb (302kg)
**Top speed:** 115mph (185kph)

**Below:** The Victory V-twin is the first modern-day large-scale challenge to Harley-Davidson built in the USA. Polaris Industries, Inc. has some horsepower.

The Victory is the first motorcycle produced by Polaris, a recreational vehicle company established in 1954. Known for its snowmobiles, watercraft and all-terrain vehicles, Polaris has now entered the V-twin cruiser fray. The Victory has a fuel injected 50-degree V-twin engine of 1507cc (91.96cu in) displacement. The overhead-cam powerplant is oil cooled, has four valves per cylinder and is rated at 75 horsepower. The wet sump engine carries six quarts (5.7lit) of oil.

The engine is solidly mounted in a stout cradle frame, with a gas-charged Fox shock absorber in back and 1.77in (45mm) Marzocchi fork up front. The single disc brakes on each wheel carry Brembo calipers, a four-piston in front and two in back. It seems Harley-Davidson has another challenger.

1999 Victory
Courtesy of Victory Motorcycles USA
Osceola, Wisconsin

# VICTORIA

**Founded:** 1886
**Factory location:** Nuremberg, Germany
**Manufacturing lifespan:** 1899-1966

This company was founded in 1886 by Max Frankenburger and Max Ottenstein as a bicycle manufacturing concern. The first motorcycles were produced in 1912 utilizing Fafnir and Zedel proprietary engines. In the years between the two World Wars production was concentrated on 493cc (30.07cu in) horizontally-opposed twins using a BMW proprietary engine. The Nuremberg company hired designer Martin Stolle, who had previously designed a new overhead-valve twin for BMW. Stolle designed a number of completely enclosed, inlet-over-exhaust, parallel twin-cylinder machines for Victoria which involved the fitting of the unit-construction engine into a pressed-steel triangular frame with sidepanels that hid the engine from view. The machines also used pressed-steel forks and were utilitarian in appearance.

The engine factory was at Sedlbauer, Germany, and made 498cc (30.37cu in) and later 598cc (36.47cu in) engines. Victoria also employed Gustav Steinlein, who designed supercharged racing bikes which broke the German speed record in 1924 with a top speed in excess of 100mph (161kph). In the late 1920s the company introduced new single-cylinder motorcycles using Sturmey Archer engines and later Horex license-built engines of the same type. During the 1930s the company made small capacity two-stroke machines and 497cc (30.32cu in) twins fitted into a triangular pressed-steel frame. ▶

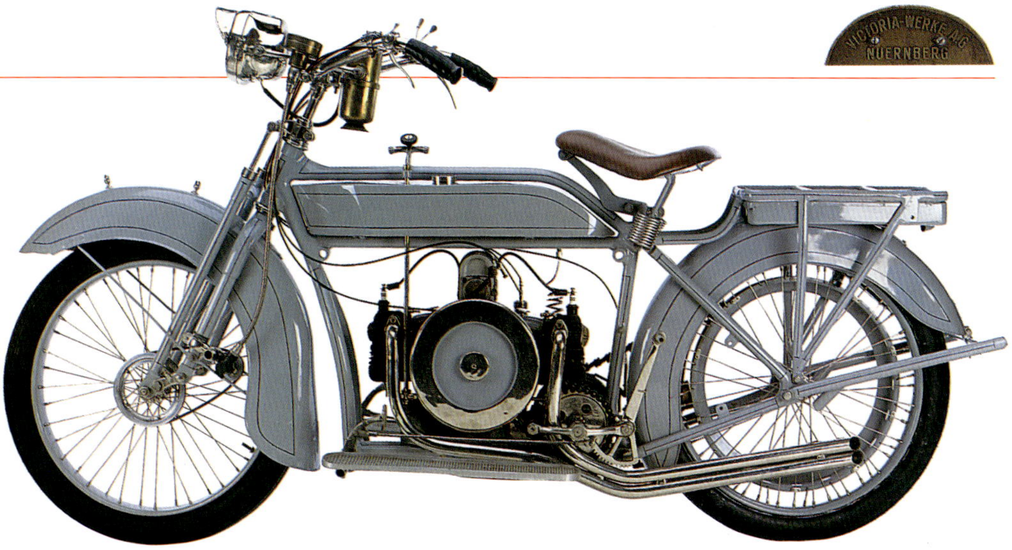

**1921 KR1**
BMW Mobile Tradition Museum
Munich, Germany

**Above:** Once the BMW engine was fitted to the Victoria KR1, the first successes in sport and a positive echo in the press served to increase sales.

**SPECIFICATIONS (1921 KR1)**
**Engine:** Four-stroke flat twin boxer
**Displacement:** 494cc (30cu in)
**Horsepower:** 6.4
**Wheelbase:** N/A
**Weight:** 260lb (120kg)
**Top speed:** 60mph (95kph)

**Below:** Seen clearly is the BMW engine M2B15, designed by Martin Stolle, fitted into the Victoria KR1. Stolle used the Douglas flat twin as a yardstick for his design, and he fitted the M2B15 to his own Douglas for the first test drives.

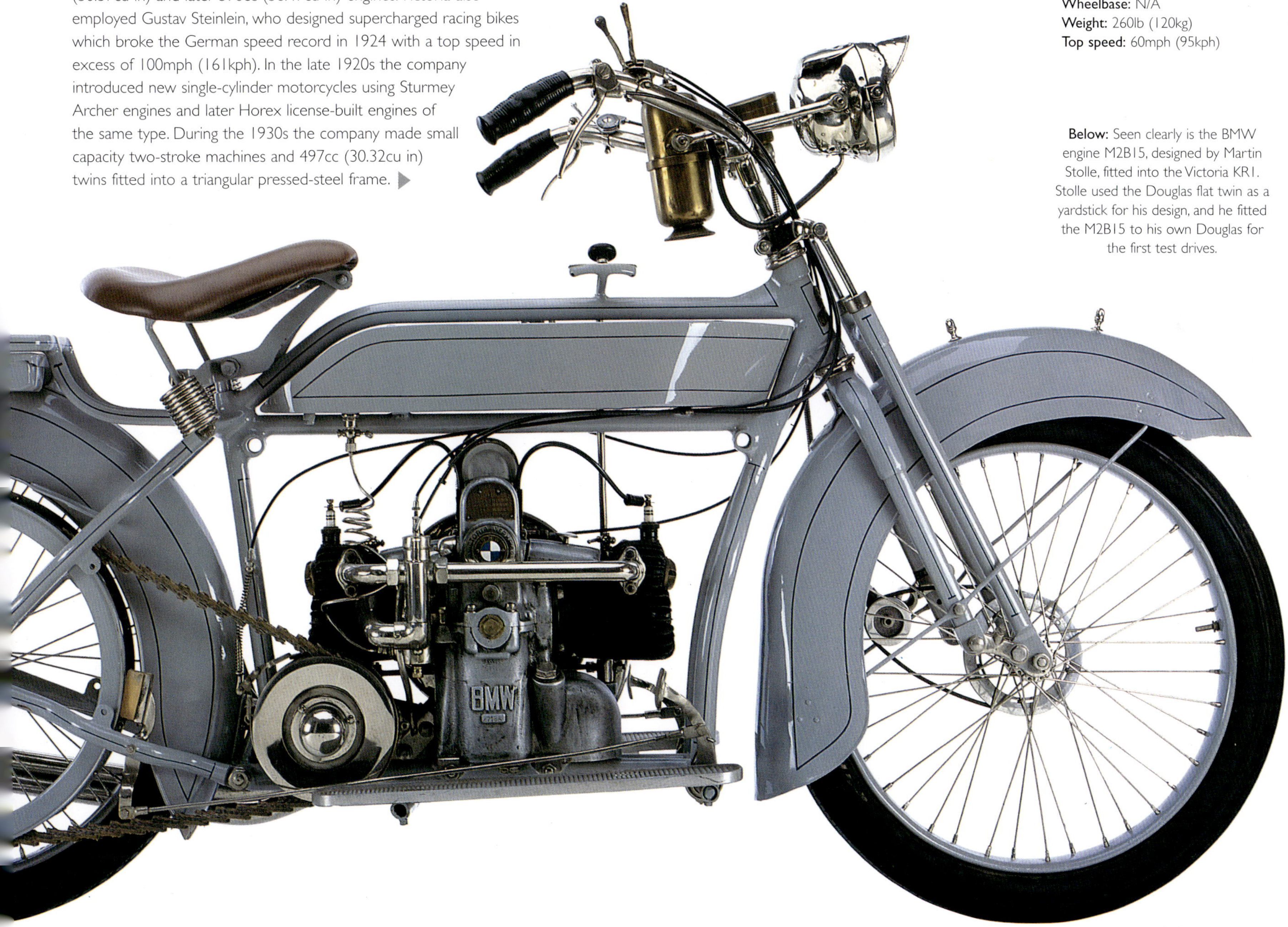

# VICTORIA

After World War II, production recommenced with small two-strokes but, in 1951, Victoria announced the sophisticated V35 Bergmeister. A clean-looking shaft-driven bike with a rubber-mounted, transverse V-twin, the layout was similar to the Moto Guzzis of many years later. Capacity was 347cc (21.17cu in). It had a four-speed transmission, telescopic forks and a plunger-style frame. Although the bike eventually performed fairly well, it almost bankrupted the company because of the long development time it took to get the engine to run smoothly. The first bikes did not go on sale until 1953, together with a wide range of lightweight singles and a new scooter.

In 1955, Victoria launched the technically extraordinary Swing. This 197cc (12.02cu in) single had short leading-link forks and an engine that pivoted with the rear suspension. Gears were changed by a set of electric push-buttons on the handlebar.

By the 1960s, production consisted of a small range of lightweights and mopeds. Victoria went into partnership with the Italian company Parilla and fitted several Parilla engines. But by 1966, continuing financial troubles led to Victoria ceasing production completely.

**SPECIFICATIONS (1951 WORLD RECORD MACHINE)**

- **Engine:** Two-stroke single
- **Displacement:** 39cc (2cu in)
- **Horsepower:** 2.15 @ 7600rpm
- **Wheelbase:** N/A
- **Weight:** N/A
- **Top speed:** 52mph (84kph)

**Below:** This rather strange-looking object is very streamlined Victoria world record machine. With this single cylinder machine, Georg Dotterweich clinched two world records in the 50cc (3.05cu in) class. Over the flying kilometer, tucked down over this machine, he managed an average speed of 46.8mph (75kph) on the return run.

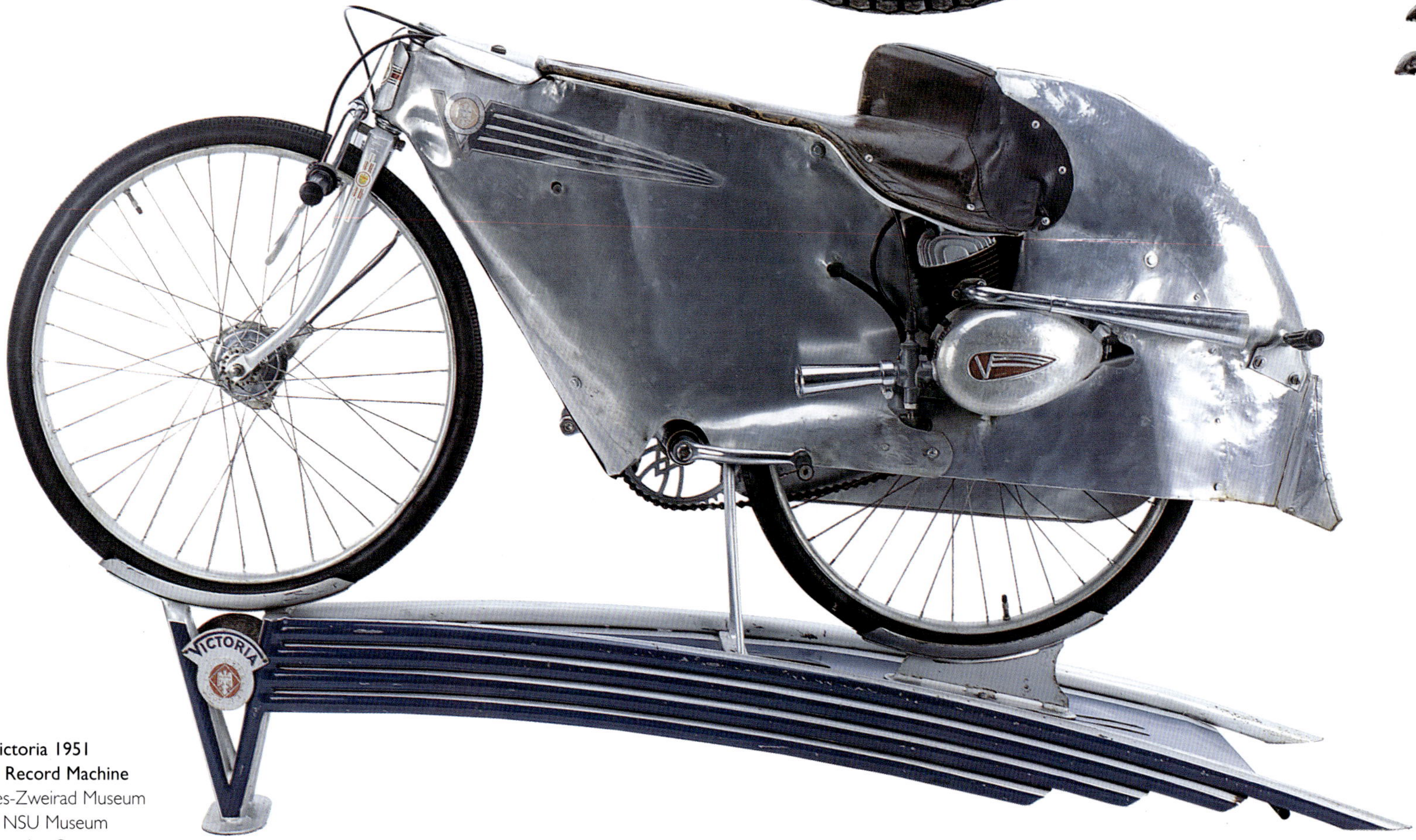


Victoria 1951
World Record Machine
Deutsches-Zweirad Museum
and NSU Museum
Neckarsulm, Germany

1954 Bergmeister
Auto & Technic Museum
Sinsheim, Germany

**Specifications (1954 Bergmeister)**
- **Engine:** Four-stroke V-twin
- **Displacement:** 347cc (21.17cu in)
- **Horsepower:** 21 @ 6300rpm
- **Wheelbase:** N/A
- **Weight:** N/A
- **Top speed:** 80mph (128kph)

**Above:** The Bergmeister used a rather odd-looking 347cc (21.16cu in) transverse twin with shaft drive to the rear wheel.

**Left:** In the years following World War II, the Victoria motorcycle company recommenced making small-capacity two-stroke machines, with one exception, the Bergmeister. The production run was from 1951 to 1958.

## Vincent-HRD

**Founded:** 1928
**Factory location:** Stevenage, Hertfordshire, England
**Manufacturing lifespan:** 1928 - 1956

Philip C. Vincent was a graduate from the University of Cambridge, England, where he had studied mechanical science. He had a low opinion of many of the features of motorcycles of the era and so decided to build his own. His first machine incorporated a Swiss MAG engine, a Moss gearbox, Webb forks, and rear suspension through a pivoting triangular rear frame section. From this experimental machine Vincent decided to go into motorcycle production and purchased the established HRD name from OK-Supreme. The HRD marque was well known as its founder Howard R. Davies had won and been placed in a number of Isle of Man TT races before and after World War I on machines of his own construction.

By 1930 Vincent–HRD was regarded as a maker of high quality, high class and hand-built motorcycles. The new company used proprietary engines from Rudge and JAP initially but later began to manufacture engines of Vincent's own design. The company offered small numbers of 490cc and 600cc (29.9cu in/36.61cu in) side-valve and overhead-valve JAP-engined machines for touring and racing, respectively. ▶

1935 Vincent-HRD
Owner – Tony East of A.R.E. Ltd
England

**Above:** Philip Vincent and his Australian engineer-designer Phil Irving created their own engine after problems with proprietary units at the 1935 Isle of Man TT races.

**Specifications (Vincent-HRD 1935)**
- **Engine:** Four-stroke ohv single
- **Displacement:** 498cc (30.4cu in)
- **Horsepower:** N/A
- **Wheelbase:** N/A
- **Weight:** 385lb (175kg)
- **Top speed:** 92mph (148kph)

Vincent stopped using proprietary engines after 1935 and all 1936 models had Vincent's own engine which had been refined in details. The 1937 range consisted of four singles and the first Vincent V-twin, the 998cc (60.80cu in) Rapide. The singles continued in production until 1939 when the company went over to war work.

The V-twin's design was arrived at by using two of the high camshaft single-cylinder engines on a single common crankshaft. The result was a fast motorcycle with the 47-degree V-twin engine fitted to a slightly longer than standard single-cylinder frame. There were problems with the clutch because of the power of the V-twin engine, but the basic idea was proven. Vincent wanted to build a sports motorcycle that was faster than a Brough Superior but, as the company stopped motorcycle production in late 1939, further developments had to wait until after the war.

Australian engineer-designer Phil Irving and Vincent redesigned the Series A Vincent Rapide during the war years and reintroduced it in redesigned form in 1945 as the Series B Rapide. Significant changes had been made to the motorcycle including a major redesign of the engine, in which the angle between the cylinders had been increased to 50 degrees to suit available magnetos better. The wheelbase had been shortened by using the engine and gearbox as a structural member which was suspended below a box-section top tube that doubled as an oil tank. Other details that met with approval were items such as the easily adjustable final drive chain and infinitely adjustable riding position. The Rapide was correctly advertised as the "world's fastest standard motorcycle" and it went into production in 1946.

A faster version, the Black Shadow, was introduced in early 1948 and, through an increased compression ratio and use of larger carburetors, this had a top speed in excess of 120mph (193kph). A racing version, the Black Lightning, was also made and these two models had some of their alloy engine parts anodized and stove-enameled black. Later variants had front forks that were upgraded by the fitment of what Vincent described as Girdraulics, a hydraulically damped girder design, while the springing of the rear suspension was damped. The racing version, the Black Lightning, was produced without lights, kickstart or stands, and with TT carburetors and unbaffled exhaust pipes.

Some single-cylinder models were produced postwar too, including the Meteor and Comet. Sales of the Comet were always small simply because many buyers viewed the single-cylinder machine as a poor relation of the V-twin. During the mid-1950s production of Vincent motorcycles was halted after a period of co-operation with the German NSU company.

**SPECIFICATIONS (1949 BLACK SHADOW SERIES C)**
- **Engine:** Four-stroke V-twin
- **Displacement:** 998cc (60.9cu in)
- **Horsepower:** 55 @ 5700rpm
- **Wheelbase:** 56.5in (143.5cm)
- **Weight:** 455lb (206kg)
- **Top speed:** 125mph (201kph)

1949 Black Shadow Series C
National Motorcycle Museum
Birmingham, England

**Above:** The 1949 Black Shadow had H.R.D. cast into the timing cover of the engine and painted on the side of the fuel tank. On later machines this would read Vincent.

**SPECIFICATIONS (1952 RAPIDE SERIES C)**
- **Engine:** Four-stroke V-twin
- **Displacement:** 998cc (60.9cu in)
- **Horsepower:** 45 @ 5700rpm
- **Wheelbase:** 56.5in (143.5cm)
- **Weight:** 455lb (206kg)
- **Top speed:** 110mph (177kph)

**Above:** The Series C models were upgraded from the Series B by the provision of hydraulic dampers under the seat in place of the friction dampers previously fitted.

**Specifications (1953 Comet)**

**Engine:** Four-stroke ohv single
**Displacement:** 499cc (30.45cu in)
**Horsepower:** 28 @ 5800rpm
**Wheelbase:** 55.75in (141.6cm)
**Weight:** 400lb (181kg)
**Top speed:** 88mph (142kph)

**Right:** Vincents used an unusual system of rear suspension that involved the shock absorbers being mounted under the front of the dual seat and which allowed the rear section of the frame to pivot.

1953 Comet
Owner – Tony East of A.R.E. Ltd
England

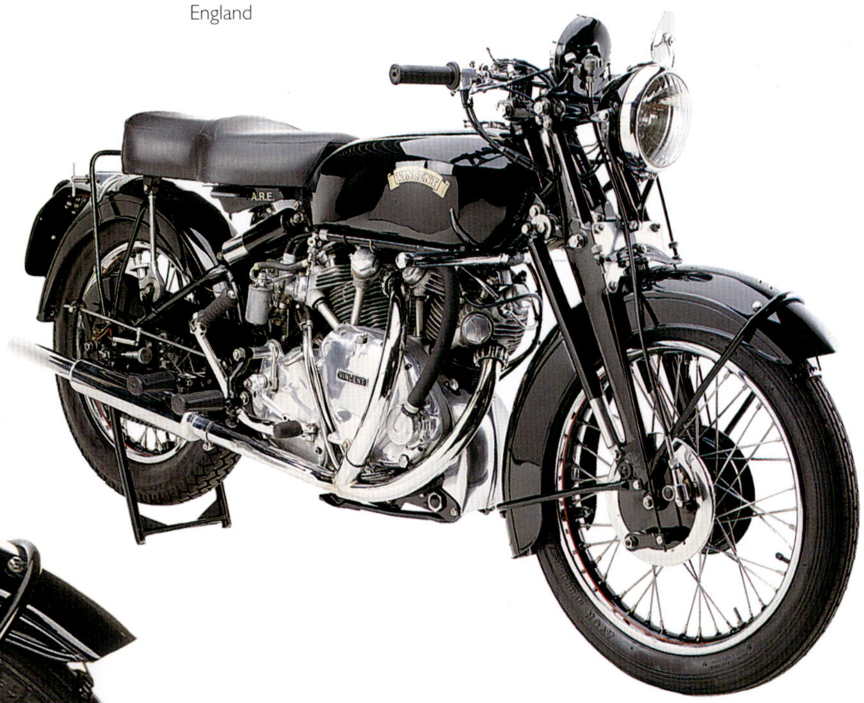


**Above:** In the construction of Vincents, like Broughs before them, quality of workmanship, engineering and finish were paramount.

**Left:** Vincent motorcycles were essentially sports bikes handbuilt in limited numbers at a time when other manufacturers were concentrating on the mass commuter market.

**Above:** The ammeter allowed the rider to check that the battery was being charged while the engine was running, especially important when the lights were on.

1952 Rapide Series C
Owner – Tony East of A.R.E. Ltd
England

## Wagner

**Founded:** 1901
**Factory location:** St Paul, Minnesota, USA
**Manufacturing lifespan:** 1901 - 1914

George Wagner took a different approach to the bicycle/motorcycle transmogrification. As a bicycle maker he recognized the design quality of the diamond frame, but also saw the value of weight distribution and strength afforded by a loop frame. So he designed a hybrid frame, grafting a forward loop on to a modified diamond chassis. In this stout platform he fitted an IOE single with atmospheric intake valve, and the exhaust routed through the front downtube.

The Wagner was offered with either V-belt or flat belt drive, and battery or magneto. Later deluxe models were equipped with a shock absorber between the seat and frame. After 1911 the exhaust system no longer used the frame as a pipe.

In 1909 Wagner also built a limited number of interesting tandem motorcycles using two engines. The upper belt run of the forward motor overlapped that of the rear, and the two were held in common tension by a twin-pulley idler arm. By 1914 sales had dwindled, and George Wagner sold the company to an accessories firm.

**Specifications (1911 Tourist)**
**Engine:** IOE single
**Displacement:** 475cc (28.88cu in)
**Horsepower:** 4
**Wheelbase:** 55in (140cm)
**Weight:** 240lb (109kg)
**Top speed:** 50mph (80kph)

1911 Wagner Tourist 4-11
Courtesy of Mike Terry
Union, New Jersey

**Below:** Exhaust exited the frame tube aft of the engine. The header pipe/clamp assembly also acted as an engine mount. The 4-11 was offered with battery or magneto.

## Wanderer

**Founded:** 1902
**Factory location:** Chemnitz, Germany
**Manufacturing lifespan:** 1902 - 1929

This company became well known as a manufacturer of quality machines with own-build 327 and 387cc (19.94 and 23.60cu in) singles and side-valve V-twins of 408 and 616cc (24.88 and 37.57cu in).

The company supplied a number of its motorcycles to the German Army in World War I. After the armistice it produced a novel 184cc (11.22cu in) machine in which the single overhead-valve cylinder was horizontal. It also manufactured larger displacement V-twins. Toward the end of the 1920s a new machine designed by Alexander Novikoff went into production. It consisted of a 498cc (30.37cu in) single-cylinder engine of unit design and shaft-driven rear wheel fitted into a pressed-steel frame. The production run was short and in 1929 the whole design and production equipment was sold off to the Janacek company of Prague, Czechoslovakia.

Perhaps ironically, the Janacek Wanderer gave a name to the company, Jawa. This sale signified the end of Wanderer bike production although later some motorized bicycles were manufactured in conjunction with NSU.

**Below:** Even this little, cheap-to-run 194cc (12cu in) Wanderer was probably too expensive for many people in mid-1920s Germany. Well over 100 motorcycle companies shut down during this terrible period.

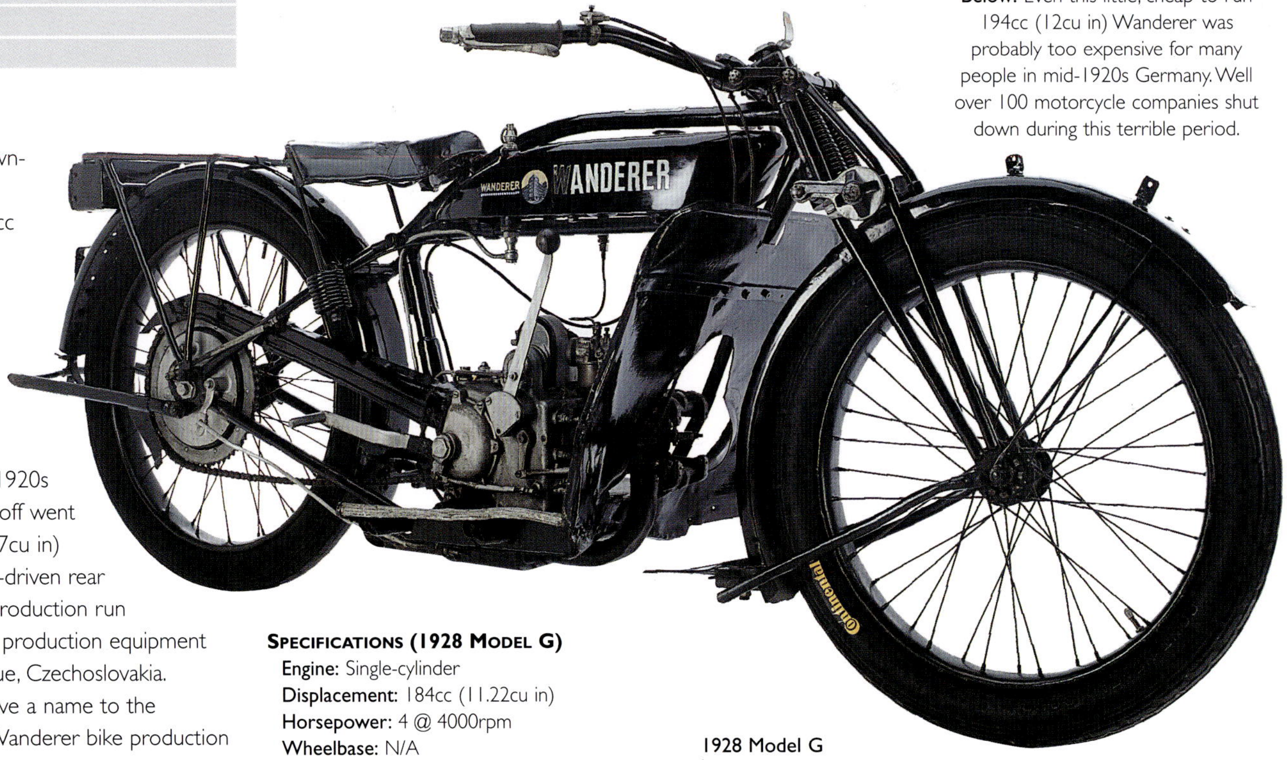


**Specifications (1928 Model G)**
**Engine:** Single-cylinder
**Displacement:** 184cc (11.22cu in)
**Horsepower:** 4 @ 4000rpm
**Wheelbase:** N/A
**Weight:** 210lb (96kg)
**Top speed:** 50mph (80kph)

1928 Model G
Auto & Technic Museum
Sinsheim, Germany

# Werner

**Founded:** 1897
**Factory location:** Paris, France
**Manufacturing lifespan:** 1897 - 1908

This company was founded by two Russian brothers, Michel and Eugene Werner, who lived in Paris, France. The brothers were among the pioneers of the motorcycle and started manufacture in 1897. Their first two-wheeled machines were powered by a Labitte engine that was installed above the front wheel of a bicycle-type machine but later motorized bicycles had the engine fitted in behind the seat down-tube. The early Werner motorcycles displaced 217cc (13.23cu in) and the later ones 230cc (14.03cu in).

An English pioneer named Lawson founded a Werner factory in Coventry, England, in 1899 and other companies, including one in Germany and one in Austria, purchased Werner patents in order to produce motorcycles. The Werner brothers went on to develop a twin-cylinder engine in 1905 but production ended in 1908 when Michel died.

**Specifications (1903 2hp)**
- **Engine:** Four-stroke single
- **Displacement:** 250cc
- **Horsepower:** 2
- **Wheelbase:** 22, 24, 26in (55.9, 61, 66cm)
- **Weight:** c.120- 130lb
- **Top speed:** c.35mph (56kph)

1903 Werner 2hp
National Motor Musuem
Beaulieu, England

**Above:** The pedals, via a chain to the rear wheel of the Werner, were used to start the machine and then the flat drive belt running from the engine pulley to the rear wheel would take over as the final drive.

**Below:** Werner was among the earliest of production motorcycles. This is a 1903 two-horsepower model, with a single cylinder engine of the Werner brothers' own design. Front brakes were standard bicycle style operated from the levers on the handlebars.

# WHIZZER

**Founded:** 1939
**Factory location:** Los Angeles, California, USA
**Manufacturing lifespan:** 1939 - 1962

The Whizzer properly belongs in the motorbike category, for the little tyke probably launched more American motorcycling enthusiasts than any other vehicle. The 138cc (8.421cu in) side-valve single didn't generate much horsepower (about two), but it was enough to eliminate most of the pedaling its absence would require.

For many years the Whizzer engine and drive system were sold only in kit form, and were most widely attached to Schwinn bicycles. So, for a kid with a bicycle, only about $80 stood between him and motorized freedom.

In the 1940s the Whizzer Motor Company moved from Los Angeles to Pontiac, Michigan, and the postwar engines were larger and more powerful, up to three horsepower. Then the company offered a complete motorbike called the Pacemaker, and all the paperboys without toolkits or handy dads could buy one. And many did. One stylish package – the 1952 Whizzer 700, also designated the Schwinn WZ – featured swooping one-into-two twice pipes and various shiny accessories.

With the influx of imported scooters and mopeds in the 1960s, Whizzer went out of business.

**SPECIFICATIONS (PACEMAKER)**
**Engine:** Side-valve single
**Displacement:** 138cc (8.42cu in)
**Horsepower:** 2-3
**Wheelbase:** 45in (114cm)
**Weight:** 105lb (48kg)
**Top speed:** 40mph (64kph)

1949 Whizzer Pacemaker
Owner – Stan Stanton
Overland Park, Kansas

**Above:** The Whizzer Pacemaker introduced more American youngsters to the sport of motorcycling than any other machine on two wheels.

# WIMMER

**Founded:** 1921
**Factory location:** Germany
**Manufacturing lifespan:** 1921-39

Wimmer began by making 134cc (8.177cu in) engines that could be used to power a bicycle. By 1925, the company had progressed to making complete motorcycles, including an advanced 173cc (10.557cu in) overhead-valve design. The single-cylinder engine was water-cooled and included a gearbox in unit with the engine, although final drive was by belt to a rim mounted on the rear wheel. In this configuration, Wimmer motorcycles were very successful in racing.

From 1928, Wimmer built a range of air-cooled bikes ranging from 198cc (12.082cu in) to 497cc (30.329cu in), and in the 1930s added a 198cc (12.082cu in) two-stroke and 346cc (21.114cu in) four-stroke trials model with high-level exhaust pipe and mufflers. Both these used engines made by Bark.

World War II brought motorcycle manufacture to an end and the factory diversified into other production. Wimmer never went back to building motorbikes.

**SPECIFICATIONS (1932 GG35)**
**Engine:** Four-stroke twin
**Displacement:** 344cc (21.30cu in)
**Horsepower:** 16
**Wheelbase:** N/A
**Weight:** N/A
**Top speed:** N/A

**Right:** Before World War II, Wimmer produced a number of motorcycles including water-cooled ohv singles and air-cooled models. This is an air-cooled twin of the 1932 period.

# YALE

**Founded:** 1902
**Factory location:** Toledo, Ohio, USA
**Manufacturing lifespan:** 1902 - 1915

Yale was a major player in the first decade of American motorcycling. The Consolidated Manufacturing Company of Toledo, Ohio, was attracted to the market in 1902. Rather than start from scratch it bought the California Motorcycle Company in 1903, seeking to complement its lines of Snell and Yale bicycles. For its first five years, the motorcycle was sold as the Yale-California.

In 1908 the motorcycle gained a few pounds with an improved front fork, and a quarter-inch bigger bore that was good for another quarter-horsepower. The wheelbase had contracted to 51.5 inches (131cm). The tanned leather drivebelt was said to be good for 5,000 miles (8,000km). The following year the big single grew to a mighty 473cc (28.85cu in) in displacement, with a 3.5-horsepower rating. The three inches (7.62cm) of missing wheelbase were restored, and overall weight was up to 175 pounds (79kg). The flywheel, which prior to 1909 had lived outdoors, moved within the crankcases. ▶

1905 Yale-California
Owner – Dale Walksler
Mt. Vernon, Illinois

**SPECIFICATIONS (1905 CALIFORNIA)**
**Engine:** IOE single
**Displacement:** 292cc 17.82cu in)
**Horsepower:** 2
**Wheelbase:** 54in (137cm)
**Weight:** 125lb (57kg)
**Top speed:** 35mph (56kph)

**Above:** The hyphenated Yale resulted from the Ohio firm's acquisition of the California Motorcycle Company in 1903. The California had become the first motorized vehicle to cross the United States the same year.

1932 Wimmer GG35
Deutsches-Zweirad Museum and NSU Museum
Neckarsulm, Germany

**Left:** The handlebars of this machine are very straight. The twin pipes can be seen folding round either side of the engine, flowing back to the silencers. Large headlight helped visibility at night.

# YALE

Yale was not among the contenders in national championship racing, but it did compete in numerous endurance contests. In 1909 the first three riders home in the 600-mile (960km) Chicago Motorcycle Club endurance run were aboard Yales.

In 1912 the company switched to chain drive as standard equipment, with belt drive an option. The Yale V-twin was distinguished by the all-horizontal cooling fins, and the muffler remained at the front leading edge of the engine. The later models (1913-1915) had the exhaust pipe routed below the engine and the muffler fitted just forward of the rear wheel.

The engine in the last Yales was a 998cc (60.89cu in) V-twin with a two-speed planetary transmission. The new frame had the upper tube angled down to the seatpost, and wheelbase had grown to 57.5 inches (146cm). The two-speed sold for $285 and the single with a two-speed was $235.

Although Yale was only in business for thirteen years, it held the distinction of tracing its lineage to the first motorcycle to cross the United States in 1902. By the end of 1915 the market for war materials looked more promising than that for motorcycles, and Yale suspended production.

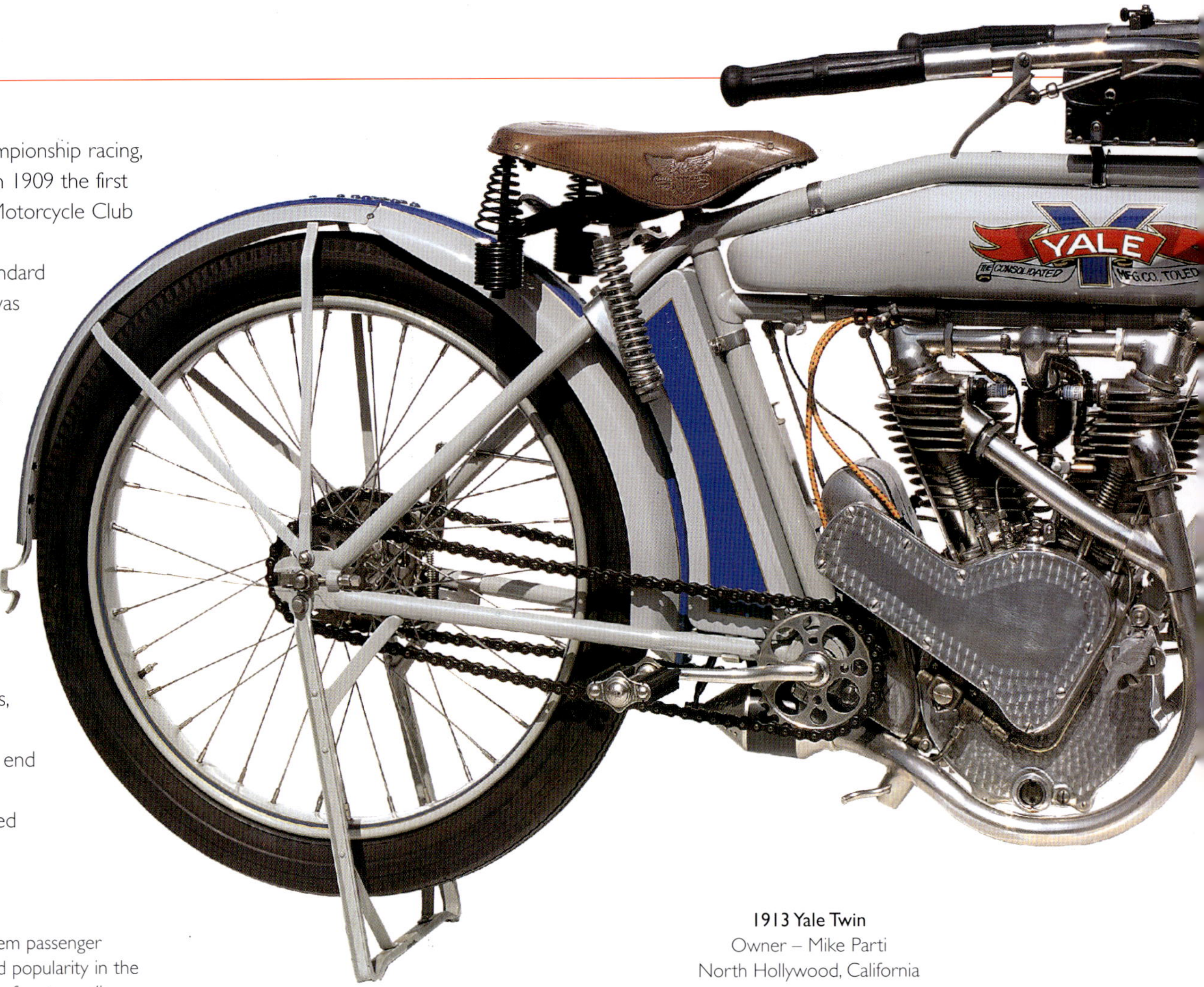


**1913 Yale Twin**
Owner – Mike Parti
North Hollywood, California

**Specifications (1911 Single)**
- **Engine:** IOE single
- **Displacement:** 473cc (28.86cu in)
- **Horsepower:** 4
- **Wheelbase:** 53.25 (135cm)
- **Weight:** 165lb (75kg)
- **Top speed:** 45mph (72kph)

**Below:** Tandem passenger accessories gained popularity in the second decade of motorcycling. Weight distribution looks somewhat dodgy here.

**1911 Yale**
Owner – Mike Lange
Big Bend, Wisconsin

**Specifications (1913 Twin)**
- **Engine:** IOE twin
- **Displacement:** 998cc (60.89cu in)
- **Horsepower:** 8
- **Wheelbase:** 57.5in (146cm)
- **Weight:** 325lb (147kg)
- **Top speed:** 55mph (89kph)

**Left:** 1913 was the last year for the option of belt drive, with the switch to chains. The top frame tube was no longer straight, and a new tank and logo appeared.

**Right:** In 1912 Yale introduced the distinctive horizontal cylinder fins on the V-twin. By 1913 the muffler had moved behind the engine.

## Yamaha

**Founded:** 1955
**Factory location:** Iwata, Tokyo, Japan
**Manufacturing lifespan:** 1955 - to date

Musical instrument manufacturer Yamaha, founded 1887, diversified into motorcycle production in 1955. The first machine, the YA1, was a 125cc (7.62cu in) two-stroke based closely on the prewar DKW RT125. It was soon followed by 175 and 250cc (10.67 and 15.25cu in) models. Soon the range included 175 and 250cc (15.25cu in) models in duplex cradle frames, as well as a 173cc (10.55cu in) scooter and a moped.

By 1960 Yamaha was exporting motorcycles to the USA and developing specialized race bikes. In 1961 the company entered machines in its first Isle of Man TT race and introduced the first use of a rotary valve engine in a production machine with the YA5. Reed valves and automatic lubrication were introduced on 1964 models. The YAS1 of 1967 had a five-valve head to improve engine efficiency. By the end of the 1960s, riders on Yamaha machines had won five World Championships.

In 1969 Yamaha introduced its first four-stroke, the XS1. This had a 654cc (39.89cu in) overhead-camshaft, parallel-twin engine and was a motorcycle not unlike many British bikes of the 1960s and 1970s. It was followed by a range of larger and smaller four-stroke twins, including the compact RD200. ▶

**Specifications (1972 RD200)**
- **Engine:** Two-stroke twin
- **Displacement:** 195cc (11.9cu in)
- **Horsepower:** 16.7
- **Wheelbase:** 30in (124cm)
- **Weight:** 274lb (124.5kg)
- **Top speed:** 82mph (131kph)

**Below:** This sophisticated little 195cc Yamaha is equipped with front brake drum, indicator lamps, speedometer driven from the front wheel and comfortable-looking dual seat.

1972 RD200
National Motor Museum
Beaulieu, England

# YAMAHA

While early on Yamaha had had a total commitment to two-strokes, as emission legislation became tighter it made sense for the technology to diversify. The range now tended towards two-stroke dirt bikes and four-stroke road bikes, although there were several exceptions.

The 1970s saw a glut of tiny-engined mopeds. Cheap to produce and buy, these were usually ridden by students as transportation to and from colleges. The SS50 was introduced at this time and was the predecessor of the famous FS1E, which became known as the "Fizzy," a nickname given to other similar machines that were regarded by other road users a hazard to all and sundry at the time.

By 1977 the company had developed a new generation of four-strokes including the three-cylinder XS750 with shaft drive. The new motorcycle was traditional in appearance but was technically rather unusual for its time. It featured a double overhead-camshaft triple with shaft drive, cast alloy wheels and disc brakes. The package was aimed at touring rather than sporting riders.

The long-lived parallel-twin first introduced in 1969 as the XS1 had been sequentially improved. The brakes were upgraded from drums to discs, an electric starter was fitted, the wheels were changed from spokes to cast alloy items, and so on.

By 1979 the fashion for custom-styled bikes had arrived and the XS650SE was introduced. This model featured the same reliable parallel-twin engine but had a number of custom touches including a slightly stepped seat, alloy wheels, pullback handlebars and several other detail changes.

Yamaha had been enjoying great racing success both on-road and off-road. The howling two-strokes of 250cc and 350cc were so fast around circuits of the world that catching them was a real problem. Larger models were also successful. The Formula 750 championship was taken by Yamaha in 1977 and Kenny Roberts won the 500cc World Championship in 1978. Heikki Mikkola won the 1977 and 1978 World Motocross Championship titles on his 400cc (24.4cu in) two-stroke. As time went by Yamaha became one of the biggest forces ever seen in the world of motorcycle racing as new bikes were developed over the years and became racing legends, along with their riders.

By the late 1970s, Yamaha was making even larger four-strokes including the XS1100 four. The company also reinvented the big single with the off-road XT500 and the roadster SR500, which influenced many other manufacturers to return to this format. Yamaha's first four-stroke V-twin was unveiled in 1982.

**SPECIFICATIONS (1973 SS50)**
**Engine:** Two-stroke single
**Displacement:** 50cc (3.05cu in)
**Horsepower:** N/A
**Wheelbase:** 45in (114cm)
**Weight:** 158lb (71.8kg)
**Top speed:** 30mph (48.3kph)

1973 SS50
Courtesy of Yamaha
Tokyo, Japan

**Above:** During the mid- to late-1970s, bikes like SS50 of 1973 this were snapped up by students as cheap transportation. The more sporty models, even the smaller-capacity machines, were fast and lethal.

**Right:** The Yamaha XS650 four-stroke twin became a very popular machine. Its reliability, simple maintenance and wide power band were a few reasons why. It was distinctive by its fat rear tire. It was equipped with fade-resistant disc brakes attached to cast aluminum front and rear wheels.

1977 XS750 2D
Owner – Eamon Maloney
England

**SPECIFICATIONS (1977 XS750 2D)**
**Engine:** Four-stroke dohc triple
**Displacement:** 747cc (45cu in)
**Horsepower:** 62 @ 7200 rpm
**Wheelbase:** N/A
**Weight:** 519lb (236kg)
**Top speed:** 119mph (190.4kph)

**Above:** The XS750 triple had a unique sound in full flight: deep and throaty is probably a good description. Although it did not come equipped with a fairing, it was a good touring machine and was equipped with shaft final drive.

1979 XS650 Special
Owner – Steve Kirkby
England

**SPECIFICATIONS (1979 XS650 SPECIAL)**
**Engine:** Four-stroke twin
**Displacement:** 650cc (39.65cu in)
**Horsepower:** 50.1 @ 7200rpm
**Wheelbase:** 56.5in (143.5cm)
**Weight:** 468lb (213kg)
**Top speed:** N/A

**Left:** The two-tier seat and pull-back handlebars gave the XS650 Special a very laid-back, US-style custom bike feel. The instrumentation was comprehensive and included a tachometer, odometer, speedometer, neutral gear indicator. It also had a self-canceling indicator mechanism.

# YAMAHA

Renowned for fast 250 and 350cc sporting two-strokes, such as the TZ250, Yamaha two-stroke technology reached its zenith in the mid-1980s, at which point (1984) the road-going 499cc (30.43cu in) V4 was marketed. Increasingly tight emissions legislation and accelerating four-stroke technology meant that the company would in future concentrate its efforts on four-stroke sports bikes. The V4 was originally introduced in 1982 as the OW61 and evolved into the OW81 of 1985. It continued evolving, although the basic design stayed the same. The liquid-cooled engine was not a true V4 as it had two crankshafts with two separate pairs of cylinders arranged in a V and geared together to drive the multiplate clutch.

Other notable 1980s releases were the brutal-looking, American-influenced V-Max, based around the liquid-cooled V4 engine from the Venture Royale tourer, boasting 145bhp in standard form but restricted to 95bhp in some markets; and the FJ1200, the first Japanese production bike to be marketed with anti-lock brakes.

In 1990 came the TDM850, styled on the off-road bikes used in desert races although the bike was designed with an on-road emphasis, while 1993 saw the advanced GTS1000 with many interesting features including hub-center steering incorporated into a single-sided front swinging arm suspension assembly. Rear suspension was a monoshock and the two assemblies were connected to what Yamaha called the "Omega" chassis. Much of this was concealed behind bodywork that was integral with the fairing.

Yamaha also launched a wide range of motorcycles for the developing cruiser market. The 1996 Royal Star was typical. Its styling was not dissimilar to that of a big twin Harley-Davidson although the power came from a liquid-cooled, 70-degree, double overhead camshaft, V-four engine, derived from the successful V-Max unit although in a lower state of tune.

The XVS650 Drag Star big cruiser was also introduced in 650cc and 1100cc (39.65 and 67.10cu in) versions. But 1998 saw a bike that became an instant legend: the awsome YZF-R1 was a machine that could be counted as a "god" in the motorcycling world, setting standards that every other sports bike producer would have to look up to.

**Specifications (1979 TZ250)**

**Engine:** Two-stroke twin
**Displacement:** 250cc (15.20cu in)
**Horsepower:** 53 @ 10500rpm
**Wheelbase:** N/A
**Weight:** 239lb 108.6kg)
**Top speed:** N/A

**Right:** The TZ250 that Dieter Braun raced. Braun captured world titles in the 125cc (7.62cu in) and the 250cc (15.26cu in) classes.

1979 TZ250
Deutsches-Zweirad Museum
and NSU Museum
Neckarsulm, Germany

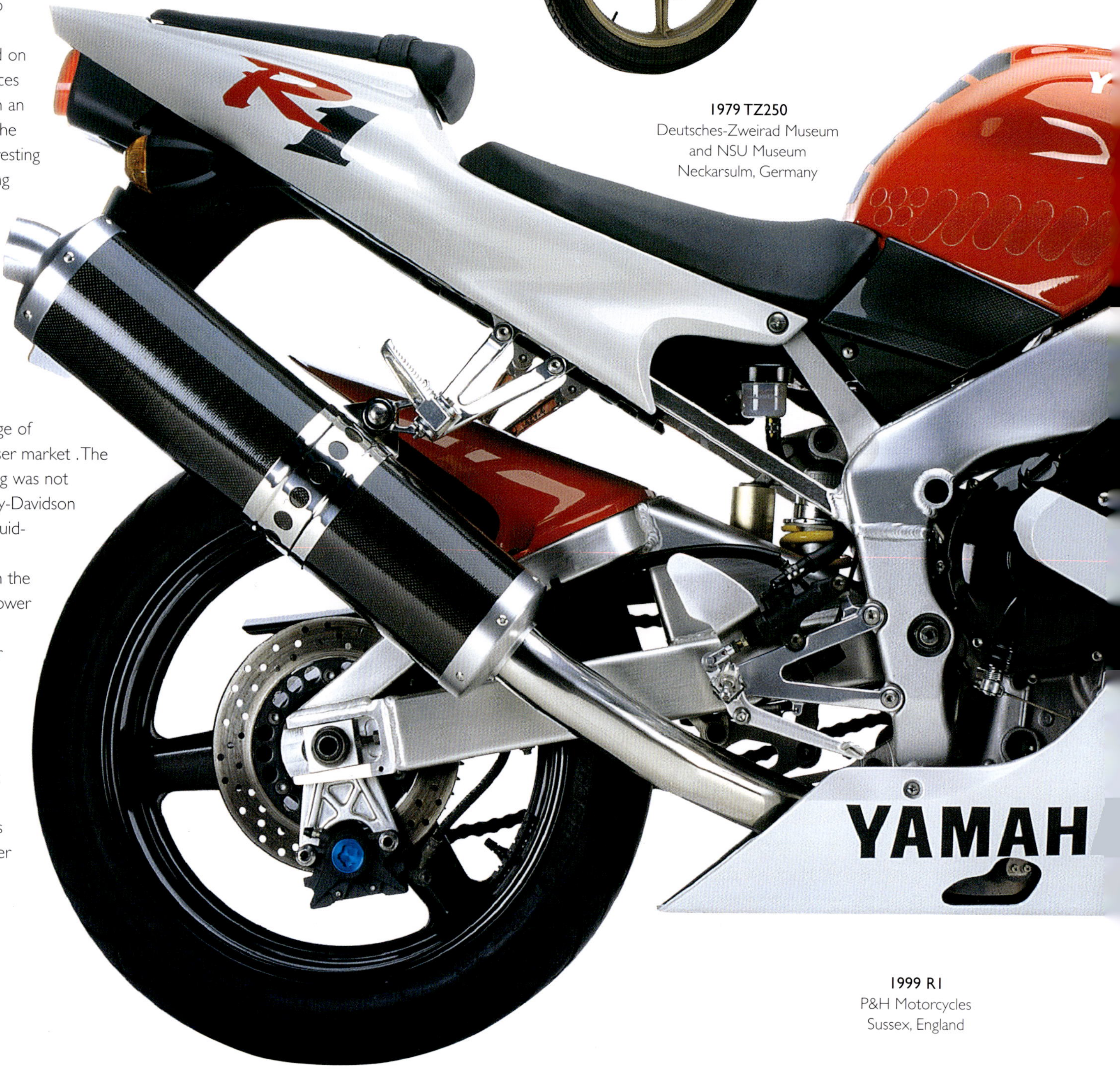


**Right:** The R1 brakes are twin-drilled discs at the front and single at the back. The brake caliper can be seen hanging on the bottom end of the disc. The front and rear wheels are 17 inch (43cm).

1999 R1
P&H Motorcycles
Sussex, England

**Specifications (1997 XVS650 Drag Star)**
**Engine:** Four-stroke V-twin
**Displacement:** 649cc (39cu in)
**Horsepower:** 32 @ 6500rpm
**Wheelbase:** 63.5in (161cm)
**Weight:** 508lb (231kg)
**Top speed:** N/A

**Below:** The Drag Star brought the original cruiser look to the middleweight class. What makes this bike special is the long wheelbase double-cradle tubular frame and ultra-low seat height.

1997 XVS650 Drag Star
Courtesy of Yamaha
Tokyo, Japan

**Below:** The R1 comes in two colors: this beautiful red-and-white livery or blue-and-white. Either way it stands out from the crowd.

**Specifications (1999 R1)**
**Engine:** Four-stroke dohc four
**Displacement:** 998cc (61cu in)
**Horsepower:** 150 @ 10500rpm
**Wheelbase:** N/A
**Weight:** 410lb (177kg)
**Top speed:** 172mph (275kph)

**Above:** The rear of the R1 points rapidly upwards from the main seat, which has a height of 32 inches (81.5cm). The silencer follows the line of the rear, its adjoining pipe disappearing into the fairing below the footpeg.

**Left:** At the front end of the R1, suspension is telescopic forks; at the rear is a monocross system. Discs at front are 11.75 inches (29.8cm), whereas on the rear the size is 9.75 inches (24.5cm).

## Yamaha

The year 2000 delivered the Diversion 900 for the economy-minded rider looking for reliability and comfort, although it should not be misjudged since it moves with speed and agility even though it looks big.

As one would expect from a company that produces in excess of a quarter of Japan's annual motorcycle output, Yamaha today offers a wide range of new and upgraded machines to suit practically all riders. Touring/cruiser stars include the Venture and Royal Star models with liquid-cooled V4 powerplants, long cross-country legs, and oodles of comfort features. The new Road Star Midnight Star has chrome forks, blacked-out engine, chrome highlights and studded saddles.

In the super sports field, the FZ1, derived from the legendary R1-based 1000cc engine, with redesigned cylinder head and four side-draft carburetors, boasts power and comfort, perimeter-style frame with fully adjustable suspension, and an upright seating position.

Yamaha's 2001 competition and off-road bikes include the YZ250F four-stroke motocross machine with titanium valves and high performance, weighing in at less than some 250cc two-strokes, and also the PW50, smallest Yamaha off-roader with 49cc (2.99cu in) two-stroke engine with a simple, single-speed automatic transmission.

Yamaha says it is committed to continuing to make people's "dreams and expectations" come true with technology and creative passion. Throughout its history of diversification, two principles have guided the company's technological development, "concern for the environment" and "union of man and machine." Looking back on the past few years, with machines like the R1, R6 and the environmentally friendly scooters rolling off the production lines, Yamaha appears to be heading in the right direction.

**Specifications (2000 XJ900 Diversion)**
**Engine:** Four-stroke dohc four
**Displacement:** 892cc (54cu in)
**Horsepower:** 89.5 @ 8200rpm
**Wheelbase:** 61in (150.5cm)
**Weight:** 520lb (239kg)
**Top speed:** 127mph (203kph)

**Above:** The Yamaha XJ900 Diversion is one of those rare machines that successfully combines a genuine long-distance capability with a lively, sporting feel.

**2000 XJ900 Diversion**
P&H Motorcycles
Sussex, England

## Zundapp

**Founded:** 1917
**Factory location:** Nuremberg, Germany
**Manufacturing lifespan:** 1917 - 1984

The Zünder und Apparatebau Company was founded by Fritz Neumeyer in 1917 to make fuses for artillery ammunition. After World War I the company began making motorcycles. Its first model, a 211cc (12.87cu in) two-stroke, appeared in 1921. More two-strokes were introduced at the end of the 1920s as was a motorcycle using a 498cc (30.37cu in) British Rudge engine. By 1933 the company had manufactured 100,000 motorcycles, and during World War II Zundapp was a prolific supplier to Germany's Wehrmacht which made great use of the company's flat-twins and flat-fours in both solo and sidecar configurations. Although the KS600 and KS800 models were intended for all theaters of operations, in practice, the diverse conditions of desert sands and Eastern Front proved too tough, so a heavyweight shaft-driven special, the KS750, with theater-driven modifications (such as foot-heaters for the cold, and extra air filters for North Africa) was developed.

After the war, Zundapp reintroduced its popular two-strokes and flat-twins, and created the Bella line of scooters. Its 1980 KS175 two-stroke was intended as basic transportation with a number of sports-type details such as a mini-fairing and cast alloy wheels.

By then the company had grown to be the biggest motorcycle manufacturer in Germany, but by 1984 the company had collapsed.

**Specifications (1938 K800)**
**Engine:** Four-stroke four
**Displacement:** 791cc (48cu in)
**Horsepower:** 22 @ 4300rpm
**Wheelbase:** N/A
**Weight:** N/A
**Top speed:** 78mph (125kph)

**Right:** The Zundapp K800 of 1938 had a horizontally opposed 800cc (48.82cu in) engine. The "K" stands for Karden (shaft), the bike being driven by a shaft to the rear wheel. This was the largest capacity engine that Zundapp ever made.

**Specifications (1953 KS601)**
**Engine:** Twin-cylinder boxer
**Displacement:** 597cc (48cu in)
**Horsepower:** 28 @ 4700rpm
**Wheelbase:** N/A
**Weight:** N/A
**Top speed:** 81mph (130kph)

1953 KS601
Deutsches-Zweirad Museum
and NSU Museum
Neckarsulm, Germany

**Left:** When introduced in 1951 the KS601 replaced the KS600 and was the fastest German roadster. Besides it's solo performance the bike was ideal with a sidecar. This 1953 example was kitted out and used for a trip around the world.

**Below:** The K800 used a pressed-steel frame, had a manual gearbox (see the gearchange handle at the side of the engine) and a front drum brake.

**Below:** While the K800 saw wartime action, in civilian garb it was renowned for being a luxury sports machine.

1938 K800
Deutsches-Zweirad Museum
and NSU Museum
Neckarsulm, Germany

# INDEX

**Cyklon 1900 Model**
Deutsches-Zweirad Museum
and NSU Museum
Neckarsulm, German

**Ducati 1976 350 Desmo**
Deutsches-Zweirad Museum
and NSU Museum
Neckarsulm, German

**Suzuki 2000 GSX-R600**
P&H Motorcycles
Sussex, England